Mathematics for Elementary Teachers

An Activity Approach

Ninth Edition

Mathematics for Elementary Teachers

An Activity Approach

Albert B. Bennett, Jr.
University of New Hampshire

Laurie J. Burton
Western Oregon University

L. Ted Nelson
Portland State University

Connect
Learn
Succeed™

MATHEMATICS FOR ELEMENTARY TEACHERS: AN ACTIVITY APPROACH, NINTH EDITION

Published by McGraw-Hill, a business unit of The McGraw-Hill Companies, Inc., 1221 Avenue of the Americas, New York, NY 10020. Copyright © 2012 by The McGraw-Hill Companies, Inc. All rights reserved. Previous editions © 2010, 2007, and 2004. No part of this publication may be reproduced or distributed in any form or by any means, or stored in a database or retrieval system, without the prior written consent of The McGraw-Hill Companies, Inc., including, but not limited to, in any network or other electronic storage or transmission, or broadcast for distance learning.

Some ancillaries, including electronic and print components, may not be available to customers outside the United States.

This book is printed on acid-free paper.
Printed in China

2 3 4 5 6 7 8 9 0 CTP/CTP 1 0 9 8 7 6 5 4 3

ISBN 978-0-07-743091-7
MHID 0-07-743091-3

Vice President, Editor-in-Chief: *Marty Lange*
Vice President, EDP: *Kimberly Meriwether David*
Senior Director of Development: *Kristine Tibbetts*
Editorial Director: *Stewart K. Mattson*
Sponsoring Editor: *John R. Osgood*
Developmental Editor: *Liz Recker*
Marketing Manager: *Kevin M. Ernzen*
Senior Project Manager: *Vicki Krug*
Buyer II: *Sherry L. Kane*
Senior Media Project Manager: *Christina Nelson*
Designer: *Tara McDermott*
Cover Designer: *Ellen Pettengell*
Cover Image: *COLORCUBE: 3D Color Puzzle, Copyright © 2000 by Spittin' Image Software, Inc., Suite #102, 416 Sixth Street, New Westminister, British Columbia, Canada V3L 3B2, web: www.colorcube.com, e-mail: info@colorcube.com, phone: 604-525-2170. Photograph by UNH Photo Graphic Services/McGraw-Hill.*
Lead Photo Research Coordinator: *Carrie K. Burger*
Photo Research: *LouAnn K. Wilson*
Compositor: *Aptara®, Inc.*
Typeface: *10/12 Times Roman*
Printer: *CTPS*

All credits appearing on page or at the end of the book are considered to be an extension of the copyright page.

To Future Teachers

This book was written to help you teach elementary and middle school mathematics. You will experience firsthand how the use of models and manipulatives contribute to the understanding of mathematics concepts.

You will find that the models and manipulatives used in the activities in this book are commonly used for teaching elementary and middle school mathematics. Many of these activities can be easily adapted for use in school classrooms, and we encourage you to do this. To assist you, there is a one-page lesson, *Activities for the Elementary School Classroom*, at the end of each chapter to illustrate how ideas from the chapter can be adapted for use in the elementary classroom. If you have the opportunity, we encourage you to try these adapted activities with children.

In this course, you are the student. Each activity in this book asks you to look for patterns and relationships and to explain in your own words how they make sense.[†] This is the same process you will someday be using with your students.

This is an important time for you to begin thinking like the teacher you are becoming and about the process of teaching and learning mathematics. You can do this by

- Monitoring your own thoughts and feelings about math as you learn to explore and investigate

- Thinking about how you can use, change, or adapt the activities in this book for use in an elementary or middle school classroom

- Observing your classmates and asking them questions to try to understand how they are thinking about mathematics

This book offers a variety of resources to help you achieve these goals.

The **Manipulative Kit** bundled with this book contains 10 colorful manipulatives commonly used in elementary schools. The Activity Sets in this book require the use of manipulatives from this kit as well as additional materials found on **Material Cards** at the back of the book.

You can enter the website www.mhhe.com/bbn without a password and to access:

- **Virtual Manipulatives,** electronic versions of the items in the **Manipulative Kit**

- Eleven interactive applets (Taking a Chance is shown here)

- Math Investigations

- Puzzlers

- Geometer's Sketchpad Modules

- Grid and Dot Paper

- Color Transparencies

- Internet Resources

- And more

[†]Answers to selected questions in the Activity Sets (marked *) are available in the back of the book.

Just for Fun Activities

Contents

Activity Sets

Material Cards

1. Algebra Pieces (1.3)
2. Algebraic Expression Cards (1.3)
3. Attribute Label Cards (2.1)
4. Attribute-Game Grid (2.1)
5. Two-Circle Venn Diagram (2.1)
6. Three-Circle Venn Diagram (2.1, 9.1)
7. Exercises and Activities No. 3 (2.1)
8. Rectangular Geoboard Template (2.2, 6.4, 9.1, 10.2)
9. Coordinate Guessing and Hide-a-Region Grids (2.2)
10. Logic Problem Clue Cards and People Pieces (Problem 1) (2.3)
11. Logic Problem Clue Cards and People Pieces (Problem 2) (2.3)
12. Logic Problem Clue Cards, Prize and People Pieces (Problem 3) (2.3)
13. Logic Problem Clue Cards, Career, Singer, People, and Location Pieces (Problem 4) (2.3)
14. Logic Problem Clue Cards (Problem 5) (2.3)
15. Logic Problem Object Pieces (Problem 5) (2.3)
16. Pica-Centro Recording Sheet (2.3)
17. Mind-Reading Cards (3.1)
18. Interest Gameboard (6.3)
19. Pythagorean Puzzle Visual Proof and Square Me Puzzle (6.4)
20. Metric Ruler, Protractor, and Compass (7.1, 9.1, 10.1, 10.3, 11.1, 11.2, 11.3)
21. Table of Random Digits (7.2, 7.3, 8.1)
22. Two-Penny Grid (8.1)
23. Three-Penny Grid (8.1)
24. Simulation Spinners (8.2)
25. Trick Dice (8.2)
26. Geoboard Recording Paper (9.1)
27. Circular Geoboard Template (9.1)
28. Grids for Game of Hex (9.2)
29. Regular Polyhedra (9.3)
30. Regular Polyhedra (9.3)
31. Two-Centimeter Grid Paper (9.3)
32. Cube Patterns for Instant Insanity (9.3)
33. Perpendicular Lines for Symmetry (9.4)
34. Metric Measuring Tape (10.1)
35. Centimeter Racing Mat (10.1)
36. Pentominoes (10.2)
37. Pentomino Game Grid (10.2)
38. Prism, Pyramid, and Cylinder (10.3)
39. Hypsometer-Clinometer (11.3)

Preface

The primary purpose of *Mathematics for Elementary Teachers: An Activity Approach* is to engage prospective elementary and middle school teachers in mathematical activities that will enhance their conceptual knowledge, introduce them to important manipulatives, and model the kind of mathematical learning experiences they will be expected to provide for their students.

The National Council of Teachers of Mathematics' *Principles and Standards for School Mathematics* and its predecessor, *Curriculum and Evaluation Standards for School Mathematics*, strongly assert that students learn mathematics well when they construct their own mathematical thinking. Information can be transmitted from one person to another, but mathematical understanding and knowledge come from within the learner as that individual explores, discovers, and makes connections.

The National Council of Teachers of Mathematics' *Professional Standards for Teaching Mathematics* presents a vision of mathematics teaching that "redirects mathematics instruction from a focus on presenting content through lecture and demonstration to a focus on active participation and involvement." In this vision, "mathematics instructors do not simply deliver content; rather, they facilitate learners' construction of their own knowledge of mathematics."

This book contains activities and materials to actively engage students in mathematical explorations. It provides prospective elementary and middle school teachers the opportunity to examine and learn mathematics in a meaningful way. It also provides instructors with a variety of resources for making an interactive approach to mathematics the focus of their teaching.

OUR PHILOSOPHY

Mathematics for Elementary Teachers: An Activity Approach is a collection of activities for prospective teachers that involves and develops inductive and deductive reasoning. The activities enable students to think deeply about how manipulatives and visual models contribute to understanding mathematical concepts. Students experience mathematics directly by using models that embody concepts and promote mathematical thinking. This book reflects the beliefs that:

- Prospective teachers who learn mathematics through appropriate use of manipulatives, models, and diagrams are more likely to develop a solid conceptual basis and a deeper understanding of the mathematics they will teach.
- Prospective teachers who learn mathematics by being actively involved in doing mathematics will be more likely to teach in the same manner.
- Prospective teachers who use manipulatives effectively in their learning will experience how manipulatives assist understanding and will be more likely to use them effectively in their teaching.
- Becoming familiar with manipulatives and models in structured activities will give prospective teachers confidence to develop lessons that use manipulatives and models.
- A concrete approach diminishes the mathematical anxiety that often accompanies a more abstract approach.
- Tactile and visual approaches provide mental images that, for some students, can be easily retained to provide understanding for symbolic representations.

COOPERATIVE LEARNING AND USING MANIPULATIVES

Each Activity Set can be done individually or in small groups. Small group instruction provides opportunities for discussion and for listening to others explain their reasoning. Guidelines for cooperative learning in small groups are outlined in Activity Set 2.3.

It is well known that effective teachers have a good understanding of the mathematics they teach and are skillful in choosing and using a variety of appropriate instructional techniques. The importance of using manipulatives in mathematics teaching and learning is well documented and amply illustrated in the pages of NCTM's *Principles and Standards for School Mathematics*. Research has shown that the appropriate use of manipulative materials has a significant positive effect on students' attitudes to learning and potential for achievement in mathematics.

Interviews with teachers successfully using manipulatives in classrooms revealed the following commonalities:

- The teachers all received training for using manipulatives.
- They designed their own lessons and worked through them using manipulatives themselves.
- They prepared for classroom use of the manipulatives by anticipating how the class would react to each activity.

FEATURES OF THE NINTH EDITION

Mathematics for Elementary Teachers: An Activity Approach consists of 34 Activity Sets and accompanying materials, which, collectively, constitute a self-contained mathematics laboratory. It contains many special features designed to enhance learning.

Discovery Based Activity Sets   Each Activity Set uses materials and/or visual models to provide a context for understanding. The questions and activities in each Activity Set are sequentially developed to encourage discovery and to provide an in-depth exploration of a topic. Students are asked to describe patterns, form conjectures, look for relationships, and discuss their thinking.

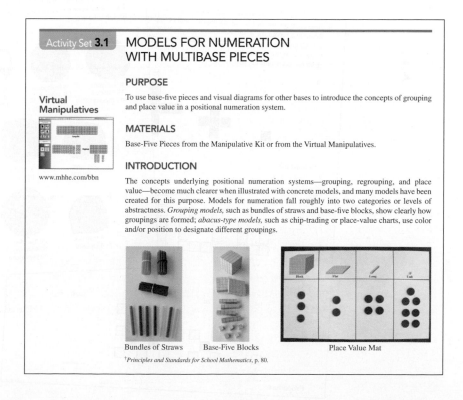

Activity Set **3.1**   MODELS FOR NUMERATION WITH MULTIBASE PIECES

Virtual Manipulatives

www.mhhe.com/bbn

PURPOSE

To use base-five pieces and visual diagrams for other bases to introduce the concepts of grouping and place value in a positional numeration system.

MATERIALS

Base-Five Pieces from the Manipulative Kit or from the Virtual Manipulatives.

INTRODUCTION

The concepts underlying positional numeration systems—grouping, regrouping, and place value—become much clearer when illustrated with concrete models, and many models have been created for this purpose. Models for numeration fall roughly into two categories or levels of abstractness. *Grouping models,* such as bundles of straws and base-five blocks, show clearly how groupings are formed; *abacus-type models,* such as chip-trading or place-value charts, use color and/or position to designate different groupings.

Bundles of Straws   Base-Five Blocks   Place Value Mat

†*Principles and Standards for School Mathematics*, p. 80.

Full-Color Diagrams Using color diagrams that match the actual manipulatives strengthens pedagogy and conceptual learning.

Exploring Attributes

1. Place your *small blue square, small red squar*...
   squares of the grid below. In the first row of th...
   small red square in exactly one attribute—co...
   differs from the small yellow circle in exact...
   remaining small attribute pieces to fill the...
   exactly one attribute and adjacent pieces in...
   your results on the grid. There are many possi...

5. The tiles for the figures in the tile sequence for consecutive odd numbers can be rearranged as follows:

Original sequence

Rearranged tiles

Repositioned tiles

3. Here are three sets of tile figures and the number sequen...
   figure and record the fourth number in each number se...
   in each number sequence by imagining how you would...
   sequence. Write a procedure using words or an algebr...
   reader to determine the number of tiles in any figure, g...

a.   1st   2d   3d

1   5

Procedure:

*b.   1st   2d

8   12

Procedure:

c.   1st   2d   3d   4th

1   5   13

Procedure:

5. **Archimedean Solids:** A *semiregular polyhedron* is a polyhedron that has as faces two or more regular polygons and the same arrangement of polygons about each vertex. There are a total of 13 semiregular polyhedra shown below, and they are called *Archimedean solids.* These were known to Archimedes (287–212 B.C.E.) who wrote a book on these solids, but the book has been lost.

a.   b.   c.   d.   e.

8 hexagons   8 hexagons   20 hexagons   8 triangles   20 hexagons
12 squares   6 squares   30 squares   18 squares   12 pentagons
6 octagons   12 decagons

f.   g.   h.   i.

8 triangles   20 triangles   20 triangles   32 triangles
6 octagons   12 pentagons   12 decagons   6 squares

j.   k.   l.   m.

8 triangles   20 triangles   80 triangles   4 triangles
6 squares   30 squares   12 pentagons   4 hexagons
                 12 pentagons

Colored Cardstock Manipulatives   Manipulatives designed for use with each Activity Set (and selected *Exercises and Activities*) are packaged with each text. A Manipulative Kit holds resealable, labeled envelopes for each type of manipulative.

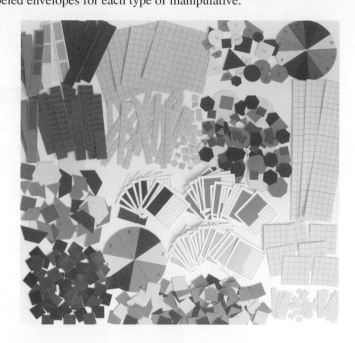

Virtual Manipulatives   There are corresponding Virtual Manipulatives and work areas on the companion website (www.mhhe.com/bbn).

Material Cards   In addition to the Manipulative Kit, the *Activity Approach* text also offers 39 Material Cards (some of which are colored) with additional manipulatives, models, grids, templates, and game mats.

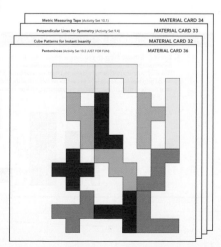

Activities for the Elementary School Classroom   At the end of each chapter, there is an Elementary School lesson plan showing how the manipulatives, instructional strategies, and concepts from the chapter can be adapted for use in elementary classrooms. The activities are not designed for a specific grade level but can easily be varied to fit a specific level. The objective is to demonstrate how the ideas from an Activity Set can be used in elementary school classrooms. Each activity is illustrated with engaging photographs of elementary school students using manipulatives.

ACTIVITIES FOR THE ELEMENTARY SCHOOL CLASSROOM

Finding Averages with Color Tiles

Purpose: To provide elementary school students with a visual introduction and meaning to finding the average of whole numbers.

Connections: Ask the class what the word "average" means. They may suggest several meanings, such as an average person or an average score. Discuss a few meanings of this word and tell them that today we are going to discover the meaning of the word "average" in mathematics.

Materials: Sets of color tiles may be created by copying 2-centimeter grid paper on four different colors of cardstock or by copying the color tile images from the companion website. Color tile transparencies can also be made with the color tile images. Sets of 20 of each of four colors can be placed in plastic sealable bags for storage. Each group of two to four students will need one set of color tiles. Students will also need centimeter grid paper for recording averages with fractional parts.

1. Place two towers of tile on the overhead, one of height 7 and the other of height 3 and have the students form the same towers at their tables. Ask the students to level off the towers by shifting tiles so that towers both have the same height. Tell them that this leveling off process can be used to find the average of numbers. Ask them, "What is the average of 7 and 3?"

2. Ask the students to find the average of 1 and 5 by building two towers and leveling them off. Then, without building towers, ask them to imagine towers of heights 20 and 26 and mentally find the average of 20 and 26. Have student volunteers share the different ways they determined the average was 23.

3. Ask the students to find the average of 5 and 8 by building towers or doing it mentally. Discuss that it is permissible to use half tiles (or fractions of tiles). Allow students to use grid paper to record this new idea. See the two towers at the left.

4. Place the five towers shown at the left on the overhead and ask the students to find the average of the five numbers by leveling off the towers. Discuss the average and then pose questions like the following (keep the original towers of heights 4, 5, 2, 1, and 3 on your overhead so students can refer back to the original towers):

   a. Tell the students that each tower represents the feet of snow that fell in Nisswa, Minnesota, for each of the past 5 years. Ask each group to discuss and report what they believe is the average snowfall for Nisswa during this 5-year period.

   b. If it snowed 6 feet the next year, have them use their tile and grid paper to determine the 6-year average.

   c. If it did not snow at all during the sixth year ask them to discuss and determine what the 6-year average would be.

Students find the average of 7, 2, and 6 by leveling off towers of 7 cubes, 2 cubes, and 6 cubes to a height of 5 cubes.

Exercises and Activities   Exercises and Activities at the end of each Activity Set ask students to relate the content and ideas of the Activity Set to three important areas:

- School Classroom
- Math Concepts
- NCTM Standards

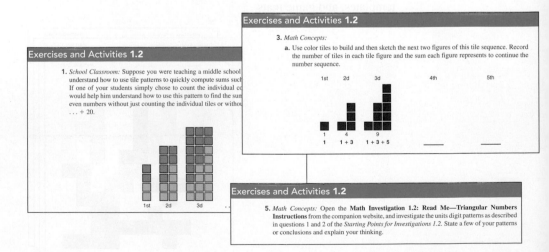

Exercises and Activities **1.2**

1. *School Classroom:* Suppose you were teaching a middle school understand how to use tile patterns to quickly compute sums such If one of your students simply chose to count the individual co would help him understand how to use this pattern to find the sum even numbers without just counting the individual tiles or withou . . . + 20.

1st   2d   3d

Exercises and Activities **1.2**

3. *Math Concepts:*

   a. Use color tiles to build and then sketch the next two figures of this tile sequence. Record the number of tiles in each tile figure and the sum each figure represents to continue the number sequence.

   1st   2d   3d   4th   5th

   1   4   9
   1   1 + 3   1 + 3 + 5   _____   _____

Exercises and Activities **1.2**

5. *Math Concepts:* Open the **Math Investigation 1.2: Read Me—Triangular Numbers Instructions** from the companion website, and investigate the units digit patterns as described in questions 1 and 2 of the *Starting Points for Investigations 1.2.* State a few of your patterns or conclusions and explain your thinking.

NCTM Standards and Expectations   A durable, removable cardstock table of the **NCTM Standards and Expectations for Grades PreK–2, 3–5, and 6–8** is provided in the back of the book so students can answer end of section *Exercises and Activities* and see what mathematics is recommended at various grade levels.

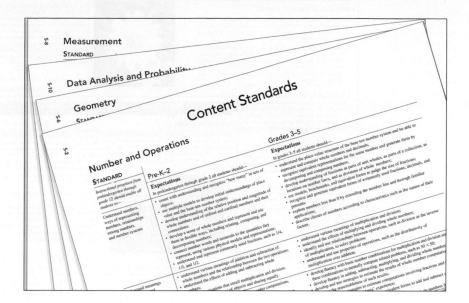

Technology Connection Through Applets   Each chapter directs students to an appropriate interactive applet from the companion website (www.mhhe.com/bbn). The applets pose questions for student explorations.

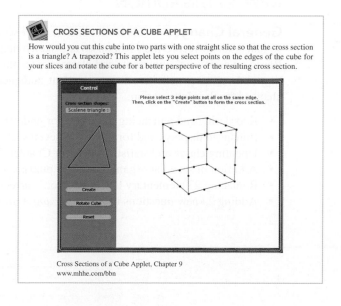

Just for Fun   Each Activity Set is followed by a *Just for Fun* activity. These are related to the topics of the Activity Sets and often relate to recreational activities or have an artistic aspect.

Answer Section   Answers to selected questions (marked with an asterisk) in the Activity Sets appear in the back of the book.

NEW TO THIS EDITION

General Changes   This book consists of 34 sections of inductive activities and is designed so that students record their responses and sketch diagrams in the spaces following each activity. Based on reviewers' comments and classroom testing, many changes have been made in formatting and restating activities for the student audience. Here is a summary of student-centered changes for the ninth edition:

- Reordering and enhancing questions for understanding in nine sections
- Enhanced displays and formatting in seven sections
- Updating charts and statistical data for Chapter 7
- Addition of seven new games and two puzzles into the activity sets
- Replacing 23 elementary text pages from current elementary school texts
- Adding 23 new questions to *Exercises and Activities* questions.

New Elementary School Text Book Pages

In order to make the connection between this text and elementary school curricula, sample pages from current elementary school textbooks were carefully chosen to demonstrate the relevance between a course based on this text and the elementary classroom. Twenty-three new pages were chosen, roughly equally distributed from grades 1 through 8.

New Exercises and Activities Questions for Elementary School Text Pages

Each of the 23 new Elementary School Text pages has an associated question in the *Exercises and Activities* section. The questions relate the concepts and activities of the section to the school text pages in order to demonstrate the relevance of the text sections to elementary classroom materials.

The questions often ask the students to take a position and make a case for the inclusion or exclusion of certain elementary classroom activities. Other times they are asked to cross-check the timing and grade placement of activities with the NCTM Content Standards. Often students simply answer and reflect on questions from the elementary text pages.

Exercises and Activities 3.1

3. *School Classroom:* Read through the activity on the **Elementary School Text** page at the beginning of this section. Notice that elementary students are asked to use base-ten pieces to model the same number in different ways. Explain in writing how use students understand the base-ten numeration system and place va against using different base pieces, such as base-five pieces, as w develop the concepts of numeration systems and place value for sc

Exercises and Activities 6.1

3. *School Classroom:* The **Elementary School Text** page at the beginning of this section shows four models for illustrating the decimal 1.65.

a. Using the three models (1) *Money,* (2) *Decimal Model,* and (3) *Base-Ten Blocks,* illustrate and explain how you would use each model to help an elementary school student see that 2.3 > 2.29.

b. Explain how you would relate each model in part a to the *Place-Value Chart* model also shown on the school page.

New Games and Problem-Solving Puzzles

The previous edition has a total of 28 conceptual games and 13 puzzles in the Activity Sets and in sections following the Activity Sets, called *Just for Fun* sections. In this edition seven new conceptual games and two puzzles have been included within the Activity Sets. These hands-on games and puzzles have been classroom tested for the past two years.

There are several reasons for including these new games and puzzles. Certainly they do promote small-group work and communication. Most also include some logical reasoning in addition to chance. Because they are included in the Activity Sets, they are played and then analyzed and discussed through follow-up questions in the Activity Set. Perhaps an even more subtle reason for introducing them in certain Activity Sets had to do with motivation. We found that in many of the activities the manipulatives themselves were novel and engaging. However, in some of the later Activity Sets, students moved through the sets with less enthusiasm. Adding these new games and activities to sections 2.2, 5.2, 5.3, 6.1, 6.2, and 6.6 brought more student energy and interaction to our classes.

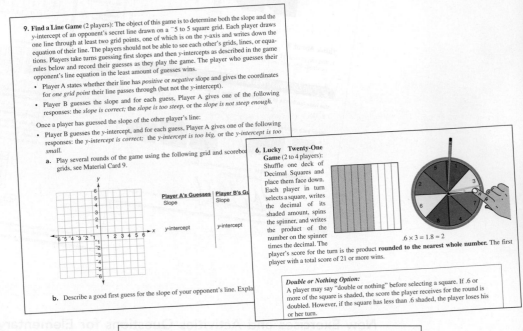

9. Find a Line Game (2 players): The object of this game is to determine both the slope and the y-intercept of an opponent's secret line drawn on a ⁻5 to 5 square grid. Each player draws one line through at least two grid points, one of which is on the y-axis and writes down the equation of their line. The players should not be able to see each other's grids, lines, or equations. Players take turns guessing first slopes and then y-intercepts as described in the game rules below and record their guesses as they play the game. The player who guesses their opponent's line equation in the least amount of guesses wins.

- Player A states whether their line has *positive* or *negative* slope and gives the coordinates for *one grid point* their line passes through (but not the y-intercept).
- Player B guesses the slope and for each guess, Player A gives one of the following responses: the *slope is correct;* the *slope is too steep,* or the *slope is not steep enough.*

Once a player has guessed the slope of the other player's line:

- Player B guesses the y-intercept, and for each guess, Player A gives one of the following responses: the *y-intercept is correct;* the *y-intercept is too big,* or the *y-intercept is too small.*

    a. Play several rounds of the game using the following grid and scoreboard grids, see Material Card 9.

Player A's Guesses	Player B's Gu
Slope	Slope
y-intercept	y-intercept

    b. Describe a good first guess for the slope of your opponent's line. Expla

**6. Lucky   Twenty-One
Game** (2 to 4 players): Shuffle one deck of Decimal Squares and place them face down. Each player in turn selects a square, writes the decimal of its shaded amount, spins the spinner, and writes the product of the number on the spinner times the decimal. The player's score for the turn is the product **rounded to the nearest whole number.** The first player with a total score of 21 or more wins.

$$.6 \times 3 = 1.8 = 2$$

Double or Nothing Option:
A player may say "double or nothing" before selecting a square. If .6 or more of the square is shaded, the score the player receives for the round is doubled. However, if the square has less than .6 shaded, the player loses his or her turn.

PYTHAGOREAN PUZZLE VISUAL PROOF

FEATURES OF THE COMPANION WEBSITE
(www.mhhe.com/bbn)

The companion website for the ninth edition of *Mathematics for Elementary Teachers: An Activity Approach* features improved and updated resources. There are three major headings: Information Center, Instructor Center, and Student Center. Instructors can obtain a password from their local McGraw-Hill representative; the Student Center is accessible without a password.

Student and Instructor Centers

Interactive Mathematics Applets demonstrate key mathematical concepts in engaging contexts. The applets include Solving Tower Puzzles, Hunting for Hidden Polygons, Deciphering Ancient Numeration Systems, Analyzing Star Polygons, Taking a Chance, Competing at Place Value, Distributions, Door Prizes, Cross-Sections of a Cube, Filling 3-D Figures, and Tessellations.

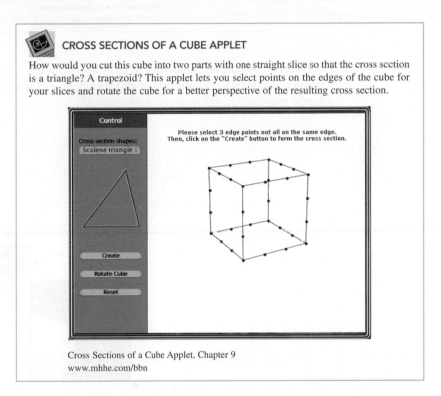

Cross Sections of a Cube Applet, Chapter 9
www.mhhe.com/bbn

Virtual Manipulatives, interactive versions of the cardstock Manipulative Kit pieces, are available for carrying out the Math Activities in the text. Each manipulative has a toolbar, a work area, a note pad, and a menu for easy access to the corresponding activities.

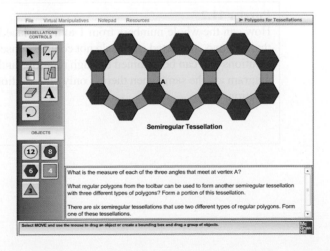

Math Investigations are offered for each section to promote a deeper understanding of topics from the text through the use of computers, calculators, and laboratory activities. Data for 14 of the investigations can be generated using the *Mathematics Investigator* software available on the site.

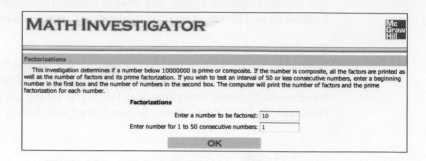

Geometer's Sketchpad Modules can be downloaded for eight of the Math Investigations. Each module is designed to facilitate open-ended student explorations while simultaneously providing a gentle introduction to Geometer's Sketchpad®.

Puzzlers for each section can be used to engage and entertain students.

Puzzler 11.2

How can the whole numbers from 1 to 8 be placed in the circles of the figure shown here so that any two connected circles do not contain consecutive whole numbers? If we agree that all solutions that can be obtained through rotations and reflections of this diagram are the same, then there is only one solution. Find this unique solution.

Grid and Dot Paper are available in a variety of formats, along with black-and-white masters for geoboards, regular polygons, Decimal Squares, base-ten grids, the coordinate system, and the random-number chart.

Color Transparency Masters for the Manipulative Kit items can be downloaded for producing transparencies for in-class use.

Internet Resources for further reading are provided for each section of the text.

Logo Instruction on the site includes special commands, worked examples, and exercises. Answers for the odd-numbered Logo exercises are included in the Student Center of the companion website and answers for the even-numbered exercises are included in the Instructor's Center of the companion website.

Network Graphs Instruction on the site includes worked examples and exercises. Answers for the odd-numbered Network exercises are included on the companion website and answers for the even-numbered exercises are in the *Instructor's Manual*.

Instructor-Only Center
Daily Planning Guides have ideas for teaching each section of the *Activity Approach* text. For each Activity Set, the guides include:

1. A brief summary of the purpose of the Activity Set
2. Student and Instructor material lists
3. Comments, tips, and teaching suggestions
4. Suggested Projects and Additional Assignments

Locating Sets of Points in the Plane
ACTIVITY SET 11.1 PLANNING GUIDE

Activity Set Summary

This section explores what were traditionally called *locus* problems. Students are asked to determine, and then describe, sets of points in the plane that satisfy certain given conditions.

Activity Set

Student Materials: A Ruler, Compass, and Protractor from Material Card 19, pieces of paper, two index cards and scissors. A piece of string about 20 cm long for each pair of students if you choose to do the Lead In activity.

Instructor Materials: No additional materials are needed.

I.   Lead In

Ask the students to place two points, A and B, about 8 cm apart in the middle of a clean sheet of paper. Ask them to add another point C so that distance from the C to A plus the distance from C to B is 16 cm. Discuss possible locations of C and how there are many such points satisfying these conditions that can be added to their diagrams.

Depending upon the suggestions the students give, you may wish to introduce using a string as a method for finding all possible locations for C. One way is to tie two knots in the string, 16 cm apart, and have one student hold the knots at the points A and B with pencil points while another student stretches the string and draws a curve.

Summarize by explaining to your students that this is how an ellipse is defined: An ellipse is a set of points, P, such that the sum of the distances from a fixed point A to P and a fixed point B to P is constant. Point A and point B are each called a focus of the ellipse.

Editable Chapter Tests are available for instructors to download for help with student assessment.

Complete *Instructor's Manual* with solutions to all Activity Set activities, Just for Fun activities, Exercises and Activity questions, and website Math Investigations is available for instructor download.

Additional Resources Mathematics for Elementary Teachers: A Conceptual Approach, ninth edition (ISBN-13: 978-0-07-351957-9; ISBN-10: 0-07-351957-X) This is an optional companion volume to the *Activity Approach*. Each of the 34 sections in it corresponds to one of the Activity Sets. The text also contains a one-page Math Activity at the beginning of each section that utilizes the same Manipulative Kit materials as the *Activity Approach*. The Manipulative Kit ISBN-13: 978-0-07-743093-1, ISBN-10: 0-07-743093-X is available for use with the *Activity Approach* and the *Conceptual Approach*. It can also be purchased separately.

Manipulative Kit Mathematics for Elementary Teachers, **Ninth Edition (ISBN-13: 978-0-07-743093-1 ISBN-10: 0-07-743093-X)** A Manipulative Kit containing 10 colorful manipulatives commonly used in elementary schools is available for use with this text and *Mathematics for Elementary Teachers: A Conceptual Approach*. This kit includes resealable, labeled envelopes for each type of manipulative.

Instructor's Resource Manual   The *Instructor's Resource Manual* to accompany *Mathematics for Elementary Teachers: An Activity Approach*, Ninth Edition, contains an updated set of section-by-section Planning Guides with detailed suggestions for teaching a course using the *Activity Approach*. The *Instructor's Manual* includes answers for all of the Activity Set questions and the *Just for Fun* activities, as well as selected answers for the updated end-of-section *Exercises and Activities*. The *Instructor's Manual* also provides a set of sample test questions, with answers, for each chapter of the *Activity Approach*. The *Instructor's Resource Manual* can be found at the companion website for *Mathematics for Elementary Teachers: An Activity Approach*, accessible at www.mhhe.com/bbn.

Create   Craft your teaching resources to match the way you teach! With McGraw-Hill Create™, www.mcgrawhillcreate.com, you can easily rearrange chapters, combine material from other content sources, and quickly upload content you have written like your course syllabus or teaching notes. Find the content you need in Create by searching through thousands of leading McGraw-Hill textbooks. Arrange your book to fit your teaching style. Create even allows you to personalize your book's appearance by selecting the cover and adding your name, school, and course information. Order a Create book and you'll receive a complimentary print review copy in 3–5 business days or a complimentary electronic review copy (eComp) via email in minutes. Go to www.mcgrawhill create.com today and register to experience how McGraw-Hill Create™ empowers you to teach *your* students *your* way.

Tegrity

 McGraw-Hill Tegrity Campus™ is a service that makes class time available all the time by automatically capturing every lecture in a searchable format for students to review when they study and complete assignments. With a simple one-click start-and-stop process, you capture all computer screens and corresponding audio. Students replay any part of any class with easy-to-use browser-based viewing on a PC or Mac. Educators know that the more students can see, hear, and experience class resources, the better they learn. With Tegrity Campus, students quickly recall key moments by using Tegrity Campus's unique search feature. This search helps students efficiently find what they need, when they need it across an entire semester of class recordings. Help turn all your students' study time into learning moments immediately supported by your lecture.

To learn more about Tegrity, watch a 2-minute Flash demo at http://tegritycampus.mhhe.com.

COURSE FORMATS

Many of the Activity Sets in *Mathematics for Elementary Teachers: An Activity Approach* are independent of each other and can be covered out of sequence (see the *Instructor's Resource Manual* for information on the Activity Set dependencies). The flexible coverage of the *Activity Approach* makes it possible for the book to be used effectively in a variety of course formats:

- A lab course based on the Activity Sets and supplemented with outside readings from a reference text or journals, with the *Exercises and Activities* used for assignments

- A combination lab and recitation course in which the Activity Sets are integrated with discussions or lectures extending the ideas raised in the Activity Sets and developed further in *Mathematics for Elementary Teachers: A Conceptual Approach*
- A traditional lecture/recitation course in which the Activity Sets and *Exercises and Activities Questions* in the *Activity Approach* are used to supplement *Mathematics for Elementary Teachers: A Conceptual Approach*

COMMON PACKAGING OPTIONS

Mathematics for Elementary Teachers: An Activity Approach, Ninth Edition, packaged with *Manipulative Kit Mathematics for Elementary Teachers,* Ninth Edition
(ISBN-13: 978-0-07-796887-8 ISBN-10: 0-07-796887-5)

Mathematics for Elementary Teachers: A Conceptual Approach, Ninth Edition, and *Mathematics for Elementary Teachers: An Activity Approach,* packaged with *Manipulative Kit Mathematics for Elementary Teachers,* Ninth Edition
(ISBN-13: 978-0-07-796885-4 ISBN-10: 0-07-796885-9)

Mathematics for Elementary Teachers: A Conceptual Approach, Ninth Edition, packaged with *Manipulative Kit Mathematics for Elementary Teachers,* Ninth Edition
(ISBN-13: 978-0-07-796883-0 ISBN-10: 0-07-796883-2)

For additional packaging options please consult your McGraw-Hill sales representative. To find your rep, please visit www.mhhe.com/rep.

ACKNOWLEDGMENTS

The authors would like to thank the students and instructors who have used the previous editions of this book, along with the instructors who reviewed this book and *Mathematics for Elementary Teachers: A Conceptual Approach.* The following reviewers contributed excellent advice and suggestions for the ninth edition of *Mathematics for Elementary Teachers: An Activity Approach:*

Reviewers of This Edition
Shari Beck, *Navarro College*
Chris Christopher, *Bridgewater College*
Ivette Chuca, *El Paso Community College*
Tandy Del Vecchio, *University of Maine*
Krista Hands, *Ashland University*
Karen Heinz, *Rowan University*
Kurt Killion, *Missouri State University*
Greg Klein, *Texas A&M University*
Elsa Lopez, *El Paso Community College*
Nicole Muth, *Concordia University—Wisconsin*
Winnie Peterson, *Kutztown University*
Michael Price, *University of Oregon*
Elizabeth Smith, *University of Louisiana— Monroe*
Mary Ann Teel, *University of North Texas*
William N. Thomas, Jr., *University of Toledo*
Tammy Voepel, *Southern Illinois University—Edwardsville*
Candide Walton, *Southeast Missouri State University*

Laurie Burton would like to especially thank all of the Western Oregon University students and faculty, in particular, Dr. Cheryl Beaver, who have willingly class-tested new materials and provided many helpful suggestions and corrections. The authors are sincerely grateful for all of this continued support as we seek to update and improve our materials. Finally, we would like to thank the people at McGraw-Hill who have dedicated their time and creativity to enhance and improve this edition of *Mathematics for Elementary Teachers: An Activity Approach.*

CHAPTER

1

Problem Solving

In grades 3–5, students should investigate numerical and geometric patterns and express them mathematically in words or symbols. They should analyze the structure of the pattern and how it grows or changes, organize this information systemically, and use their analysis to develop generalizations about the mathematical relationships in the pattern.[†]

Activity Set 1.1 | SEEING AND EXTENDING PATTERNS WITH PATTERN BLOCKS

PURPOSE

To recognize, describe, construct, and extend geometric patterns.

Virtual Manipulatives

www.mhhe.com/bbn

MATERIALS

Pattern Blocks and Color Tiles from the Manipulative Kit or from the Virtual Manipulatives.

INTRODUCTION

In this first activity set, colored geometric shapes called pattern blocks will be used to recognize, study, and extend geometric patterns. The set of pattern blocks consists of six different polygons: a green triangle, an orange square, a red trapezoid, a blue rhombus, a tan rhombus, and a yellow hexagon.

Human beings are pattern-seeking creatures. Babies begin life's journey listening for verbal patterns and looking for visual patterns. Scientists in search of extraterrestrial intelligence send patterned signals into the universe and listen for incoming patterns on radio telescopes. Mathematics is also concerned with patterns. Many mathematicians and educators involved in reforming mathematics teaching and learning at the elementary and middle school levels are suggesting that the notion of mathematics as the study of number and shape needs to be expanded. Some suggest that "mathematics is an exploratory science that seeks to understand every kind of pattern."[‡]

In this set we will look at a variety of sequences. A **sequence** is an ordered set of objects. There are many possibilities for sequences. A few examples of sequences are a sequence of pattern block figures, a sequence of tile figures, a sequence of letter groupings, a sequence of whole numbers, and a sequence of fractions.

[†]*Principles and Standards for School Mathematics*, p. 159.

[‡]Lynn A. Steen, *On the Shoulders of Giants: New Approaches to Numeracy*, pp. 1–8.

Name _____

Create a Pattern

Get Ready

Main Idea

I will create a pattern.

Mario is making a pattern. The pattern unit is three shapes long. It repeats over and over.

✓ Check

Use pattern blocks. Create a pattern.
Trace the pattern blocks. Then color.

1. Use ▪ ▲ .

2. Use ▲ ▪ .

3. **Talk About It** Look at your pattern in Exercise 1. Identify the pattern unit and describe the pattern.

Exercises and Activities 1.1

1. *School Classroom:* A second-grade teacher started the following pattern block sequence and asked her students to continue the pattern by adding five more pattern blocks.

   a. One student looked at the sequence and said he did not know what to do. Describe what you would say or do as the teacher.

   b. Another student continued the pattern block sequence as follows. Describe what you believe this student was thinking. What questions can you ask to encourage the student to reveal how she perceived and extended the pattern?

2. *School Classroom:* Design a pattern block sequence that you believe is appropriate for an elementary school student and write a few questions that you can ask about your sequence. Try this activity on an elementary school age child of your choice. Record your sequence, your questions, and the student's responses.

3. *School Classroom:* The example from the **Elementary School Text** at the beginning of this section shows a student using pattern blocks to create and extend a pattern. At the bottom of the page, students are asked to create a pattern, and then to identify the pattern unit and describe the pattern. Explain what you would say or do as the teacher to help a student who is struggling to create a pattern with pattern blocks, without just telling the student what to do.

4. *Math Concepts:* Make up two secret pattern block or color tile sequences that have the same first four figures but different figures after that. Show the first four figures to a partner and challenge your partner to find both of your secret sequences. Illustrate your sequences and explain the results of your challenge.

5. *Math Concepts:* A pattern block figure is shown below.

   Figure 1

   a. Use your pattern blocks to create a pattern block sequence for which Figure 1 is the *second* figure in the sequence. Sketch diagrams of the first, third, and fourth figures in your sequence, and write a rule for extending the pattern you created so that the reader is able to build the next few figures in your sequence.

   b. Use your pattern blocks to create a second pattern block sequence for which Figure 1 is the *fourth* figure in the sequence. Sketch diagrams of the first, second, third, and fifth figures in your sequence, and write a rule for extending the pattern you created so that the reader is able to build the next few figures in your second sequence.

6. *Math Concepts:* The first two figures in a color tile sequence are shown below. Extend this color tile sequence in two different ways and answer the following questions for each of your sequences.

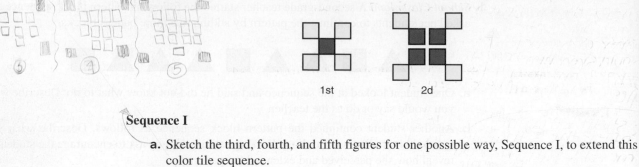

1st   2d

Sequence I

a. Sketch the third, fourth, and fifth figures for one possible way, Sequence I, to extend this color tile sequence.

b. How many color tiles are in the 100th and 101st figures in your Sequence I? Explain how you determined your answer.

c. Write a rule for extending your Sequence I so that a reader is able to build any figure in the sequence.

Sequence II

a. Sketch the third, fourth, and fifth figures for a second possible way, Sequence II, to extend this color tile sequence.

b. How many color tiles are in the 100th and 101st figures in your Sequence II? Explain how you determined your answer.

c. Write a rule for extending your Sequence II so that a reader is able to build any figure in the sequence.

7. *NCTM Standards:* The National Council of Teachers of Mathematics (NCTM) is a professional organization whose goal is to improve the teaching and learning of mathematics. Go to the NCTM website, www.nctm.org, to locate information on their publication, *The Principles and Standards for School Mathematics.* Write a short description of the purpose of this publication and give the specific URL where you found this information.

8. *NCTM Standards:* Go to the **Pre-K–2 Standards** in the back pages of this book, and find the *Expectation* where studying patterns is recommended. State the *Expectation* and the *Content Standard* the *Expectation* is under, and explain why you think the study of patterns is under this particular *Standard.*

---

www.mhhe.com/bbn

bennett-burton-nelson website

Virtual Manipulatives   Grid and Dot Paper   Links and Readings
Interactive Chapter Applets   Color Transparencies   Geometer Sketchpad Modules
Puzzlers   Extended Bibliography

JUST FOR FUN

FIBONACCI NUMBERS IN NATURE

The Fibonacci numbers 1, 1, 2, 3, 5, 8, 13, . . . occur in nature in a variety of unexpected ways. Following the first two numbers of this sequence, each number is obtained by adding the previous two numbers. What are the next five numbers in this sequence?

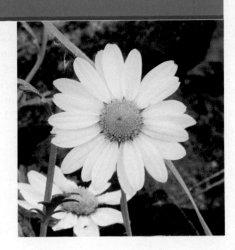

*1. Daisies: Field daisies often have 21, 34, 55, or 89 petals. If you are playing the game "loves me, loves me not" with a daisy, which numbers of petals will result in a yes answer? Would the daisy shown here be a good one to play this game? The centers of daisies have clockwise and counterclockwise spirals. The numbers of these spirals are also Fibonacci numbers.

2. Sunflowers: The seeds of the sunflower form two spiral patterns, one proceeding in a clockwise direction and one in a counterclockwise direction. The numbers of spirals in the two directions are consecutive Fibonacci numbers. In the photograph, there are 34 counterclockwise and 55 clockwise spirals. In larger sunflowers, there are spirals of 89 and 144. Find a sunflower and count its spirals.

3. Cones: Pine, hemlock, and spruce cones have spirals of scalelike structures called bracts. The numbers of these spirals are almost always Fibonacci numbers. In the pinecone photograph below, a clockwise spiral is identified by Xs and a counterclockwise spiral with Ys. See if you can find the 8 clockwise and 13 counterclockwise spirals.

4. Pineapples: The sections of a pineapple are also arranged in spirals that represent Fibonacci number patterns. Find a pineapple, and count its spirals from upper left to lower right and from lower left to upper right.

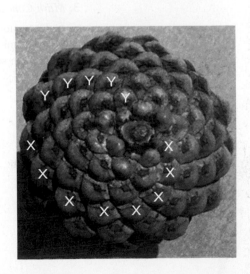

Exercises and Activities **1.2**

1. *School Classroom:* Suppose you were teaching a middle school class and helping students understand how to use tile patterns to quickly compute sums such as 2 + 4 + 6 + ... + 20. If one of your students simply chose to count the individual color tiles, explain how you would help him understand how to use this pattern to find the sum of the first 10 consecutive even numbers without just counting the individual tiles or without just adding 2 + 4 + 6 + ... + 20.

1st   2d   3d   . . .

2. *School Classroom:* One *Expectation* in the **Pre-K–2 Algebra Standard** in the back pages of this book says that students should be able to transfer from one representation of a pattern to another.

   a. Create a pattern with color tiles that you believe children at the Pre-K–2 level can "transfer" from a tile pattern to a number pattern. Record your tile pattern and the corresponding number pattern. 2, 4, 6, 8, ...

   b. Create a number pattern that you believe children at the Pre-K–2 level can transfer from a number pattern to a color tile pattern. Record your number pattern and the corresponding tile pattern. 1, 3, 5, 7, ...

   c. If you were to try the patterns you created with children at the Pre-K–2 level, what difficulties might you expect them to encounter, and how would you prepare them to overcome those difficulties?

3. *Math Concepts:*

   a. Use color tiles to build and then sketch the next two figures of this tile sequence. Record the number of tiles in each tile figure and the sum each figure represents to continue the number sequence.

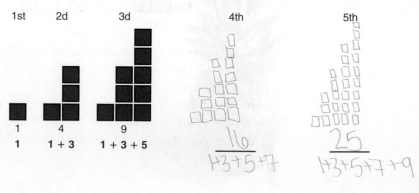

1st   2d   3d   4th   5th

1   4   9   16   25

1   1 + 3   1 + 3 + 5   1+3+5+7   1+3+5+7+9

b. By duplicating each of the figures in part a and inverting the duplicate copy, rectangles are formed. Build and sketch the 4th figure in the sequence of rectangles. Explain how you can use the 4th rectangular array in the tile sequence to find the sum of the odd numbers $1 + 3 + 5 + 7$ without just adding. *There are double the amt of 16, so it is 32.*

1st   2d   3d   4th

c. Explain how you can use rectangular arrays to obtain the sum of the odd numbers from 1 to 191 without just adding $1 + 3 + 5 + 7 + 9 + \ldots + 191$.

4. *Math Concepts:* Design and sketch the first three figures of a color tile sequence that grows in an interesting pattern such as the tile sequences in activities 2 and 3.

    a. Write a procedure in words that enables you to determine the number of tiles in the 10th figure of your tile sequence without actually constructing the 10th figure. How many tiles are in the 10th figure of your tile sequence?

    b. Write a procedure using words or an algebraic expression to determine the number of tiles for any figure, *n*, in your tile sequence. Explain your thinking.

5. *Math Concepts:* Open the **Math Investigation 1.2: Read Me—Triangular Numbers Instructions** from the companion website, and investigate the units digit patterns as described in questions 1 and 2 of the *Starting Points for Investigations 1.2.* State a few of your patterns or conclusions and explain your thinking.

6. *Math Concepts:* Here are the first three figures in a color tile sequence.

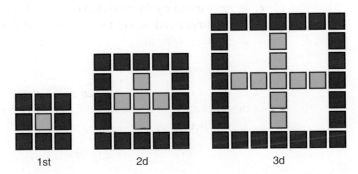

1st   2d   3d

    a. Write directions for constructing the eighth figure of this color tile sequence so that someone who has not seen any of the figures could build the figure by following your directions.

    b. What are the first eight terms in the number sequence represented by the total number of tiles in each of the first eight figures in the above color tile sequence?

    c. Determine the total number of tiles in the 15th figure. How many tiles are red? How many tiles are blue?

d. Write a procedure using words or an algebraic expression to determine the number of red tiles for any figure, *n*. Write a procedure using words or an algebraic expression to determine the number of blue tiles for any figure, *n*.

e. Write a procedure using words or an algebraic expression to determine the total number of tiles for any figure, *n*.

7. *NCTM Standards:* Go to the **Algebra Standards** in the back pages of this book, and for each grade level, Pre-K–2, 3–5, and 6–8 find: "Understand patterns, relations and functions." Using the tile sequence in question 3a, describe how a child at each level is expected to work with this tile sequence.

---

bennett-burton-nelson website

Virtual Manipulatives   Grid and Dot Paper   Links and Readings
Interactive Chapter Applets   Color Transparencies   Geometer Sketchpad Modules
Puzzlers   Extended Bibliography

SOLVING STORY PROBLEMS WITH ALGEBRA PIECES

PURPOSE

To use algebra pieces as a visual model for representing and solving algebra story problems.

MATERIALS

Algebra Pieces on Material Card 1 and scissors to cut them out.

INTRODUCTION

The Greek algebra of the Pythagoreans (ca. 540 B.C.E.) and Euclid (ca. 300 B.C.E.) was not symbolic with letters for variables, as we think of algebra, but geometric. An arbitrary number was expressed as a line segment. To express the sum of two arbitrary numbers, the Greeks joined the two segments end to end. The product of two numbers was represented as the area of a rectangle with the two segments as sides.

Two numbers   Sum of two numbers   Product of two numbers

In this activity set, we will represent and solve algebra story problems using a geometric model similar to that of the Greeks. Our model will consist of two types of pieces: a variable piece and a unit piece. The variable piece will be used to represent an arbitrary line segment or an arbitrary number. Each unit piece will represent a length of 1 unit.

Unit   Variable piece

The algebra pieces can be placed together to form different expressions.

An arbitrary number

Twice a number

3 more than a number

2 more than 3 times a number

---

1. If one variable piece represents a whole number, then two consecutive whole numbers are represented by the algebra pieces in figure a. Figure b illustrates the sum of the two consecutive whole numbers.

Number

Number + 1

Two consecutive whole numbers
(a)

Number   +   Number + 1

The sum of two consecutive whole numbers
(b)

a. Represent four consecutive whole numbers with your algebra pieces. Sketch them here.

b. Using your model and mental arithmetic, determine four consecutive whole numbers, which have a sum of 58. Explain your thinking.

2. Use your algebra pieces to represent the sides of the triangle described as follows:

The second side of the triangle is twice the length of the first side. The third side of the triangle is 6 units longer than the second side.

*a. Draw a sketch of your algebra-piece model of the triangle.

*b. Using your model and mental arithmetic, determine the length of each side of the triangle if the perimeter of the triangle is 66 units. Explain your thinking.

*3. Two pieces of rope differ in length by 7 meters. End to end, their total length is 75 meters. Let one variable piece represent the length of the shorter rope, and let the unit piece represent 1 meter. Use the algebra pieces and mental arithmetic to find the lengths of the pieces of rope. Sketch your pieces and explain your process.

4. There are 3 boys on the school playground for every girl on the playground. Altogether there are 76 children. Let one variable piece represent the number of girls on the playground. Use the algebra pieces and mental arithmetic to find the number of boys and the number of girls on the playground. Sketch your pieces and explain your process.

5. A box contains $2.25 in nickels and dimes. There are three times as many nickels as dimes.

Number of dimes   Number of nickels

a. If one variable piece represents the *number of dimes* in the box, explain why the variable pieces shown above represent the *total number* of nickels and dimes.

b. Suppose each dime is replaced by two nickels so that there are only nickels in the box. Explain why the *total number* of coins is now represented by the following pieces.

c. The total amount of money in the box is $2.25. Explain how the model in part a can be used to determine the *total value* of nickels represented by each variable piece.

d. Explain how you can use the information in part b to determine the original number of dimes and nickels in the box.

*6. Andrea has a collection of nickels, and Greg has a collection of dimes. The number of nickels Andrea has is four times the number of dimes that Greg has. Andrea has 80 cents more than Greg. Let one variable piece represent the number of dimes Greg has. What pieces represent the number of nickels Andrea has? Use the algebra pieces, mental arithmetic, and the techniques in activity 5 to determine how much money Greg has. Sketch your pieces and explain your process.

7. The length of a rectangle is 5 feet more than three times its width. Determine the length and the width if the perimeter is 130 feet. Use your algebra pieces and mental arithmetic to represent this information and solve the question. Sketch your pieces and explain your process.

*8. Three-fifths of the students in a class are women. If the number of men in the class were doubled and the number of women were increased by 9, there would be an equal number of men and women. Represent the number of women by three variable pieces and the number of men by two variable pieces. Use the algebra pieces and mental arithmetic to find the number of students. Sketch your pieces and explain your process.

9. The sum of three numbers is 43. The first number is 5 more than the second number, and the third number is 8 less than twice the first number. Let one variable piece represent the second number, construct the first and third numbers, and add. Use the algebra pieces and mental arithmetic to find the three numbers. Sketch your pieces and explain your process.

JUST FOR FUN

ALGEBRAIC EXPRESSIONS GAME[†] (2 teams)

In this game, players match algebraic expressions to word descriptions. Copies of algebraic expression cards appear on Material Card 2. There are two decks with 12 cards in each deck, one for each team of 12 students. Each student has an expression card similar to the samples shown here.

Play: Team A plays through its 12 cards and the amount of time required is recorded. Then team B plays through its 12 cards and records its time. On team A, the player who has the $n + 1$ card begins by saying, "I have $n + 1$. Who has two less than a number?" Then the player on team A, who has the card with $n - 2$, says, "I have $n - 2$. Who has one more than two times a number?" The game continues in this manner.

On team B, the first player is the player with the $n + 2$ card, and the next player is the player with an algebraic expression matching the word description on the first player's card.

Each deck of 12 cards is circular. That is, the last card in the deck calls the first card. Therefore, all the cards in the deck should be used. If there are fewer than 12 students on a team, some students can use more than one card. If there are more than 12 students on a team, two students can share a card, or more cards can be made.

Objective: The two teams compete against each other to complete the cycle of cards in the shortest amount of time.

First Player

I have
$n + 1$
Who has
two less than a number

Next Player

I have
$n - 2$
Who has
one more than two times a number

Variation: The game can be changed so that word descriptions are matched to algebraic expressions. Two sample cards are shown here. In this case, player 1 says, "I have two more than three times a number. Who has $4x - 1$?" Player 2 says, "I have one less than four times a number. Who has $3x + 5$?" Make a deck of these cards and play this version of the game.

First Player

I have
two more than three times a number
Who has
$4x - 1$

Next Player

I have
one less than four times a number
Who has
$3x + 5$

[†]T. Giambrone, "I HAVE . . . WHO HAS . . .?" *The Mathematics Teacher* 73, 504–506.

Exercises and Activities 1.3

1. *School Classroom:* Suppose you were working with a student who was struggling with the idea of using a variable and could not understand that the variable was not a fixed value. Explain how you could use algebra pieces to help the student understand how the variable is just a placeholder. Give an example question and solution with an algebra piece sketch that you would use to help the student.

2. *School Classroom:* Devise a problem that you believe is appropriate for an upper elementary school student to solve using algebra pieces and mental arithmetic. Write out the problem and notes on "getting started" questions you may wish to ask your student. Try this activity on an upper elementary school age child of your choice. Record your problem, questions or hints you posed, and the student's responses.

3. *Math Concepts:* Use algebra pieces and mental arithmetic to determine four consecutive odd numbers whose sum is 64. Sketch and label your algebra piece model, and explain how you solved the problem.

4. *Math Concepts:* Use your algebra pieces to construct a rectangle whose length is twice its width. Draw a sketch of this rectangle. Using algebra pieces and mental arithmetic, explain how you can determine the length and width of this rectangle if you know the perimeter of the rectangle is 54 units.

5. *Math Concepts:* Five-eighths of the pieces of candy in a bowl of candy are chocolate, one-fourth of the pieces are strawberry, and the remaining pieces are sour apple. If the number of strawberry pieces is tripled, there will be 108 pieces of candy all together. Use algebra pieces and mental arithmetic to determine how many pieces of chocolate candy are in the bowl. Sketch and label your algebra piece model, and explain how you solved the problem.

6. *Math Concepts:* A box contains a total of $11.40 in nickels, dimes, and quarters. There are twice as many nickels as dimes and three times as many quarters as dimes. Use algebra pieces and mental arithmetic to determine how many of each coin are in the box. Sketch and label your algebra piece model, and explain how you solved the problem.

7. *NCTM Standards:* Go to http://illuminations.nctm.org/ and under "Lessons" select grade levels K–2 and 3–5 and the **Algebra** and **Geometry Standards.** Search for the keyword "pattern." Choose a lesson that involves extending and analyzing patterns.

   a. State the title of the lesson and briefly summarize the lesson.

   b. Referring to the **Standards Summary** in the back pages of this book as necessary, list the *Problem-Solving Standard Expectations* that the lesson addresses, and explain how the lesson addresses these *Expectations*.

8. *NCTM Standards:* One of the **Grades 3–5 Algebra Expectations** in the back of this book states, "Model problem situations with objects and use representations such as graphs, tables and equations to draw conclusions." Explain why you think using algebra pieces and mental arithmetic as a problem-solving tool addresses this *Expectation*.

---

www.mhhe.com/bbn

bennett-burton-nelson website

Virtual Manipulatives   Grid and Dot Paper   Links and Readings
Interactive Chapter Applets   Color Transparencies   Geometer Sketchpad Modules
Puzzlers   Extended Bibliography

ACTIVITIES FOR THE ELEMENTARY SCHOOL CLASSROOM

Exploring Patterns with Color Tiles

Purpose: To introduce elementary school students to recognizing, describing, and extending geometric patterns.

Connections: Ask the class what the word "patterns" means. They may suggest several meanings, such as a pattern in cloth, a pattern used to make a piece of clothing, etc. Discuss a few meanings of this word and tell them that "We will look at some mathematical patterns!"

Materials: Sets of color tiles can be created by copying 2-centimeter grid paper on four different colors of cardstock or by downloading the color tile images from the companion website. Color tile transparencies can also be made with the color tile images. Sets of 20 of each of four colors can be placed in plastic sealable bags. Each group of two to four students will need one set of color tiles.

This student is building a pattern that is growing to the right, to the left, and away from her.

1. Pass out sets of tiles to each group. Form the following sequence of four tile figures at the overhead and ask each group to form these four figures with their own tiles.

   - Ask the class what they think the pattern is, what the 5th figure might look like, and to explain their reasoning. You may wish to have volunteers go to the overhead to demonstrate as they explain.

   - Once the class agrees on a pattern, such as 5 tiles in a row for the 5th figure, ask each group to build the next two figures.

   - Ask the class to describe what the 10th and the 50th tile figures in the sequence look like.

2. Repeat activity 1 for the following tile sequences, or depending on your students, create more challenging sequences.

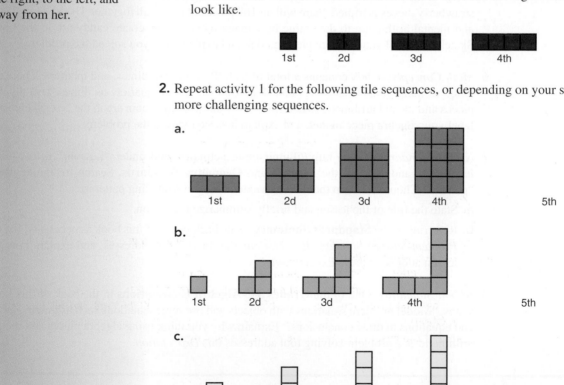

3. Ask each group to build a tile sequence of four figures so there is a pattern in how the figures change. Select a few examples to be shown at the overhead, and have the children describe their patterns.

2 Sets, Functions, and Reasoning

Being able to reason is essential to understanding mathematics. By developing ideas, exploring phenomena, justifying results, and using mathematical conjectures in all content areas and—with different expectations of sophistication—at all grade levels, students should see and expect that mathematics makes sense. Building on the considerable reasoning skills that children bring to school, teachers can help students learn what mathematical reasoning entails.[†]

SORTING AND CLASSIFYING WITH ATTRIBUTE PIECES

PURPOSE

To use attribute pieces in games and activities for sorting and classifying, reasoning logically, formulating and verifying hypotheses, and introducing set terminology and operations.

Virtual Manipulatives

www.mhhe.com/bbn

MATERIALS

Attribute Pieces from the Manipulative Kit or from the Virtual Manipulatives, Attribute Label Cards from Material Card 3, and scissors to cut them out, Attribute Game Grids from Material Card 4 and the Two-Circle and Three-Circle Venn Diagrams on Material Cards 5 and 6, respectively.

INTRODUCTION

"Mathematics is reasoning. One cannot do mathematics without reasoning. The standard does not suggest, however, that formal reasoning strategies be taught in grades K–4. At this level, the mathematical reasoning should involve the kind of informal thinking, conjecturing, and validating that helps children to see that mathematics makes sense."

"Manipulatives and other physical models help children relate processes to their conceptual underpinnings and give them concrete objects to talk about in explaining and justifying their thinking. Observing children interact with objects in this way allows teachers to reinforce thinking processes and evaluate any possible misunderstandings."[‡]

[†]*Principles and Standards for School Mathematics*, p. 56.

[‡]*Curriculum and Evaluation Standards for School Mathematics*, p. 29.

Name _____

Sort and Classify

Get Ready

Main Idea

I will sort and classify objects.

Vocabulary

sort

Venn diagram

You can **sort** objects using a **Venn diagram**.

These buttons are yellow.

These buttons are yellow and have four holes.

These buttons have four holes.

Check

Use pattern blocks. Sort the shapes.
Draw one way you sorted.

1.

2. **Talk About It**   How did you sort the shapes?

Exercises and Activities 2.1

1. *School Classroom:* Two students were discussing the meaning of union and intersection. One student illustrated union by figure a and argued that the union is the elements in set *A* or in set *B*. The other student illustrated union by figure b. Explain how you would help the two students understand which illustration is correct.

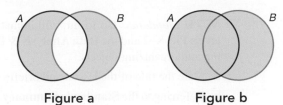

Figure a   **Figure b**

2. *School Classroom:* Devise an activity that you believe is appropriate for elementary school students to explore sorting and classifying shapes using a set of mixed buttons as a manipulative. Describe the activity and questions or hints you may pose to help students get started.

3. *School Classroom:* **The Elementary School Text** page at the beginning of this section asks students to sort buttons according to two attributes; color and number of button holes.

   a. Describe another pair of attributes a student can use to sort the 14 buttons where there is at least one button in each part of the diagram. Sketch and label a Venn diagram to show this.

   b. Devise a set of common objects with some shared characteristics that elementary school students can place in various regions of a three-circle Venn diagram. Describe the three sets, and provide a sketch of a completed and filled-out three-circle Venn diagram showing your three sets. Include a label for each circle in the Venn diagram.

4. *Math Concepts:* Set up the model for the following questions by labeling the three-circle Venn diagram on Material Card 6 with the following attribute labels: Circle 1, small pieces; Circle 2, triangular pieces; Circle 3, red pieces. Distribute all of your attribute pieces onto the correct regions of your diagram on Material Card 6.

   Let *S* represent Small, *T* represent Triangular, *R* represent Red, and *N* represent Not. For each of the following, describe the region in a complete sentence and shade the corresponding Venn diagram on Material Card 7 to show the indicated region.

   a. $(S \cup T) \cup NR$ **b.** $(S \cap T) \cup NR$

   c. $(S \cup T) \cap NR$ **d.** $(S \cap NT) \cup NR$

   e. $(NS \cup T) \cap R$ **f.** $(NS \cup NT) \cap R$

5. *Math Concepts:* Use your set of attribute pieces for the following. Let set *A* be all blue pieces and set *B* be all large pieces.

   a. Describe not $(A \cup B)$ and illustrate not $(A \cup B)$ with a shaded two-circle Venn diagram. Describe not *A* ∩ not *B* and illustrate not *A* ∩ not *B* with a shaded two-circle Venn diagram. How are the phrases not $(A \cup B)$ and not *A* ∩ not *B* related in this case?

   b. Describe not $(A \cap B)$ and illustrate not $(A \cap B)$ with a shaded two-circle Venn diagram. Describe not *A* ∪ not *B* and illustrate not *A* ∪ not *B* with a shaded two-circle Venn diagram. How are the phrases not $(A \cap B)$ and not *A* ∪ not *B* related in this case?

   c. Are the relationships you saw between not $(A \cup B)$ and not *A* ∩ not *B* and between not $(A \cap B)$ and not *A* ∪ not *B* in parts a and b true for all sets *A* and *B*? Explain your thinking.

6. *Math Concepts:* Use your set of attribute pieces to describe sets *A*, *B*, and *C* with the following properties.

   i.   Set *A* and set *B* have at least one common element.

  ii.   Set *C* is completely contained in set *B* but is not the same as set *B*.

 iii.   Set *A* and set *C* have no common elements.

Sketch a clearly labeled Venn diagram, and list the pieces in each of the appropriate regions of the diagram.

7. *NCTM Standards:* Go to http://illuminations.nctm.org/ and under "Lessons" select grade levels Pre-K–2 and the **Data Analysis & Probability Standard.** Choose a lesson about sorting and organizing objects.

  a. State the title of the lesson and briefly summarize the lesson.

  b. Referring to the **Standards Summary** in the back pages of this book as necessary, list the *Data Analysis and Probability Standard Expectations* that the lesson addresses and explain how the lesson addresses these *Expectations*.

---

www.mhhe.com/bbn

bennett-burton-nelson website

Virtual Manipulatives	Grid and Dot Paper	Links and Readings
Interactive Chapter Applets	Color Transparencies	Geometer Sketchpad Modules
Puzzlers	Extended Bibliography	

Activity Set **2.2**
GEOBOARD SLOPE AND LINEAR FUNCTIONS

PURPOSE

To become familiar with slopes of line segments and properties of lines and to write linear equations.

irtual
Manipulatives

www.mhhe.com/bbn

MATERIALS

A transparent straightedge or ruler. A rectangular geoboard and rubber bands (optional). A template for making a rectangular geoboard is on Material Card 8 and a rectangular geoboard is available in the Virtual Manipulatives.

INTRODUCTION

Starting with the idea of the slope of a geoboard line segment, the slope-intercept form of a linear equation is examined. Intuitively speaking, the slope of a line segment is its inclination from the horizontal. Slopes can be positive, negative, or zero. The slope of one of the line segments shown here is positive, and the slope of the other is negative. In going from A to B in figure 1, we move horizontally 2 spaces to the right, the run, and vertically 3 spaces up, the rise. Since slope is equal to $\frac{\text{rise}}{\text{run}}$, the slope of the line segment $\overline{AB}$ is $\frac{3}{2}$. Similarly, in going from C to D in figure 2 the run is 2 and the rise is $^-3$ (the vertical move is down), so the slope of the line segment $\overline{CD}$ is $\frac{-3}{2}$. Notice, in figure 3, that going from D to C the rise is 3 and the run is $^-2$ (the horizontal move is left), so the rise/run from D to C (right to left instead of left to right) is also $\frac{-3}{2}$.

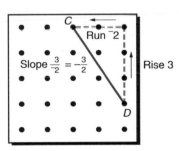

Figure 1   **Figure 2**   **Figure 3**

---

1. Sketch the rise and run triangle and label the numerical rise, run, and slope for each line segment on the geoboards.

a.   **b.**   **c.**   **d.**   **e.**

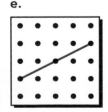

Slope: _____   _____   _____   _____   _____

2. Sketch a geoboard line segment and the rise and run triangle for each slope. Is it possible to have more than one line segment with the same slope? If so, how are the line segments with the same slope related?

a. slope $\frac{3}{4}$ **b.** slope $\frac{^{-}1}{3}$ ***c.** slope $\frac{^{-}4}{3}$ **d.** slope $\frac{0}{4}$ **e.** slope $\frac{^{-}1}{2}$

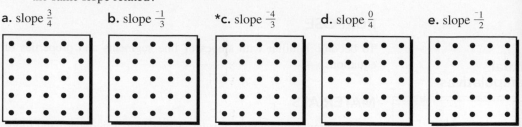

Slopes of Line Segments

In a coordinate system, slopes of line segments, and the lines that contain them, are determined as on the geoboards above. In this figure, the line segment joining the points (0, 3) and (3, 1) has slope $-\frac{2}{3}$ as does the line ℓ containing that segment.

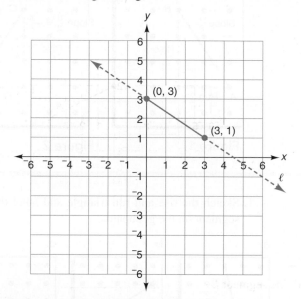

In activities 3 to 10 use the following three definitions:

> The **slope of a line segment** is the slope of the line containing the segment.
>
> **Two line segments are parallel** if the lines containing them are parallel.
>
> **Two line segments are perpendicular** if the lines containing them are perpendicular.

3. Below each diagram, compute and record the slope of each line segment *A*. Then use a ruler and carefully sketch a line segment *B* parallel to line segment *A* on the same grid. Compute and record the slope of each line segment *B*.

a.   **b.**

          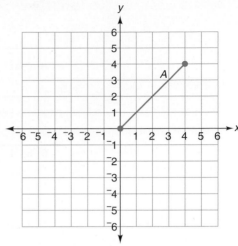

Slope of line segment *A*   _____   _____

Slope of line segment *B*   _____   _____

c.   **d.**

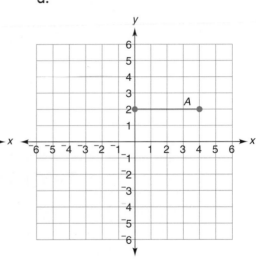

Slope of line segment *A*   _____   _____

Slope of line segment *B*   _____   _____

e. If two line segments are parallel, what is the relationship between their slopes?

4. On each of the following diagrams, use a ruler (or the corner of an index card) to carefully approximate a new line segment C perpendicular to line segment A on the same grid; sketch the new segment. Compute and record the slope of each line segment A and the slope of each line segment C.

*a.

b.

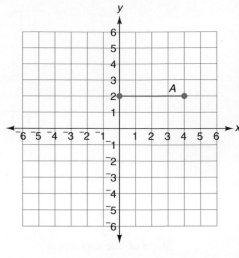

Slope of line segment A   _____   _____

Slope of line segment C   _____   _____

c.

d.

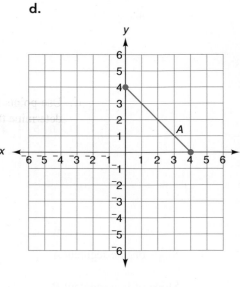

Slope of line segment A   _____   _____

Slope of line segment C   _____   _____

e. If two line segments are perpendicular, what is the relationship between their slopes?

5. Each of the following lines shows a point P with labeled coordinates and a point Q without labeled coordinates. For each line, record the coordinates of point Q and then plot one additional point R on the line and record the coordinates of point R.

a.   **b.**

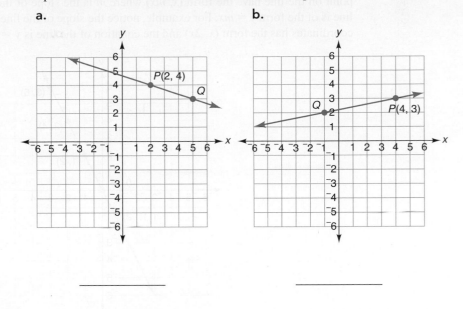

Coordinates of Q _____   _____

Coordinates of R _____   _____

*c. Use points P and Q to determine the slope of the line in part a. Use points Q and R to determine the slope of the line in part a.

d. Use points P and Q to determine the slope of the line in part b. Use points Q and R to determine the slope of the line in part b.

e. What general conclusions can you make about using points on a line to find the slope of the line?

f. Given any two points on a line, explain how you can compute the slope of the line without graphing the line on a coordinate system. Illustrate your explanation by finding the slope of the line which contains the points (1, 3) and (10, 7). Then determine the slope of the line which contains the points (⁻3, 7) and (5, ⁻6).

Lines that Pass through the Origin

Every line that passes through the origin $(0, 0)$ has a special property; the coordinates of each point on the line have the form (x, mx) where m is the slope of the line. The equation of such a line is of the form $y = mx$. For example, notice the slope of the line shown below is 2, each of the coordinates has the form $(x, 2x)$ and the equation of the line is $y = 2x$.

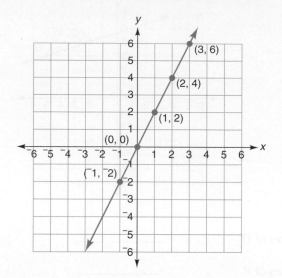

6. Mark at least two points on each of the following lines, and determine the equation of each of the lines.

    *a.   **b.**

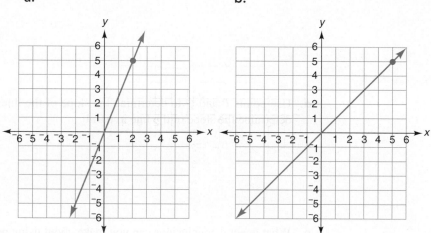

Linear Equation   _____   _____

Lines that Do Not Pass through the Origin

Every line that does not pass through the origin, such as line ℓ on the next page, is parallel to a line that does pass through the origin, such as line k below. Both lines k and ℓ have slope $\frac{1}{2}$, and the equation of line k is $y = \frac{1}{2}x$. Notice, also, that the second coordinate for each point on ℓ is 2 more than the second coordinate for the corresponding point on k. Thus, line ℓ is line k shifted vertically up by 2. Therefore the equation of line ℓ is $y = \frac{1}{2}x + 2$. That is, for any point on line k, the y-coordinate is always half the x-coordinate and for any point on line ℓ, the y-coordinate is always 2 more than half the x-coordinate.

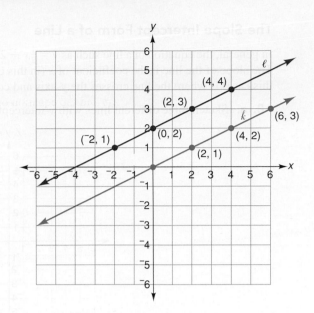

7. For each of the following lines ℓ, use a ruler and carefully sketch a parallel line k through the origin on the same grid. Determine the equation of line k, determine the coordinates of two corresponding points with the same x-coordinate on line k and line ℓ and, thinking of line ℓ as a vertical shift of line k, use this information to determine the equation of line ℓ.

*a.   **b.**

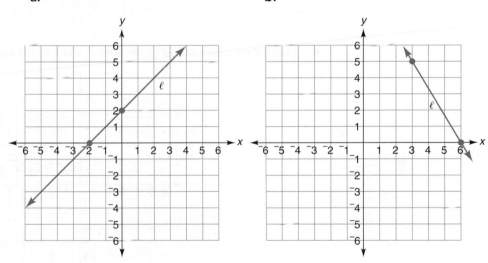

Equation of line k _____   _____

Equation of line ℓ _____   _____

c. Write a statement that will explain to the reader how to use a line and a parallel line through the origin to find the equation of the original line.

The Slope Intercept Form of a Line

In general, the equation of a line such as $y = \frac{1}{2}x + 2$ is called the slope-intercept form of the line. The slope of the line is the coefficient of x (in this case $\frac{1}{2}$) and the y-intercept (the point $(0, 2)$ in this case) is where the line crosses the y-axis and corresponds to an x value of 0.

8. a. Sketch three different lines with y-intercept 4, and give the equation of each line.

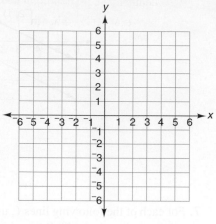

Linear Equations   i _____   ii _____   iii _____

b. How many different lines can there be with y-intercept 4? Explain.

c. Sketch three different lines with slope $\frac{3}{4}$, and give the equation of each line.

Linear Equations   i _____   ii _____   iii _____

d. How many different lines can there be with slope $\frac{3}{4}$? Explain.

e. How many different lines can there be with y-intercept 4 and slope $\frac{3}{4}$? Explain.

9. Find a Line Game (2 players): The object of this game is to determine both the slope and the *y*-intercept of an opponent's secret line drawn on a ‾5 to 5 square grid. Each player draws one line through at least two grid points, one of which is on the *y*-axis and writes down the equation of their line. The players should not be able to see each other's grids, lines, or equations. Players take turns guessing first slopes and then *y*-intercepts as described in the game rules below and record their guesses as they play the game. The player who guesses their opponent's line equation in the least amount of guesses wins.

- Player A states whether their line has *positive* or *negative* slope and gives the coordinates for *one grid point* their line passes through (but not the *y*-intercept).

- Player B guesses the slope and for each guess, Player A gives one of the following responses: the *slope is correct;* the *slope is too steep,* or the *slope is not steep enough.*

Once a player has guessed the slope of the other player's line:

- Player B guesses the *y*-intercept, and for each guess, Player A gives one of the following responses: the *y-intercept is correct;* the *y-intercept is too big,* or the *y-intercept is too small.*

  a. Play several rounds of the game using the following grid and scoreboard. For more grids, see Material Card 9.

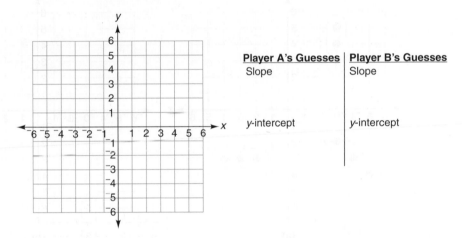

Player A's Guesses	Player B's Guesses
Slope	Slope
y-intercept	*y*-intercept

  b. Describe a good first guess for the slope of your opponent's line. Explain.

  c. Where might you place a grid point so that there could be 13 lines with positive slopes going through that point? Explain.

  d. What is the minimum number of guesses to determine the *y*-intercept if you know both the slope and one point on a line? Explain.

JUST FOR FUN

Both of the following games use coordinate grids from Material Card 9.

COORDINATE GUESSING GAME

(2 players or teams)

The object of this game is to determine the coordinates of the opponent's target. Each player uses a pair of rectangular grids such as the ones shown here (Material Card 9). Each player draws three targets on one grid and records guesses as to the opponent's targets on the other grid. A target consists of three adjacent intersection points of the grid (in rows, columns, or diagonals) whose coordinates are integers.

The players should not be able to see each other's grids. They take turns guessing three points at a time by giving the coordinates of each point. When a guessed point is on a target, the opponent must acknowledge this immediately. The game ends when one player has identified the location of one of the opponent's targets.

Variation: To speed up the game, you may wish to agree to inform your opponent whenever a guess is within 1 unit (horizontally or vertically) of a target.

Player marks three targets

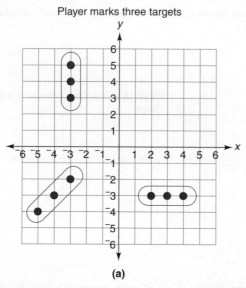

(a)

Player records guesses at opponent's targets

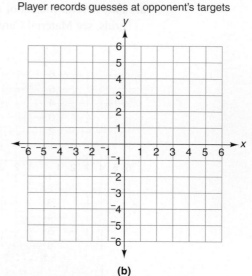

(b)

HIDE-A-REGION GAME

(2 players or teams)

This game is similar to the Coordinate Guessing Game, but players search for the opponent's rectangle. Each player uses a pair of rectangular grids (Material Card 9). The game begins with the players agreeing on the areas for the rectangles. Each player then sketches a rectangle of the given area on one grid, with the coordinates of the vertices being integers. (The players should not see each other's grids.) The players take turns guessing points by giving

coordinates. Only one guess is allowed on each turn. Each player must tell whether the opponent's guess is an exterior, interior, vertex, or boundary point. Both players keep a record of their opponent's guesses and their own guesses. The first player to locate all four vertices of the opponent's rectangle is the winner.

Variation: The players may agree to switch the shape of the region but keep all other rules the same. For example, instead of a rectangle, the region could be a right triangle, triangle, or parallelogram.

Rectangle of area 12

Record of guesses to
locate opponent's rectangle

(a)

(b)

 HUNTING FOR HIDDEN POLYGONS APPLET

In this applet, you try to find a hidden polygon on a coordinate system. You are given the number of sides and the slopes of the sides, and you are told if the points you select are inside (black), outside (yellow), on the boundary (blue), or at a vertex of the hidden polygon (white). Where would you select your next point or points for the information shown here? Use the interactive applet from the companion website to explore this idea further.

Hidden Polygons Applet, Chapter 2
www.mhhe.com/bbn

Exercises and Activities 2.2

1. *School Classroom:* A fourth-grade student was confused about how a negative slope could be referred to as rise over run; they argued that you "rise up" and that you "run over (to the right)." Explain how you would help this student make sense of using the idea of rise over run for negative slope and for slopes of 0. Illustrate your explanation.

2. *School Classroom:* Suppose that after you introduced your students to slopes, a student asks you if it is possible to have a line with slope $2\frac{1}{3}$. Explain how you would help the student understand that this is possible. Write a series of questions you could ask the student to bring about his understanding and ability to draw lines given similar mixed number slopes.

3. *Math Concepts:* With a classmate, play the Hide-a-Region game described in the **Just for Fun Activity** in this section. List several strategies that helped you determine the hidden target and explain how they helped you.

4. *Math Concepts:*
   a. Of all possible lines, how many lines have a *y*-intercept of 3? Explain your thinking and write equations in slope-intercept form to illustrate your answer.
   b. Of all possible lines, how many lines have a slope of 3? Explain your thinking and write equations in slope-intercept form to illustrate your answer.
   c. Of all possible lines, how many lines have a slope of 3 and a *y*-intercept of 3? Explain your thinking and write equations in slope-intercept form to illustrate your answer.

5. *Math Concepts:* Consider the following lines:

$y = \frac{1}{3}x + 3$	$y = \frac{1}{3}x - 3$	$y = -\frac{1}{3}x + 3$	$y = -\frac{1}{3}x - 3$
$y = 3x + \frac{1}{3}$	$y = 3x - \frac{1}{3}$	$y = -3x + \frac{1}{3}$	$y = -3x - \frac{1}{3}$

Determine three different ways to categorize this set of lines into groups. Illustrate your categories and explain your thinking.

6. *Math Concepts:* Twelve different line segments, each with different nonnegative slopes, can be formed on the 5-pin × 5-pin geoboard. *Note:* Vertical line segments have undefined slopes.

   a. Sketch and count the number of line segments with different nonnegative slopes that can be formed on 2-pin × 2-pin, 3-pin × 3-pin, and 4-pin × 4-pin geoboards. Copy Rectangular Geoboards from the website or use printable Virtual Manipulatives.

   b. Predict the number of line segments with different nonnegative slopes that can be formed on a 6-pin × 6-pin geoboard and give your prediction. Then sketch the geoboard line segments to check your prediction. You may find it helpful to sketch the line segments on more than one geoboard. Copy Rectangular Geoboards from the website or use printable Virtual Manipulatives.

7. *NCTM Standards:*

a. In order to determine the slopes of lines, students need an understanding of the Cartesian coordinate system and how to plot points given their coordinates. Look through the **Standards** summary in the back pages of this book to determine specifically where such experience is recommended. Record the *Expectation(s),* the grade level(s), and the *Content Standard(s)* the recommendations are under.

b. Return to the **Standards** summary in the back pages of this book and find an *Expectation* that specifically mentions slope. State the *Expectation* and the *Content Standard* the *Expectation* is under, and explain why you think slope is under this particular *Standard* and grade level.

---

www.mhhe.com/bbn

bennett-burton-nelson website

Virtual Manipulatives   Grid and Dot Paper   Links and Readings
Interactive Chapter Applets   Color Transparencies   Geometer Sketchpad Modules
Puzzlers   Extended Bibliography

LOGIC PROBLEMS FOR COOPERATIVE LEARNING GROUPS

PURPOSE

To have cooperative learning groups use deductive reasoning to solve logic problems.

MATERIALS

The logic problem clue cards and other materials for the five cooperative logic problems are on Material Cards 10–15. You will also need scissors to cut the cards out.

INTRODUCTION

"In a cooperative learning situation, students' achievements of their shared goals are positively correlated; students perceive that they can reach their learning goals if and only if the other students in the learning group also reach their goals. Thus, students seek outcomes that are beneficial to all group members. When students work on mathematics assignments, they discuss the material with their group, explain how to complete the work, listen to each other's explanations, encourage each other to understand the solutions, and provide academic help and assistance."[†]

The logic problems in this activity set are designed to be solved cooperatively by a group of four people. Each member of the group will have a clue card that contains statements not found on any other person's card. No member of the group is allowed to read another member's card. The group is to work as a team to solve the problem cooperatively. When the activity begins, members of the group read their clues to the group. The clues may be read as often as requested by the group. The tasks of the group members are to (1) identify the problem that is to be solved; (2) agree on a process (Will there be one group recorder? Will the solution be arrived at mentally, or will diagrams, charts, or models be used?); (3) listen carefully when clues are read; and (4) make sure that all members of the group understand each step toward the solution.

Inductive reasoning is the process of forming conclusions on the basis of observations and experiments; it involves making an educated guess. *Deductive reasoning* is the process of deriving conclusions from given statements. The cooperative logic problems in this activity set will require deductive reasoning.

Cooperative Logic Problems

Form a team of four people. Using one set of clue cards per team, follow these guidelines as you solve the problems:

- Each team member takes one clue card. (If there are not enough people to form a group of four, some members may hold more than one card.)
- Each person reads the clues aloud but should not show the clue card to another person.
- The team is to identify the problem and agree on a method for solving it.
- The team members are to solve the problem cooperatively by assisting each other.
- The problem is solved when all team members understand the solution and agree that the problem has been solved.

[†]David Johnson and Roger Johnson, "Cooperative Learning in Mathematics Education," in *New Directions for Elementary School Mathematics,* 235.

Exercises and Activities **2.3**

1. *School Classroom:* Some of the students in an elementary school classroom were convinced that the two phrases, "If you do your chores, then we will go shopping" and "If we go shopping, then you will do your chores," mean the same thing. Explain how you would help the students understand that these two phrases mean different things.

2. *School Classroom:* Design a cooperative logic problem in the style of activities 1, 2, 3, and 4 in this section that is appropriate for a group of four elementary school students to solve. Design four people cards and four clue cards. Describe your people and clue cards, and give the solution to your problem. Explain your thinking and how your clues will lead the group of students to solve your problem.

3. *School Classroom:* The **Just for Fun Activity: Attribute Identity Game,** in section 2.1, stresses reasoning through classification. Pick a level: Pre-K–2, grades 3–5, or grades 6–8, and adapt the Attribute Identity Game for that level. Describe your game completely so that another person could read your directions and use them. You may use objects other than attribute pieces in your game (buttons, color tiles, etc.).

4. *School Classroom:* On the **Elementary School Text** page at the beginning of this section, students use Polya's four-step problem-solving approach and a table to solve a logic question. Pick one of the five logic problems from this section, and solve the question using a table as illustrated on the Elementary School Text page.

5. *Math Concepts:* Fiona has eight pets of varying ages. Can you use the given clues to order the pets from youngest to oldest and match each pet name to their pet type? The pets names, in alphabetical order, are Billy, Buff, Freckles, Polly, Ralph, Red, Sylvester, and Tycho.

   Clues
   i. The Gila monster, Ralph, is older than all but one other pet.
   ii. The goldfish is the youngest pet and the parrot is the oldest pet.
   iii. There is one pet older than Sylvester the ferret and younger than the chicken Buff.
   iv. There are six pets both older than Polly and younger than Red.
   v. There are two pets younger than Billy.
   vi. There is one pet older than Freckles and younger than Red.
   vii. There are five pets older than the goat.
   viii. Ralph and Red are the only pets older than the dog.
   ix. There is no pet older than the cat but younger than the dog.

6. *Math Concepts:* Four students have majors, jobs, and methods of transportation as noted in the following unordered table. Use the given clues to match the jobs, majors, and methods of transportation with the correct students. Describe and show your solution path.

Students	Freshman	Sophomore	Junior	Senior
Work	Coffee Shop	Library	Theatre	Tutor
Major	English	Computer Science	Math	Psychology
Transportation	Bike	Bus	Car	Skateboard

Clues

  i. The English major rides a bike.
 ii. The tutor is a junior and won't ride a skateboard.
iii. The sophomore takes the bus.
 iv. The freshman won't work in the coffee shop or drive a car.
  v. The skateboarder is a psychology major.
 vi. The computer science major works in the library.
vii. The math major works in the coffee shop and won't drive a car.
viii. The senior drives a car.

7. *NCTM Standards:* In the **Standards** summary in the back pages of this book there are five *Process Standards* and five *Content Standards*. The *Process Standards* discuss ways of acquiring and using content knowledge. Pick one of the cooperative logic problems you completed in this activity set and explain briefly in what way each of the *Process Standards* was (or was not) incorporated as the problem was resolved.

8. *NCTM Standards:* Locate a copy of *The Principles and Standards for School Mathematics*. Read the section on **"Reasoning and Proof"** that applies to the grade levels Pre-K–2 and summarize the recommendations by describing the type of reasoning suggested for these grade levels and the role of the teacher in developing reasoning abilities.

---

www.mhhe.com/bbn

bennett-burton-nelson website

Virtual Manipulatives	Grid and Dot Paper	Links and Readings
Interactive Chapter Applets	Color Transparencies	Geometer Sketchpad Modules
Puzzlers	Extended Bibliography	

ACTIVITIES FOR THE ELEMENTARY SCHOOL CLASSROOM

Reasoning with Attribute Pieces

Purpose: To introduce elementary school students to testing conjectures and reasoning logically by comparing and contrasting attribute pieces.

Connections: "How many of you have a dog or a cat?" "What other animals do you have?" "Have you ever looked at two animals to compare them to see how they are alike or how they are different?" Today we will use colored pieces called attribute pieces, and you will compare them to see how they are alike and how they are different.

Materials: Masters for classroom sets of attribute pieces can be downloaded from the companion website and printed on cardstock. The masters can also be used to create colored overhead transparencies. Sets of 24 attribute pieces can be placed in plastic sealable bags. Each group of two to four students will need one set of attribute pieces.

1. Pass out a set of attribute pieces to each group and allow them some time to look at them. Often students will sort the pieces by color, shape, or size. Select a few groups to describe what they noticed or what they did with the pieces. Discuss the three major ways the pieces differ: color, shape, and size.

This second grader is building a one-difference train.

2. Place these four pieces in a row on the overhead and ask how each piece differs from the previous piece. This row of pieces is called a one-difference train because each piece differs from the previous piece by one attribute. Ask students to determine some of the different pieces for the fifth piece in this train, and to use their pieces to continue building this one-difference train as long as is possible.

3. Form the following two-difference train on the overhead and repeat activity 2 by asking students to compare each piece to the next piece. Ask them what kind of a train this is (two-difference train). Ask them to form and to continue building this train. *Note:* This activity can be played like a game, with each student in turn trying to place a new piece on the train, until no further moves are possible.

4. Place the following three pieces on the overhead and ask what kind of a train this forms (three-difference train). Ask for suggestions for a few more pieces for this train.

5. Draw a circle on the overhead, and tell the students you are thinking about a set of attribute pieces for the circle, such as all the yellow pieces, or all triangular pieces, and that they can guess what type of pieces are in the circle by selecting an attribute piece, one at a time, and you will either place it in the circle or on the outside of the circle. Repeat this activity using a variety of "Secret Attribute" sets such as all yellow pieces, all square pieces, all large pieces, all large square pieces, etc.

6. (Optional) Repeat activity 5 for a two-circle Venn diagram. You may want to first show an example and note how each piece inside the overlapping part of the circles has the attributes of both circles. You may use this to lead a conversation about the intersection of sets.

3 Whole Numbers

Concrete models can help students represent numbers and develop number sense; they can also help to bring meaning to students' use of written symbols and can be useful in building place-value concepts. But using materials, especially in a rote manner, does not ensure understanding. Teachers should try to uncover students' thinking as they work with concrete materials by asking questions that elicit students' thinking and reasoning.[†]

MODELS FOR NUMERATION WITH MULTIBASE PIECES

PURPOSE

Virtual Manipulatives

www.mhhe.com/bbn

To use base-five pieces and visual diagrams for other bases to introduce the concepts of grouping and place value in a positional numeration system.

MATERIALS

Base-Five Pieces from the Manipulative Kit or from the Virtual Manipulatives.

INTRODUCTION

The concepts underlying positional numeration systems—grouping, regrouping, and place value—become much clearer when illustrated with concrete models, and many models have been created for this purpose. Models for numeration fall roughly into two categories or levels of abstractness. *Grouping models,* such as bundles of straws and base-five blocks, show clearly how groupings are formed; *abacus-type models,* such as chip-trading or place-value charts, use color and/or position to designate different groupings.

Bundles of Straws

Base-Five Blocks

Place Value Mat

[†]*Principles and Standards for School Mathematics,* p. 80.

ACTIVITY

2 Use base-ten blocks to model 1,025 in two ways.

One Way　**Use thousands, hundreds, tens, and ones.**

1 thousand　　　2 tens　　5 ones

Another Way　**Use hundreds, tens, and ones.**

10 hundreds　　　　　　　　2 tens　5 ones

Think About It

1. Why can you use different combinations of thousands, hundreds, tens, and ones to model the same number?

✓ CHECK What You Know

Use base-ten blocks to model each number in two ways.

2. 135　　　3. 304　　　4. 1,283　　　5. 1,890

Write each number modeled.

6. 　　　7.

8. **WRITING IN ▸MATH** Explain how base-ten blocks are helpful in understanding numbers.

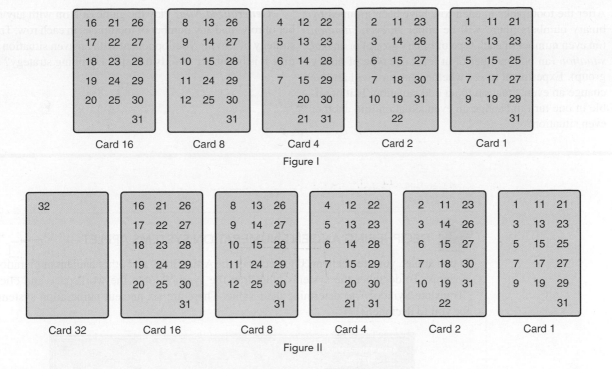

16	21	26
17	22	27
18	23	28
19	24	29
20	25	30
		31

Card 16

8	13	26
9	14	27
10	15	28
11	24	29
12	25	30
		31

Card 8

4	12	22
5	13	23
6	14	28
7	15	29
	20	30
	21	31

Card 4

2	11	23
3	14	26
6	15	27
7	18	30
10	19	31
	22	

Card 2

1	11	21
3	13	23
5	15	25
7	17	27
9	19	29
		31

Card 1

Figure I

| 32 |

Card 32

16	21	26
17	22	27
18	23	28
19	24	29
20	25	30
		31

Card 16

8	13	26
9	14	27
10	15	28
11	24	29
12	25	30
		31

Card 8

4	12	22
5	13	23
6	14	28
7	15	29
	20	30
	21	31

Card 4

2	11	23
3	14	26
6	15	27
7	18	30
10	19	31
	22	

Card 2

1	11	21
3	13	23
5	15	25
7	17	27
9	19	29
		31

Card 1

Figure II

GAME OF NIM (2 players)

The game of Nim is said to be of ancient Chinese origin. In its simplest form, it is played with three rows of toothpicks or markers. On a turn, a player may take any number of toothpicks from any one row. The winner of the game is the player who takes the last toothpick or group of toothpicks. Try a few rounds of this game with a classmate.

With a little practice, it is easy to discover some situations in which you can win. For example, if it is your opponent's turn to play and there is a 1-2-3 arrangement, as shown below, you will be able to win. Sketch three more situations in which you will win if it is your opponent's turn to play.

Winning Strategy: A winning strategy for the game of Nim involves binary numbers.

1. On your turn, group the remaining toothpicks in each row by binary numbers, using the largest binary numbers possible in each row, as shown in the following example.

2. Then remove toothpicks so that there is an *even number* of each type of pile left. In the example above, you will see an even number of 4s, an even number of 2s, and an odd number of 1s. So 1 toothpick must be taken from one of the rows. Show that the 1-2-3 arrangement shown in the column at the left has an even number of binary groups.

*3. Assume it is your turn and you have the arrangement shown below. Cross out toothpick(s) so that your opponent will be left with an even number of binary groups.

*4. After the toothpicks in each row have been grouped by binary numbers, there will be either an *even situation* (an even number of each type of binary group) or an *odd situation* (an odd number of at least one type of binary group). Experiment to see whether one turn will always change an even situation to an odd situation. Is it possible in one turn to change an even situation into another even situation?

Generalized Nim: Play the game of Nim with any number of rows and any number of toothpicks in each row. Try the strategy of leaving your opponent with an even situation each time it is his or her turn. Is this still a winning strategy?

 DECIPHERING ANCIENT NUMERATION SYSTEMS APPLET

In this applet, you are challenged to decipher the Attic-Greek and other ancient numeration systems. To decipher the systems, you drag the symbols onto the workspace and click "Translate Symbols" to determine their value. There are six ancient numeration systems for you to decipher.

Deciphering Ancient Numeration Systems Applet, Chapter 3
www.mhhe.com/bbn

Exercises and Activities 3.1

1. *School Classroom:* Suppose you have asked your students to imagine there is another culture that uses base five to count and they need to devise a way to communicate numbers with this culture. Explain how you would help your students solve this problem.

2. *School Classroom:* Devise an activity you think will help elementary school students understand how the digits in a base-ten number relate to the value of the number. In your activity, use base-ten pieces and use the 1-to-6 Spinner from your Manipulative Kit to pick digits. Write a few questions you can ask your students about your activity.

3. *School Classroom:* Read through the activity on the **Elementary School Text** page at the beginning of this section. Notice that elementary students are asked to use base-ten pieces to model the same number in different ways. Explain in writing how using base pieces helps the students understand the base-ten numeration system and place values. Make a case for or against using different base pieces, such as base-five pieces, as well as base-ten pieces, to develop the concepts of numeration systems and place value for schoolchildren.

4. *Math Concepts:* Explain why the digits in a place value system with base b are 0, 1, ..., $b - 1$ and why no digits for numbers greater than $b - 1$ are needed.

5. *Math Concepts:* For any base b, the base piece after a long-flat is called a flat-flat.
   a. Sketch what you think a flat-flat should look like and explain why it is a logical choice for the next base piece regardless of the base.
   b. Determine the minimal collection of base-seven pieces and the corresponding base-seven numeral for 30,000 unit squares. Draw a generic sketch of the base-seven pieces and explain how you arrived at your answer.

6. *Math Concepts:* The place value chart model for numeration (see the Introduction to this Activity Set) consists of a chart with columns on which markers are placed. This model can represent any base, with the columns, starting on the right, representing units, longs, flats, and blocks, respectively, in the given base. Using base five, for example, each group of five markers is replaced by one marker in the next column to the left. In this diagram, 13 markers in the units column, grouped by fives, result in two markers in the longs column and three markers in the units column, or 23_{five}.

23_{five}

When grouped by fours (base four), regrouping the same starting set of 13 markers, as shown on page 68, results in three markers in the longs column and one marker in the units column, or 31_{four}.

31_{four}

a. Sketch a place value chart after 19 unit markers have been traded using base three. Record the resulting base-three numeral below the chart.

b. Sketch a place value chart after 15 unit markers have been traded using base two. Record the resulting base-two numeral below the chart.

c. Explain how this model differs conceptually from the multibase piece model that we have previously considered.

7. *Math Concepts:* A common elementary school activity is to create a display to show sticks, stick bundles, and stick bundles of bundles to count the number of days, so far, in the school year. Each school day a stick (or coffee stirrer) is added to the ones pocket; the sticks are rebundled and moved as needed, and the children write out the corresponding base-ten numeral modeled by the sticks and stick bundles.

a. What base-ten numeral is modeled by the following display?

Hundreds   Tens   Ones

b. If there are 190 school days in the school year; how many times will the children rebundle sticks from the beginning to the end of the school year? Describe and list each rebundling.

8. *Math Concepts:* Use centimeter grid paper to cut a collection of base pieces for base two up to a flat-flat.

a. Use the pieces to represent a minimal collection of 21 units. Sketch your result and then write the base-two numeral for that collection of units.

b. Form the collection of base pieces that represents the base-two number 11011_{two}. Sketch that collection and then determine the corresponding base-ten numeral for the collection. Explain how you arrived at your answer.

9. *NCTM Standards:* The five **Process Standards** in the summary in the back pages of this book discuss ways of acquiring and using content knowledge. Read through those **Process Standards,** list the *Expectations* that can be met by working with base-five pieces, and briefly explain how they are met by working with base-five pieces.

---

www.mhhe.com/bbn

bennett-burton-nelson website

Virtual Manipulatives   Grid and Dot Paper   Links and Readings
Interactive Chapter Applets   Color Transparencies   Geometer Sketchpad Modules
Puzzlers   Extended Bibliography

Activity Set 3.2

ADDING AND SUBTRACTING WITH MULTIBASE PIECES

Virtual Manipulatives

www.mhhe.com/bbn

PURPOSE

To use base-five pieces to visually illustrate addition and subtraction.

MATERIALS

A pair of dice and Base-Five Pieces from the Manipulative Kit or from the Virtual Manipulatives.

INTRODUCTION

The operations of addition and subtraction are inverses of each other. *Addition* is explained by putting together sets of objects, and *subtraction* can be explained by taking away a subset of objects from a given set. This dual relationship between subtraction and addition can be seen in the trading-up game, which introduces addition, and the trading-down game, which introduces subtraction.

Algorithms for addition and subtraction are step-by-step procedures for adding and subtracting numbers. One of the best ways to gain insight into the addition and subtraction algorithms is by thinking the process through using manipulatives that represent other number bases. The base-five pieces will be used in the following activities.

Addition

1. **Trading-Up Game** (2 to 5 players): Use your base-five pieces and a pair of dice to play. On a player's turn, two dice are rolled. The total number of dots facing up on the dice is the number of base-five units the player wins. At the end of a player's turn, the player's pieces should be traded (regrouped), if necessary, so that the total winnings are represented by the fewest number of base-five pieces (minimal collection). The base-five numeral for the minimal collection should be recorded. The first player to get one long-flat wins the game.

   Example: On the player's first turn, shown below, the eight units won were traded for a minimal collection and the corresponding base-five numeral was recorded.

   On the player's second turn, seven additional pieces won were added to the player's collection. After trading to get a minimal collection, the player recorded the base-five numeral for the total collection.

	Dice	Collection	Minimal collection	Numeral
1st turn	⚁ ⚄			13_{five}
2d turn	⚄ ⚁			30_{five}

Exercises and Activities 3.2

1. *School Classroom:* Write three different short story problems appropriate for elementary school students that illustrate the three subtraction methods. Explain your thinking.

2. *School Classroom:* A student in your class repeatedly makes the same type of addition error. Here are two examples: $23 + 18 = 311$ and $34 + 18 = 412$. What error is the student making? Explain how you would use base-ten pieces to help this student understand how to resolve this issue.

3. *School Classroom:* The **Elementary School Text** page at the beginning of this section illustrates how the standard subtraction algorithm corresponds to subtracting with base-ten pieces. Illustrate with similar diagrams what the steps would look like if the students decided to subtract from left to right. That is, subtract the hundreds before subtracting the tens and subtract the tens before subtracting the units in $300 - 134$. Explain why you believe one method is better than the other or why you believe both methods are equally useful.

4. *Math Concepts:* For each of the following, sketch a multibase piece model to compute the sum or difference and explain how the base pieces can be used to model the standard paper-and-pencil algorithm. Give the base-five numeral for each result.

   a. $431_{\text{five}} + 233_{\text{five}}$ **b.** $1982 + 2189$

   c. $431_{\text{five}} - 233_{\text{five}}$ **d.** $2912 - 1189$

5. *Math Concepts:* Using sticks bundled for base-five (see Introduction to Activity Set 3.1), sketch a simple stick bundle model to compute each of the following sums or differences and explain how the stick bundles can be used to model the standard paper-and-pencil algorithm. Give the base-five numeral for each result.

   a. $432_{\text{five}} + 144_{\text{five}}$ **b.** $411_{\text{five}} - 333_{\text{five}}$

6. *Math Concepts:* With beans as single units (1), gluing 10 beans on a popsicle stick for a bean stick (10) and gluing 10 bean sticks together for a bean raft (100) is another easy and inexpensive manipulative to use in the elementary school classroom. For each of the following, sketch a bean stick model to compute the sum or difference and explain how the beans and bean sticks can be used to model the standard paper-and-pencil algorithm (use very simple outline sketches to save time). *Hint:* You can trade 1 bean stick for 10 beans, etc.

   a. $335 + 134$ **b.** $3000 - 1982$

7. *Math Concepts:* Do an Internet search and find a website that features a game or math applet focused on whole number addition or subtraction. Describe the game or applet and critique its quality and usefulness. Give the URL of the game or math applet you found.

8. *NCTM Standards:* Read the *Expectation* in the **Pre-K–2 Number and Operations Standards** in the back pages of this book under the *Standard* "Understand meanings of operations . . ." that involves "understand the effects of adding . . ." Give examples of how the activities in this activity set address this expectation.

9. *NCTM Standards:* Go to http://illuminations.nctm.org/ and under "Lessons" select grade levels **Pre-K–2** and the **Number and Operation Standard.** Choose a lesson that involves adding or subtracting whole numbers.

   a. State the title of the lesson and briefly summarize the lesson.

   b. Referring to the **Standards Summary** in the back pages of this book as necessary, list the *Number and Operation Standard Expectations* that the lesson addresses and explain how the lesson addresses these *Expectations*.

---

www.mhhe.com/bbn

bennett-burton-nelson website

Virtual Manipulatives	Grid and Dot Paper	Links and Readings
Interactive Chapter Applets	Color Transparencies	Geometer Sketchpad Modules
Puzzlers	Extended Bibliography	

| Activity Set **3.3** | # MULTIPLYING WITH BASE-TEN PIECES |

PURPOSE

To use base-ten pieces to build visual models for multiplication.

Virtual Manipulatives

www.mhhe.com/bbn

MATERIALS

Base-Ten Pieces from the Manipulative Kit or from the Virtual Manipulatives.

INTRODUCTION

Multiplication is often thought of as repeated addition. For example,

$$4 \times 8$$

can be thought of as 4 copies of 8, or

$$8 + 8 + 8 + 8$$

If repeated addition is illustrated with 4 sets of 8 tiles, the tiles can be pushed together to form a rectangular array of squares with dimensions 4 by 8.

So, one possibility for a conceptual model for multiplication is a rectangle. The two factors are the dimensions of the rectangle, and the number of squares in the rectangle is the product. This rectangular model (or area model) and base-ten pieces will be used to illustrate multiplication algorithms.

---

1. The product 7 × 12 can be represented with base-ten pieces as 7 copies of 12. When the pieces are pushed together, they form a rectangle with dimensions 7 × 12. By regrouping the base pieces to form a minimal collection of 8 longs and 4 units, we can determine that the product is 84.

Determine the following product by forming a rectangle with your base-ten pieces and then regrouping to obtain the minimal collection. Sketch the rectangle of base-ten pieces, and write the numeral representing the minimal collection beneath it.

7 × 23

7-4 Multiply Two-Digit Numbers

MAIN IDEA

I will multiply two-digit numbers.

Math Online

macmillanmh.com
- Extra Examples
- Personal Tutor
- Self-Check Quiz

GET READY to Learn

A coyote travels 27 miles per hour. How far would a coyote travel in 12 hours?

There is more than one way to multiply two-digit numbers.

Real-World EXAMPLE

1 **MEASUREMENT** A coyote travels 27 miles each hour. Multiply 27×12 to find how far a coyote can travel in 12 hours.

One Way: Partial Products

```
   27
 × 12
   14    Multiply 2 × 7.
   40    Multiply 2 × 20.
   70    Multiply 10 × 7.
 +200    Multiply 10 × 20.
  324    Add partial products.
```

	20	7
10	200	70
2	40	14

Another Way: Paper and Pencil

Step 1 Multiply the ones.

```
    1
   27
 × 12
   54  ←  2 × 27
```

Step 2 Multiply the tens.

```
    1
   27
 × 12
   54   ← 2 × 27
  270   ← 10 × 27
```

Step 3 Add the products.

```
    1
   27
 × 12
   54
 +270
  324   ← Add.
```

So, a coyote can travel 324 miles in 12 hours.

2. The product 12 × 13 is represented below with base-ten pieces as 12 copies of 13. When pushed together, the pieces form a rectangle with dimensions 12 × 13. Several exchanges can be made without affecting the dimensions of the rectangle. Ten longs can be exchanged for 1 flat, and groups of 10 adjacent units can be exchanged for longs. The resulting rectangle is composed of 1 flat, 5 longs, and 6 units, so the product of 12 and 13 is 156.

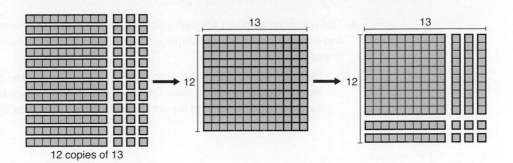

12 copies of 13

Use your base-ten pieces to determine the following products. Use as few base pieces as you can when building your rectangle. Sketch each rectangle, regroup to show the minimal set of base-ten pieces, and record the numeral for this collection.

a. 13 × 13

*b. 21 × 23

*3. Using your results from activity 2, explain why it is possible, using only base-ten pieces, to multiply a two-digit number by a two-digit number without knowing any multiplication facts.

4. The rectangular model for multiplication corresponds very closely to the traditional paper-and-pencil algorithm for multiplication. Use your base-ten pieces to form the rectangle representing 23×24.

*a. Here is a paper-and-pencil procedure that uses four partial products for multiplication. Sketch a diagram of the base-ten piece rectangle representing 23×24. Clearly match each partial product with the corresponding region of your diagram.

$$
\begin{array}{r}
24 \\
\times\ 23 \\
\hline
12 \quad (3 \times 4) \\
60 \quad (3 \times 20) \\
80 \quad (20 \times 4) \\
400 \quad (20 \times 20) \\
\hline
552
\end{array}
$$

Partial products

b. The following procedure uses two partial products for multiplication. Make another sketch of your base-ten piece rectangle, and match the parts of the rectangle with the corresponding partial products.

$$
\begin{array}{r}
24 \\
\times\ 23 \\
\hline
72 \quad (3 \times 24) \\
480 \quad (20 \times 24) \\
\hline
552
\end{array}
$$

Partial products

5. Once you become familiar with the base-ten piece model, it is easy to sketch diagrams of rectangles in order to compute products. For example, to compute 33×41, you would outline the rectangle as in the Figure 1 below and fill it with flats, longs, and units as in the second sketch. The product is obtained by counting the base-ten pieces, 12 hundreds, 15 tens, and 3 units, and regrouping to obtain 1 thousand, 3 hundreds, 5 tens, and 3 units (1353).

Figure 1

Figure 2

For each of the products on the following page,

(1) Draw a base-ten piece sketch, similar to Figure 2, in the first column.

(2) Determine the product from the sketch and record it below the sketch.

(3) In column 2, compute the product using the paper-and-pencil algorithm with *four* partial products and match the partial products to the corresponding parts of your sketch by marking the partial products on the sketch.

(4) In column 3 compute the product using the paper-and-pencil algorithm with *two* partial products and match the partial products to the corresponding parts of your sketch by marking the partial products on the sketch.

a. 12 × 23

Sketch and Product from Sketch	Four Partial-Product Algorithm	Two Partial-Product Algorithm

*b. 22 × 43

Sketch and Product from Sketch	Four Partial-Product Algorithm	Two Partial-Product Algorithm

6. Examine the relationship between the four partial-product algorithm and the two-partial-product algorithm in activity 5 and explain how they are related.

JUST FOR FUN

CROSS-NUMBERS FOR CALCULATORS

Sit back, relax, and exercise your calculator's multiplication key with this cross-number puzzle.

Across

1. $[(18 + 2) \times 4] + 19$

5. $\dfrac{14 + 3}{9 + 8} \times 66$

6. $500{,}000{,}000 \div 9$ (Omit the decimal part of the number.)

8. The middle two digits of the product of $2 \times 2 \times 2 \times 2 \times 3 \times 37$

12. $\dfrac{(41 - 29) \times (63 - 23)}{95 \div 19}$

15. The sum of the digits in the product of $13 \times 9004 \times 77$

16. The sum of the first seven odd numbers

17. March 30, 1974: A "freeze model" in a department store posed motionless for 5 hours, 32 minutes. How many minutes in all did he pose?

23. $\dfrac{13{,}334 - 6566}{8 \times 9} \times \dfrac{992 \div 4}{17 + 4}$

27. $(10{,}000{,}000 \div 81) \times 100$ (nearest whole number)

28. Take the current year, subtract 17, multiply by 2, add 6, divide by 4, add 21, subtract $\frac{1}{2}$ of the current year.

29. The first two digits of the product of 150×12.

Down

3. $(34 \times 53) - (137 \times 2)$

4. Asphalt roof shingles are sold in bundles of 27. Three bundles cover 100 ft². How many bundles are needed for 11,700 ft² of roofing in a housing development?

5. $\dfrac{88{,}984 \times 493}{17 \times 392}$

7. $\dfrac{51 \times 153 \times 62 \times 57}{17 \times 969 \times 31}$

11. $\dfrac{(62 \times 21) + 23}{25} - 11$

14. The number of different combinations of U.S. coins into which a dollar can be changed. (This number is a palindrome, and the sum of its digits is 13.)

17. Remainder of $1816 \div 35$

18. $(343 \times 5 + 242) \times 2$

19. $4 \times [(37 \times 24) - 1]$

21. The number halfway between 7741 and 8611

26. $\dfrac{119 \times 207 \times 415}{23 \times 747}$

Exercises and Activities 3.3

1. *School Classroom:* How would you answer the following elementary school student's question: "I know that to multiply a number by 10 you just put a zero at the end, but why?" Write your reply and include any necessary diagrams or sketches.

2. *School Classroom:* Design an activity that you believe is appropriate for helping an elementary school student understand what partial products are and how they work while multiplying one two-digit number by another two-digit number. Write a few questions to go with your activity. Explain how your activity will help a typical child learning about multiplication.

3. *School Classroom:* Explain how the distributive property of multiplication over addition is illustrated visually in the model for 27×12 in the **Elementary School Text** page at the beginning of this section.

4. *Math Concepts:* Using your base-five pieces only (no pencil and paper), build a rectangle similar to the base-ten rectangle in activity 2 in this activity set to determine the product $12_{five} \times 13_{five}$. Draw a sketch of your rectangle, label the dimensions, and record the product in base five. Explain how you used the base-five pieces to determine the product.

5. *Math Concepts:* Use a place value chart (see Exercises and Activities 3.1) and answer the following questions:

   a. Sketch a base-five place-value chart with 4 markers in the units column, 1 marker in the long column, and 3 markers in the flat column to represent 314_{five}. Explain, using place-value chart diagrams, how you can multiply $3 \times 314_{five}$ using just the markers and the chart.

   b. Explain, using place-value chart diagrams, how you can multiply $10_{five} \times 314_{five}$ using just the markers and the chart.

6. *Math Concepts:* Select 2 flats, 8 longs, and 6 units from your base-ten pieces.

   a. Using only these pieces (all of them), and making no exchanges, form a rectangle. Sketch the rectangle and label the edge dimensions. What is the multiplication problem represented by the sketch? What are the *two* partial products for this multiplication problem, and how do they correspond to the sketch?

   b. Still using only these pieces (all of them), form a different rectangle with different edge dimensions using exactly the same base-ten pieces with no exchanges. What is the multiplication problem represented by the sketch? What are the *four* partial products for this multiplication problem, and how do they correspond to the sketch?

7. *NCTM Standards:* Read the **Grades 3–5 Number and Operations Standards** in the back pages of this book. Pick two *Expectations* that the activities in this section address. State the *Expectations* and the *Standards* they are under. Explain which activities address these *Expectations* and how they do so.

---

bennett-burton-nelson website

Virtual Manipulatives	Grid and Dot Paper	Links and Readings
Interactive Chapter Applets	Color Transparencies	Geometer Sketchpad Modules
Puzzlers	Extended Bibliography	

Activity Set **3.4**   DIVIDING WITH BASE-TEN PIECES

**Virtual
Manipulatives**

www.mhhe.com/bbn

PURPOSE

To use base-ten pieces to illustrate two physical interpretations of division and the long-division algorithm.

MATERIALS

Base-Ten Pieces from the Manipulative Kit or from the Virtual Manipulatives.

INTRODUCTION

In this activity set we will begin by using base-ten pieces to look at two different ways to approach division. The *measurement* or *subtractive* concept of division is illustrated by answering the question, "How many piles of 3 cards can you make from a total of 39 cards?"

The *sharing* or *partitive* concept of division is illustrated by answering the question, "If 39 cards are separated into 3 piles, how many are in each pile?"

Each question can be answered by computing $39 \div 3$. The answer to both questions is 13. With physical objects, however, the first question would be modeled by repeatedly subtracting groups of 3 objects and counting the number of groups, and the second by dividing the objects into 3 groups and counting the number of objects in each group.

Base-ten pieces can also be used to illustrate the inverse relationship between multiplication and division and to provide a concrete interpretation of the long-division algorithm.

---

1. Using base-ten pieces, we can determine the quotient $36 \div 3$ by simple counting procedures. We start with 3 longs and 6 units (36).

With the *sharing* concept of division (Figure 1), 36 is shared equally among 3 groups. Each group has 1 long and 2 units.

The *measurement* concept of division (Figure 2) asks how many groups of 3 can be formed from 36. In this case, all the longs must be traded for units so that groups of 3 can be formed.

$36 \div 3 = 12$ (12 in each of 3 equal groups)
Sharing Concept
Figure 1

$36 \div 3 = 12$ (12 groups of 3)
Measurement Concept
Figure 2

a. Represent 24 as a minimal collection of base-ten pieces. Then, regrouping when necessary, determine 24 ÷ 6 using the measurement concept of division. Record your results with sketches of base-ten pieces.

*b. Represent 132 as a minimal collection of base-ten pieces. Determine 132 ÷ 12 using the sharing concept of division. Record your results with sketches of base-ten pieces.

2. Many times division with whole numbers does not come out evenly, so there is a remainder. When we divide 20 by 3 using the measurement concept, there are 6 groups of 3 units and 2 remaining units. Dividing 20 by 3 using the sharing concept, we have 3 groups of 6 with 2 remaining.

20 ÷ 3 = 6 R 2   20 ÷ 3 = 6 R 2
(6 groups of 3 with 2 remaining)   (6 in each of 3 groups with 2 remaining)

Measurement Concept   **Sharing Concept**

Use base-ten pieces to determine each of the following quotients and record your results in a diagram.

a. 57 ÷ 4 (sharing)

*b. 114 ÷ 12 (measurement)

Explore

Math Activity for 4-3
Use Division Models

You can use base-ten blocks to help you divide.

ACTIVITY

1 At the fair, you need tickets to ride the rides. Three friends share 336 tickets equally. How many tickets will each friend receive?

Represent 336 using base-ten blocks.

Regroup the base-ten blocks to make 3 equal groups.

When you divide 336 into three groups, there are 112 in each group.

So, 336 ÷ 3 = 112.

Use multiplication to check your answer. ✔

112 × 3 = 336.

ACTIVITY

2 Find 252 ÷ 4.

Represent 252 using base-ten blocks.

Regroup the base-ten blocks to make 4 equal groups.

3. Division often arises naturally in a school classroom. For example, suppose two students are discussing dividing up a package of 20 stickers.

  a. Which division concept is it if the students wish to divide the stickers evenly among 5 students? Support your answer with a sketch of base-ten pieces, a short explanation, and give the resulting division sentence.

  b. Which division concept is it if the students wish to give out 5 stickers at a time? Support your answer with a sketch of base-ten pieces, a short explanation, and give the resulting division sentence.

4. When 36 was divided by 3 in activity 1, the answer 12 was obtained in two different ways. Notice that with either concept the base-ten pieces can be pushed together to form a rectangular array of 36 squares with one dimension of 3. So *division can be thought of as finding the missing dimension of a rectangle when the total number of unit squares and one dimension are known.*

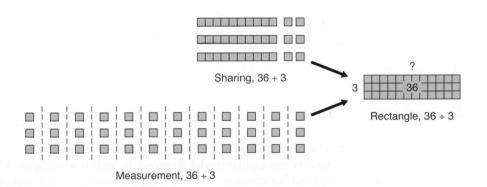

In a similar fashion, to divide 143 by 11 using the base-ten pieces, form the minimal collection of base-ten pieces for 143. Then draw a line segment of length 11 units to represent one dimension of the rectangle. Finally, distribute the base pieces representing 143 (regrouping as necessary) until a rectangle has been formed. In this example we can see that the other dimension is 13, so 143 ÷ 11 = 13.

Minimal collection for 143   Known dimension of the rectangle   Rectangle with 143 unit squares and dimensions 11 by 13

Use your base-ten pieces to determine each of the following quotients. Sometimes you may need to trade pieces. For each, sketch a diagram of your result, record the missing dimension of the rectangle, and give the resulting division sentence. (*Note:* If there is a remainder, you will get a rectangle with pieces left over.)

a. 96 ÷ 4

b. 221 ÷ 17

*c. 529 ÷ 23

d. 397 ÷ 34

5. The paper-and-pencil algorithm for long division can be visualized using base-ten pieces and the rectangular model. Suppose the goal is to compute 477 ÷ 14. Notice that the usual symbol for division, 14⟌477, suggests two sides of a rectangle, where the length of one side is 14, the total number of units is 477, and the length of the other side (the quotient) is unknown. The following steps show how the rectangular model for division is related to the long-division algorithm.

Step 1: First select the base-ten pieces to represent 477.

Step 1

4 flats,
7 longs,
7 units

Step 2: Draw a line segment of length 14 units to represent one dimension of the rectangle. Begin distributing the base-ten pieces representing 477 to form a rectangle of width 14.

Step 3: Three sections each of width 10 can be incorporated into the rectangle. This requires 4 flats and 2 longs and leaves 5 longs and 7 units, which is not enough to complete another section of width 10 (1 flat had to be traded for 10 longs to build this much).

Step 4: Four sections of width 1 can be added onto the rectangle (1 long was traded for 10 units). This uses 5 longs and 6 units and leaves 1 unit remaining—not enough to make the rectangle any wider unless the remaining unit is cut into pieces.

Step 5: The desired dimension of the rectangle (the quotient) is 34, and there is a remainder of 1.

Compute the following quotients using your base-ten pieces and the rectangular model illustrated on page 92 and page 93. Record your results by sketching each final base-ten piece rectangle and showing how each digit in the quotient relates to the long-division algorithm.

a. $144 \div 6$

$$6\overline{)144}$$

b. $134 \div 3$

$$3\overline{)134}$$

*c. $587 \div 23$

$$23\overline{)587}$$

JUST FOR FUN

Here are several games and number tricks to try using a calculator.

ARABIAN NIGHTS MYSTERY

Select any three-digit number, such as 837, and enter it on your calculator twice to form a six-digit number (in this case, 837837). Then carry out the following steps: divide this number by 11, then divide the result by 7, and finally divide the result by 13. You may be surprised by the outcome. This trick has been called the Arabian Nights Mystery because it can be explained by using the number 1001, in reference to the book *Tales from the Thousand and One Nights*. Try this trick for some other three-digit numbers. Explain why it works.

KEYBOARD GAME (2 players)

The first player begins the game by entering a whole number on a calculator. The players then take turns subtracting single-digit numbers, with the following restriction: each player must subtract a nonzero digit, using a digit button adjacent to the one used by the preceding player. For example, if a player subtracts 6, the next player must subtract 9, 8, 5, 2, or 3. When a player's turn results in a number less than 0, that player loses the game.

MAGIC FORMULAS

Usually if someone asks you to select a number on which to perform some operations, you will choose an easy one. With the aid of a calculator, however, you do not have to be so careful about the number you select. For example, try a three- or four-digit number in the following formula.

- Select any number (remember this number, as it will be needed later), add 221, multiply by 2652, subtract 1326, divide by 663, subtract 870, divide by 4, and subtract the number you started with. Your result will be 3.

Exercises and Activities **3.4**

1. *School Classroom:*

   a. Describe two real-world examples, appropriate for elementary school students, of using the sharing division concept.

   b. Describe two real-world examples, appropriate for elementary school students, of using the measurement division concept.

2. *School Classroom:* How would you help this student? Carlie was watching Adam divide 12 by 3 using the measurement concept and then declared the answer to $12 \div 3$ to be 3. Carlie explained her method as: If you put 12 chips in 3 piles and then count the number of piles, you get 3.

3. *School Classroom:* Write a story problem suitable for elementary school students for each of the following:

   a. A problem that illustrates $48 \div 6 = 8$ using the sharing concept of division.

   b. A problem that illustrates $48 \div 6 = 8$ using the measurement concept of division.

4. *School Classroom:* The division example on the **Elementary School Text** page at the beginning of this section uses the partitive or sharing concept to determine $336 \div 3$ and $252 \div 4$.

   a. Draw a sketch to show how you would divide 252 by 4 using the rectangular model, as illustrated in activity 5 in this activity set.

   b. Write a story problem for $252 \div 4$, appropriate for elementary school students, in which the solution makes the most sense as a rectangular division model rather than a sharing concept or a measurement concept.

5. *Math Concepts:* Using your base-five pieces only (no pencil and paper), build a rectangle similar to the base-ten rectangle in activity 4 in this activity set to determine the quotient $1402_{\text{five}} \div 22_{\text{five}}$. Draw a sketch of your rectangle, label the dimensions, and record the quotient in base five. Explain how you used the base-five pieces to determine the solution.

6. *Math Concepts:* Read the Arabian Nights Mystery described in the **Just for Fun Activity** for this section. Explain why the mystery always works.

7. *Math Concepts:* Open the **Math Calculator Investigation 3.4: Read Me—Sums and Differences of Squares Instructions** from the companion website and investigate the divisibility of the sums and differences of the squares as described in questions 1, 2, 3, and 4 of the *Starting Points for Investigations 3.4.* Give a few of your examples and explain your thinking.

8. *NCTM Standards:* Read the *Expectation* in the **Grades 3–5 Number and Operations Standards** in the back pages of this book under the *Standard* "Understand meanings of operations . . ." that involves "division as the inverse of multiplication." Explain how the base-ten piece models can be used to see this relationship.

---

bennett-burton-nelson website

Virtual Manipulatives   Grid and Dot Paper   Links and Readings
Interactive Chapter Applets   Color Transparencies   Geometer Sketchpad Modules
Puzzlers   Extended Bibliography

ACTIVITIES FOR THE ELEMENTARY SCHOOL CLASSROOM

Introducing Place Value with Base-Ten Pieces

Purpose: To provide elementary school students with an understanding of base-ten positional numeration.

Connections: "Thousands of years ago before we had cities, automobiles, planes, and computers, we lived in caves and did not have numbers like we have today. One early number system used marks like / / / / to write the number four. How do you think the number for nine was written? We will use base-ten pieces to help you learn about the types of numbers that are used today."

Flat   Long Unit

This student is modeling 2237 with 3-dimensional base-ten blocks that are commonly found in schools.

Materials: Sets of base-ten pieces may be created by copying base-ten grid paper from the companion website onto cardstock and cutting out units, longs, and flats. Base-ten piece transparencies can also be made with the base-ten pieces image. Sets of base-ten pieces can be placed in plastic sealable bags. Each group of two to four students will need one set of base-ten pieces.

1. Pass out sets of base-ten pieces to pairs of students and ask them what they notice about the pieces. Discuss the relationship of the pieces to each other and the value of each piece, if the smallest piece has value 1. (*Note:* Depending on the level of the students, you may want to use only units and longs and adjust the numbers in the following activities as needed.)

2. Write numbers such as 36 and 253 on the board and ask students to represent the number with their base-ten pieces. Have the students discuss other collections of base-ten pieces that also represent these numbers. Discuss finding or using the fewest number of pieces (minimal collection) for these numbers and make sure the children are comfortable with trading (such as 10 units for 1 long or 1 long for 10 units). Ask the students how the early cave people might have written the number for 36 and discuss the convenience of today's numbers. (*Note:* The purpose of this portion of the activity is to encourage students to think in terms of units, tens, and hundreds.)

3. Ask students to use their base-ten pieces to compute the results of the following expressions. You may adjust the numbers and operations to match the level of the students you are working with. Have the students discuss their methods and reasoning with the class.

   a. $68 + 57$ **b.** $274 + 63$ **c.** $321 - 74$ **d.** 4×13 **e.** $141 \div 3$

4. Using the preceding expressions, ask students to make up a story problem involving the given numbers and operation. (*Note:* Depending on the level of the students, examples or explanations may be needed, such as, thinking of division by 3 as sharing among 3 people.)

5. (Optional) Chips numbered from 0 to 9 in a bag are needed for each pair of students. Have each student sketch a place-value table as shown here. Taking turns, each student selects one chip from the bag and writes this number in one of the columns of their table. Each player takes three turns and the object is to form the greatest three-digit number.

Hundreds	Tens	Ones

4 Number Theory

Number theory offers many rich opportunities for explorations that are interesting, enjoyable, and useful.

. . . Challenging but accessible problems from number theory can be easily formulated and explored by students. For example, building rectangular arrays with a set of tile can stimulate questions about divisibility and prime, composite, square, even, and odd numbers. . . .[†]

Activity Set 4.1

MODELS FOR EVEN NUMBERS, ODD NUMBERS, FACTORS, AND PRIMES

Virtual Manipulatives

www.mhhe.com/bbn

PURPOSE

To use models to provide visual images of basic concepts of number theory.

MATERIALS

Color Tiles from the Manipulative Kit or from the Virtual Manipulatives.

INTRODUCTION

Some problems in number theory are simple enough for children to understand yet are unsolvable by mathematicians. Maybe that is why this branch of mathematics has intrigued so many people, novices and professionals alike, for over 2000 years. For example, is it true that every *even number* greater than 2 can be expressed as the sum of two *prime numbers?* It is true for the first few even numbers:

$$4 = 2 + 2 \qquad 6 = 3 + 3 \qquad 8 = 3 + 5 \qquad 10 = 5 + 5 \qquad 12 = 5 + 7 \qquad 14 = 7 + 7$$

However, mathematicians have not been able to prove it is true for all even numbers greater than 2.

The ideas of odd, even, factors, and primes are basic concepts of number theory. In this activity set, these ideas will be given geometric form to show that visual images can be associated with them.

[†]*Curriculum and Evaluation Standards for School Mathematics*, pp. 91–93.

Even and Odd Numbers

1. The nonzero whole numbers (counting numbers) can be represented geometrically in many different ways. Here the first five consecutive numbers are represented as a sequence of tile figures. Extend the sequence by drawing the figures for the numbers 6, 7, and 8.

Describe, in your own words, how the figures for the even counting numbers differ from those for the odd counting numbers in the sequence above.

2. Here is a tile sequence for the first four *even numbers*.

a. Draw the figure for the seventh even number above. What is the seventh even number?

Seventh even number _____

*b. Describe in words what the figure for the 125th even number would look like. What is the 125th even number?

125th even number _____

c. Describe in words what the figure for the *n*th even number would look like. Write a mathematical expression for the *n*th even number.

*n*th even number _____

3. This tile sequence represents the first four *odd numbers*.

    1st   2d   3d   4th   5th   8th

    1   3   5   7

a. Draw the figures for the fifth and eighth odd numbers. What is the fifth odd number? What is the eighth odd number?

5th odd number _____   8th odd number _____

*b. Describe in words how to draw the figure representing the 15th odd number. What is the 15th odd number?

15th odd number _____

c. Determine the 50th, 100th, and *n*th odd numbers by imagining what their figures would look like, based on the model shown above.

50th odd number _____   100th odd number _____   *n*th odd number _____

*d. When the odd numbers, beginning with 1, are arranged in consecutive order, 7 is in the fourth position and 11 is in the sixth position. In what position is 79? 117? (*Hint:* Think about the tile figures for these numbers. You may wish to draw a rough sketch of the figures.)

79 is in the _____ position.   117 is in the _____ position.

4. The following diagram illustrates that when an even number is added to an odd number, the sum is an odd number. Determine the oddness or evenness of each of the sums and differences below by drawing similar diagrams.

   Even number   Odd number   Even + Odd number = Odd number

a. The sum of any two even numbers.

*b. The sum of any two odd numbers.

c. The sum of any two consecutive counting numbers.

d. The sum of any three consecutive counting numbers.

*e. The difference of any two odd numbers.

f. The sum of any three odd numbers and two even numbers.

5. The tiles for the figures in the tile sequence for consecutive odd numbers can be rearranged as follows:

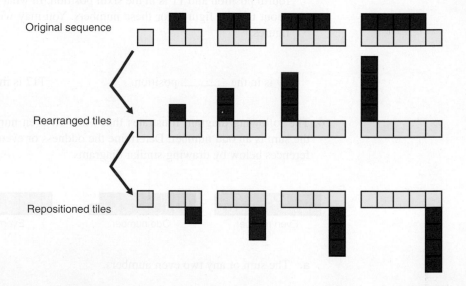

Original sequence

Rearranged tiles

Repositioned tiles

a. The L-shaped figures for the first five consecutive odd numbers can be pushed together to form a square. What does this tell you about the sum of the first five consecutive odd numbers?

*b. Visualize the L-shaped figures for the first 10 consecutive odd numbers. What size square can be formed from these figures? What is the sum of the first 10 consecutive odd numbers?

c. Consider the sum of all odd numbers from 1 to 79.

$$1 + 3 + 5 + 7 + \ldots + 77 + 79$$

How many numbers are in this sum? Determine the sum of the consecutive odd numbers from 1 through 79 by visualizing L-shaped figures forming a square.

Factors and Primes

6. All possible rectangular arrays that can be constructed with exactly 4 tiles, exactly 7 tiles, and exactly 12 tiles are diagrammed below. Use the tiles from your Manipulative Kit or from the Virtual Manipulatives to form all possible rectangular arrays that can be constructed for the remaining numbers from 1 through 12 (remember a square is a rectangle and rectangles with the same dimensions, regardless of orientation, are the same rectangle). Sketch these arrays in the spaces provided below.

Rectangles with 1 tile	Rectangles with 2 tiles	Rectangles with 3 tiles

Rectangles with 4 tiles	Rectangles with 5 tiles	Rectangles with 6 tiles

Rectangles with 7 tiles	Rectangles with 8 tiles	Rectangles with 9 tiles

Rectangles with 10 tiles	Rectangles with 11 tiles	Rectangles with 12 tiles

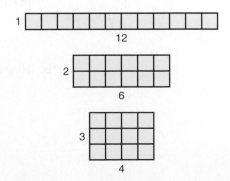

7. The dimensions of a rectangular array are factors of the number the array represents. For example, the number 12 has a 1 × 12 array, 2 × 6 array, and 3 × 4 array, and the factors of 12 are 1, 2, 3, 4, 6, and 12. Use your results from activity 6 to complete the following table by listing all the factors of each number and the total number of factors. Then extend the table to numbers through 20.

Number	Factors	Number of Factors
1	_____	_____
2	_____	_____
3	_____	_____
4	1, 2, 4	3
5	_____	_____
6	_____	_____
7	1, 7	2
8	_____	_____
9	_____	_____
10	_____	_____
11	_____	_____
12	1, 2, 3, 4, 6, 12	6
13	_____	_____
14	_____	_____
15	_____	_____
16	_____	_____
17	_____	_____
18	_____	_____
19	_____	_____
20	_____	_____

8. Numbers with more than one rectangle, such as 12 and 4, are called **composite numbers.** Except for the number 1, all numbers that have exactly one rectangle are called **prime numbers.**

   a. Write a sentence or two to explain how you can describe prime and composite numbers in terms of *numbers of factors.*

   *b. How does the number 1 differ from the prime and composite numbers?

c. Is there another counting number, like 1, that is neither prime nor composite? Explain why or why not in terms of rectangles.

d. Some numbers are called *square numbers* or *perfect squares*. Look at the sketches in activity 6. Which numbers from 1 through 12 do you think could be called square numbers? State your reason.

*e. Examine the rectangles representing numbers that have an odd number of factors. What conclusions can you draw about numbers that have an odd number of factors?

9. The numbers listed in your chart have either 1, 2, 3, 4, 5, or 6 factors.

a. Identify another number that has exactly 5 factors. Are there other numbers with exactly 5 factors? Explain.

b. Find two numbers greater than 20 that have more rectangles than the number 12. What are the factors of each of these numbers?

10. There are five numbers in your table in activity 7 that have exactly 4 factors.

a. The number 8 is the cube of a prime number, $8 = 2^3$, and it has exactly 4 factors. Look at the factors of 3^3 and 5^3. Will the cubes of all prime numbers have exactly 4 factors? Explain your reasoning.

b. Each of the numbers 6, 10, 14, and 15 also have exactly 4 factors. Looking at the factors for these numbers, determine what special characteristics these numbers with exactly 4 factors possess. List a few more numbers with exactly 4 factors, and explain how you could generate more of the numbers.

JUST FOR FUN

NUMBER CHART PRIMES AND MULTIPLES

A seventh-grade student, Keith, chose to do a math project based on identifying prime numbers with the sieve of Eratosthenes.[†] Keith's innovation to the sieve added extra information. He used a number chart like the one here and put a triangle around 1 because it is neither prime nor composite. Then he circled 2 because it was prime and put a black dot above each multiple of 2. Next he moved from 2 to the next undotted number, 3, circled 3 and put a blue dot to the right of each multiple of 3.

The chart below has been started using Keith's method. The multiples of 2 have a black dot above them. Circle 3 and put a blue dot to the right of each multiple of 3. Circle 5 and put a green dot beneath all multiples of 5. Circle 7 and put a red dot to the left of all multiples of 7. Finally, circle all the remaining numbers which have no colored dots in their squares.

1. How can we be sure that all the circled numbers are prime?

2. How can you use the chart to find all numbers which are multiples of 3 and 5?

3. Keith's chart actually included all numbers up to 1000. How many different colors did he use?

△1	②2	3	•4	5	•6	7	•8	9	•10
11	•12	13	•14	15	•16	17	•18	19	•20
21	•22	23	•24	25	•26	27	•28	29	•30
31	•32	33	•34	35	•36	37	•38	39	•40
41	•42	43	•44	45	•46	47	•48	49	•50
51	•52	53	•54	55	•56	57	•58	59	•60
61	•62	63	•64	65	•66	67	•68	69	•70
71	•72	73	•74	75	•76	77	•78	79	•80
81	•82	83	•84	85	•86	87	•88	89	•90
91	•92	93	•94	95	•96	97	•98	99	•100
101	•102	103	•104	105	•106	107	•108	109	•110
111	•112	113	•114	115	•116	117	•118	119	•120

△ neither prime nor composite

◯ prime numbers

black dot   multiple of 2
blue dot   multiple of 3
green dot   multiple of 5
red dot   multiple of 7

[†]C. L. Bradford, "Keith's Secret Discovery of the Sieve of Eratosthenes," pp. 239–241.

Exercises and Activities 4.1

1. *School Classroom:* How would you help a student in your class who, after building rectangular arrays to find factors, insisted that the factors of 16 are 1, 2, 4, 4, 8, and 16 because "every side of the array has to have a number that goes with it"?

2. *School Classroom:* One of the students in your class said that it was easy to find the sum of the first n odd numbers because it is just n^2. However, when asked to find the sum of consecutive odd numbers from 1 through 219 she couldn't do it because she didn't know how many odd numbers there were from 1 through 219. Explain how you would help her understand how to find the number of consecutive odd numbers from 1 to any other odd number.

3. *School Classroom:* Suppose that your students were working on sketching all rectangles for the numbers 7 through 20 and recording their dimensions. After finishing, one group of students insisted that 1 was a prime number because it has only one rectangle like 2, 3, 5, and the other primes. Explain how you would resolve this issue without simply telling them a rule to remember.

4. *Math Concepts:* The tile sequence below represents the first four consecutive odd numbers. Sketch a tile figure that represents the nth odd number. Write an algebraic expression for this nth odd number and describe how your algebraic expression can be seen in the shape of the tile figure you have sketched.

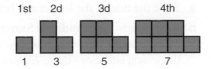

1st   2d   3d   4th

1   3   5   7

5. *Math Concepts:*

   a. How many numbers less than or equal to 100 have an odd number of factors? Explain your answer in terms of rectangular arrays.

   b. How many numbers less than or equal to 100 have an even number of factors? Explain your answer in terms of rectangular arrays.

6. *Math Concepts:* For the following questions, use specific prime number examples to help draw conclusions about the general statements.

   a. If p is a prime number, how many factors does p^2 have? Explain whether or not the number of factors of p^2 varies with different primes.

   b. If p is a prime number and n is a counting number, how many factors does p^n have?

   c. Explain how you can use the results in part b to find a number with exactly 6 factors? Exactly 8 factors?

7. *Math Concepts:*

   a. The number 32 is the fifth power of 2, $32 = 2^5$, and it has exactly 6 factors. Is this true for the fifth power of any number? Are there any special conditions on the base number? Give three more numbers, like 32, that have exactly 6 factors. Explain your reasoning.

   b. Each of the numbers 12, 18, and 20 also have exactly 6 factors. Looking at the factors for these numbers, determine what special characteristics these types of numbers with exactly 6 factors possess. List a few more numbers of this type with exactly 6 factors, and explain how you could generate more of these numbers with exactly 6 factors.

8. *Math Concepts:* If p, q, and r, are three different prime numbers, determine the number of factors for each of the following numbers. Use specific prime number examples to help draw conclusions about the general statements.

   a. $p \times q$

   b. $p^2 \times q$

   c. $p^2 \times q^2$

   d. $p \times q \times r$

9. *NCTM Standards:*

   a. In the **Grades 3–5 Number and Operations Standards** in the back pages of this book, one *Expectation* says, "Describe classes of numbers according to characteristics such as the nature of their factors." As a grades 3–5 teacher, explain what this statement would mean to you.

   b. Determine if there are any other *Expectations* at the grades 3–5 level or higher that specifically refer to the number theory topics explored in the activities in this activity set, and, if so, record what they suggest.

10. *NCTM Standards:* Go to http://illuminations.nctm.org/ and under "Lessons" select grade levels 3–5 and the **Number and Operations Standards.** Choose a lesson that involves even and odd numbers or factors of whole numbers; search for the keyword "factor."

    a. State the title of the lesson and briefly summarize the lesson.

    b. Referring to the **Standards Summary** in the back pages of this book as necessary, list the *Number and Operation Standard Expectations* that the lesson addresses and explain how the lesson addresses these *Expectations.*

---

www.mhhe.com/bbn

bennett-burton-nelson website

Virtual Manipulatives	Grid and Dot Paper	Links and Readings
Interactive Chapter Applets	Color Transparencies	Geometer Sketchpad Modules
Puzzlers	Extended Bibliography	

MODELS FOR GREATEST COMMON FACTOR AND LEAST COMMON MULTIPLE

PURPOSE

To use a linear model to illustrate the concepts of greatest common factor and least common multiple and show how they are related.

MATERIALS

No supplementary materials are needed.

INTRODUCTION

Greatest common factor (GCF) and least common multiple (LCM) are important concepts that occur frequently in mathematics. The GCF of two numbers is usually introduced by listing all the factors of two numbers, identifying the *common factors*, and then choosing the *greatest* of the common factors.

Factors of 12: 1, 2, 3, 4, ⑥, 12

Factors of 18: 1, 2, 3, ⑥, 9, 18

The LCM of two numbers is often introduced by listing multiples of each number, identifying *common multiples*, and choosing the *least* of the common multiples.

Multiples of 12: 12, 24, ㉟, 48, 60, 72, 84, 96, 108, 120, 132, 144, . . .

Multiples of 18: 18, ㉟, 54, 72, 90, 108, 126, 144, 162, 180, 198, . . .

In this activity set, the concepts of GCF and LCM will be visually represented by rods. The GCF will be viewed as the greatest common length into which two (or more) rods can be cut.

The LCM will be viewed as the shortest common length into which two (or more) rods will fit. This will be determined by placing copies of each rod end to end.

4-1   Greatest Common Factor

EXAMPLE   Find the GCF by Listing Factors

2 Find the GCF of 60 and 54.

First make an organized list of the factors for each number.

60: $1 \times 60, 2 \times 30, 3 \times 20, 4 \times 15, 5 \times 12, 6 \times 10 \longrightarrow$ 1, 2, 3, 4, 5, 6, 10, 12, 15, 20, 30, 60

54: $1 \times 54, 2 \times 27, 3 \times 18, 6 \times 9 \longrightarrow$ 1, 2, 3, 6, 9, 18, 27, 54

The common factors are 1, 2, 3, and 6, and the greatest of these is 6.
So, the greatest common factor or GCF of 60 and 54 is 6.

Use a Venn diagram to show the factors. Notice that the factors 1, 2, 3, and 6 are the common factors of 60 and 54 and the GCF is 6.

CHECK Your Progress

Find the GCF of each set of numbers.

c. 35, 60   d. 15, 45   e. 12, 19

EXAMPLE   Find the GCF by Using Prime Factors

3 Find the GCF of 18 and 30.

Review Vocabulary

prime number a whole number that has exactly two factors, 1 and the number itself; *Example:* 7 (Lesson 1-2)

prime factorization a composite number expressed as a product of prime numbers; *Example:* $12 = 2 \times 2 \times 3$ (Lesson 1-2)

METHOD 1   Write the prime factorization.

2 and 3 are common factors.

METHOD 2   Divide by prime numbers.

2)18   30   Divide both 18 and 30 by 2.
3) 9   15   Divide the quotients by 3.
    3   5

Using either method, the common prime factors are 2 and 3.
So, the GCF of 18 and 30 is 2×3 or 6.

CHOOSE Your Method

Find the GCF of each set of numbers.

f. 12, 66   g. 36, 45   h. 32, 48

Greatest Common Factor

1. Here are rods of length 24 units and 36 units. Both rods can be cut evenly into pieces with a common length of 6 units, since 6 is a factor of 24 and 6 is a factor of 36.

a. There are five other ways to cut both rods evenly into pieces of common length. Mark those on the following five pairs of rods.

*b. Because rods of length 24 and 36 can both be cut evenly into pieces of length 6, 6 is called a *common factor* of 24 and 36. List the other common factors of 24 and 36.

Common factors of 24 and 36: 6, _____, _____, _____, _____, _____

c. Circle the *greatest common factor*[†] of 24 and 36. The greatest common factor of 24 and 36 is abbreviated as GCF(24, 36).

2. Determine the greatest common factor of each pair of numbers below by indicating how you would cut the rods into common pieces of greatest length. Record your answer next to the diagram.

a. 32

24

GCF(32, 24) =

*b. 18

25

GCF(18, 25) =

c. 42

28

GCF(42, 28) =

[†]Also commonly called the *greatest common divisor* or *GCD*.

3. a. Determine the greatest common factor of the numbers 20 and 12 by indicating how you would cut the two rods below into pieces of greatest common length.

20

12

GCF(20, 12) =

b. The amount by which one rod exceeds the other is represented by the **difference rod.** Determine the GCF of the difference rod and the shorter of the first two rods using the second diagram below.

Difference rod

20

12

Difference rod

8

12

GCF(8, 12) =

Shorter rod
(of first two rods)

4. For each pair of rods shown below, determine the GCF of the shorter rod and the difference rod. Indicate how you would cut the difference rod and the smaller rod on the diagrams, and fill in the blanks to record the GCF of the difference rod and the shorter rod.

Difference rod

*a. 40

24

GCF(_____, 24) = _____

Difference rod

b. 42

28

GCF(_____, 28) = _____

Difference rod

c. 21

12

GCF(_____, 12) = _____

*5. You may have noticed in activities 1–4 that the longer rod is always cut at a point coinciding with the end of the shorter rod, which illustrates that all common factors of the shorter rod and the difference rod are also factors of the longer rod. So, the GCF of two numbers can be determined by computing the GCF of the difference rod and the shorter of the first two rods. Use your results from activity 4 to determine the following.

GCF(40, 24) = GCF(_____, 24) =   GCF(42, 28) = GCF(_____, 28) =

GCF(21, 12) = GCF(_____, 12) =

6. The preceding activity illustrates that the GCF of two numbers can be determined by computing the difference of the two numbers and then finding the GCF of the difference and the smaller of the two numbers. If the GCF is not then apparent, this method can be continued, as shown in the following example. Notice in the first step the larger number, 198, is replaced by the difference of 198 and 126 (72), then in the second step, 126 is now the larger number, and so 126 is replaced by the difference of 126 and 72 (54).

GCF(198, 126) = GCF(72, 126) = GCF(72, 54) = GCF(18, 54)
= GCF(18, 36)   = GCF(18, 18) = 18

Use this difference method to find the GCF of the following pairs of numbers. Show each step.

  a. GCF(144, 27) =

  *b. GCF(280, 168) =

  c. GCF(714, 420) =

  *d. GCF(306, 187) =

Least Common Multiple

7. In the following diagram, the numbers 3 and 5 are represented by rods. When the rods of length 3 are arranged end to end alongside a similar arrangement of rods of length 5, the distances at which the ends evenly match are **common multiples** of 3 and 5 (15, 30, 45, etc.). The least distance at which they match, 15, is the **least common multiple** of 3 and 5. This least common multiple is written LCM(3, 5) = 15.

Find the LCM of each of the following pairs of numbers by drawing the minimum number of end-to-end rods of each length needed to make both rows the same length.

  a. 8
    12

LCM(8, 12) = _____

  *b. 14
    21

LCM(14, 21) = _____

  c. 5
    7

LCM(5, 7) = _____

  *d. 8
    10

LCM(8, 10) = _____

8. There is a relationship between the GCF and the LCM of two numbers. The first figure below shows the numbers 6 and 15; GCF(6, 15) = 3 is indicated by marks on the rods. The second figure shows that LCM(6, 15) = 30.

a. GCF(6, 15) = 3 and 3 divides the 6-unit rod into 2 parts and the 15-unit rod into 5 parts. Notice that 2 rods of length 15 or 5 rods of length 6 equal 30, the LCM(6, 15). Use the rod diagrams in activity 7 to complete the following table. Look for a relationship involving the GCF, LCM, and the product of the two numbers.

	A	B	GCF(A, B)	LCM(A, B)	A × B
(1)	6	15	3	30	90
(2)	8	12	_____	_____	_____
*(3)	14	21	_____	_____	_____
(4)	5	7	_____	_____	_____
*(5)	8	10	_____	_____	_____

b. Based on your observations from the table in part a, write a brief set of directions for finding the LCM of two numbers, A and B, once you have determined the GCF of A and B.

9. For each of the following pairs of numbers, first compute the GCF of the pair and then use the relationship from activity 8b to compute the LCM.

*a. GCF(9, 15) =

LCM(9, 15) =

b. GCF(8, 18) =

LCM(8, 18) =

*c. GCF(140, 350) =

LCM(140, 350) =

d. GCF(135, 42) =

LCM(135, 42) =

JUST FOR FUN

STAR POLYGONS

Star polygons are often constructed to provide decorative and artistic patterns. The star polygon pictured here was formed from colored yarn around a circle of 16 equally spaced tacks on a piece of plywood. Starting at the red tack in the lower left and moving in a clockwise direction, the yarn goes a step of 5 to the next red tack and then another step of 5 to a third red tack. This procedure continues until the yarn gets back to its starting point. In the following activities, star polygons are analyzed by using the concepts of factor, multiple, greatest common factor, and least common multiple.[†]

Star polygons can be constructed by taking steps of a given size around a circle of points. The following star (14, 3) was constructed by beginning at point p and taking a step of 3 spaces to point q. Three spaces from q is point r. Through this process we eventually come back to point p, after having hit all 14 points. The resulting figure is a star polygon.

In general, for whole numbers n and s, where $n \geq 3$ and $s < n$, star (n, s) denotes a star polygon with n points and steps of s.

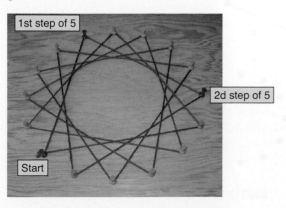

[†]A. B. Bennett, Jr., "Star Patterns," *Arithmetic Teacher*, pp. 12–14.

*1. Sketch the star polygons, given below, by beginning at point *x* and taking steps of *s* in a clockwise direction.

Will the same star polygons be obtained if the steps are taken in a counterclockwise direction?

Star (8, 3)   Star (9, 4)   Star (7, 2)   Star (7, 4)

*2. Sketch the following pairs of star polygons. Make a conjecture about star (n, s) and star (n, r), where $r + s = n$.

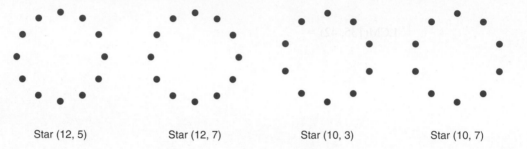

Star (12, 5)   Star (12, 7)   Star (10, 3)   Star (10, 7)

Conjecture:

*3. The star polygons in activities 1 and 2 can each be completed by beginning at any point and drawing one continuous path. In each of those examples, the path returns to the starting point after hitting all points. For star (15, 3), however, the path closes after hitting only 5 points. To complete this star, 3 different paths are needed. Determine the number of different paths to complete each of the following star polygons.

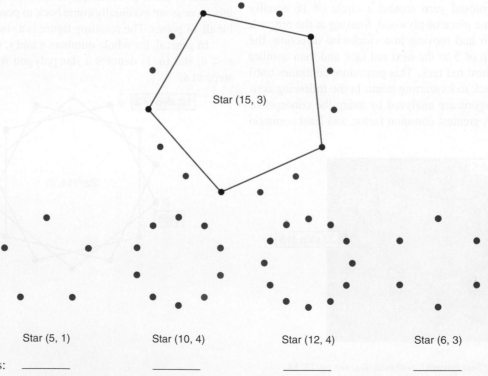

Star (15, 3)

Star (5, 1)   Star (10, 4)   Star (12, 4)   Star (6, 3)

Number of paths: _____   _____   _____   _____

*4. What conditions must *n* and *s* satisfy in order for star (*n*, *s*) to be formed with 1 continuous path? Use your conjecture to sketch 15-point star polygons that can be formed by 1 continuous path. There are 4 of these star polygons.

Star (15, 1), which is congruent to star (15, 14), is one of them. Determine and sketch the remaining three star polygons, and write the size of the steps for each.

Star (15,   )   Star (15,   )   Star (15,   )

Size of step: _____   _____   _____

*5. Star (14, 3) (shown at the right) was constructed by beginning at point *p* and taking steps of 3 to points *q*, *r*, *s*, *t*, and so forth. After point *t*, the next step of 3 passes the starting point, *p*, completes the first *orbit* (once around the circle, shown as red edges) and starts us on the second orbit (shown as blue edges). When the last step in the second orbit passes *p*, the third and final orbit (shown as black edges) begins. For star (14, 3) it takes three orbits before the path returns to the starting point, *p*. The individual orbits are shown below.

Star (14, 3)

Orbit 1 starting at *p*   Orbit 2   Orbit 3

For the star polygons given below, how many orbits are needed before a given path will return to its starting point? For each star polygon, you may pick any point as the starting point.

Star (9, 2)   Star (8, 6)   Star (14, 4)

Number of orbits: _____   _____   _____

6. Star (7, 3) was drawn by starting at point 1 and connecting the points in the following order: 1, 4, 7, 3, 6, 2, 5, and 1. Three orbits are needed to complete this star. The number of orbits is just the number of times we need to go around the 7 points of the circle before the steps of 3 bring us back to the beginning point. That is, after taking steps of 3 for 21 spaces, we arrive back at the beginning point. The 21 spaces represent the least common multiple of 7 and 3.

Star (7, 3)

First orbit   Second orbit   Third orbit

a. Explain how the concept of least common multiple can be used to determine the number of orbits for 1 path of star (15, 6). Check your answer.

*b. Make a conjecture about the number of orbits needed to complete 1 path for star (n, s).

7. Create a star polygon. Any number of points can be used and any shape can be used; the points do not have to lie on a circle. Star polygons can be made by drawing with colored pencils (different colors for steps of different sizes) or by using colored thread or yarn. With a needle and thread, they can be stitched on posterboard. Several star polygons can be formed on the same set of points. Three star polygons have been stitched from 36 holes on the posterboard pictured here. One star polygon is made from green thread with steps of 6, another from red thread with steps of 11, and a third from blue thread with steps of 15.

a. The star polygon with steps of 11 is the only one of the three star polygons in this photograph that can be constructed by 1 continuous path. Why?

*b. How many orbits are needed to complete star (36, 11)?

ANALYZING STAR POLYGONS APPLET

In this applet, you will draw star polygons by choosing the number of points and size of the steps. Star (9, 2) was drawn by beginning at one of 9 points and taking steps of size 2 around the circle of points until returning to the original point. What is the relationship between the numbers of points and sizes of steps? This applet enables you to form more than one star polygon on a given set of points to create colorful designs.

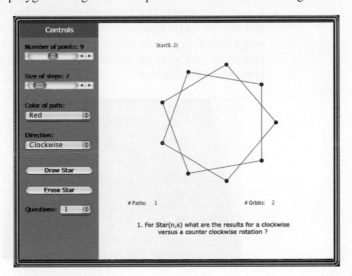

Analyzing Star Polygons Applet, Chapter 4
www.mhhe.com/bbn

Exercises and Activities **4.2**

1. *School Classroom:* Devon's teacher has told his class that *Relatively Prime* numbers are numbers whose greatest common factor is 1. Devon would like to know how 4 and 9 can be relatively prime since neither 4 nor 9 are prime numbers. How can you help Devon's teacher explain this idea?

2. *School Classroom:* Star Polygons are described in the **Just for Fun** activity in this section and also on the companion website under Interactive Math Applets. Describe how you could adapt Star Polygons to create a math-art project for children using, for example, colored pencils or yarn as in the photo. Explain how the project you design contributes to the math curriculum for children.

Yarn and tack star polygon created by a student at Western Oregon University.

3. *School Classroom:* The **Elementary School Text** page at the beginning of this section gives two methods for finding the GCF of two numbers.

   a. Use each of these methods to find the GCF(198, 126). Show your computations and sketches.

   b. Compare the two methods in part a to the example in activity 6 in this activity set. Explain which method you believe is more conceptually clear and which method is easier to use for a GCF computation.

4. *Math Concepts:* For each of the given number pairs (A, B), determine the GCF(A, B) and the LCM(A, B). Then record the prime factorizations of A, B, GCF(A, B), and LCM(A, B) as demonstrated here:

			Prime Factorizations			
(A, B)	GCF(A, B)	LCM(A, B)	A	B	GCF(A, B)	LCM(A, B)
(8, 12)	4	24	$2 \times 2 \times 2$	$2 \times 2 \times 3$	2×2	$2 \times 2 \times 2 \times 3$
(20, 24)						
(12, 25)						
(15, 60)						

   a. Find the relationship between the prime factors of each of the two numbers and the prime factors of the GCF of the two numbers. Explain how you can determine the GCF of two numbers by using the prime factorizations of both numbers.

   b. Find a relationship between the prime factors of each of the two numbers and the prime factors of the LCM of the two numbers. Explain how you can determine the LCM of two numbers by using the prime factorizations of both numbers.

5. *Math Concepts:*

    a. Let Set *A* be all multiples of 8 and let Set *B* be all multiples of 12. How can you use these two sets and a two-circle Venn diagram to find the LCM(8, 12)? Explain your solution path and illustrate it with a two-circle Venn diagram.

    b. Let Set *C* be all factors of 8 and let Set *D* be all factors of 12. How can you use these two sets and a two-circle Venn diagram to find the GCF(8, 12)? Explain your solution path and illustrate it with a two-circle Venn diagram.

6. *Math Concepts:* Color rods such as Cuisenaire Rods[†] shown here are often found in elementary schools.

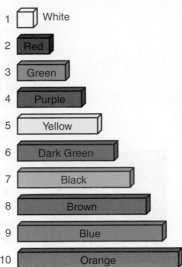

1   White
2   Red
3   Green
4   Purple
5   Yellow
6   Dark Green
7   Black
8   Brown
9   Blue
10   Orange

    a. Putting several same-color rods end to end forms a train. Using the rods, is it possible to make a purple train and a black train that are the same length? Explain your answer.

    b. Can any two different nonwhite trains always be made the same length? Are different lengths possible? What do these lengths represent? Explain your reasoning.

    c. How would you explain the concept of *least common multiple* in terms of same-color trains? Demonstrate your explanation by showing how to use rods to find LCM(12, 15).

7. *Math Concepts:* Any whole number can be represented by joining various rods. For example, 18 can be represented by putting an orange and brown rod end to end and 12 can be formed with an orange and a red rod. Explain how you can illustrate the concepts of *common factors* and *greatest common factor* using Cuisenaire rods. You'll need trains of rods for your original numbers and comparison trains of other (shorter) rods. Demonstrate your explanation by showing how to use rods to find the common factors of 12 and 16 and then the GCF(12, 16).

8. *Math Concepts:* In this activity set we explored the relationship between the greatest common factor and the least common multiple of two numbers. Does this relationship hold if you are considering the greatest common factor or the least common multiple of three numbers? Experiment with several sets of three numbers. Explain your thinking.

9. *NCTM Standards:* Explain where you believe the concepts of GCF and LCM are used in elementary and middle school mathematics, then look through the **Number and Operations Standards** in the back pages of this book to determine whether or not GCF and LCM are referenced. If the GCF and LCM are not mentioned specifically, what *Expectations* address these topics? Explain your thinking.

bennett-burton-nelson website

Virtual Manipulatives   Grid and Dot Paper   Links and Readings
Interactive Chapter Applets   Color Transparencies   Geometer Sketchpad Modules
Puzzlers   Extended Bibliography

[†]Cuisenaire Rods is a registered trademark of the Cuisenaire Company of America, Inc.

ACTIVITIES FOR THE ELEMENTARY SCHOOL CLASSROOM

Exploring Factors and Primes with Color Tiles

Purpose: To introduce elementary school students to a visual model for prime and composite numbers.

Connection: Prime numbers are usually defined as numbers with exactly two factors. By representing numbers as rectangular arrays and looking at factors of numbers as the dimensions of rectangles, students have a visual model for partitioning the counting numbers into three distinct groups; prime numbers, composite numbers, and 1.

Materials: Sets of color tiles may be created by copying 2-centimeter grid paper from the companion website on four different colors of cardstock. Color tile transparencies may also be made with the color tile images. Sets of 20 of each of four colors can be placed in plastic sealable bags. Each group of two to four students will need one set of color tiles. Students will also need centimeter grid paper for recording rectangles.

This sixth grader has formed all the possible rectangles with 12 or fewer tiles.

1. Form the three figures shown here on the overhead. Point out that rectangular arrays must be solid (no holes) and that two arrays are the same if one can fit exactly on top of the other. Ask the students to build other rectangular arrays with 12 color tiles. To summarize and make sure that everyone understands, display the three different arrays of 12 tiles with their dimensions written beneath each. (The one other 12-tile array is the 2 by 6 array.)

Not an array   1 × 12 array   3 × 4 array

2. Point out that the numbers in the dimensions of the rectangles, 1, 12, 3, 4, 2 and 6, are all factors of 12. Ask them if they can find any other factors of 12 and have them make a chart with headings like the one here. Show them how to record the data for the number 12.

Number	Number of Rectangles	Dimensions	Factors of the Number
12	3	1 × 12, 2 × 6, 3 × 4	1, 2, 3, 4, 6, 12

3. Ask each pair of students to form all possible rectangles with fewer than 12 tiles and record their results in descending order in the chart.

Number	Number of Rectangles	Dimensions	Factors of the Number
11			
10			
⋮			

4. Tell the students numbers like 7, with exactly one possible rectangle with exactly two different dimensions, are called prime numbers. Numbers with more than one possible rectangle are called composite numbers. The number 1 is different than the others because it has only one possible rectangle and the dimensions are both the same. The number 1 is neither prime nor composite. Ask the students to list the prime numbers from their chart and then use their tiles to find and record all the prime numbers less than 20.

5. (Optional) Ask the students which numbers less than 12 have arrays that are squares (*Answer:* 1, 4, 9). Tell them that these are called square numbers. Ask them to find two more square numbers.

5

Integers and Fractions

> By using an area model in which part of a region is shaded, students can see how fractions are related to a unit whole, compare fractional parts of a whole, and find equivalent fractions. . . . Students who have a solid conceptual foundation in fractions should be less prone to committing computational errors than students who do not have such a foundation.[†]

Activity Set 5.1   BLACK AND RED TILE MODEL FOR INTEGERS

PURPOSE

To use black and red tiles to provide a model for adding, subtracting, multiplying, and dividing integers.

Virtual Manipulatives

www.mhhe.com/bbn

MATERIALS

Black and Red Tiles from the Manipulative Kit or from the Virtual Manipulatives.

INTRODUCTION

The *integers* (sometimes called *positive and negative numbers* or *signed numbers*) are the numbers . . . , $^-6$, $^-5$, $^-4$, $^-3$, $^-2$, $^-1$, 0, $^+1$, $^+2$, $^+3$, $^+4$, $^+5$, $^+6$, ... Two thousand years ago, the Chinese dealt with positive and negative numbers by using black and red rods. We will use a similar model, black and red tiles, to illustrate addition, subtraction, multiplication, and division of integers. Black tiles will represent positive numbers and red tiles will represent negative numbers. One black tile has a value of $^+1$, one red tile has a value of $^-1$, and a pair with one black tile and one red tile has a value of 0.

In this model every collection of red and black tiles has a *net value.* The **net value** of a collection is the value of the number of red or black tiles remaining after all possible red and black tiles have been matched. As the figures below show, an excess of red tiles will be designated by a negative integer and an excess of black tiles by a positive integer. The + and − signs are usually written as superscripts so as not to be confused with the operations of addition and subtraction.

Net value $^-3$ Net value $^+4$

[†]*Principles and Standards for School Mathematics*, pp. 150, 218.

Explore 2-5

Algebra Lab
Subtracting Integers

MAIN IDEA

Use counters to model the subtraction of integers.

You can also use counters to model subtraction of integers. Remember one meaning of subtraction is to *take away*.

 ACTIVITY

Use counters to find each difference.

1 $5 - 2$

Place 5 positive counters on the mat. Remove 2 positive counters.

So, $5 - 2 = 3$.

2 $4 - (-3)$

Place 4 positive counters on the mat. Remove 3 negative counters. However, there are 0 negative counters.

Add 3 zero pairs to the set.

Now you can remove 3 negative counters. Find the remaining number of counters.

So, $4 - (-3) = 7$.

 CHECK Your Progress

Use counters or a drawing to find each difference.

a. $7 - 6$ **b.** $5 - (-3)$ **c.** $6 - (-3)$ **d.** $5 - 8$

Using this model every integer can be represented in many ways. For example, the following three collections of tiles each have a net value of $^-2$ because when pairs of red and black are matched there is an excess of 2 red tiles in each collection.

Collections with the same number of black tiles and red tiles have *net value 0*. In this case, the positive integer for the black tiles and the negative integer for the red tiles are called *opposites* of each other.

1. Take a small handful of red and black tiles from the Manipulative Kit (or use the random tile feature in the Virtual Manipulatives) and drop them on a flat surface. Record the information about your collection in part a of the following table. Repeat the above directions three times and record the information in parts b, c, and d.

	Total Number of Tiles	Number of Red Tiles	Number of Black Tiles	Net Value
a.	_____	_____	_____	_____
b.	_____	_____	_____	_____
c.	_____	_____	_____	_____
d.	_____	_____	_____	_____

2. The following table contains partial results from collections of red and black tiles that have been dropped. Use your red and black tiles to determine the missing table entries.

	Total Number of Tiles	Number of Red Tiles	Number of Black Tiles	Net Value
*a.	_____	8	29	_____
b.	42	26	_____	_____
*c.	_____	_____	14	$^+8$
d.	17	_____	_____	$^+5$
e.	20	_____	_____	$^-4$
*f.	_____	_____	11	$^-2$

Addition

3. These two collections represent the integers $^-3$ and $^+2$, respectively. Form each collection with your tiles. Combine the two collections to determine the sum, $^-3 + {}^+2$. What integer represents the sum of the two collections?

Collection I

$^-3$

Collection II

$^+2$

a. Represent $^-3$ with the fewest number of tiles. Do the same for $^+2$. Sketch these collections and show that, when combined, they represent the same sum as the preceding collections.

b. Use your red and black tiles to determine these sums. Draw a sketch to indicate how you got your answer.

$^+7 + {}^-3 =$

$^-4 + {}^-3 =$

$^-8 + {}^+2 =$

*c. Try to visualize black and red tiles as you determine these sums.

$^+50 + {}^-37 =$ $^-34 + {}^-25 =$ $^-132 + {}^+70 =$

4. Write directions that will enable the reader to perform the following operations. Use the black and red tile terminology in your directions.

   a. Add any two negative integers.

   *b. Add a positive integer and a negative integer.

Subtraction

5. The collections A and B show one way to compute $^+5 - {}^+8$ with black and red tiles. It is not possible to take 8 black tiles from collection A, but collection A can be changed to collection B by adding 3 black tiles and 3 red tiles. Collection B still represents 5, but now 8 black tiles can be removed to determine that $^+5 - {}^+8 - {}^-3$.

Use your tiles to form the following collections. Then change each collection to one that represents the same number but has enough tiles so that the appropriate number of tiles can be taken away. In each example, sketch the new collection. Use the results to complete the equations.

   a. Change this collection to show $^-4 - {}^+3$.

   *b. Change this collection to show $^+5 - {}^-2$.

   c. Change this collection to show $^-3 - {}^-5$.

*6. Explain how parts a, b, and c of activity 5 can be used to show that subtraction can be performed by adding the opposite. That is, taking away a given number of one color is the same as adding the same number of the opposite color. Symbolically, for positive numbers, this is written $a - b = a +\ ^-b$. (*Hint:* Reconstruct the sets in parts a, b, and c with your black and red tiles and watch what happens when you bring in extra tiles and then subtract.)

Multiplication†

7. The red and black tiles can be used to illustrate a model for multiplication if we agree that in the product $n \times s$, n tells the number of times we *put in* (+) or *take out* (−) s red or black tiles. For example, $^-2 \times\ ^+3$ means that 2 times we take out 3 black tiles. This changes set A, which represents 0, to set B, which represents $^-6$. This shows that $^-2 \times\ ^+3 =\ ^-6$.

Two times, take out 3 black tiles
$^-2 \times\ ^+3 =\ ^-6$

For each of the following activities, start with a collection of 8 red and 8 black tiles, that is, a set that has net value zero. Make the described changes to the collection. Sketch the resulting collection and record its value. Then write the complete number equation that has been illustrated.

a. Three times, put in 2 red tiles.

*b. Two times, take out 4 red tiles.

c. Three times, take out 2 black tiles.

8. Use your tiles to show how you would illustrate $^-3 \times\ ^-4$ with red and black tiles. Illustrate your results by drawing a sketch. Explain how you determined the number of red and black tiles you used in the initial collection.

---

†This model for multiplication can be described as the mail-delivery model. Bringing mail to you is a positive action and taking mail from you is a negative action. The mail contains bills for $1 each (debts) or checks for $1 each (assets). The mail carrier can bring (positive) or take away (negative) bills (negative) or checks (positive). Then, for example, $^-2 \times\ ^+4$ signifies that 2 times the mail carrier takes away four $1 checks, and your net worth has decreased by $8.

Division

9. Review the measurement and sharing concepts to whole number division discussed in Activity Set 3.4.

   a. Form a collection of 12 red tiles and use the sharing concept to determine the quotient $^-12 \div {}^+3$. Draw a sketch of your tiles to indicate how you obtained your answer.

   b. Form a collection of 12 red tiles and use the measurement concept to determine the quotient $^-12 \div {}^-3$. Draw a sketch of your tiles to indicate how you obtained your result.

   *c. Explain why neither the sharing nor measurement concept can be used to illustrate $^+12 \div {}^-3$.

10. In whole number arithmetic we know that $6 \div 2 = 3$ because $2 \times 3 = 6$; that is, division can be defined in terms of multiplication. This same approach can be used for integer division.

a. Show that this approach gives the same answers as the methods in 9a and 9b on the previous page.

b. What answer does it give for 9c?

c. Determine each of the following.

    *i. $^{+}15 \div {}^{+}3$ **ii.** $^{+}15 \div {}^{-}3$ ***iii.** $^{-}15 \div {}^{+}3$ **iv.** $^{-}15 \div {}^{-}3$

d. Which of the operations in part c cannot be illustrated using black and red tiles?

JUST FOR FUN

The following four games for negative numbers require two dice, one white and one red. The white die represents positive numbers, and the red die represents negative numbers.

ADDITION GAME (2 to 4 players)

Each player begins the game with a marker on the zero point of the number line. On a turn, the player rolls the dice and adds the positive number represented by the white die to the negative number represented by the red die. This sum determines the amount of movement on the number line. If it is positive, the marker moves to the right, and if it is negative, the marker moves to the left. If the sum is zero, the player rolls again. The first player to reach either $^{-}10$ or 10 wins the game. If this game is played at first by moving the marker separately for each die—to the right for the white die and to the left for the red die—it will quickly lead to the rule for adding positive and negative numbers.

ADDITION AND SUBTRACTION GAME (2 to 6 players)

Each player selects one of the cards shown below. On a player's turn, the dice are rolled and the two numbers are either added or subtracted. Suppose, for example, that you rolled $^{+}4$ and $^{-}6$; you could add $^{+}4 + {}^{-}6 = {}^{-}2$, subtract $^{+}4 - {}^{-}6 = 10$, or subtract $^{-}6 - {}^{+}4 = {}^{-}10$. The answer is then marked on the player's card. The first player to complete a row, column, or diagonal wins the game.

GAME 1

GAME 2

$^{-}9$	$^{-}11$	$^{-}1$	8	10
12	3	$^{-}10$	$^{-}2$	$^{-}6$
8	$^{-}12$	$^{-}7$	$^{-}4$	$^{-}5$
2	6	11	7	1
$^{-}3$	0	5	9	4

Card 1

5	12	10	$^{-}1$	$^{-}9$
$^{-}10$	$^{-}3$	7	11	$^{-}8$
$^{-}4$	2	4	$^{-}6$	$^{-}2$
9	$^{-}7$	$^{-}5$	$^{-}11$	1
8	6	3	0	$^{-}12$

Card 2

$^{-}1$	7	9	4	$^{-}6$
8	$^{-}5$	11	$^{-}12$	6
$^{-}11$	1	$^{-}2$	7	$^{-}9$
$^{-}3$	10	12	$^{-}4$	3
2	$^{-}8$	5	0	$^{-}10$

Card 3

$^{-}8$	$^{-}10$	10	5	9
11	7	$^{-}11$	$^{-}9$	3
6	$^{-}7$	4	0	$^{-}1$
$^{-}4$	12	2	$^{-}12$	8
1	$^{-}5$	$^{-}3$	$^{-}2$	$^{-}6$

Card 4

6	$^{-}2$	$^{-}12$	$^{-}11$	$^{-}10$
$^{-}5$	12	1	$^{-}9$	8
4	11	10	2	0
$^{-}7$	5	9	$^{-}3$	3
$^{-}4$	$^{-}8$	$^{-}6$	7	$^{-}1$

Card 5

$^{-}5$	$^{-}3$	2	$^{-}2$	11
4	5	$^{-}6$	$^{-}1$	$^{-}9$
$^{-}12$	$^{-}11$	$^{-}7$	8	$^{-}8$
12	7	6	$^{-}4$	3
1	0	$^{-}10$	5	10

Card 6

MULTIPLICATION AND INEQUALITY
GAME (2 to 4 players)

On a turn, the player rolls the dice and multiplies the positive number from the white die by the negative number from the red die. This operation is repeated a second time, and the player then selects the greater of the two products. In the example shown at the right, each player has had four turns. The greater product in each case has been circled. Player B is ahead at this point with the greater score: a total of $^-12$. After 5 rounds, the player with the greater total wins the game.

Chance Option: If a player obtains two undesirable numbers, such as $^-25$ and $^-15$, he or she may use the *chance option*, which involves rolling the dice a third time. If the third product is greater than the other two—say, $^-12$—the player may select this number. If the third product is less than or equal to either of the other two—say, $^-18$—then the smallest of the three numbers ($^-25$ in this example) must be kept as the player's score.

	Player A		Player B	
GAME 3	(⁻4)	⁻6	(⁻1)	⁻3
	(⁻2)	⁻18	⁻6	(⁻2)
	(⁻6)	⁻30	(⁻5)	⁻16
	⁻15	(⁻6)	⁻24	(⁻4)
	Total	⁻18	Total	⁻12

ALL FOUR BASIC OPERATIONS GAME
(1 to 4 players)

Roll the dice four times, and record the four negative numbers from the red die and the four positive numbers from the white die. Using each number no more than once, write as many as possible in the eight blanks of the equations under Round 1 to complete the equations. Repeat this activity for Round 2 and Round 3. You receive 1 point for each equation. If you complete all four equations for a given round, you receive 4 points plus 2 bonus points. The total number of points for the three rounds is your score.

	Round 1	Round 2	Round 3
GAME 4	_____ + $^-1$ = _____	$^+3$ + _____ = _____	_____ + _____ = $^-6$
	_____ $^-4$ = _____	$^-1$ − _____ = _____	_____ − $^-5$ = _____
	$^-2$ × _____ = _____	$^-1$ × _____ = _____	$^+3$ × _____ = _____
	_____ ÷ $^+3$ = _____	_____ ÷ _____ = $^+2$	_____ ÷ $^-1$ = _____

Exercises and Activities **5.1**

1. *School Classroom:* Write a short word problem appropriate for an elementary school student for each of the following integer addition and subtraction sentences.

   a. $^{+}7 + {}^{-}3 = ?$ **b.** $^{-}4 + {}^{-}3 = ?$

   c. $^{-}4 - {}^{+}3 = ?$ **d.** $^{+}5 - {}^{-}2 = ?$

   e. $^{-}3 - {}^{-}7 = ?$

2. *School Classroom:* A seventh-grade student said his father told him to subtract a negative number you just "change the sign and add." So, for example, $^{+}5 - {}^{-}7 = {}^{+}5 + {}^{+}7 = {}^{+}12$. How can you use the red and black tile model to help the student see why this rule works?

3. *School Classroom:* Read the integer subtraction activity described in the **Elementary School Text** page at the beginning of this section.

   a. Describe what prerequisite knowledge about the red and yellow counter model students need before they can complete this activity.

   b. Draw a sketch to show how you would subtract $^{-}5 - (^{+}3)$ using the model on the school page. Explain your steps.

4. *School Classroom:* Design an activity that you believe is appropriate for helping an elementary school student understand adding and subtracting integers using a temperature model. Write a few questions that you can ask about your activity. Try this activity on an upper elementary or middle school age child of your choice. Record your questions and record the student's responses.

5. *Math Concepts:* For each of the following, sketch a black and red tile model to show computing the sum or difference. In each case, explain your thinking.

   a. $^{+}7 + {}^{-}3 = ?$ **b.** $^{-}4 + {}^{-}3 = ?$

   c. $^{-}4 - {}^{+}3 = ?$ **d.** $^{+}5 - {}^{-}2 = ?$

   e. $^{-}3 - {}^{-}7 = ?$

6. *Math Concepts:* For each of the following, sketch a black and red tile model to show computing the product or quotient. In each case, explain your thinking.

   a. $^{+}6 \times {}^{-}2 = ?$ **b.** $^{-}6 \times {}^{+}2 = ?$

   c. $^{-}6 \times {}^{-}2 = ?$ **d.** $^{-}6 \div {}^{+}2 = ?$

   e. $^{-}6 \div {}^{-}2 = ?$

7. *NCTM Standards:* Go to the **Number and Operations Standards** in the back pages of this book and find the *Expectation* that specifically mentions integer operations. State the *Expectation* and the *Standard* it is under. Explain how the activities in this activity set will help students achieve this *Expectation*.

---

bennett-burton-nelson website

Virtual Manipulatives	Grid and Dot Paper	Links and Readings
Interactive Chapter Applets	Color Transparencies	Geometer Sketchpad Modules
Puzzlers	Extended Bibliography	

FRACTION BAR MODEL FOR EQUALITY AND INEQUALITY

PURPOSE

Virtual Manipulatives

To use Fraction Bars to provide a visual model for the *part-to-whole* and *division* concepts of fractions, fraction equality and inequality, and fraction rounding and estimation.[†]

MATERIALS

Fraction Bars from the Manipulative Kit or from the Virtual Manipulatives.

www.mhhe.com/bbn

INTRODUCTION

The set of Fraction Bars consists of 32 bars divided into 2, 3, 4, 6, or 12 equal parts. The bars are colored (halves—green, thirds—yellow, fourths—blue, sixths—red, and twelfths—orange) so that the user can easily distinguish bars with different numbers of parts. Various fractions are named by shading parts of the bars. For example, the bar to the left represents $\frac{5}{6}$ (five-sixths). The top number in the fraction, the *numerator*, tells the number of shaded parts, and the bottom number, the *denominator*, tells the number of equal parts into which the bar is divided. This model illustrates the *part-to-whole* concept of fractions. It emphasizes the unit and models fractions in relation to this unit. The *fraction-quotient* concept of fractions is introduced in activity 9.

$\frac{5}{6}$

A Fraction Bar with all of its parts shaded is called a whole bar and its fraction equals 1. A bar with no parts shaded is called a zero bar and its fraction equals zero.

$$\frac{3}{3} = 1 \qquad\qquad \frac{0}{4} = 0$$

$\frac{2}{3}$

$\frac{8}{12}$

1. The fractions for the bars in the figure to the left are equal because both bars have the same amount of shading. In the set of 32 Fraction Bars, there are three bars whose fractions equal $\frac{2}{3}$. Sort your set of bars into piles so that the bars with the same shaded amount are in the same pile.

   *a. There are five bars whose fractions are equal to $\frac{0}{4}$. How many bars represent the other fractions listed here?

Fraction	Number of Bars with Equal Fractions
$\frac{0}{4}$	5
$\frac{1}{2}$	_____
$\frac{2}{3}$	_____
$\frac{6}{6}$	_____
$\frac{1}{4}$	_____

[†]Fraction Bars is a registered trademark of American Education Products, LLC

b. Complete this table by writing in the sixths, fourths, thirds, and halves that are equal to the twelfths. (*Note:* Many of the spaces will be blank.)

Twelfths	$\frac{0}{12}$	$\frac{1}{12}$	$\frac{2}{12}$	$\frac{3}{12}$	$\frac{4}{12}$	$\frac{5}{12}$	$\frac{6}{12}$	$\frac{7}{12}$	$\frac{8}{12}$	$\frac{9}{12}$	$\frac{10}{12}$	$\frac{11}{12}$	$\frac{12}{12}$
Sixths													
Fourths													
Thirds													
Halves													

2. The $\frac{1}{3}$ bar has more shading than the $\frac{1}{4}$ bar, so $\frac{1}{3}$ is greater than $\frac{1}{4}$. This is written $\frac{1}{3} > \frac{1}{4}$ (or $\frac{1}{4} < \frac{1}{3}$).

*a. Select the following Fraction Bars from your set of bars:

$$\frac{5}{6}, \frac{1}{4}, \frac{11}{12}, \frac{2}{3}, \frac{1}{6}, \frac{5}{12}, \frac{3}{4}, \frac{1}{3}, \frac{7}{12}, \frac{1}{2}, \text{ and } \frac{1}{12}$$

Place these bars in increasing order from the smallest shaded amount to the largest shaded amount and complete the following inequalities.

$$\underline{\quad} < \frac{1}{6} < \underline{\quad} < \underline{\quad} < \underline{\quad} < \frac{1}{2} < \underline{\quad} < \underline{\quad} < \underline{\quad} < \underline{\quad} < \frac{11}{12}$$

b. Each of the fractions in part a has a common denominator of 12. Rewrite these inequalities using only fractions with a denominator of 12.

$$\underline{\quad} < \frac{2}{12} < \underline{\quad} < \underline{\quad} < \underline{\quad} < \underline{\quad} < \underline{\quad} < \underline{\quad} < \underline{\quad} < \underline{\quad} < \frac{11}{12}$$

3. Buy Cheap Game (2 players): Shuffle one deck of Fraction Bars, deal each player eight bars, and set the unused bars aside. Player A lays down one bar face up and names the fraction on his or her bar. Player B lays down a bar and names the fraction on his or her bar. If the shaded amount of Player B's bar is *greater than or equal to* that on Player A's bar, Player B wins both bars (and sets them aside). Otherwise, Player A wins the bars. This is the end of the first play. The player who **won** the two bars begins the next play.

When the players have both used their eight bars, deal eight more bars from the unused bars to continue the game. After all of the bars have been played, the player with the most bars wins.

Variation: For 3 players, deal five bars to each player and adjust the rules accordingly.

Example: For the bars shown here, the second player can win two bars by playing any of the bars for the fractions $\frac{3}{4}, \frac{7}{12}, \frac{3}{3},$ or $\frac{5}{6}$.

First bar played

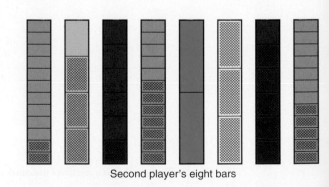

Second player's eight bars

a. Play at least one full *Buy Cheap* game.

*b. What is the best bar for the second player to play in the example on the previous page? (*Hint:* Why is this game called *Buy Cheap?*)

c. Suppose Player 2 in the example started the game. Explain why it might not be a good strategy to start the game by laying down the zero bar.

4. Rounding fractions to the nearest whole number can be facilitated by sketching or visualizing Fraction Bars. For example, with the bars representing $1\frac{2}{7}$, the shaded amount is closer to 1 whole bar than to 2 whole bars. So, to the nearest whole number, $1\frac{2}{7}$ rounds to 1.

$$1\frac{2}{7} \text{ rounds to } 1$$

On the other hand, on the bars representing $1\frac{4}{7}$, the shaded amount is closer to 2 whole bars than to 1 whole bar. So, to the nearest whole number, $1\frac{4}{7}$ rounds to 2.

$$1\frac{4}{7} \text{ rounds to } 2$$

Round the fractions in the table at the top of the next page to the nearest whole number. For each fraction, draw a Fraction Bar sketch to justify your answer.

Fraction	Diagram	Nearest Whole Number
*a. $4\frac{2}{3}$		_____
b. $\frac{1}{8}$		_____
*c. $\frac{10}{12}$		_____
d. $2\frac{5}{7}$		_____

5. Each part of this $\frac{3}{4}$ bar has been split into 2 equal parts. There are now 8 parts, and 6 of these are shaded. Because this splitting has neither increased nor decreased the total shaded amount of the bar, both $\frac{3}{4}$ and $\frac{6}{8}$ are fractions for the same amount.

$$\frac{3}{4} = \frac{2 \times 3}{2 \times 4} = \frac{6}{8}$$

a. Split each part of these bars into 2 equal parts, and complete the equations.

$$\frac{4}{9} = \qquad\qquad \frac{3}{10} = \qquad\qquad \frac{1}{5} =$$

*b. Split each part of these bars into 3 equal parts, and complete the equations.

$$\frac{6}{7} = \qquad\qquad \frac{5}{8} = \qquad\qquad \frac{1}{6} =$$

c. Split each part of these bars into 4 equal parts, and complete the equations.

$$\frac{0}{3} = \qquad\qquad \frac{3}{4} = \qquad\qquad \frac{1}{2} =$$

d. Suppose that each part of the Fraction Bar for $\frac{a}{b}$ is split into 3 equal parts. How many of the parts will be shaded? _____ How many parts will there be in all? _____ Write the fraction for this bar. _____

6. There are an infinite number of fractions that are equal to $\frac{2}{3}$. These fractions can be generated by equally splitting the parts of a $\frac{2}{3}$ bar.

$$\frac{2}{3} = \frac{2 \times 2}{2 \times 3} = \frac{4}{6} \qquad \frac{2}{3} = \frac{3 \times 2}{3 \times 3} = \frac{6}{9} \qquad \frac{2}{3} = \frac{4 \times 2}{4 \times 3} = \frac{8}{12}$$

  a. If each part of a $\frac{2}{3}$ bar is split into 5 equal parts, what equality of fractions does the bar represent?

  *b. If each part of a $\frac{2}{3}$ bar is split into 17 equal parts, what equality of fractions does the bar represent?

  c. What effect does splitting each part of any Fraction Bar into 17 equal parts have on the numerator and denominator of the fraction for the bar?

  *d. Split each of the following bars to illustrate the given equality.

$$\frac{5}{6} = \frac{10}{12} \qquad\qquad \frac{5}{6} = \frac{15}{18} \qquad\qquad \frac{5}{6} = \frac{20}{24}$$

7. Each part of a $\frac{2}{3}$ bar is bigger than each part of a $\frac{3}{4}$ bar. If each part of the $\frac{2}{3}$ bar is split into 4 equal parts and each part of the $\frac{3}{4}$ bar is split into 3 equal parts, both bars will then have 12 parts of equal size. The new fractions for these bars will have a common denominator of 12.

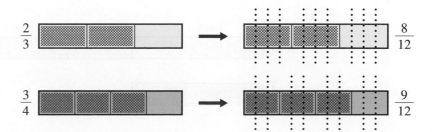

For each of the following pairs of bars, use the fewest number of splits so that all the new parts for both bars are the same size. The corresponding fractions will have the same denominator. Complete the equations.

*a. $\dfrac{1}{2} =$

$\dfrac{5}{7} =$

b. $\dfrac{1}{3} =$

$\dfrac{3}{8} =$

c. $\dfrac{4}{10} =$

$\dfrac{4}{6} =$

8. Sketch bars, at the left, for $\frac{3}{5}$ and $\frac{5}{7}$. Sometimes it is difficult to tell from a sketch which fraction is greater.

   a. When both bars are split so that all parts have the same size, the two fractions for these bars will have the same denominator. Complete these equations so that both fractions have the same denominator.

   $$\dfrac{3}{5} = \qquad\qquad \dfrac{5}{7} =$$

   b. Which is greater, $\frac{3}{5}$ or $\frac{5}{7}$?

   Replace the fractions in each of the following pairs with fractions having the same denominator. Circle the greater fraction in each pair (or state that they are equal).

   c. $\dfrac{1}{3} =$ *d. $\dfrac{7}{9} =$ e. $\dfrac{4}{6} =$ *f. $\dfrac{11}{15} =$

   $\dfrac{2}{7} =$ $\dfrac{8}{10} =$ $\dfrac{6}{9} =$ $\dfrac{8}{11} =$

9. The *fraction-quotient* concept of fractions relates quotients of whole numbers to fractions. For example, 3 whole bars are placed end to end to represent the number 3. If this 3-bar is divided into 4 equal parts, each part will be $\frac{3}{4}$ of a whole bar. This shows that $3 \div 4 = \frac{3}{4}$.

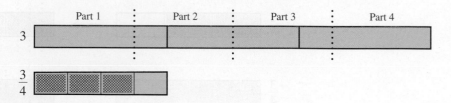

Illustrate each quotient of whole numbers by dividing the given big bar into equal parts. Then complete the equation by writing a fraction or mixed number.[†]

a. $3 \div 2 =$

*b. $2 \div 3 =$

c. $4 \div 3 =$

JUST FOR FUN

These two fraction games provide extra practice in comparing fractions. In FRIO[‡] you compare unequal fractions, and in Fraction Bingo you search for equal fractions.

FRIO (2 to 4 players)

Each player is dealt five bars in a row face up. These bars should be left in the order in which they are dealt. The remaining bars are spread face down. Each player, in turn, takes a bar that is face down and uses it to replace any one of the five bars. The object of the game is to get five bars in order from the *smallest* shaded amount to the *largest* or from the

largest to the *smallest*. In this example the five bars will be in order if the $\frac{2}{6}$ bar is replaced by a whole bar and the $\frac{1}{4}$ bar is replaced by an $\frac{11}{12}$ bar. The first player to get five Fraction Bars in decreasing or increasing order wins the game.

FRACTION BINGO (2 to 4 players)

Each player selects a fraction bingo mat from those shown below. The deck of 32 bars is spread face down. Each player, in turn, takes a bar and circles the fraction or fractions on his or her mat that equal the fraction from the bar. The first player to circle four fractions in any row, column, or diagonal is the winner.

Strategy: If the bars are colored green, yellow, blue, red, and orange for halves, thirds, fourths, sixths, and twelfths, respectively, you can increase your chances of winning by selecting bars of the appropriate color.

Mat 1

$\frac{4}{6}$	$\frac{1}{6}$	$\frac{0}{4}$	$\frac{11}{12}$
$\frac{5}{12}$	$\frac{1}{4}$	$\frac{5}{6}$	$\frac{3}{6}$
$\frac{3}{4}$	$\frac{1}{12}$	$\frac{1}{3}$	$\frac{11}{12}$
$\frac{6}{12}$	$\frac{4}{4}$	$\frac{9}{12}$	$\frac{10}{12}$

Mat 2

$\frac{1}{3}$	$\frac{1}{4}$	$\frac{1}{6}$	$\frac{0}{3}$
$\frac{7}{12}$	$\frac{0}{6}$	$\frac{1}{12}$	$\frac{4}{6}$
$\frac{2}{3}$	$\frac{3}{4}$	$\frac{5}{6}$	$\frac{5}{12}$
$\frac{11}{12}$	$\frac{2}{2}$	$\frac{3}{12}$	$\frac{1}{2}$

Mat 3

$\frac{2}{3}$	$\frac{1}{4}$	$\frac{2}{6}$	$\frac{6}{12}$
$\frac{5}{6}$	$\frac{0}{3}$	$\frac{5}{12}$	$\frac{1}{6}$
$\frac{7}{12}$	$\frac{4}{4}$	$\frac{1}{2}$	$\frac{11}{12}$
$\frac{3}{4}$	$\frac{8}{12}$	$\frac{1}{1}$	$\frac{1}{3}$

Mat 4

$\frac{1}{4}$	$\frac{1}{6}$	$\frac{7}{12}$	$\frac{1}{2}$
$\frac{0}{3}$	$\frac{5}{12}$	$\frac{2}{3}$	$\frac{4}{4}$
$\frac{1}{12}$	$\frac{5}{6}$	$\frac{11}{12}$	$\frac{2}{12}$
$\frac{6}{6}$	$\frac{3}{4}$	$\frac{0}{12}$	$\frac{1}{3}$

[†]If long strips of paper are available, the big bars such as the 2-bar (the length of 2 whole bars) and the 3-bar (the length of 3 whole bars) can be cut to actual length. A strip can then be folded and the folded amount compared to the Fraction Bars.

[‡]R. Drizigacker, "FRIO, or Fractions In Order," *Arithmetic Teacher* 13, pp. 684–685.

Exercises and Activities 5.2

1. *School Classroom:* Jeremy believes that $\frac{1}{6}$ is greater than $\frac{1}{4}$ because 6 is greater than 4. Explain how you would use Fraction Bars to help him determine the correct inequality.

2. *School Classroom:* One of your students says that you can't always say that $\frac{2}{3}$ is greater than $\frac{1}{2}$ because $\frac{1}{2}$ of a large pizza is more than $\frac{2}{3}$ of a small pizza. Describe how you could help the student come to an understanding about fraction inequality by starting with his pizza example.

3. *Math Concepts:* How can you use the Fraction Bars to find fractions between $\frac{1}{4}$ and $\frac{1}{3}$? Explain your thinking.

4. *Math Concepts:* Illustrate and explain two different ways to show the equality relationship between $\frac{1}{6}$ and $\frac{2}{12}$ with Fraction Bars.

5. *Math Concepts:* Illustrate and explain two different ways to show the inequality relationship between $\frac{1}{3}$ and $\frac{1}{4}$ with Fraction Bars.

6. *Math Concepts:* Illustrate and explain how to use Fraction Bars to show $5 \div 4 = ?$, then complete the equation by writing the correct mixed number quotient.

7. *NCTM Standards:* Go to http://illuminations.nctm.org/ and under "Lessons" select grade levels 3–5 and the **Number and Operations Standard.** Choose a lesson about fun with fractions.

   a. State the title of the lesson and briefly summarize the lesson.

   b. Referring to the **Standards Summary** in the back pages of this book as necessary, list the *Number and Operation Standard Expectations* that the lesson addresses and explain how the lesson addresses these *Expectations*.

8. *NCTM Standards:* In the **Grades 3–5 Number and Operations Standards** in the back pages of this book, it is suggested that students need to understand fractions as locations on the number line. Describe how you can use the Fraction Bar model to help students make the transition to the placement of fractions on the number line with understanding.

---

www.mhhe.com/bbn

bennett-burton-nelson website

Virtual Manipulatives	Grid and Dot Paper	Links and Readings
Interactive Chapter Applets	Color Transparencies	Geometer Sketchpad Modules
Puzzlers	Extended Bibliography	

Activity Set **5.3**

COMPUTING WITH FRACTION BARS

PURPOSE

To use Fraction Bars to perform the basic operations of addition, subtraction, multiplication, and division in a visual and intuitive manner.

MATERIALS

Fraction Bars from the Manipulative Kit or from the Virtual Manipulatives.

INTRODUCTION

Piaget has charted the cognitive development of preadolescents, and his research indicates that even at the age of 12, most children deal only with symbols that are closely tied to their perceptions. For example, the symbolic representation $\frac{1}{6} + \frac{2}{3} = \frac{5}{6}$ has meaning for most elementary school children only if they can relate it directly to concrete or pictorial representations.[†]

$$\frac{1}{6} + \frac{2}{3} = \frac{5}{6}$$

The following table documents the lack of conceptual understanding of fractions and fraction addition exhibited by 13-year-olds when they were asked to estimate the answer to $\frac{12}{13} + \frac{7}{8}$.[‡] Over 50 percent of the students responded with the incorrect answers 19 and 21. What is a reasonable explanation of how students may have arrived at the incorrect answers 19 and 21?

Responses	Percent Responding, Age 13
○ 1	7
● 2	24
○ 19	28
○ 21	27
○ I don't know	14

Students may learn fraction skills at a rote manipulation level, but when their memory fails or they encounter a nonstandard application, they have no conceptual basis to fall back on.

In this activity set, Fraction Bars will be used to develop visual images of fraction operations. These images will provide a conceptual basis for computations, estimations, and problem solving.

[†]M. J. Driscoll, "The Role of Manipulatives in Elementary School Mathematics," *Research within Reach: Elementary School Mathematics,* p. 1.

[‡]T. P. Carpenter, H. Kepner, M. K. Corbitt, M. M. Lindquist, and R. E. Reys, "Results and Implications of the Second NAEP Mathematics Assessment: Elementary School," *Arithmetic Teacher* 27, pp. 10–12, 44–46.

Multiplying Fractions

ACTIVITY

2 Find $\frac{3}{5} \times \frac{2}{3}$ using a model. Write in simplest form.

To find $\frac{3}{5} \times \frac{2}{3}$, find $\frac{3}{5}$ of $\frac{2}{3}$.

Begin with a square to represent 1.

Shade $\frac{2}{3}$ of the square yellow.

Shade $\frac{3}{5}$ of the square blue.

Six out of 15 parts are shaded green. So, $\frac{3}{5} \times \frac{2}{3} = \frac{6}{15}$ or $\frac{2}{5}$.

Study Tip

Multiplying Fractions
Finding $\frac{3}{5} \times \frac{2}{3}$ is the same as finding $\frac{2}{3} \times \frac{3}{5}$. So, you could also begin by shading $\frac{3}{5}$ of the square yellow and then $\frac{2}{3}$ of the square blue.

✓ **CHECK Your Progress**

Find each product using a model. Then write in simplest form.

d. $\frac{3}{4} \times \frac{2}{3}$ e. $\frac{2}{5} \times \frac{5}{6}$ f. $\frac{4}{5} \times \frac{3}{8}$

ANALYZE THE RESULTS

2. Draw a model to show that $\frac{2}{3} \times \frac{5}{6} = \frac{10}{18}$. Then explain how the model shows that $\frac{10}{18}$ simplifies to $\frac{5}{9}$.

3. Explain the relationship between the numerators of the problem and the numerator of the product. What do you notice about the denominators of the problem and the denominator of the product?

4. **MAKE A CONJECTURE** Write a rule you can use to multiply fractions.

Addition and Subtraction

1. **Addition and Subtraction:** Determine the missing fractions and the sum or difference of the fractions for each pair of bars. For addition, use Fraction Bars to determine the sum by comparing the addend bars to a third sum bar as shown in the Sum Example below. For subtraction, use a third Fraction Bar to determine the difference by drawing two vertical lines on the minuend and subtrahend bars to indicate the difference on the difference bar as illustrated in the Difference Example below.

Sum Example:

Difference Example:

*a. $\frac{1}{3} + \underline{\quad} = \underline{\quad}$ b. $\frac{5}{6} - \underline{\quad} = \underline{\quad}$

*c. $\frac{1}{3} + \underline{\quad} = \underline{\quad}$ d. $\frac{3}{4} - \underline{\quad} = \underline{\quad}$

*e. $\frac{3}{8} + \underline{\quad} = \underline{\quad}$ f. $\frac{4}{5} - \underline{\quad} = \underline{\quad}$

2. **Match Game** (2 to 4 players): Shuffle one deck of Fraction Bars, and turn three bars face up to form the beginning of the *Board*. Place the remaining bars face down to form the *Stack*. Each player, in turn, takes the top bar from the *Stack* and compares it to the bars on the *Board*. On a player's turn, he or she has three options and can pick up all of the bars that match one or more of these options:

- If his or her *Stack* bar has the **same shaded amount** as one of the bars on the *Board*, the player wins the two bars;

- If the shaded amount of his or her *Stack* bar **equals the sum of the shaded amounts of two bars** on the *Board*, the player wins the three bars; or

- If the shaded amount of his or her *Stack* bar **equals the difference between the shaded amounts of two bars** on the *Board*, the player wins the three bars.

Stack   Board

If a player wins two or three bars, he or she continues by taking another bar from the *Stack* and plays again; if not, the player places his or her *Stack* bar on the *Board* and the player's turn ends. As play progresses; turn up new bars from the *Stack* so there are always at least three bars on the *Board*. After each bar in the *Stack* has been used, the player with the most bars wins.

> *Challenge Option:*
> If a player does not see the bars that can be won on his or her turn, the next player may pick up these bars before beginning his or her turn.

a. Play at least one full game of *Match*.

b. Using fractions from the *Match* game, write four equality sentences that demonstrate the following option: The shaded amount of one bar equals the same shaded amount as another bar.

*c. Using fractions from the *Match* game, write four addition sentences that demonstrate the following option: The shaded amount of one bar equals the total shaded amounts of two bars.

d. Using fractions from the *Match* game, write four subtraction sentences that demonstrate the following option: The shaded amount of one bar equals the difference between the total shaded amounts of two bars.

3. Obtaining Common Denominators: If each part of the $\frac{2}{3}$ bar is split into 4 equal parts and each part of the $\frac{1}{4}$ bar is split into 3 equal parts, both bars will have 12 parts of the same size. These new bars show that $\frac{2}{3} + \frac{1}{4} = \frac{11}{12}$ and $\frac{2}{3} - \frac{1}{4} = \frac{5}{12}$.

Use the fewest number of splits for the following pairs of Fraction Bars so that each pair of bars has the same number of parts of the same size. Then write two fraction equalities under each pair. For example, in part a, $\frac{5}{6} = \frac{10}{12}$ and $\frac{1}{4} = \frac{3}{12}$.

____ = ____ , ____ = ____   ____ = ____ , ____ = ____   ____ = ____ , ____ = ____

Use the bars from parts a, b, and c above to compute the following sums and differences.

*d. $\dfrac{5}{6} + \dfrac{1}{4} =$ **e.** $\dfrac{3}{5} + \dfrac{2}{3} =$

f. $\dfrac{2}{9} + \dfrac{3}{6} =$ ***g.** $\dfrac{5}{6} - \dfrac{1}{4} =$

h. $\dfrac{2}{3} - \dfrac{3}{5} =$ **i.** $\dfrac{3}{6} - \dfrac{2}{9} =$

Multiplication

4. You can determine $\frac{1}{3} \times \frac{1}{6}$ by splitting the shaded part of a $\frac{1}{6}$ bar into 3 equal parts. One of these smaller parts is $\frac{1}{18}$ of a bar, because there are 18 of these parts in a whole bar. (You can think of this as having $\frac{1}{6}$ of an amount and taking $\frac{1}{3}$ of it.)

To determine $\frac{1}{3} \times \frac{4}{5}$, split each shaded part of the $\frac{4}{5}$ bar into 3 equal parts. One of these split parts is $\frac{1}{15}$ of the whole bar, and 4 of these split parts is $\frac{4}{15}$ of the whole bar. (You can think of this as having $\frac{4}{5}$ of an amount and taking $\frac{1}{3}$ of each fifth.)

a. Split each part of each bar into 2 equal parts. Use this result to complete the given equations.

$\frac{1}{2} \times \frac{1}{3} =$ $\qquad$ $\frac{1}{2} \times \frac{3}{5} =$ $\qquad$ $\frac{3}{2} \times \frac{6}{8} =$

*b. Split each shaded part of each bar into 3 equal parts, and complete the equations.

$\frac{1}{3} \times \frac{1}{4} =$ $\qquad$ $\frac{2}{3} \times \frac{1}{6} =$ $\qquad$ $\frac{2}{3} \times \frac{4}{5} =$

c. Split each shaded part of each bar into 4 equal parts, and complete the equations.

$\frac{1}{4} \times \frac{1}{2} =$ $\qquad$ $\frac{3}{4} \times \frac{2}{5} =$ $\qquad$ $\frac{3}{4} \times \frac{2}{3} =$

Division

5. Using the *measurement* concept of division (see Activity Set 3.4), we can write $\frac{1}{2} \div \frac{1}{6} = 3$, because the shaded portion of the $\frac{1}{6}$ bar (the *divisor* bar) can be measured off (or fits into) exactly 3 times on the shaded part of the $\frac{1}{2}$ bar (the *dividend* bar).

Similarly, $\frac{5}{6} \div \frac{1}{3} = 2\frac{1}{2}$, because the shaded portion of the $\frac{1}{3}$ bar can be measured off (or fits into) $2\frac{1}{2}$ times on the shaded part of the $\frac{5}{6}$ bar.

Dividend bar

Divisor bar

$$\frac{5}{6} \div \frac{1}{3} = 2\frac{1}{2}$$

Sketch Fraction Bars to determine the following quotients. Use your sketch to explain your reasoning. The dividend bars have been drawn for you.

a. $\frac{3}{4} \div \frac{1}{2} =$ ***b.** $\frac{10}{12} \div \frac{1}{6} =$ **c.** $\frac{7}{8} \div \frac{1}{4} =$

*d. $1 \div \frac{2}{3} =$ **e.** $\frac{3}{2} \div \frac{3}{4} =$

Estimation

6. It is often helpful to draw a sketch or visualize a fraction model when you are trying to estimate with fractions. For example, to estimate the quotient $1\frac{5}{7} \div \frac{1}{8}$, you can compare Fraction Bars representing $1\frac{5}{7}$ to bars representing eighths. There are 8 eighths in 1 whole bar and about 6 eighths in the $\frac{5}{7}$ bar. So, $\frac{1}{8}$ can be measured off about 14 times, and $1\frac{5}{7} \div \frac{1}{8} \approx 14$.

$$1\frac{5}{7} \div \frac{1}{8} \approx 14$$

Use a visual approach to estimate the following fraction operations. Draw Fraction Bar sketches and explain how you arrived at your estimation.

a. $1\frac{3}{4} \div \frac{1}{3}$ ***b.** $\frac{5}{8} - \frac{1}{6}$

c. $\frac{4}{5} + \frac{1}{2}$ ***d.** $\frac{2}{3} \times \frac{5}{6}$

All Four Operations

7. *a. The following 10 fractions are from the set of Fraction Bars:

$$\frac{1}{6}, \frac{2}{4}, \frac{5}{12}, \frac{2}{6}, \frac{0}{3}, \frac{3}{4}, \frac{3}{12}, \frac{2}{3}, \frac{1}{2}, \frac{1}{4}$$

Using each fraction only once, place these fractions in the 10 blanks to form four equations.

_____ + _____ = _____   3 × _____ = _____

_____ − _____ = _____   _____ ÷ _____ = 2

b. Spread your bars face down and select any 10. Using the fraction from each bar only once, complete as many of these four equations as possible.

Fractions selected: _____ , _____ , _____ , _____ , _____ ,

_____ , _____ , _____ , _____ , _____

_____ + _____ = _____   3 × _____ = _____

_____ − _____ = _____   _____ ÷ _____ = 2

c. **Solitaire:** The activity in part b can be played like a solitaire game. See how many turns it takes you to complete the four equations by selecting only 10 bars on each turn.

JUST FOR FUN

These three games provide opportunities to perform operations on fractions.

FRACTION BAR BLACKJACK
(Addition—2 to 4 players)

Spread the bars face down. The object is to select one or more bars so that the fraction or the sum of fractions is as close to 1 as possible, but not greater than 1. Each player selects bars one at a time, trying to get close to 1 without going over. (A player may wish to take only 1 bar.) Each player finishes his or her turn by saying "I'm holding." After every player in turn has finished, the players show their bars. The player who is closest to 1 or to a sum of 1, but not over, wins the round.

Examples: Player 1 has a sum greater than 1 and is over. Player 2 has a greater sum than player 3 and wins the round.

SOLITAIRE (Subtraction)

Spread the Fraction Bars face down. Turn over two bars and compare their shaded amounts. If the difference between the two fractions is less than $\frac{1}{2}$, you win the two bars. If not, you lose the bars. See how many bars you can win by playing through the deck. Will you win the top pair of bars shown here? The bottom pair?

GREATEST QUOTIENT GAME

(Division—2 to 4 players)

Remove the zero bars from your set of 32 bars and spread the remaining bars face down. Each player takes two bars. The object of the game is to get the greatest possible quotient by dividing one of the fractions by the other. The greatest *whole* number of times that one fraction divides into the other is the player's score. Each player has the option of taking another bar to improve his or her score or passing. If the player wishes to select another bar, he or she must first discard one bar. The first player to score 21 points wins the game.

Examples: The whole number part of the quotient can be determined by comparing the shaded amounts of the bars. The score for the top two bars is 4, because the shaded amount of the $\frac{2}{3}$ bar is 4 times greater than the shaded amount of the $\frac{1}{6}$ bar. The score for the bottom two bars is 1, because the shaded amount of the $\frac{1}{2}$ bar fits into the shaded amount of the $\frac{8}{12}$ bar once but not twice.

 TAKE A CHANCE APPLET

In this applet you can play a game with a deck of fractions between 0 and 1 having denominators of 2 through 10. As cards are turned up, you make decisions involving inequalities of two fractions, or four fractions if you decide to take a chance. The sample screen below shows four fractions and asks, "Are two of the fractions less than $\frac{1}{2}$ and the other two greater than or equal to $\frac{1}{2}$?" How would you answer this question to win four cards? If you end up winning 35 cards you beat the deck.

Take a Chance Applet, Chapter 5
www.mhhe.com/bbn

Exercises and Activities 5.3

1. *School Classroom:* One of your students multiplies fractions by getting a common denominator and multiplying the numerators (for example, $\frac{2}{3} \times \frac{3}{4} = \frac{8}{12} \times \frac{9}{12} = \frac{72}{12}$). The student says she does this because you add fractions by getting a common denominator and then adding the numerators. How can you help this student understand why her answer is unreasonable?

2. *School Classroom:* **The Elementary School Text** page at the beginning of this section describes a model for multiplying fractions.

   a. Study this page, and then explain using the model on the page why $\frac{2}{3} \times \frac{3}{5}$ will equal $\frac{3}{5} \times \frac{2}{3}$ without the need to draw another diagram.

   b. Start with a rectangle whose dimensions are 1 by $1\frac{1}{4}$ and use this rectangle model to compute the product of $\frac{2}{3}$ and $1\frac{1}{4}$. Explain how you determine the product from your diagram.

3. *School Classroom:* Illustrate and explain how you would introduce division of fractions by modeling $\frac{3}{4} \div \frac{1}{6}$ with Fraction Bars.

4. *Math Concepts:* Illustrate and explain each of the steps you would use to model each of the following with Fraction Bars.

   a. $\frac{2}{3} + \frac{3}{4}$

   b. $\frac{5}{6} - \frac{3}{4}$

5. *Math Concepts:*

   a. Illustrate and explain each of the steps you would use to model $\frac{1}{6} \times \frac{3}{4}$ with Fraction Bars.

   b. Illustrate and explain each of the steps you would use to model $\frac{5}{6} \times \frac{3}{4}$ with Fraction Bars.

   c. How are part a and part b similar? How are they different? Explain.

6. *Math Concepts:* Open the **Math Laboratory Investigation 5.3: Read Me—Fraction Patterns Instructions** from the companion website and investigate the fraction patterns described in questions 2 and 3 of the *Starting Points for Investigations 5.3*. State a few of your patterns or conclusions and explain your thinking.

7. *NCTM Standards:* Go to the **Grade 6–8 Number and Operations Standards** in the back pages of this book and find the "Compute Fluently" *Standard*. How will the use of Fraction Bar models for fraction operations help students achieve the first *Expectation* in this *Standard* as it relates to fractions?

---

www.mhhe.com/bbn

bennett-burton-nelson website

Virtual Manipulatives	Grid and Dot Paper	Links and Readings
Interactive Chapter Applets	Color Transparencies	Geometer Sketchpad Modules
Puzzlers	Extended Bibliography	

ACTIVITIES FOR THE ELEMENTARY SCHOOL CLASSROOM

Introducing Fractions with Fraction Bars

Purpose: To introduce elementary school students to fraction notation, equality, and inequality using Fraction Bars.

Connections: Ask the students if they know the meaning of the word "fracture." Discuss some meanings of the word including, "to break into pieces." Tell them that fraction is related to the word fracture and that a fraction is used to talk about a part of something.

Materials: Sets of Fraction Bars can be printed by copying the Fraction Bar images from the companion website. Fraction Bar transparencies can also be made with the Fraction Bar images. Sets of Fraction Bars can be placed in plastic sealable bags. Each pair of students will need one set of Fraction Bars.

Students turn over bars, and the greater shaded amount wins the two bars.

1. Ask each group of students to examine their set of bars to see what they notice. Discuss their observations. (*Examples:* All red bars have 6 parts; all blue bars have 4 parts; some bars have shaded parts and unshaded parts; etc.)

2. Show them a red bar with 5 parts shaded and ask if anyone knows its fraction. Write $\frac{5}{6}$ and ask them where the "5" comes from and where the "6" comes from. Have them each select a bar and write its fraction. Ask a few volunteers to describe their bar and its fraction.

3. Show them two bars with the same amount of shading and write the equation showing the equality of their fractions. Ask each student to select two new bars with the same amount of shading and to write the equality. Discuss a few examples of fraction equality.

$$\frac{2}{3} = \frac{4}{6} \text{ bars}$$

4. Show them two bars with different amounts of shading and write the inequality for their fractions. Ask each student to select two bars with different shaded amounts and write the inequality for their fractions. Ask volunteers for descriptions of the bars and the inequalities.

$$\frac{1}{4} < \frac{1}{3} \text{ bars}$$

5. Show two bars whose total shaded amount is one whole bar. Point out that the shaded amount of one bar can be used to "fill in" the other bar to make one whole shaded bar and show the sum is equal to 1 (see the example). Ask them to find two bars that make a whole bar and to write the equation for its sum.

$$\frac{1}{3} + \frac{2}{3} = \frac{3}{3}$$

6. Have each pair turn all of their bars face down and then ask each student to select any two bars and determine if the total shaded amount is less than, equal to, or greater than one whole bar. To make sure that everyone understands, ask for volunteers to describe their amounts. This can be made into a game where the student with the greater total shaded amount wins.

6

Decimals: Rational and Irrational

The approach to decimals should be similar to work with fractions, namely placing strong and continued emphasis on models and oral language and then connecting this work with symbols. . . . Exploring ideas of tenths and hundredths with models can include preliminary work with equivalent decimals.[†]

.4

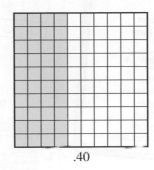
.40

Activity Set **6.1** ## DECIMAL SQUARES MODEL

PURPOSE

To use Decimal Squares[‡] as a visual model for the part-to-whole concept of decimals and for illustrating decimal equality, inequality, place value, and estimation.

irtual
lanipulatives

www.mhhe.com/bbn

MATERIALS

Decimal Squares from the Manipulative Kit or from the Virtual Manipulatives.

INTRODUCTION

The results of the second mathematics assessment of the National Assessment of Educational Progress (NAEP) have implications for the use of models in the teaching of decimal concepts.

> In analyzing the computational errors made on the decimal exercises it is evident that much of the difficulty lies in a lack of conceptual understanding. . . . It is important that decimals be thought of as numbers and the ability to relate them to models should assist in understanding.[§]

[†]*Curriculum and Evaluation Standards for School Mathematics,* p. 59.

[‡]Decimal Squares is a registered trademark of American Education Products, LLC

[§]Carpenter, Corbitt, Kepner, Lindquist, and Reys, "Decimals: Results and Implications from National Assessment," *Arithmetic Teacher* 28, pp. 34–37.

Representing Decimals

▷ **MINI Lab**

The models below show some ways to represent the decimal 1.65.

Place-Value Chart

1,000	100	10	1	0.1	0.01	0.001
thousands	hundreds	tens	ones	tenths	hundredths	thousandths
O	O	O	1	6	5	O

Money

1 dollar   6 dimes   5 pennies

Decimal Model

one   65 hundredths

Base-Ten Blocks

1 one   6 tenths   5 hundredths

Model each decimal using a place-value chart, money, a decimal model, and base-ten blocks.

1. 1.56   2. 0.85   3. 0.08   4. $2.25

1–4. See Ch. 3 Answer Appendix.

Decimals, like whole numbers, are based on the number ten. In a place-value chart, the place to the right of the ones place has a value of one tenth. The next place has a value of one hundredth. Numbers that have digits in the tenths place and beyond are called **decimals.**

Place-Value Chart

1,000	100	10	1	0.1	0.01	0.001	0.0001
thousands	hundreds	tens	ones	tenths	hundredths	thousandths	ten-thousandths
O	O	O	1	6	5	O	O

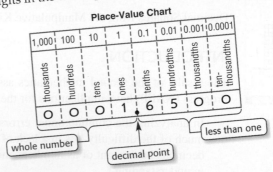

whole number   decimal point   less than one

The Decimal Squares model for decimals is an extension of the base-ten multibase piece model that was used for whole numbers in Chapter 3. The base-ten piece model started with a unit and the pieces increased in size by a factor of 10 (10 units equal 1 long, 10 longs equal 1 flat, etc.). The Decimal Squares model starts with the unit, but the number pieces decrease in size by a factor of 10, as shown below. The number pieces representing 1, $\frac{1}{10}$, $\frac{1}{100}$, and $\frac{1}{1000}$ are indicated by shading one part of each unit number piece.

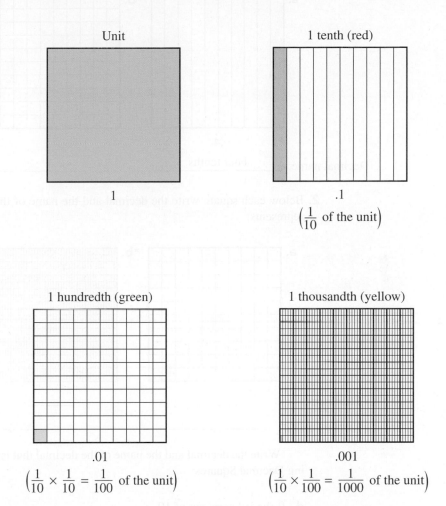

The decimals 3 tenths, 37 hundredths, and 379 thousandths are illustrated by the following Decimal Squares.

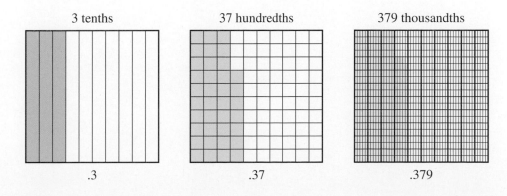

Part to Whole

1. Find the Decimal Squares that represent each of the following decimals. For each decimal, shade the blank Decimal Square to show the decimal and write the name of the decimal below the given decimal.

a.   *b.   c.

        .4   .75   .325

Decimal name: ___Four tenths___   _____   _____

2. Below each square write the decimal and the name of the decimal that the shaded amount represents.

 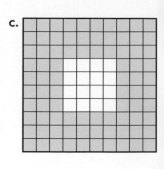

a.   *b.   c.

Decimal: _____   _____   _____

Decimal name: _____   _____   _____

Write the decimal and the name of the decimal that is represented by each of the following Decimal Squares:

d. 9 shaded parts out of 10   _____

e. 13 shaded parts out of 100   _____

*f. 954 shaded parts out of 1000 _____

3. **High-Low Game** (2 players): Shuffle one deck of Decimal Squares and place them face down in a *Draw* stack. Player A takes the top square from the *Draw* stack, states the color of the card, but does not show the card to Player B. Using decimal names, Player B tries to guess the number of shaded parts and has the following number of guesses:

Draw   Discard

- Red square, three guesses,
- Green square, four guesses, and
- Yellow square, five guesses.

After each guess, Player A tells Player B if the guess is **too high** or **too low.** If one of the guesses is correct, Player B wins the square. If not, the square is placed face up in the *Discard* stack. In either case, Player B takes the next square from the *Draw* stack, and it is Player A's turn to guess the number of shaded parts. The first player to win three Decimal Squares wins the game.

a. Play at least one game of *High-Low*.

b. Can you always win a red Decimal Square with three guesses? If not, what is the minimum number of guesses that you need to guarantee winning a red square the first time a red square is played?

c. Describe a winning strategy for guessing the value of a red Decimal Square.

d. Describe a winning strategy for guessing the value of a green Decimal Square.

e. Describe a winning strategy for guessing the value of a yellow Decimal Square.

Equality

The decimals for the following Decimal Squares are equivalent because each Decimal Square is the same size and has the same amount of shading. That is, 4 parts out of 10 is equal to 40 parts out of 100, and 40 parts out of 100 is equal to 400 parts out of 1000.

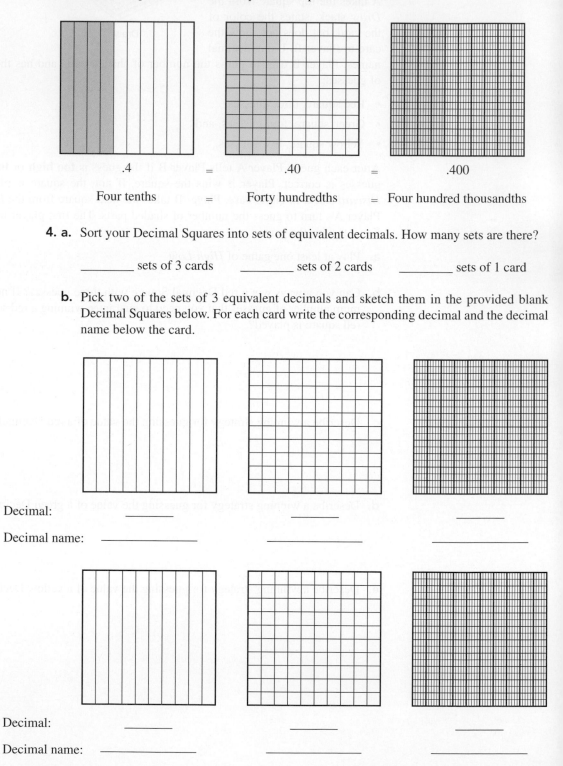

.4   =   .40   =   .400

Four tenths   =   Forty hundredths   =   Four hundred thousandths

4. a. Sort your Decimal Squares into sets of equivalent decimals. How many sets are there?

_____ sets of 3 cards   _____ sets of 2 cards   _____ sets of 1 card

b. Pick two of the sets of 3 equivalent decimals and sketch them in the provided blank Decimal Squares below. For each card write the corresponding decimal and the decimal name below the card.

Decimal: _____   _____   _____

Decimal name: _____   _____   _____

Decimal: _____   _____   _____

Decimal name: _____   _____   _____

Fill in the boxes below each Decimal Square to complete the statement and the equation.

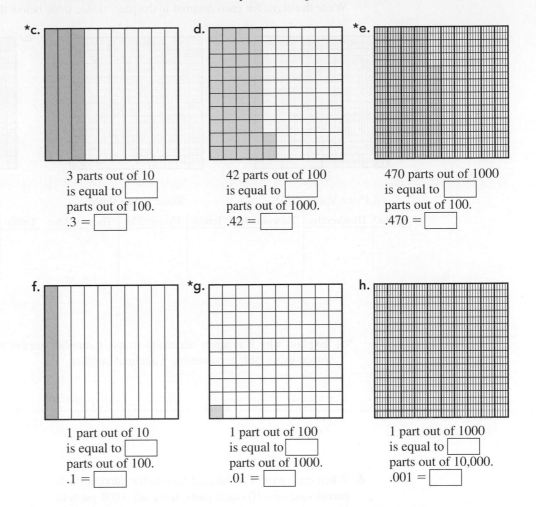

*c.

3 parts out of 10
is equal to ☐
parts out of 100.
.3 = ☐

d.

42 parts out of 100
is equal to ☐
parts out of 1000.
.42 = ☐

*e.

470 parts out of 1000
is equal to ☐
parts out of 100.
.470 = ☐

f.

1 part out of 10
is equal to ☐
parts out of 100.
.1 = ☐

*g.

1 part out of 100
is equal to ☐
parts out of 1000.
.01 = ☐

h.

1 part out of 1000
is equal to ☐
parts out of 10,000.
.001 = ☐

Place Value

The decimal .435 is represented by the shaded parts in both Decimal Squares below. Figure a represents .435 and we say its decimal name is "four hundred thirty-five thousandths," because 435 parts out of 1000 are shaded. In Figure b, the encircled parts of the square show that .435 can also be thought of as 4 tenths, 3 hundredths, and 5 thousandths and that each digit has *place value* as recorded in the table.

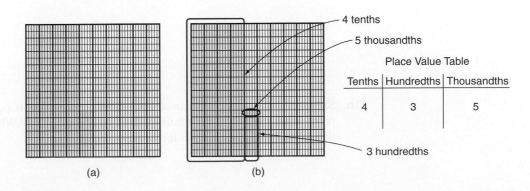

4 tenths

5 thousandths

Place Value Table

Tenths	Hundredths	Thousandths
4	3	5

3 hundredths

(a)   (b)

5. For each of the Decimal Squares, circle the parts that show the decimal in place-value form. Write the digits for each decimal in the place-value table below the square.

a.
.832

Place Value Table

Tenths	Hundredths	Thousandths

*b.
.055

Place Value Table

Tenths	Hundredths	Thousandths

c.
.705

Place Value Table

Tenths	Hundredths	Thousandths

*d. Explain why it is never necessary to use a number greater than 9 in any column of a place-value table representing a decimal number.

6. When each part of a Decimal Square for hundredths is partitioned into 10 equal parts, there are 1000 parts in the whole square. One of these parts is 1 thousandth of the whole square and represents the decimal .001 as shown here.

.001 →

a. Suppose each part of a Decimal Square for thousandths is partitioned into 10 equal parts. What fraction of the whole square is 1 of these parts? What is the decimal for 1 of these small parts, and what is the name of the decimal?

*b. Suppose each part of a Decimal Square for thousandths is partitioned into 100 equal parts. What fraction of the whole square is 1 of these parts? What is the decimal for 1 of these small parts, and what is the name of the decimal?

Inequality

The Decimal Squares for .62 and .610 show that .62 is greater than .610, because its square has the greater shaded amount. We can also determine that .62 > .610 by thinking in terms of place value. The digit 6 in .62 and .610 tells us that 6 tenths of both squares are shaded. That is, 6 full columns of both squares are shaded. Looking at the next column, we see that the square for .62 has 2 hundredths (or 20 thousandths) shaded, whereas the square for .610 has 1 hundredth (or 10 thousandths) shaded. So, .62 > .610.

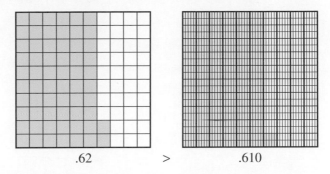

.62   >   .610

7. Determine an inequality for each pair of decimals, and explain the reason for the inequality by describing their Decimal Squares. For example, .4 > .27 because the Decimal Square for .4 has 4 full columns shaded, and the square for .27 has less than 3 full columns shaded.

   a. .7   .43

   *b. .042   .04

   c. .3   .285

Place all of your Decimal Squares face down. For each of parts d–f pick three Decimal Squares at random, place the cards in order, and then write the corresponding decimal equalities or inequalities. For example, for cards representing .2, .15, and .175, rewrite the inequalities as .150 < .175 < .200.

   d. _____   _____   _____

   e. _____   _____   _____

   f. _____   _____   _____

8. The following question is from a mathematics assessment test that was given to students entering college.

Question: Which of the following numbers is the smallest?

a. .07   b. 1.003   c. .08   d. .075   e. .3

Less than 30 percent of 7100 students answered this question correctly.[†] Explain how to determine the correct answer by describing Decimal Squares for these decimals.

Approximation

9. a. Using a blank Decimal Square for tenths, determine how many complete parts should be shaded to best approximate $\frac{1}{3}$ of the whole square. Shade these parts. Beneath the square, record the decimal that represents the shaded part.

—————

b. Shade complete parts of each of these two blank Decimal Squares to best approximate $\frac{1}{3}$ of a whole square. Beneath each square, record the decimal that represents the shaded portion of the square.

—————   —————

[†]A. Grossman, "Decimal Notation: An Important Research Finding," *Arithmetic Teacher* 30, pp. 32–33.

*c. Shade complete parts of each of these Decimal Squares to best approximate $\frac{1}{6}$ of a whole square. Write the decimal that represents the shaded part of each square.

_____   _____   _____

  ## JUST FOR FUN

In Decimal Bingo you practice identifying equal decimals. The Decimal Place-Value Game provides more insight on place values.

DECIMAL BINGO (2 to 4 players)

Each player selects one of the following four bingo mats with decimals. The deck of Decimal Squares should be spread face down. Each player in turn takes a square and circles the decimal or decimals on the bingo mat that equal the decimal for the square. The winner is the first player to circle four decimals in any row, column, or diagonal.

.30	.400	.1	.70
.7	.55	.3	.8
.10	.40	.85	.95
.8	.300	.05	.550

Mat 1

.60	.50	.3	.10
.1	.75	.600	.5
.450	.30	.15	.525
.500	.45	.425	.750

Mat 2

.70	.2	.50	.40
.5	.4	.450	.65
.20	.700	.375	.675
.400	.45	.475	.650

Mat 3

.75	.300	.60	.4
.600	.9	.30	.350
.40	.750	.325	.25
.35	.6	.575	.90

Mat 4

DECIMAL PLACE-VALUE GAME (2 to 4 players)

Players each draw a place-value table like the one next to the dice. Each player in turn rolls two dice until he or she obtains a sum less than 10. The player then records this number in one of the three columns in his or her place-value table. Only one number is written in one column on each turn, and the number cannot be moved to another column after it has been written down. After each player has had three turns, the player with the greatest three-place decimal is the winner. The first player to win five rounds wins the game.[†]

Variation: Use a place-value table with four columns, and roll the dice to obtain the digits in a four-place decimal.

Place Value Table

Tenths	Hundredths	Thousandths

[†]Another way to generate numbers for this game is to write each digit from 0 to 9 on a separate card and then draw one card at random from this deck. Replace the card before the next draw.

Exercises and Activities **6.1**

1. *School Classroom:* The students in your class are discussing the relative values of several decimals. Richard claims that .15 is smaller than .125 since 15 parts is always less than 125 parts and Susan insists he has it backward but cannot explain why. How might you help these students use a Decimal Square model and correct decimal language to resolve this discussion?

2. *School Classroom:* Elementary students learn that one or more zeros can be placed at the end of a decimal without changing its value, but they usually do not understand why. Use Decimal Squares to illustrate .3 = .30 = .300 and write an explanation involving the use of additional zeros that would make sense to students. Copy Blank Decimal Squares from the companion website.

3. *School Classroom:* **The Elementary School Text** page at the beginning of this section shows four models for illustrating the decimal 1.65.
   a. Using the three models (1) *Money,* (2) *Decimal Model,* and (3) *Base-Ten Blocks,* illustrate and explain how you would use each model to help an elementary school student see that 2.3 > 2.29.
   b. Explain how you would relate each model in part a to the *Place-Value Chart* model also shown on the school page.

4. *Math Concepts:* Use Decimal Squares to find a few decimal numbers between .5 and .6, a few decimal numbers between .49 and .5, and a few decimal numbers between .311 and .312. In each case, give the name of the decimal, illustrate the decimal with a Decimal Square sketch and explain your thinking. Copy Blank Decimal Squares from the companion website.

5. *Math Concepts:* Open the **Math Investigation 6.1: Read Me—Repeating Decimals Instructions** from the companion website and investigate the relationship between fractions and their decimal expansions as described in question 1 of the *Starting Points for Investigations 6.1.* Describe your investigation and explain your thinking.

6. *Math Concepts:* Sketch each of the following decimals on a blank Decimal Square and describe how you can use the Decimal Square representation to express each of these decimals as fraction. Copy Blank Decimal Squares from the companion website.
   a. .7
   b. .15
   c. .250
   d. .125

7. *NCTM Standards:* Read the **Grades 3–5 and 6–8 Number and Operations Standards** in the back pages of this book. Pick two *Expectations,* one from each level, which the activities in this activity set address. State the *Expectations* and the *Standards* they are under. Explain which activities from this activity set address these *Expectations* and how they do so.

---

www.mhhe.com/bbn

bennett-burton-nelson website

Virtual Manipulatives   Grid and Dot Paper   Links and Readings
Interactive Chapter Applets Color Transparencies   Geometer Sketchpad Modules
Puzzlers   Extended Bibliography

irtual
lanipulatives

ww.mhhe.com/bbn

Activity Set 6.2

OPERATIONS WITH DECIMAL SQUARES

PURPOSE

To use Decimal Squares to illustrate decimal addition, subtraction, multiplication, and division.

MATERIALS

Decimal Squares and the 1-to-8 Spinner from the Manipulative Kit or from the Virtual Manipulatives.

INTRODUCTION

It is common when computing on a calculator to get decimal numbers. Because of our technology and the frequent occurrence of decimals, it has been suggested that decimal concepts be taught earlier in the elementary school curriculum.

> Calculators create whole new opportunities for ordering the curriculum and for integrating mathematics into science. No longer need teachers be constrained by the artificial restriction to numbers that children know how to employ in the paper-and-pencil algorithms of arithmetic. Decimals can be introduced much earlier since they arise naturally on the calculator. Real measurements from science experiments can be used in mathematics lessons because the calculator will be able to add or multiply the data even if the children have not yet learned how. They may learn first what addition and multiplication mean and when to use them, and only later how to perform these operations manually in all possible cases.[†]

Early introduction of the decimal concepts of addition, subtraction, multiplication, and division in the elementary school curriculum makes it imperative that children have good physical and visual models that embody these concepts. The goal is to develop concepts and a decimal number sense rather than paper-and-pencil manipulative skills. For example, a child may not know the traditional moving-the-decimal-point algorithm of computing $.35 \div .05$ but may "see" that the answer is 7 by using the Decimal Squares model—and then verify this result by using a calculator. These figures show that the shaded part for .05 fits into the shaded part for .35 seven times.

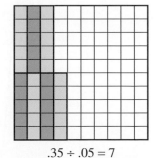

.35 $.35 \div .05 = 7$

[†]National Research Council, *Everybody Counts: A Report to the Nation on the Future of Mathematics Education*, pp. 47–48.

15-6   Subtract Decimals

GET READY to Learn

Albert Einstein was a very intelligent man who made many important scientific discoveries. His brain had a mass of 1.23 kilograms. This is less than the mass of an average adult male brain, which has a mass of about 1.4 kilograms. What is the difference in mass?

MAIN IDEA

I will subtract decimals.

Math Online

macmillanmh.com

- Extra Examples
- Personal Tutor
- Self-Check Quiz

In the previous Explore Activity, you used models to subtract decimals.

Real-World EXAMPLE   Subtract Decimals

1   **MEASUREMENT** What is the difference in mass between Albert Einstein's brain and the mass of an average adult male brain?

Step 1   Draw a model of 1.4 on a hundredths grid.

Step 2   Subtract 1.23.

$$1.4 - 1.23 = 0.17$$

So, Einstein's brain had a mass of 0.17 kilogram less than the mass of an average adult male brain.

Addition

1. Addition of decimals can be illustrated by determining the total shaded amount of two or more Decimal Squares. Fill in the missing number (addend), and compute the sum by counting the total number of shaded parts.

a.

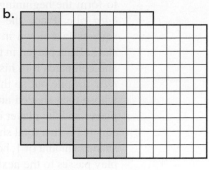

.3 + _____ = _____

b.

.38 + _____ = _____

c.

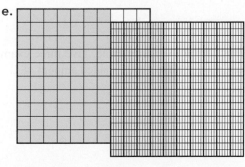

_____ + .355 = _____

d.

.8 + _____ = _____

e.

_____ + .470 = _____

f.

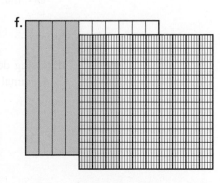

.4 + _____ = _____

2. **Units Game** (2 to 4 players): Remove the yellow squares from one deck of Decimal Squares and shuffle the red and green squares. Deal each player four squares. Turn one square face up to form the beginning of a *Discard* pile. Place the remaining squares face down in a *Playing*

Draw   Discard

stack. Each player, in turn, takes one square from either the *Playing* stack or the *Discard* pile and compares it to his or her own squares. Throughout the game, spread the squares in the *Discard* pile out so that any square may be taken. When a player has two or more squares whose total shaded amount is 1 whole square, these squares are placed face up beside the player and the player draws again. On the first turn, a player may have more than one set of squares with a total shaded amount of 1. If a player cannot combine squares to make a total shaded amount of 1, he or she places one of his or her squares face up in the *Discard* pile, and play passes to the next player. The first player who lays all of his or her squares down ends the round. At the end of each round, a player earns one point for each square laid down and loses one point for each square left in his or her hand. The player with the most points wins the game.

> **Challenge Option:**
> If a player discards a square that creates a set that adds to 1 in the *Discard* pile, another player who sees this may pick up this set of cards.

a. Play at least one *Units* game.

b. Using decimals from the *Units* game, give three examples of pairs of decimals whose Decimal Squares have a total shaded amount of 1.

c. Using decimals from the *Units* game, give three examples of triples of decimals whose Decimal Squares have a total shaded amount of 1.

d. Using decimals from the *Units* game, give three examples of sets of more than three Decimal Squares that have a total shaded amount of 1.

Subtraction

3. Subtraction of decimals can be illustrated with Decimal Squares by circling the amount to be taken away—*take-away concept for subtraction*—and counting the number of shaded parts that remain.

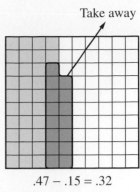

Take away

$.47 - .15 = .32$

For each of the following, outline the amount to be taken away and complete the equation.

a.

$.25 - .19 = \underline{\hspace{1cm}}$

b.

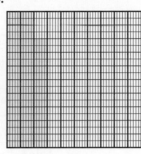

$.280 - .175 = \underline{\hspace{1cm}}$

c.

$.75 - .08 = \underline{\hspace{1cm}}$

4. Greater Difference Game (2 to 4 players): Shuffle one deck of Decimal Squares and place them face down to form the *Draw* pile. During each round, each player takes two squares from the *Draw* pile and gives the decimal name of the difference of the decimals for the two squares. The player with the greater difference wins the round. The first player to win three rounds wins the game.

Draw

> ***Chance Option:***
> Before announcing the differences, each player has the option of replacing one of their Decimal Squares by discarding a square and drawing a new square from the *Draw* pile.

a. Play at least one *Greater Difference* game.

b. What is the greatest difference you can obtain using the deck of Decimal Squares? Give an example.

c. What is the least (positive) difference you can obtain using the deck of Decimal Squares? Give an example.

d. Give an example of two Decimal Squares where the best strategy is to replace a square with the *Chance* option. Explain.

Multiplication

5. Here is the Decimal Square for .45. If there are 3 sets of these 45 shaded parts, as shown below, there are a total of $3 \times 45 = 135$ shaded parts. Since there are 100 parts in each whole square, the total shaded amount would be 1 whole square and 35 parts out of 100.

.45

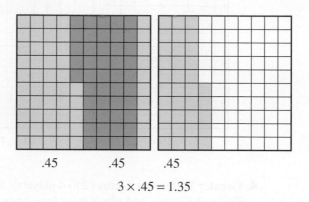

.45   .45   .45

$$3 \times .45 = 1.35$$

In a similar manner, compute the following products and explain your answers in terms of the shaded parts of Decimal Squares.

a. $6 \times .83 =$ _____

*b. $4 \times .725 =$ _____

*c. Explain, using a Decimal Square for .35, why multiplication by 10 results in a decimal number with the same digits but with the decimal point in a different place.

6. **Lucky Twenty-One Game** (2 to 4 players): Shuffle one deck of Decimal Squares and place them face down. Each player in turn selects a square, writes the decimal of its shaded amount, spins the spinner, and writes the product of the number on the spinner times the decimal. The player's score for the turn is the product **rounded to the nearest whole number.** The first player with a total score of 21 or more wins.

$.6 \times 3 = 1.8 \approx 2$

> *Double or Nothing Option:*
> A player may say "double or nothing" before selecting a square. If .6 or more of the square is shaded, the score the player receives for the round is doubled. However, if the square has less than .6 shaded, the player loses his or her turn.

a. Play at least one *Lucky Twenty-One* game. This game should be played without a calculator.

b. What is the smallest *product* you can obtain using your deck of Decimal Squares and 1-to-8 Spinner? What is the corresponding score? List three cards and spinner numbers for which you will get this score.

c. What is the largest product you can obtain using your deck of Decimal Squares and 1-to-8 Spinner? What is the corresponding score? List the cards and spinner numbers for which you will get this score.

d. Is *Double or Nothing* a good strategy? Explain.

7. The product .3 × .2 means "take 3 tenths of 2 tenths." To do this, we split the shaded amount of the .2 square into 10 equal parts and take 3 of them. The result is 6 hundredths. This blue region shows that .3 × .2 = .06.

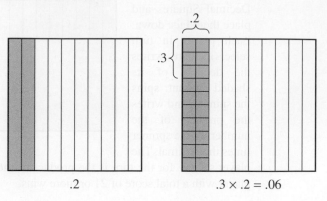

.3 × .2 = .06

The shaded portion of the first figure below represents the decimal 1.2. When the shaded amount representing 1.2 is split into 10 equal parts and 3 are taken, as shown by the blue region in the second figure, the result is 3 tenths and 6 hundredths, or 36 hundredths. This shows that .3 × 1.2 = .36.

Notice in the second figure that .3 and 1.2 are also the lengths of the edges of the blue rectangle. That is, we are using a rectangular model for decimal multiplication, similar to the rectangular model for multiplying two two-digit whole numbers in Activity Set 5.3.

1.2

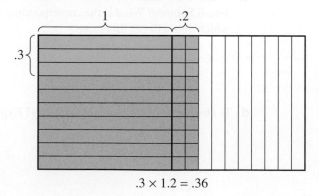

.3 × 1.2 = .36

The product 1.3×1.2 can be found by forming a rectangle with dimensions 1.3×1.2, as shown below. The blue rectangular region represents 1 unit, 5 tenths, and 6 hundredths, so $1.3 \times 1.2 = 1.56$. Notice the top portion of the blue rectangle model shows 1×1.2 and the lower portion of the model shows $.3 \times 1.2$. The sum of these two partial products is 1.56. You can also think of this model as showing the four partial products ($1 \times 1, 1 \times .2, .3 \times 1,$ $.3 \times .2$) whose sum is also 1.56.

1×1.2

$(1 \times 1.2) + (.3 \times 1.2) = 1.56$
or
$1.3 \times 1.2 = 1.56$

$.3 \times 1.2$

In a similar manner, sketch a Decimal Squares diagram to illustrate each of the following products. Label the dimensions of the rectangle, determine the product from the diagram, and explain your reasoning.

a. $.4 \times .3 =$ _____

*b. $1.4 \times 1.3 =$ _____

Division

8. The *sharing method of division* can be used to illustrate the division of a decimal by a whole number. In the Decimal Square shown here, the shaded portion representing .60 has been divided into 3 equal parts to illustrate .60 ÷ 3. Since each of these parts has 20 shaded parts (out of 100), .60 divided by 3 is .20.

.60 ÷ 3 = .20

3 equal parts

Divide each Decimal Square into the given number of parts, and use the result to determine the quotient.

a.

.8 ÷ 4 = _____

b.

.75 ÷ 3 = _____

c.

.200 ÷ 4 = _____

9. Use the following Decimal Squares to determine the indicated quotients. Record each quotient beneath the square, and shade that amount for the quotient on the Decimal Square.

a.

1 ÷ 10 = _____

b.

.1 ÷ 10 = _____

c.

.01 ÷ 10 = _____

*d. Explain, using Decimal Squares, why dividing a decimal number, such as 2.87, by 10 results in a decimal with the same digits but the decimal point moved one place to the left.

10. The *measurement concept of division* involves repeatedly measuring off or subtracting one amount from another. It can be seen in the Decimal Square shown here that 15 of the shaded parts can be measured off from 75 parts 5 times.

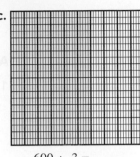

$.75 \div .15 = 5$

Draw lines on the following Decimal Squares to indicate how the measurement concept of division can be used to obtain each indicated quotient.

a.

$.8 \div .2 =$ _____

*b.

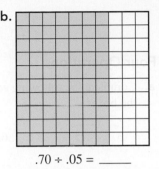

$.70 \div .05 =$ _____

c.

$.600 \div .3 =$ _____

*d. On the Second National Assessment of Educational Progress, students were asked to estimate $250 \div .5$. Only 39 percent of the 17-year-olds correctly estimated this quotient; 47 percent ignored the decimal point, giving an answer of 50.[†] Use the measurement concept of division to explain why $250 \div .5 = 500$.

11. Greater Quotient Game (2 to 4 players): Shuffle one deck of Decimal Squares and place all of them face down to form the *Draw* pile. During each round, each player takes two squares from the *Draw* pile. The player obtaining the greatest possible quotient by dividing one of the decimals by the other wins the round. The first player to win three rounds wins the game.

Draw

Chance Option:
Each player has the option of replacing one of their Decimal Squares by discarding a square and drawing a new square from the *Draw* pile.

a. Play at least one *Greater Quotient* game.

b. What is the greatest quotient you can obtain using the deck of Decimal Squares?

[†]National Assessment of Educational Progress, "Math Achievement Is Plus and Minus," p. 2.

c. What is the least quotient you can obtain using the deck of Decimal Squares (if you are trying to actually win the round)?

d. Give an example of two Decimal Squares where the best strategy is to replace a square with the *Chance* option. Explain.

All Four Operations

12. a. Complete the following equations by placing each of these 10 decimals in exactly one of the boxes.

.3   .75   .8   .650   .15   .2   .35   .45   .400   .350

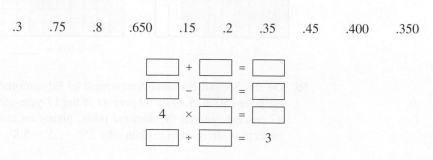

b. Spread your Decimal Squares face down and select 10 of them. List your 10 decimals below. Using each of your decimals only once, complete as many of the following four equations as possible.

10 decimals selected: _____, _____, _____, _____, _____,

_____, _____, _____, _____, _____,

c. *Solitaire:* The activity in part b can be played like a solitaire game. See how many turns it takes you to complete the four equations by selecting only 10 Decimal Squares on each turn.

JUST FOR FUN

Build skills in performing operations on decimals with this addition game.

DECIMAL SQUARES BLACKJACK
(2 to 4 players)

The dealer shuffles the deck of Decimal Squares and deals one square face down to each player. The dealer also gets one square. The object of the game is to use one or more squares to get a decimal or a sum of two or more decimals that is less than or equal to 1, without going over. To get an additional square from the dealer, a player says "Hit me." When a player wants no more additional squares, he or she says "I'm holding." After every player has said "I'm holding," the players show their squares. The player whose sum is closest to 1, but not greater than 1, wins 1 point. The winner is the first player to win 5 points.

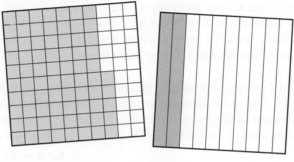

I'm holding!

Exercises and Activities **6.2**

1. *School Classroom:* One of your students cannot understand how to add decimals by using the standard algorithm where decimal points are aligned before adding. Illustrate how you can use the Decimal Square model and correct decimal language to help the student resolve this issue using the sum of the decimals .5, .15, and .175 as an example.

2. *School Classroom:* Design a few questions that you believe are appropriate for helping an upper elementary school student understand how to subtract decimals using a Decimal Squares model and the comparison method of subtraction. Try this activity on an upper elementary school age child of your choice. Record your questions and the student's responses.

3. *School Classroom:* The Decimal Squares subtraction modeled on the **Elementary School Text** page at the beginning of this section used the *Take Away Subtraction Method* (see activity 7 in Activity Set 3.2). Draw sketches and describe how this same subtraction would be modeled using Decimal Squares and both the *Missing Addend Method* and the *Comparison Method* for subtraction (see activities 7 and 8 in Activity Set 3.2).

4. *Math Concepts:* For each of the following, draw a sketch to show how a Decimal Squares model is used to compute the sum or difference and explain how the model matches the placement of decimal points in the standard paper-and-pencil algorithm. Copy Blank Decimal Squares or use the Virtual Decimal Squares from the companion website.

   a. .3 + .5   **b.** .4 + .65

   c. .85 − .2   **d.** .7 − .15

5. *Math Concepts:* For each of the following, draw a sketch to show how a Decimal Squares model is used to compute the product and explain how the model matches the standard paper-and-pencil algorithm. Copy Blank Decimal Squares or use the Virtual Decimal Squares from the companion website.

   a. .2 × .5   **b.** 1.2 × 1.5

6. *Math Concepts:* For each of the following, draw a sketch to show how a Decimal Squares model is used to compute the quotient. Which division concept are you using? Explain. Copy Blank Decimal Squares or use the Virtual Decimal Squares from the companion website.

   a. .75 ÷ .15   **b.** .750 ÷ 3

7. *Math Concepts:* In activity 10 in this activity set, the measurement concept of division is used as an approach to divide one decimal by another decimal. However, another way to compute the quotient is to multiply the dividend and the divisor by the same power of 10 and just do whole number division. For example, .75 ÷ .15 = 75 ÷ 15, .8 ÷ .2 = 8 ÷ 2, and .70 ÷ .05 = 70 ÷ 5. Use the Decimal Square model to explain why division of decimals like these can be replaced by division involving whole numbers.

8. *NCTM Standards:* Go to the **Grade 6–8 Number and Operations Standards** in the back pages of this book and find the *"Understand Meanings of Operations" Standard.* Explain how using a Decimal Square model can help a middle school student understand the meaning of decimal addition and subtraction.

---

bennett-burton-nelson website

Virtual Manipulatives	Grid and Dot Paper	Links and Readings
Interactive Chapter Applets	Color Transparencies	Geometer Sketchpad Modules
Puzzlers	Extended Bibliography	

A MODEL FOR INTRODUCING PERCENT

PURPOSE

To use base-ten pieces to introduce the concept of percent and to illustrate and solve various percent problems.

MATERIALS

Base-Ten Pieces from the Manipulative Kit or from the Virtual Manipulatives.

INTRODUCTION

Percent is a common and widely used mathematical concept. From television to newspapers to shopping, the word percent enters our life almost daily, as noted in the following passage.

> Percentages are everywhere—in the food we eat ([a serving of] cornflakes contains 25% of our recommended daily allowance of vitamin A), in the clothes we wear (35% cotton), in our favorite television programs (watched by 55% of the television audience), and in the money we earn (27% tax bracket) and spend ($5\frac{1}{2}$% sales tax). In modern society, people who do not understand percentages will have difficulty reading articles and advertisements that appear in newspapers, determining if they are being cheated by financial institutions or retail establishments, or knowing if they are being misled by politicians.[†]

When something is divided into 100 equal parts, one part is called *one percent* and written 1%. If a 10 by 10 grid from the base-ten pieces is considered to represent a unit, then one part of the grid is 1 percent and the whole grid is 100 percent. The base-ten number pieces will be used to explore the concept of percent and solve various percent problems.

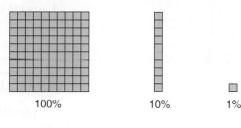

100%   10%   1%

The classical three cases of percent are visualized in this activity set using this model.

Percent and whole:	25% of 150 = ?
Part and whole:	?% of 150 = 90
Percent and part:	6% of ? = 24

At the end of this activity set, Fraction Bars are split into approximately 100 parts to provide percent and decimal estimations for fractions.

---

1. If the 10 by 10 grid represents 100%, determine what percent is represented by each of these collections of base-ten pieces.

    *a.   b.   *c.   *d.   e.

Percent: _____   _____   _____   _____   _____

[†]James H. Wiebe, "Manipulating Percentages," *The Mathematics Teacher*, pp. 23–26.

Explore 7-1

Math Lab
Modeling Percents

MAIN IDEA
Use models to illustrate the meaning of percents.

In Lesson 3-1, you learned that a 10 × 10 grid can be used to represent *hundredths*. The word *percent* (%) means *out of one hundred*, so you can also use a 10 × 10 grid to model percents.

ACTIVITY

1 Model 18%.

18% means 18 out of 100.
So, shade 18 of the 100 squares on the decimal model.

✔ **CHECK Your Progress   Model each percent.**

a. 30%   b. 8%   c. 42%   d. 75%

ACTIVITIES

Identify each percent that is modeled.

2

There are 40 out of 100 squares shaded.

So, the model shows 40%.

3

There are 25 out of 100 squares shaded.

So, the model shows 25%.

✔ **CHECK Your Progress   Identify each percent modeled.**

e.   f.   g.

ANALYZE THE RESULTS

1. Identify the fraction of each model in Exercises a–g that is shaded.
2. **MAKE A CONJECTURE** How can you write a percent as a fraction? How can you write a fraction with a denominator of 100 as a percent?

2. If the 10 by 10 grid represents 100%, use your base-ten pieces to form a collection to represent each of the percentages below. Draw sketches to record your answers.

    *a. 23%   **b.** 98%   ***c.** 105%

    d. 123%   **e.** 202%   ***f.** $\frac{1}{2}$%

Value 300

3. Suppose that a value of 300 is assigned to the 10 by 10 grid and that this value is spread evenly among all the small squares. Use this value for parts a–e.

    *a. Describe an easy method for performing a mental calculation to find the value of one small square.

Using mental calculations, determine the value of each of the following collections of base-ten pieces:

b.

Value: _____

*c.

Value: _____

d.

Value: _____

e.

Value: _____

Percent and Whole

Value 150

4. Suppose the 10 by 10 grid is assigned a value of 150 and this value is spread evenly among all the small squares. For each part a–e, select and sketch the collection of base-ten pieces that represents the given **percent** of a 10 by 10 grid. Determine the **value** of each collection without just doing paper-and-pencil computations.

*a. The value of 30% of 150 = ?

b. The value of 75% of 150 = ?

*c. The value of 7% of 150 = ?

d. The value of 111% of 150 = ?

e. The value of 210% of 150 = ?

f. Explain how you can use base-ten pieces to determine the value of a percent of a whole.

Part and Whole

Value 450

5. Assign a value of 450 to the 10 by 10 grid. For each part a–e, select and sketch the collection of base-ten pieces that represents the given **value.** Determine what **percent** of the 10 by 10 grid the value represents.

*a. ? % of 450 = 45

b. ? % of 450 = 108

*c. ? % of 450 = 441

d. ? % of 450 = 585

e. ? % of 450 = 909

f. Explain how you can use base-ten pieces to determine what percent of the whole a given value (part) is.

Percent and Part

6. For each part a–d, select and sketch the collection of base-ten pieces that represents the given **percent** of a 10 by 10 grid. In each part, if the collection has the given **value,** what is the value of the entire 10 by 10 grid?

   *a. 6% of ? = 24   b. 40% of ? = 30

   *c. 55% of ? = 132   d. 125% of ? = 180

   e. Explain how you can use base-ten pieces to determine the value of a whole given the value of a percent of the whole.

Some Percent Statements

7. Many statements that deal with percent can be represented with the base-ten piece model. Consider the statement: "Last year the charity benefit raised $6720, which was 120% of its goal." 120% can be represented with the following collection of base-ten pieces.

   There are several observations that can be made by looking at the model:

   (1) Because 120% has a value of $6720, one can see from the model that each long has a value of $560 ($6720 ÷ 12) or that each small square has a value of $56 ($6720 ÷ 120).

   (2) Last year's goal (100%) must have been $5600 (10 × $560 or 100 × $56).

   (3) The goal was exceeded by $1120 ($6720 − $5600).

   Model each of the following statements with your base-ten pieces. Sketch your model, record at least one *percent* observation, and explain how you arrived at it.

   *a. 65% of the firm's 320 employees were women.

   *b. 280 of the school's 800 students were absent.

    c. I bought this sweater for $126 at the store's 30% off sale.

    d. This year the charity benefit had a goal of $7000 and it raised 135% of its goal.

    e. In a certain county, 57 of the schools have a student-to-teacher ratio that is greater than the recommendations for accreditation. The 57 schools are 38% of the number of schools in the county.

    f. A new company entered the New York Stock Exchange in July, and by December the price of each share of stock had risen (increased) 223% to $32.50 a share.

Fractions as Percents

8. Fractions with denominators that are factors of 100 can be readily expressed as percents. For example, if each part of a $\frac{3}{4}$ Fraction Bar is split into 25 equal parts, the bar will have 75 parts shaded out of 100 equal parts. So, $\frac{3}{4}$ equals 75%, or the decimal .75.

$$\frac{3}{4} = \frac{75}{100} = 75\% = .75$$

Imagine splitting each of the following Fraction Bars into 100 equal parts. Indicate above each part of a bar the number of new parts after splitting, and then determine the percent and decimal equivalents for each fraction.

a.

$$\frac{1}{2} = \frac{}{100} = \underline{\hspace{1cm}} \% = .\underline{\hspace{1cm}}$$

*b.

$$\frac{2}{5} = \frac{}{100} = \underline{\hspace{1cm}} \% = .\underline{\hspace{1cm}}$$

c.

$$\frac{3}{10} = \frac{}{100} = \underline{\hspace{1cm}} \% = .\underline{\hspace{1cm}}$$

*d.

$$\frac{13}{20} = \frac{}{100} = \underline{\hspace{1cm}} \% = .\underline{\hspace{1cm}}$$

Fractions as Approximate Percents

9. To obtain an approximate percent for the fraction $\frac{1}{7}$, visualize a $\frac{1}{7}$ Fraction Bar. This bar has 1 part shaded out of 7 parts. If each part of the bar is split into 14 equal parts, the result will be 14 shaded parts out of 98 parts.

14 parts

$$\frac{1}{7} = \frac{1 \times 14}{7 \times 14} = \frac{14}{98}$$

If each part of the $\frac{1}{7}$ bar is split in 15 equal parts, there will be 15 shaded parts out of 105 parts.

15 parts

$$\frac{1}{7} = \frac{1 \times 15}{7 \times 15} = \frac{15}{105}$$

Because 105 is not as close to 100 as 98 is, we can say that $\frac{1}{7}$ is approximately 14%. Since 14% is $\frac{14}{100}$, the decimal .14 is also an approximation for $\frac{1}{7}$.

Determine a percent and decimal approximation for each of the following fractions by imagining splitting the corresponding Fraction Bar into approximately 100 parts. Explain how you arrived at your percent for each fraction by indicating the number of parts due to splitting above each part of the bar.

a.

$$\frac{1}{3} \approx \frac{}{100} = \underline{\hspace{2cm}} \% = . \underline{\hspace{2cm}}$$

*b.

$$\frac{5}{6} \approx \frac{}{100} = \underline{\hspace{2cm}} \% = . \underline{\hspace{2cm}}$$

c.

$$\frac{2}{9} \approx \frac{}{100} = \underline{\hspace{2cm}} \% = . \underline{\hspace{2cm}}$$

JUST FOR FUN

GAME OF INTEREST (2 to 4 players)

This game requires the Color Tiles (for markers), the 1-to-12 Spinner from the Manipulative Kit, and the game mat on Material Card 18.

Each player chooses markers of one color and players spin to see who will play first (high number). In turns, players spin to obtain a percent with the number 1–10 representing 1% to 10%. (If the spinner ends on the numbers 11 or 12, spin again.) The player spinning then mentally computes

that percent of one of the following amounts, $50, $100, $200, $300, $400, $500, or $600, and places a marker on the number in the table corresponding to the correct percent of that amount (the *interest*). The game continues until one player, the winner, gets 4 adjacent markers in a row either vertically, horizontally, or diagonally.

Example: Spin 7%; choose to take 7% of $400, which is $28; place a color marker on the number 28 on the gameboard.

INTEREST GAMEBOARD

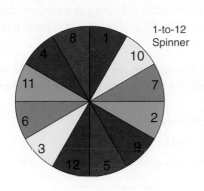

1-to-12 Spinner

$50	$100	$200	$300	$400	$500	$600
.5	1	1.5	2	2.5	3	3.5	4	4.5	5
1	2	3	4	5	6	7	8	9	10
2	4	6	8	10	12	14	16	18	20
3	6	9	12	15	18	21	24	27	30
4	8	12	16	20	24	28	32	36	40
5	10	15	20	25	30	35	40	45	50
6	12	18	24	30	36	42	48	54	60

 ## COMPETING AT PLACE VALUE APPLET

This applet is a two-person game in which each player tries to form the largest possible four-place decimal by placing digits from the spinner into the place value table. In the following example, you are playing against the Robot. In which box of the place value table would you place the "5" from the spinner? As you play this game, try to determine the Robot's strategy in placing digits in the table. For example, since you have one more random number to place in the last box, in which box of the place value table would you place the "5" from the spinner?

Competing at Place Value, Chapter 6
www.mhhe.com/bbn

Exercises and Activities 6.3

1. *School Classroom:* Several of your students are unsure about how to determine the original price of an item, and their savings, when an item is advertised as "On sale for $10.99 at 30% of the original cost." How can you use the base-ten piece percent model to help your students? Include diagrams with your explanation.

2. *School Classroom:* Some of your students are in disagreement about the answer to the following question. Explain how you can use base-ten pieces or percent grids to help them with this problem.

   If an amount first increases in value by 50% and then decreases in value by 50%, will it return to its original value or to more or less than its original value?

3. *School Classroom:* Refer to the **Elementary School Text** page at the beginning of this section. Express each of the shaded portions of the grids in parts e, f, and g as a percent, decimal, and fraction. Explain how thinking of percent on a 10 by 10 grid helps you express a percent as a fraction or a decimal.

4. *Math Concepts:* Model each of the following with your base-ten pieces; sketch the model, label the sketch clearly, and record at least one percent observation about each statement. In each case, explain your reasoning.

   a. 70 percent of the 120 students in the class are women.

   b. 10 of the 30 students in the class want to teach middle school.

   c. Jane spent $25 on teaching supplies at the education center's 35 percent off sale.

5. *Math Concepts:*

   a. If an amount doubles in value, by what percent has the amount increased? Include base-ten piece diagrams with your explanation of the solution.

   b. If an amount triples in value, by what percent has the amount increased? Include base-ten piece diagrams with your explanation of the solution.

6. *Math Concepts:* For each of the following, explain your thinking and include diagrams or sketches of base-ten pieces or percent grids to justify your solution.

   a. If 3% of an amount has a value of $45, what is the value of 100%?

   b. If 45% of an amount has a value of $3, what is the value of 100%?

   c. Are part a and part b the same question or different questions? Explain your thinking.

7. *Math Concepts:* How can you use Fraction Bars to obtain a percent for each of the following fractions? Is the percent exact or an approximation? Sketch and mark Fraction Bars, as in activities 8 and 9 in this activity set, to help explain your answers.

   a. $\frac{1}{4}$ **b.** $\frac{3}{8}$ **c.** $\frac{2}{11}$ **d.** $\frac{7}{15}$

8. *NCTM Standards:* Go to http://illuminations.nctm.org/ and under "Lessons" select grade levels 6–8 and the **Number and Operations Standard.** Choose a lesson about percents.

   a. State the title of the lesson and briefly summarize the lesson.

   b. Referring to the **Standards Summary** in the back pages of this book as necessary, list the *Number and Operation Standard Expectations* that the lesson addresses and explain how the lesson addresses these *Expectations*.

---

bennett-burton-nelson website

Virtual Manipulatives	Grid and Dot Paper	Links and Readings
Interactive Chapter Applets	Color Transparencies	Geometer Sketchpad Modules
Puzzlers	Extended Bibliography	

IRRATIONAL NUMBERS ON THE GEOBOARD

PURPOSE

To use geoboards and/or dot paper to represent figures whose sides and perimeters have lengths that are irrational numbers.

Virtual Manipulatives

www.mhhe.com/bbn

MATERIALS

A Rectangular Geoboard and rubber bands (optional). There is a template for making a Rectangular Geoboard on Material Card 8, or you may wish to use the Rectangular Geoboard in the Virtual Manipulatives.

INTRODUCTION

When we used the rod model for greatest common factors (Activity Set 4.2), we saw that any two rods with whole number lengths could be cut evenly into pieces of equal common length. In some cases, the lengths of the rods may be relatively prime, like 3 and 8, but the rods can still be cut evenly into pieces with common length 1.

If two rods do not have whole number lengths but do have rational number lengths, can they still be cut evenly into rods of equal common length? Again, the answer is yes. Suppose, for example, the rods have lengths $3\frac{1}{3}$ and $5\frac{1}{2}$. Because these numbers are equal to $3\frac{2}{6}$ and $5\frac{3}{6}$, the rods can both be cut evenly into pieces of length $\frac{1}{6}$.

Does it then follow that any two lengths can be evenly cut into pieces of equal common length? About 2300 years ago, mathematicians would have answered yes. They thought that any two lengths are *commensurable*—that is, have a common unit of measure. This unit might be very small, such as a millionth or a billionth of an inch, but surely there would always be such a length. When the Greek mathematician Hippasus (470 B.C.E.) discovered that the side and the diagonals of squares are *incommensurable*—that is, do not have a common unit of measure—he caused such a crisis in mathematics that, reportedly, he was taken to sea and never returned. His discovery ultimately led to new types of numbers, called *irrational numbers,* which are represented by infinite nonrepeating decimals.

In a square, diagonal $\overline{AB}$ and side $\overline{AC}$ cannot be cut into pieces of equal common length

Explore 3-5

Geometry Lab
The Pythagorean Theorem

MAIN IDEA

Find the relationship among the sides of a right triangle.

You can use centimeter grid paper to find the area of squares and triangles. In this lab, you will investigate the relationship among the sides of a right triangle.

Area = 1 cm²

Area = $\frac{1}{2}$ cm²

Area = 1 cm²

ACTIVITY

STEP 1 Draw each figure on centimeter grid paper. In each figure, the sides of three squares form a right triangle.

Triangle 1   Triangle 2   Triangle 3

STEP 2 Find the area of each square that is attached to the triangle. Record this information in a table like the one shown.

Triangle	Area of Blue Square (cm²)	Area of Green Square (cm²)	Area of Yellow Square (cm²)
1			
2			
3			

ANALYZE THE RESULTS

1. What relationship exists among the areas of the three squares in each triangle?

2. On centimeter grid paper, draw a right triangle with the two shorter sides 3 centimeters and 4 centimeters long. If squares were attached to each side of this triangle, what would be the area of each square? Use a ruler to measure the length of the third side of the triangle.

3. **MAKE A CONJECTURE** Determine the length of the longest side of a right triangle if the length of the two shorter sides are 6 centimeters and 8 centimeters long.

1. One way to determine the area of the yellow square *W* is to enclose it inside the larger 3 by 3 square. If each small square represents 1 square unit (1 u^2), then the larger square surrounding square *W* has an area of 9 square units. Each triangular region between square *W* and the large square is half of a rectangle of area 2 square units, so each has an area of 1 square unit. Thus, the area of square *W* is 9 square units − 4 square units = 5 square units.

Here are seven other squares that can be constructed on the geoboard. Determine the area of each square. Record the areas inside the squares.

2. For any square, the length of a side times itself gives the area of the square.

side length × side length = area

Square *W* in activity 1 has an area of 5 square units. The length of a side of square *W* is $\sqrt{5}$ units because by definition $\sqrt{5}$ is *the positive number that, when multiplied times itself, gives 5.* That is, $\sqrt{5} \times \sqrt{5} = 5$. One of the squares in activity 1 has an area of 9 square units, and the length of a side is $\sqrt{9} = 3$ units.

Finish recording the areas (from least to greatest) and the corresponding side lengths for the eight squares in activity 1.

Area of square (square units): ____ ____ ____ 5 ____ 9 ____ ____

Length of side (units):   ____ ____ ____ $\sqrt{5}$ ____ 3 ____ ____

*3. Determine the lengths of the three line segments in the next figure by first drawing a square on each segment and finding the area of the square. (The corners of a sheet of paper can be used to draw the sides and locate the corners of the square. The corners of each square will be on the grid dots. The dotted lines form a square on segment a.) Record the side lengths by the line segments.

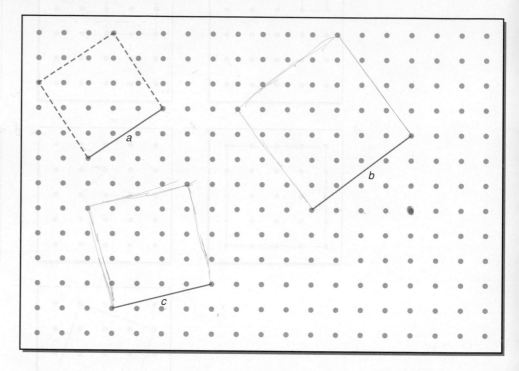

4. Calculator Activity: If n is a positive integer and not a perfect square (that is, n is not 1, 4, 9, 16, 25, 36, . . .), then $\sqrt{n}$ is an *irrational number*. For example, $\sqrt{5}$ is an irrational number. When written as decimals, irrational numbers have infinite and nonrepeating decimal expansions.

a. Use the $\sqrt{}$ key on your calculator to obtain an approximate value for $\sqrt{5}$. Record the decimal from your calculator display. (If you do not have a square root key you can raise 5 to the $\frac{1}{2}$ or .5 power.)

b. Multiply the calculator's decimal for $\sqrt{5}$ times itself and record the result. Did you get 5? Explain why a calculator might, or might not, produce a 5.

c. Explain the advantages of labeling the length of a segment with a symbol like $\sqrt{5}$ rather than writing out the decimal digits for $\sqrt{5}$ that appear on a calculator display.

5. Each of the following figures has three squares surrounding a right triangle (a right triangle has one angle of 90°). For each figure, use the techniques from activity 1 to determine the area of each square and complete the table.

		Square A	Square B	Square C
a.	Figure 1	————	————	————
*b.	Figure 2	————	————	————
c.	Figure 3	————	————	————
*d.	Figure 4	————	————	————

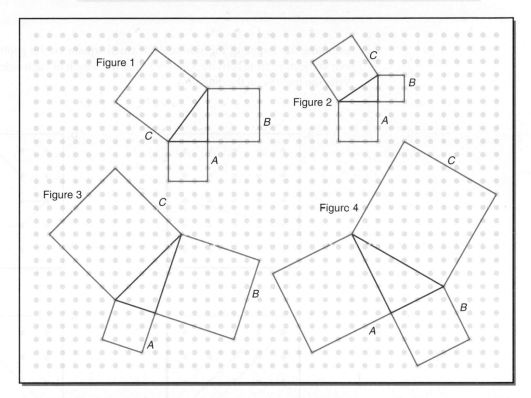

6. For every right triangle, the same relationship holds between the area of the square on the longest side (the hypotenuse) and the total area of the squares on the other two sides (the legs).

a. Use the data from activity 5 to complete this table.

		Total Area of Squares on Two Legs	Area of Square on Hypotenuse
(1)	Figure 1	————	————
(2)	Figure 2	————	————
(3)	Figure 3	————	————
(4)	Figure 4	————	————

b. Use the data from part a to make a conjecture, in writing, about the relationship between the total area of the squares on the two legs of a right triangle and the area of the square on the hypotenuse.

c. Use the relationship from part b to find the area of the square on the hypotenuse and the length of the hypotenuse for each of the figures in activity 5.

		Area of Square on Hypotenuse	Length of Hypotenuse
(1)	Figure 1	_____	_____
*(2)	Figure 2	_____	_____
(3)	Figure 3	_____	_____
*(4)	Figure 4	_____	_____

7. Assuming the length of the side of each small square on the geoboard is 1 linear unit, use your conjecture from activity 5 to determine the length of each side of the following figures. Write the lengths on the diagrams.

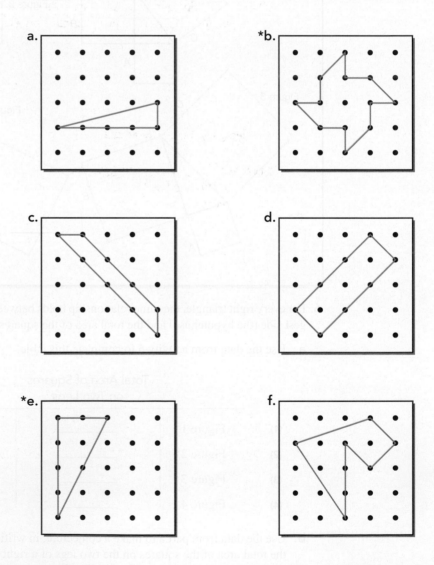

a.

*b.

c.

d.

*e.

f.

8. *Pythagorean Theorem Visual Proof Puzzle*

    a. Cut out all five *Pythagorean Theorem Visual Proof Puzzle* pieces on Material Card 19 (1 big square and four identical triangles). Fit the four triangles into the big square without overlapping the pieces. Leave the yellow center square open. You may wish to tape your pieces together.

    b. Determine the area of the big square, the area of each triangle, and the area of the open yellow center square in terms of a and b. (*Hint:* What is each side length of the small yellow square in terms of a and b?)

    c. The area of the big square is the same as the sum of the areas of the five inside pieces. How can you use this to give a proof of the Pythagorean theorem? Explain.

9. Challenge question: *Square Me Puzzle*

    a. Cut out all five *Square Me Puzzle* pieces on Material Card 19. These five pieces fit together to form one "big" square; can you do it? (*Hint:* Neither of the right angles in piece 3 are corners of the big square.)

    b. Assuming the length of each side of the small square (piece 1) is 1 linear unit, what is the exact perimeter of each piece of the puzzle? Use square roots to report the exact values.

    c. What is the area of each piece of the puzzle?

    d. What is the area of the "big" square? What is the length of each side of the "big" square?

JUST FOR FUN

GOLDEN RECTANGLES

Some rectangles are more aesthetically pleasing than others. One in particular, the *golden rectangle,* has been the favorite of architects, sculptors, and artists for over 3000 years. The Greeks of the fifth century B.C.E. were fond of this rectangle. The front of the Parthenon in Athens fits into a golden rectangle.

Parthenon

In the nineteenth century, the German psychologist Gustav Fechner found that most people unconsciously favor the golden rectangle. Which one of the following rectangles do you feel has the most pleasing dimensions?

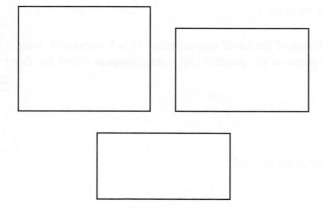

The length of a golden rectangle divided by its width is an irrational number that, when rounded to three decimal places, is 1.618. Measure the preceding rectangles to determine which is closest to a golden rectangle. Measure some other rectangles, such as greeting cards, credit cards, business cards, index cards, pictures, and mirrors, to see if you can find a golden rectangle. (A ratio of 1.6 is close enough.) Check the ratio of the length of the front of the Parthenon to its width in the diagram on this page.

A golden rectangle can be constructed from a square such as $ABCD$ by placing a compass on the midpoint of side $\overline{AB}$ and swinging an arc DF. Then $FBCE$ is a golden rectangle.

Make a golden rectangle, and check the ratio of its sides. If the sides of the square have length 2, then $BF = 1 + \sqrt{5}$. Use your calculator to determine $(1 + \sqrt{5}) \div 2$ (the ratio of the sides of the rectangle) to three decimal places. Cut out your rectangle and fold it in half along its longer side. Is the result another golden rectangle?

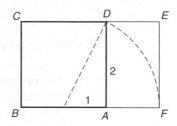

The ratio of the sides of a golden rectangle is called the *golden mean* or *golden ratio.*[†] It is surprising that this number (approximately 1.618) is also associated with the Fibonacci numbers: 1, 1, 2, 3, 5, 8, 13, ... The ratios of successive terms in this sequence ($\frac{1}{1}, \frac{2}{1}, \frac{3}{2}, \frac{5}{3}, \frac{5}{8}, \dots$) get closer and closer to the golden ratio. The ratio $\frac{8}{5}$, for example, is 1.6. Use your calculator to determine how far you must go in the Fibonacci sequence before the ratio of numbers is approximately 1.618.

[†]Several occurrences of the golden ratio are described in C. F. Linn, *The Golden Mean* (New York: Doubleday, 1974).

Exercises and Activities **6.4**

Downloadable Dot Paper, Rectangular Geoboards, and printable Virtual Rectangular Geoboards are available at the companion website.

1. *School Classroom:* Marthona often mixes up the Pythagorean theorem and will use $a^2 + b^2 = c^2$ as well as $a^2 = b^2 + c^2$ or $b^2 = a^2 + c^2$ when a and b are the legs and c is the hypotenuse of a right triangle. How can you help her understand the theorem and resolve this issue?

2. *School Classroom:* Suppose that you are teaching an elementary school class that is studying decimal operations. Design an activity for the class that uses decimal operations and that involves the golden rectangle (described in the **Just for Fun** activity in this section), the golden ratio (1.618 rounded), and measuring. Describe your activity in detail.

3. *School Classroom:* On the **Elementary School Text** page at the beginning of this section complete the table in *Step 2* of the activity.
   a. Continue the table for Triangles 4 and 5 by drawing blue, green, and yellow squares where (1) Triangle 4 has a 2 cm by 2 cm blue square on one edge and a 3 cm by 3 cm green square on the other edge; and (2) Triangle 5 has a 3 cm by 3 cm blue square on one edge and a 3 cm by 3 cm green square on the other edge.
   b. Answer the three questions posed at the end of the school page in *Analyze the Results*.

4. *School Classroom:* Draw an obtuse triangle on a virtual or paper geoboard. Construct a square on each side of this triangle and then determine the area of each square. Compare the sum of the areas of the two squares on the short sides of the triangle to the area of the square on the long side of the triangle. Repeat for two different obtuse triangles. Form a conjecture about the relationship between the sums of the areas of squares on the short sides of an obtuse triangle and the area of the square on the long side. Include your drawings as you explain your conjecture.

5. *Math Concepts:* For each of the following use the small square on the geoboard as the unit square, and create your shapes on a virtual or paper geoboards.
   a. Create a fun shape that would fit on a 5-pin × 5-pin geoboard by using only line segments with rational lengths.
   b. Determine the area of the shape you created in part a. Show your work clearly.
   c. Create a fun shape that would fit on a 5-pin × 5-pin geoboard using at least three line segments with irrational lengths and at least one line segment with rational length for the edges of your shape.
   d. Determine the area of the shape you created in part c. Show your work clearly.
   e. Create a fun shape that would fit on a 5-pin × 5-pin geoboard by using only line segments with irrational lengths.
   f. Determine the area of the shape you created in part e. Show your work clearly.

6. *Math Concepts:* How many line segments of different length can be constructed on a 5-pin × 5-pin geoboard? Sketch the segments and record the length of each segment. Explain your thinking.

7. *Math Concepts:* Golden rectangles, described in the **Just for Fun** activity in this section, have proportions that have been favored by people since antiquity. Two familiar rectangles are the 3" by 5" index card and the common business card (2" by 3.5"). Which of these two cards has proportions closest to a golden rectangle? Explain your answer and how you arrived at it.

8. *Math Concepts:* Do an Internet or library search on visual proofs of the Pythagorean theorem. Find a visual proof different from the proof in activity 7 in this activity set. Demonstrate the proof and explain why it works. Give the reference for your source.

9. *Math Concepts:* Open the **Math Laboratory Investigation 6.4: Read Me—Pythagorean Theorem Instructions** on the companion website and investigate the physical model of the Pythagorean theorem as described in questions 1 and 2 of the *Starting Points for Investigations 6.4.* Describe your investigation and explain your thinking.

10. *NCTM Standards:* The Pythagorean relationship is only specifically mentioned in the **Grade 6–8 Geometry Standards** in the back pages of this book, but understanding the theorem and being computationally fluent with the theorem addresses other *Expectations* in other *Content Standards.* List two such *Expectations* and describe how fluency with the Pythagorean theorem addresses these *Expectations.*

---

www.mhhe.com/bbn

bennett-burton-nelson website

Virtual Manipulatives	Grid and Dot Paper	Links and Readings
Interactive Chapter Applets	Color Transparencies	Geometer Sketchpad Modules
Puzzlers	Extended Bibliography	

ACTIVITIES FOR THE ELEMENTARY SCHOOL CLASSROOM

Introducing Decimals with Base-Ten Pieces

Purpose: To introduce elementary school students to decimals using base-ten pieces.

Connection: Ask each student to write an example of a decimal on a piece of paper. Record some of their examples on the overhead and ask them where they have seen decimals written. Pick one of their examples, or write the decimal .3 on the overhead and ask them to draw a picture or sketch to represent that decimal. Let them share their examples with the class and, if no one has a part-to-whole sketch showing 3 out of 10 parts, then provide an example. Tell them that today they are going to look at decimals using base-ten pieces.

Materials: Sets of base-ten pieces can be created by copying base-ten grid paper from the companion website onto cardstock and cutting out units, longs, and base-ten pieces. Transparencies can also be made with the base-ten pieces image. Sets of base-ten pieces can be placed in plastic sealable bags. Each group of two to four students will need one set of base-ten pieces.

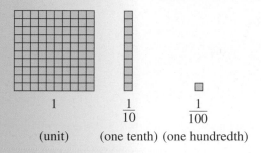

1

(unit)

$\dfrac{1}{10}$

(one tenth)

$\dfrac{1}{100}$

(one hundredth)

1. Have the students select one piece of each size from their base-ten pieces. Ask each group to discuss how the pieces are related and to determine a value for each piece if the largest piece represents 1 unit. Ask for volunteers to describe their findings.

2. Put 11 hundredth pieces and 12 tenths pieces on the overhead and ask the students for suggestions about how the same collection could be represented by the fewest pieces. Then, if no one suggests it, model exchanging 10 hundredth pieces for 1 tenth piece and 10 tenths for 1 unit piece. When all agree that no more trades can reduce the number of pieces, record the minimum number of pieces in a table like the following.

Unit pieces	$\frac{1}{10}$ pieces	$\frac{1}{100}$ pieces
1	3	1

Using a 10 by 10 grid as the unit, this third grader is representing the decimal 2.563.

3. Ask the students to form each of the following collections, find the minimum collection, and record their results in a table like the one above.

   a. 9 tenths and 12 hundredths   **b.** 1 unit, 4 tenths, and 11 hundredths

   c. 14 tenths   **d.** 16 hundredths

   e. 1 unit, 9 tenths, and 10 hundredths   **f.** 2 units, 13 tenths, and 15 hundredths

4. Ask the students what the number 102 means. Tell them that the collection in part a of the table they just made will be written as 1.02 so it is not confused with 102. The period or dot separates the units from the tenths and 1.02 means 1 unit, no tenths, and 2 hundredths. Ask them to write numbers with decimal points for the collections in parts b through f of their table.

5. Tell the students that decimal numbers like 1.32 can be read in several ways. Discuss the reason for each way.

   a. As "one point three two"

   b. As "one and thirty-two hundredths"

   c. As "one and three tenths and two hundredths"

6. Write the following numbers on the overhead and ask each group to form the collection of base-ten pieces represented by each of the numbers. Ask for volunteers to show or describe their collections.

1.21   2.03   .23   .04   1.07

7

Statistics

In grades K–4, students begin to explore basic ideas of statistics by gathering data appropriate to their grade level, organizing them in charts or graphs, and reading information from displays of data. These concepts should be expanded in the middle grades. . . . Instruction in statistics should focus on the active involvement of students in the entire process: formulating key questions; collecting and organizing data; representing the data using graphs, tables, frequency distributions, and summary statistics; analyzing the data; making conjectures; and communicating information in a convincing way.[†]

COLLECTING AND GRAPHING DATA

PURPOSE

To collect and display data and to look for relationships or trends between two sets of data.

MATERIALS

A protractor and a tape measure from Material Card 20 or a ruler and string.

INTRODUCTION

Graphs provide a visual means of looking at sets of data and examining relationships and trends in the data. There are many ways to display data and a decision on which type of display to use often depends on the type of data you wish to display and on which display best illustrates the results.

Pie Graphs

Pie graphs, like this one displaying percentage of fruit juices in a fruit drink, show the relative sizes of certain quantities by dividing a circle into sectors with the same proportions.

Fruit Juice Percentage Breakdown in Fruit Drink

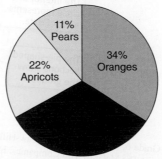

11% Pears

34% Oranges

22% Apricots

[†]*Curriculum and Evaluation Standards for School Mathematics,* p. 105.

7-2 Circle Graphs

▷ **MiNi Lab**

The table below shows the results of a survey about which sport people prefer to watch. These data can be displayed in a circle graph.

Sport	Percent
auto racing	4
baseball	11
basketball	12
football	43
none	12
other	18

Source: The Gallup Poll

STEP 1 For each category, let 1 centimeter equal 1%. On a piece of adding machine tape, mark the length, in centimeters, that represents each percent. Label each section.

auto racing 4%	baseball 11%	basketball 12%	football 43%	none 12%	other 18%

STEP 2 Tape the ends together to form a circle.

STEP 3 Tape one end of a piece of string to the center of the circle. Tape the other end to the point where two sections meet. Repeat with four more pieces of string.

1. Make a bar graph of the data.
2. Which graph represents the data better, a circle graph or a bar graph? Explain.

A **circle graph** is used to compare data that are parts of a whole.

Favorite Sport to Watch

The interior of the circle represents a set of data.

The pie-shaped sections show the groups.

4% Auto Racing
11% Baseball
12% Basketball
43% Football
12% None
18% Other

The percents add up to 100%.

Bar Graphs

Bar graphs, such as the triple bar graph showing votes cast in presidential elections,[†] show data classified into distinct categories with equal width bars representing frequencies.

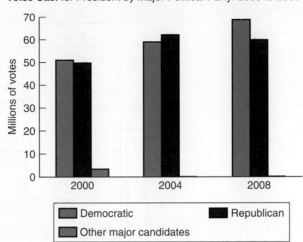

Votes Cast for President by Major Political Party: 2000 to 2008

Line Plots

Line plots, such as the plot shown below displaying the number of books read by a class of students, are often used to display numerical data that naturally falls into distinct numerical categories.

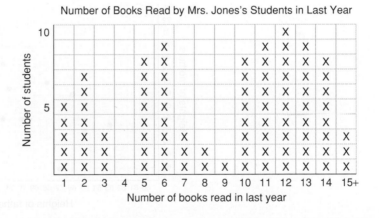

Number of Books Read by Mrs. Jones's Students in Last Year

Stem-and-Leaf Plots and Histograms

The stem-and-leaf plot and the histogram on the next page both display a graphical representation of the same set of homework scores. The histogram shows the total number of scores within the noted interval (for example, there are 4 scores in the 20 to 29 range). The stem-and-leaf plot also shows scores in the same intervals but retains the actual data (for example, in the interval 20 to 29 the four scores, with stem 2 for 20 and leaves 2, 7, 8, and 8 for the unit digits, are 22, 27, 28, and 28).

[†]*Statistical Abstract of the United States* (Washington, DC: Board of Census, 2009): Tables 385 and 386.

Homework Scores	
Stem	Leaf
1	9
2	2788
3	022447779
4	01335567889
5	00

Homework Scores

Scatter Plots

Scatter plots provide a visual means of looking for relationships between two sets of data. In this scatter plot, a middle school student collected the heights of the mothers and fathers of her classmates. By plotting a point that paired the heights of each set of parents she can look for a trend: Do taller mothers tend to be married to taller fathers?

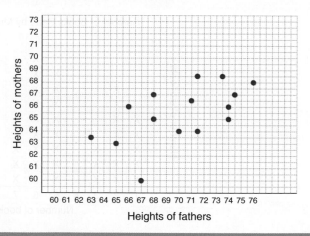

Bar and Pie Graphs

1. As a class, gather data on the eye color of the students in the class. Organize the data in the provided table.

Eye Color	Number of Students
Brown	
Blue	
Green	
Hazel	
Gray	

*a. Sketch a *single bar graph* corresponding to this data set by first marking a scale on the vertical axis, then marking the heights of the bars, and then sketching single bars of those heights centered over the eye colors. The bar edges in each data category should not touch, but each bar should be the same width.

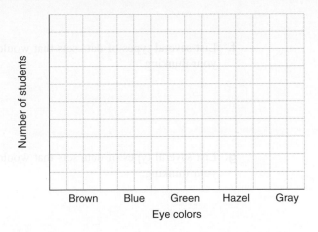

Number of students

Brown   Blue   Green   Hazel   Gray

Eye colors

*b. Sketch a *pie graph* corresponding to the class data set of eye color by using a protractor to divide the circle into a set of pie slices of the appropriate size. To determine the appropriate size you must compute the central angle of each pie slice by multiplying the percentage of students with a particular eye color by 360°. Label each slice with the correct percentage and the correct eye color.

Eye Color	Number of Students	Percentage of Students	Central Angle
Brown			
Blue			
Green			
Hazel			
Gray			
Total			

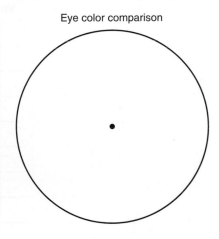

Eye color comparison

c. Which is the most common eye color? The least common?

d. In your opinion, does the bar graph or the pie graph display the eye color data the best? Explain your thinking.

e. List at least three observations each about these two data displays; what features does each display emphasize?

f. List several types of data sets that would be good to display with a bar graph. Explain your thinking.

g. List several types of data sets that would be good to display with a pie graph. Explain your thinking.

Line Plots

2. As a class, gather data on the number of individual writing tools (pencils, pens, highlighters, markers, etc.) that each student in the class has with them today. Organize the data in the provided table.

Number of Writing Tools	Number of Students	Number of Writing Tools	Number of Students
1		9	
2		10	
3		11	
4		12	
5		13	
6		14	
7		15+	
8			

*a. Complete the *line plot* corresponding to this data set by marking an X for each student with the indicated number of writing tools above the number.

Number of Writing Tools in Math Class

   b. What is the most popular number of writing tools? The least popular?

   c. List at least three observations about this data display; what feature does this display emphasize?

   d. List several types of data sets that would be good to display with a line plot. Explain your thinking.

Stem-and-Leaf Plots and Histograms

3. The following stem-and-leaf plot displays one randomly chosen temperature reading for each of the 50 U.S. states on February 14, 2010, at 12 noon PST (Pacific standard time).

Temperature	
Stem	Leaf
2	0678
3	025567777899
4	11246689
5	00555567789
6	0123344456
7	22344

   a. How many states had temperatures 50° or less?

   b. What is the highest temperature? The lowest?

   *c. Another way to organize the temperature data would be to divide the data range into several intervals and note the frequency at which the temperatures in these intervals occurs. Organize your temperatures by frequency in the provided table.

Interval	15–24	25–34	35–44	45–54	55–64	65–74
Frequency						

d. Sketch a *histogram* displaying the temperature data by sketching bars of the correct height above the intervals on the horizontal axis. Consecutive bars should touch.

Current Temperature, February 14, 12 noon

e. What is the most common range of temperatures?

f. In your opinion; which graph, stem-and-leaf plot or histogram, displays the temperature data the best? Explain your thinking.

g. List at least three observations each about these two data displays; what features does each display emphasize?

h. List several types of data sets that would be good to display with a stem-and-leaf plot. Explain your thinking.

i. List several types of data sets that would be good to display with a histogram. Explain your thinking.

Scatter Plots

4. a. As a class, gather data on the height of your mothers and fathers (in inches); give your best approximations if you don't know their exact heights. Organize the class data in the provided table.

Father's Height	Mother's Height	Father's Height	Mother's Height	Father's Height	Mother's Height	Father's Height	Mother's Height

b. Form a *scatter plot* of these data on the following grid:

Use the scatter plot you formed in part b to answer the following questions.

c. What is the height of the shortest mother? The tallest mother?

d. What are the heights of the shortest and tallest fathers?

e. What is the difference in height between the shortest and tallest mother? The shortest and tallest father?

f. For how many couples was the woman taller than the man?

5. One method for determining a relationship or trend on a scatter plot is to draw a single straight line or curve that approximates the location of the points.

    a. On the scatter plot in activity 4, draw a single straight line through the set of points that you believe best represents the trend of the plotted points. This is called a *trend line*. (One strategy: Look for a directional pattern of the points from left to right and then draw a line in a similar direction so that approximately half the points are above the line and half of the points are below the line.)

    b. Do you think there is a trend or relationship between the two sets of data? That is, from the data collected, do taller people seem to marry taller people? Justify your conjecture in a sentence or two.

*6. a. Suppose that the middle school student's scatter plot in the introduction had looked as follows. Draw a trend line that you believe best represents this data set. Write a sentence or two summarizing the relationship between heights of fathers and mothers for this data.

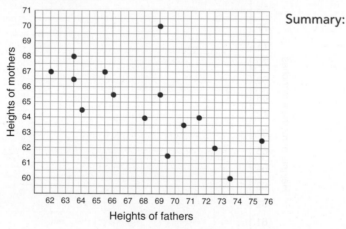

Summary:

    *b. Now suppose that the student's data had looked like the scatter plot below. Draw a trend line for these points. Would you say there is a trend or relationship between the heights of the fathers and mothers for this data? Explain your reasoning.

Summary:

c. The relationship between two sets of data can be described as positive, negative, or no relationship, depending on the slope of the trend line. Classify the relationships for the scatter plots in activities 4 and 6 on the preceding pages as positive, negative, or no relationship.

4b. _____   6a. _____   6b. _____

d. For a negative relationship, one set of data increases while the other corresponding set of data decreases; and for a positive relationship, as one set of data increases the corresponding data also increases. Describe two sets of data that will have a negative relationship and two that will have a positive relationship.

7. Form a scatter plot for each of the following sets of data and in each case sketch a trend line. Determine if there is a positive or negative relationship, or no relationship.

a. This table contains data on one aspect of child development—the time required to hop a given distance. The age of each child is rounded to the nearest half year. Use your trend line to predict the hopping time for an average 7.5-year-old and record it in the table.

Age (years)	5	5	5.5	5.5	6	6	6.5	7	7	7.5	8	8	8.5	8.5	9	9	9.5	10	11
Time (seconds) to hop 50 feet	10.8	10.8	10.5	9.0	8.4	7.5	9.0	7.1	6.7		7.5	6.3	7.5	6.8	6.7	6.3	6.3	4.8	4.4

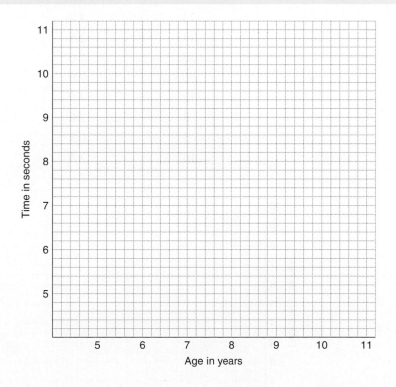

b. The following table was recorded by a forester who did a sample cutting of oak trees and recorded their diameters (in inches) and age (by counting rings). Use your trend line to predict the age of a tree that is 5.5 inches in diameter and the diameter of a tree that is 40 years old.

Age (years)	Diameter (inches)
10	2.0
8	1.0
22	5.8
30	6.0
18	4.6
13	3.5
38	7.0
38	5.0
25	6.5
8	3.0
16	4.5
28	6.0
34	6.5
29	4.5
20	5.5
4	0.8
33	8.0
23	4.7
14	2.5
35	7.0
30	7.0
12	4.9
8	2.0
5	0.8
10	3.5

Age of a tree that is 5.5

inches in diameter: _____

Diameter of a tree that

is 40 years old: _____

JUST FOR FUN

M&M'S®

Bag Number

	1	2	3	4	5	6	7	8	9	10	11	12	13	14	15	16	17	18	19	20	21	22	23	24
Red	9	12	5	10	9	11	11	11	11	14	10	14	12	8	11	11	12	5	10	18	14	13	11	9
Yellow	16	13	16	17	17	8	14	19	13	15	19	12	20	15	14	18	18	16	24	13	10	17	17	9
Blue	12	7	11	11	11	8	11	8	7	11	11	7	7	12	8	11	11	9	5	9	15	8	12	4
Orange	5	12	9	9	9	5	8	5	9	6	9	11	6	9	8	11	5	8	8	7	7	10	5	6
Green	6	5	5	6	9	10	6	7	8	2	2	4	10	7	9	2	8	5	4	5	6	4	9	16
Brown	8	6	9	5	1	12	5	5	8	8	3	10	5	5	7	5	2	12	10	5	5	3	3	11
Totals	56	55	55	58	56	54	55	55	56	56	54	58	60	56	57	58	56	55	61	57	57	55	57	55

The table above lists the color distributions in 24 bags of M&M's milk chocolate candies (net wt. 1.69 oz.).

*1. The total number of pieces of candy varies little from bag to bag, but some color combinations vary greatly. As the number of one color changes in a bag, does it affect the number of any other color? For example, if the number of brown increases in a bag, does it affect the number of any other particular color? At the right is a grid for a scatter plot comparison for the two colors, blue and brown. Each bag determines a point on the grid. For example, on the grid point (12, 8) represents 12 blue and 8 brown from bag 1 and (7, 6) represents 7 blue and 6 brown from bag 2. Plot all blue/brown pairs on the grid. Draw a trend line to see if there is any relationship. (*Note:* If the number of brown increases as the number of blue increases, there is a positive relationship. If the number of brown decreases as the number of blue increases, there is a negative relationship. Or, there may be no relationship.)

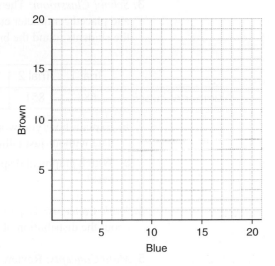

*2. Assume that you purchase the same size bag of candy as those in the table. If your bag had 14 blue pieces, about how many brown pieces would you predict using your trend line? If there where 14 brown, how many blue would you predict?

*3. Try comparing yellow and green. Make a scatter plot and draw the trend line.

4. Pick other pairs of colors to compare.

Exercises and Activities 7.1

1. *School Classroom:* Students studying a scatter plot comparing *Monthly Income* to *Frequency of Dining Out* are having trouble answering interpretive questions that don't correspond to plotted points on the scatter plot. For example, they don't know how to answer, "How often do families with a monthly income of $4000 eat out?" The students say their trend line does not go through a point for $4000. How can you help these students?

2. *School Classroom:* Read through the *Mini-Lab* on the **Elementary School Text** page at the beginning of this section.

   a. Explain what prerequisite knowledge the students would have to know before using this technique to make this circle graph.

   b. Compare the construction of the pictured circle graph with the construction of the circle (pie) graph you made at the beginning of this activity set. What additional skills did you need to construct the latter?

3. *School Classroom:* The students in a middle school class have built identical paper bridges and placed centimeter cubes on the bridges to determine bridge load strengths. In nine trials the students found the bridges broke under the following weights (in cm cubes):

	Trial 1	Trial 2	Trial 3	Trial 4	Trial 5	Trial 6	Trial 7	Trial 8	Trial 9
Number of cubes	688	851	787	832	1000	187	120	481	730

   a. Explain how you would help the students find effective graphical ways to display their data without just telling them which graphical displays to use.

   b. Which graphical display type do you think best displays the data? Why do you think it is best?

4. *Math Concepts:* Explore scatter plots and trend lines further by answering the questions about the distribution of M&M's in the **Just for Fun Activity** in this section.

5. *Math Concepts:* Review current periodicals (newspapers or magazines) and find at least two different types of data graphs explored in the activities in this activity set. For each graph, write three observations about the data that you can read from the graph. Include a reference for each periodical with a copy of the page on which you found the data display.

6. *Math Concepts:* List at least two similarities and at least two differences between each pair of graph types:

   a. Bar graph and stem-and-leaf graph

   b. Bar graph and histogram

   c. Stem-and-leaf graph and histogram

7. *NCTM Standards:* Read the **Data Analysis and Probability Standards** in the back pages of this book for each grade level: Pre-K–2, 3–5, and 6–8. For each grade level, list at least one *Expectation* that describes the types of graphs that should be studied at that level.

---

www.mhhe.com/bbn

bennett-burton-nelson website

Virtual Manipulatives   Grid and Dot Paper   Links and Readings
Interactive Chapter Applets   Color Transparencies   Geometer Sketchpad Modules
Puzzlers   Extended Bibliography

ANALYZING DATA, SAMPLING, AND SIMULATION

PURPOSE

To analyze real data and apply the idea of randomness to sampling and simulations.

MATERIALS

Green and Red Tiles from the Manipulative Kit, the Table of Random Digits from Material Card 21, and containers such as boxes and bags for selecting tile samples.

INTRODUCTION

One of the main objectives of statistics is to make decisions or predictions about a population (students in schools, voters in a country, light bulbs, and fish, etc.) based on information taken from a sample of the population. A poorly chosen sample will not truly reflect the nature of the population. An important requirement is that the sample be randomly chosen. *Randomly chosen* means that every member of the population is equally likely to be selected.

Once a sample has been chosen, it is useful to determine a single number that describes the data. An *average* is one type of value or measure that represents a whole set of data. There are three averages commonly used to describe a set of numbers: mean, median, and mode. Let's use these averages to describe the following set of numbers:

2, 3, 4, 6, 8, 11, 12, 12, 12, 18

The **mean,** which is commonly referred to as the average, is the sum of the values divided by the total number of values. The sum of the 10 numbers is 88, so the mean is 8.8 (88 ÷ 10). The **median** is the middle value when all the values are arranged in order. The median for these values is 9.5, which is halfway between the two middle values 8 and 11. The **mode** is the value (or values) that occurs most frequently—in this case, the mode is 12.

Simulations are processes that help answer questions about a real problem; they are experiments that closely resemble the real situation. These experiments usually involve random samples.

In this activity set, we will analyze time intervals between eruptions and duration of eruptions for Old Faithful geyser using stem-and-leaf plots, line plots, and scatter plots; experimentally select random samples; and use the idea of randomness to simulate a real situation.

---

1. The park rangers in Yellowstone National Park make predictions on the times of eruptions for Old Faithful geyser to inform visitors at the park. The data in the table shows the length of time in minutes between 16 consecutive eruptions.

57	87	73	94	52	88	72	88	62	87	57	94	51	98	59

   *a. Examine the data and list three observations about the length of time between eruptions.

Stem	Leaf

   b. Complete the stem-and-leaf plot at the left and a line plot on page 217 for this data.

8-8 Using Sampling to Predict

▷ GET READY for the Lesson

CELL PHONES The manager of a local cell phone company wants to conduct a survey to determine what kind of musical ring tones people typically use.

What Kind of Musical Ring Tone Do You Use?
Classical
Rock
Rap/Hip-Hop
Dance
Other

1. Suppose she decides to survey the listeners of a rock radio station. Do you think the results would represent the entire population? Explain.

2. Suppose she decides to survey a group of people standing in line for a symphony. Do you think the results would represent the entire population? Explain.

3. Suppose she decides to mail a survey to every 100th household in the area. Do you think the results would represent the entire population? Explain.

The manager of the cell phone company cannot survey everyone. A smaller group called a **sample** is chosen. A sample should be representative of the population.

Population	Sample
United States citizens	registered voters
California residents	homeowners
Six Flags Marine World visitors	teenagers

For valid results, a sample must be chosen very carefully. An **unbiased sample** is selected so that it is representative of the entire population. A simple random sample is the most common type of unbiased sample.

Concept Summary

Unbiased Samples

Type	Description	Example
Simple Random Sample	Each item or person in the population is as likely to be chosen as any other.	Each student's name is written on a piece of paper. The names are placed in a bowl, and names are picked without looking.

Line plot

c. What information is revealed by each of the plots in part b and what information about the data is not revealed?

d. Compute the mean, median, and mode(s) for the data.

e. Compute the mean, median, and mode(s) for eight shortest time intervals between eruptions and then for the seven longest time intervals. Explain why these averages are more important in analyzing the data than those in part d.

f. Assume that you know the time interval between two eruptions. Using the information above, describe a possible method for estimating the length of the next time interval between eruptions.

*2. The following data is for 15 consecutive eruptions of Old Faithful. For each duration of an eruption in minutes, there is an interval in minutes before the next eruption.[†]

Duration	4.4	2.0	4.7	1.9	4.2	1.6	1.6	2.1	4.5	1.7	4.5	1.9	4.6	1.7	4.6
Interval to next eruption	81	60	91	51	85	55	98	49	85	65	102	56	86	62	91

a. Form a scatter plot for the given data and sketch a trend line.

Duration of eruption in minutes

[†]For lesson plans about the eruptions of Old Faithful, see Linda C. Foreman and Albert B. Bennett, Jr., *Math Alive*, pp. 399–417.

b. The following starting times and durations are for several randomly selected eruptions from a 2-day period. Use your scatter plot and trend line to make the following predictions.

Starting Time	Duration	Predicted Interval Before Next Eruption	Predicted Time of Next Eruption
11:22 a.m.	1 min 50 sec	_____	_____
8:30 a.m.	4 min 26 sec	_____	_____
12:40 p.m.	3 min 46 sec	_____	_____

3. **Sampling and Predictions:** The objective of sampling is to make predictions about a large population. Samples are usually relatively small. For example, some national television ratings are based on a sample of only 1100 people. The following activity is designed to show how a sample can represent the given population.

Have a classmate put any one of the following three populations of tiles in a container, without your knowing the numbers of red and green tiles. *Don't look at the contents of the container until you have completed all parts of this activity.*

Population 1	Population 2	Population 3
25 red tiles	20 red tiles	10 red tiles
5 green tiles	10 green tiles	20 green tiles

Draw a tile and check off its color in the following table. Return the tile to the container and repeat this activity. After every five draws, make a prediction as to which population you think is in the container. Continue the experiment until you have selected 25 times.

a. Compute the percentage of red tiles in each of the following groups.

First 5   First 10   First 15   First 20   All 25

b. As the size of the sample increases, the likelihood that it represents the population becomes greater. Based on your sample of 25 tiles, predict which of the three given populations you have sampled. Would you have selected the same population if your sample size had been only the first 5 tiles? The first 10? Now look at the contents of the container to check your prediction.

4. Stratified Sampling: The following are the housing prices for 18 households. Write the information for each household on a separate piece of paper, and place the pieces of paper in a container.

Lake Home	Lake Home	Lake Home	Suburban Home	Suburban Home	Suburban Home	Suburban Home	Suburban Home	Suburban Home
$400,000	$250,000	$185,000	$100,000	$120,000	$105,000	$175,000	$159,000	$135,000
City Home	City Home	City Home	City Home	City Home	City Home	City Home	City Home	City Home
$179,000	$226,000	$175,000	$193,000	$221,000	$300,000	$325,000	$105,000	$168,000

a. The average of all 18 prices is $195,611.11. Select 6 pieces of paper at random from the container. Compute the average (mean) price of your sample and record it here. By how much does it differ from the average of all 18 housing prices?

*b. There are many different samples of 6 housing prices that you could have selected. Suppose, for example, your sample contained the 6 greatest housing prices. What is the average of these 6 housing prices? What is the average of the 6 smallest housing prices?

c. The average of the 6 greatest housing prices and the average of the 6 smallest housing prices differ significantly from the average of all 18 housing prices. By using a technique called *stratified sampling,* you can avoid getting an unrepresentative sample. Separate the total population of 18 housing prices by living area into 3 different containers. Notice that the lake property, suburban, and city prices represent $\frac{1}{6}$, $\frac{1}{3}$, and $\frac{1}{2}$ of the population, respectively. To obtain a proportional **stratified sample** of 6 housing prices, select 1 lake property housing price ($\frac{1}{6}$ of 6), 2 suburban housing prices ($\frac{1}{3}$ of 6), and 3 city housing prices ($\frac{1}{2}$ of 6) from their individual containers. Compute the average of these 6 housing prices. By how much does it differ from the average of all 18 housing prices?

*d. If the stratified sampling procedure in part c is used, what is the greatest possible average that can be obtained for 6 housing prices?

What is the smallest possible average that can be obtained?

Compare these averages to those in part b and discuss the advantages of stratified sampling.

5. **Simulation:** People with type O blood are called universal donors because their blood can be used in transfusions to people with different blood types. About 45 percent of the population has type O blood.

   a. If blood donors arrive at the blood bank with random blood types, how many donors, on the average, would it take to obtain five donors with type O blood? Make and record a conjecture. Explain your estimate.

   b. There are 100 pairs of digits from 00 to 99 and the pairs (00, 01, 02, . . . , 44) represent 45 percent of them. These 45 pairs of digits will represent the donors with type O blood. Without looking, put your pencil point on the table of random digits on Material Card 21. Beginning with the digit closest to the pencil point, start listing consecutive pairs of digits from the table of random digits until your list includes exactly five pairs from the list (00, 01, 02, . . . , 44). Use the *Experiment 1* row in the table in part c to record this data. If each pair of digits represents a donor, then according to this trial how many donors would have to arrive at the blood bank to obtain five donors with type O blood?

   c. The procedure you followed in part b is a *simulation*—a way to answer a problem by running an experiment which resembles the problem.[†] Assuming that blood donors who go to the blood bank have random blood types and that 45 percent have type O, your experiment simulated the number of donors needed to obtain five donors with type O blood. Use the *Experiment 2* through *Experiment 10* rows in the table to record the results of running the experiment another nine times.

	Tallies		Number of Donors Needed to Obtain 5 of Blood Type O
Experiment	Digit Pairs from 00 to 44	Digit Pairs from 45 to 99	
1			
2			
3			
4			
5			
6			
7			
8			
9			
10			
		Experimental Mean	

[†]An excellent source for simulation activities is M. Gnanadesikan, R. Scheaffer, and J. Swift, *The Art and Techniques of Simulation*.

d. The mean of the numbers of donors in the 10 experiments (third column) is the *average number* for these experiments. Based on your experimental results, what is the average number of donors the blood bank would have to receive to obtain five donors with type O blood?

JUST FOR FUN

SIMULATED RACING GAME (2 players)

In this race, one player flips a coin and the other rolls a die. At the start of play, each player rolls the die, and the high roller gets to use the die in the game. The race track is 12 steps long, and the racers move simultaneously. That is, the coin is flipped and the die is rolled at the same time. The coin tosser can move 1 step for heads and 2 steps for tails. The die roller can move the number of steps that comes up on the die. The race continues until one person lands on the last step. However, *the winner must land on the last step by exact count.* It is possible for this race to end in a tie. Find a person to race against and complete several races using a die and a coin.

1. Does this appear to be a fair race? That is, do the wins seem to be evenly distributed between the die roller and the coin tosser? You may wish to have a larger sample of completed races on which to base your conclusions. Use the table of random digits on Material Card 21 to simulate die rolling and coin flipping as follows:

- *Coin Flipping:* Select an arbitrary digit in the table of random digits. If the digit is even, call the outcome heads. If the digit is odd, call the outcome tails. For the next flip, move to the next digit in the table and do the same. Repeat this process until the game is complete.
- *Die Rolling:* Select an arbitrary digit in the table of random digits. If the closest digit is a 1, 2, 3, 4, 5, or 6, let it represent your first roll of the die. If that digit is a 0, 7, 8, or 9, move to the next digit in the table that is not a 0, 7, 8, or 9 and let that digit represent your die roll. For the succeeding roll, move to the next digit in the table and do the same. Repeat this process until the game is complete.

2. What happens when the length of the race (number of steps) is shortened? For example, will a two-step race be won more frequently by one player than the other? Try races of different lengths. List some conjectures or conclusions about the fairness of the race and its length.

Race Track												
Start	1	2	3	4	5	6	7	8	9	10	11	Finish
Coin flipping												
Die rolling												

Exercises and Activities **7.2**

1. *School Classroom:* A group of 10 students was asked to count the change in their pockets (which was 25, 25, 43, 50, 50, 50, 50, 50, 75, and 100 cents) and to compute the mean, median, and mode. The students thought a mode and a median of 50 cents made sense but a mean of 51.8 cents did not seem reasonable because that was not an amount of money anyone could have. How would you explain the meaning of mean in this case to the students?

2. *School Classroom:* Design a color tile sampling activity (for example, see activity 3 in this activity set) that you believe is appropriate for an elementary school student and write a few questions that you can ask about your activity. Try this activity on an elementary school age child of your choice. Describe your activity, record your questions, and record the student's responses.

3. *School Classroom:* Read the *Get Ready for the Lesson* section and other information on the **Elementary School Text** page at the beginning of this section. As a classroom teacher:

   a. List three questions you could ask your students *before* they begin to work that would raise their interest in the activity and also encourage them to suggest their own ideas for sampling methods.

   b. List three questions you could ask your students to promote discussion and understanding of the sampling process *after* they have completed the activity.

4. *Math Concepts:* With a classmate, play the *Racing Game* described in the **Just for Fun Activity** in this section. Answer the two questions after you and your partner have played the game.

5. *Math Concepts:* The following table displays housing prices for three types of houses in Monmouth, Oregon.

City Home	City Home	City Home	City Home	City Home	City Home
$180,000	$220,000	$150,000	$135,000	$147,000	$165,000
Luxury Home	Luxury Home	Country Home	Country Home	Country Home	Country Home
$375,000	$410,000	$200,000	$190,000	$220,000	$250,000

   a. Pick a stratified sample of six houses from the data set and explain your procedure.

   b. What is the difference between the median of the entire data set and the median of your stratified sample? Are either the median of the entire set or the median of a stratified sample a good indicator of housing prices in Monmouth?

   c. What is the largest possible difference between the median of the entire data set and the median of any stratified sample of six houses?

6. *Math Concepts:* For each of the following, design a data set with 10–15 entries satisfying the stated criteria. In each case, give a real-world example of where such a data set might occur. Explain your reasoning.

   a. The mean is a better measure of central tendency than the median or the mode.

   b. The median is a better measure of central tendency than the mean or the mode.

   c. The mode is a better measure of central tendency than the mean or the median.

7. *NCTM Standards:* Read the *Expectations* in the **Grades 6–8 Data Analysis and Probability Standards** in the back pages of this book under the *Standard* "Develop and evaluate inference . . .". For each *Expectation*, give an example of an activity from this activity set that addresses the *Expectation*.

---

www.mhhe.com/bbn

bennett-burton-nelson website

Virtual Manipulatives   Grid and Dot Paper   Links and Readings
Interactive Chapter Applets   Color Transparencies   Geometer Sketchpad Modules
Puzzlers   Extended Bibliography

Activity Set **7.3**
STATISTICAL DISTRIBUTIONS: OBSERVATIONS AND APPLICATIONS

PURPOSE

To construct and apply frequency distributions.

MATERIALS

The Table of Random Digits on Material Card 21.

Alexander Hamilton

FEDERALIST PAPERS

James Madison

INTRODUCTION

Once measurements from a population sample have been collected, they are arranged by grouping similar measurements together in a table, chart, or graph. A *frequency distribution* is a tabulation of values by categories or intervals. An interesting illustration of the use of frequency distributions was in the resolution of the controversy over authorship of the *Federalist Papers.*[†] This is a collection of 85 political papers written in the eighteenth century by Alexander Hamilton, John Jay, and James Madison. There is general agreement on the authorship of all but 12 of these papers. In order to determine who should be given credit for the 12 disputed papers, frequency distributions were compiled for certain filler words such as *by, to, of,* and *on.*

Forty-eight of Hamilton's papers and 50 of Madison's papers were analyzed to determine how many times each author used the word "by" in every 1000 words of text. You will notice from figure a on the next page, for example, that in approximately 16 papers Hamilton used the word "by" seven or eight times in every 1000 words whereas in roughly the same number of papers Madison used "by" 11 or 12 times in every 1000 words. In some papers Madison used "by" more than 13 times for every 1000 words while Hamilton never used "by" more than 12 times per 1000 words.

A comparison of the frequency distributions for usage of "by" indicates that Madison used that word more frequently than Hamilton did. Notice that Madison's distribution looks like the distribution of the word "by" in the distribution of the disputed papers in the bottom of figure a. An analysis for the use of the word "to" is shown in figure b. These and similar distributions for other filler words support the contention that Madison was the author of the disputed papers.

[†]F. Mosteller et al., *Statistics: A Guide to the Unknown,* pp. 164–175.

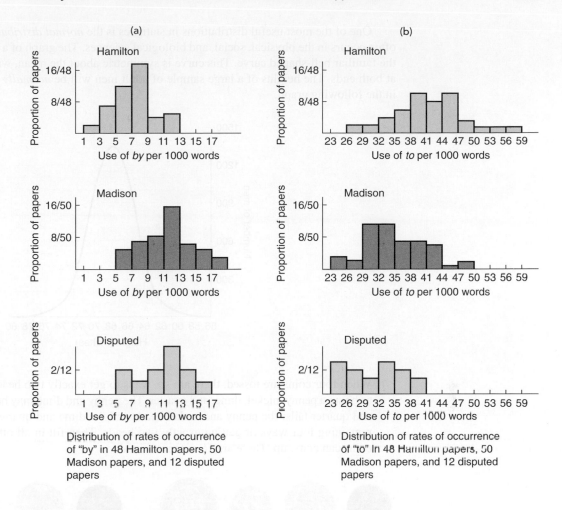

Distribution of rates of occurrence of "by" in 48 Hamilton papers, 50 Madison papers, and 12 disputed papers

Distribution of rates of occurrence of "to" In 48 Hamilton papers, 50 Madison papers, and 12 disputed papers

Several types of frequency distributions commonly occur. If each category or interval of the distribution has approximately the same number of values, the distribution is called a **uniform distribution.** For example, the following histogram shows the frequency distribution for the outcomes of rolling a die 3000 times. The frequency of each outcome varies between approximately 480 and 520.

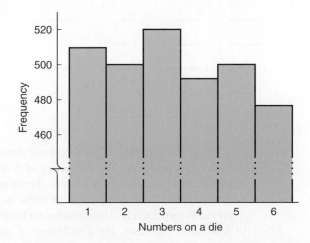

One of the most useful distributions in statistics is the *normal distribution.* This distribution often occurs in the physical, social, and biological sciences. The graph of a normal distribution is the familiar bell-shaped curve. This curve is symmetric about the mean, with a gradual decrease at both ends. The heights of a large sample of adult men will be *normally distributed,* as shown in the following graph.

1. When four coins are tossed, there are six ways to get exactly two heads. Think of the coins as being a penny, nickel, dime, and quarter. The penny and dime may be heads and the nickel and quarter tails; the penny and nickel heads and the dime and quarter tails, etc. Fill in the remaining four ways of getting exactly two heads. Then fill in all other possible ways the coins can come up. There are 16 outcomes in all.

The graph at the top of the next page shows the number of different outcomes for tosses of four coins at a time. The frequency of 6 above 2 heads corresponds to the six different outcomes that have exactly two heads. There are frequencies of 1 above 0 heads and 4 heads, because each of these two events can occur in only one way, if the tosses result in all tails or in all heads respectively. This distribution looks like a normal curve. As the number of tosses of four coins increases, the distribution of outcomes theoretically gets closer to a normal curve.

Outcomes (number of heads when tossing 4 coins)

a. Use the table of random digits on Material Card 21 to simulate the tossing of six coins. Pick an arbitrary starting point in the table and look at the first six digits. Count each even digit as heads and each odd digit as tails and record the number of heads on line one of the table below. Then look at the next six random digits and record the number of heads on line two. Continue to use groups of six random digits to simulate 64 tosses of six coins, and record the number of heads for each toss in the table below.

1	2	3	4	5	6	7	8	9	10	11	12	13
14	15	16	17	18	19	20	21	22	23	24	25	26
27	28	29	30	31	32	33	34	35	36	37	38	39
40	41	42	43	44	45	46	47	48	49	50	51	52
53	54	55	56	57	58	59	60	61	62	63	64	

b. Plot the frequency of each outcome. For example, the number of times you got exactly two heads should be plotted above 2H on the graph. Theoretically, about 78 percent (50 possibilities out of 64) of the outcomes should be 2, 3, or 4 heads. What percent of the outcomes in your experiment are 2, 3, or 4 heads?

Outcomes (number of heads when tossing 6 coins)

*c. Suppose that an outcome of heads represents the birth of a girl and an outcome of tails represents that of a boy. In addition, suppose that each of the coin tosses in part a represents a family that is planning to have six children. Explain how you would use your experimental data to predict approximately what percent of those families will have *at least* three girls.

2. When measurements such as weight, range of eyesight, or IQ are compiled for a large number of people, they are usually normally distributed. The following list contains the pulse rates of 60 students.

Pulse rates (beats per minute)

Pulse rate	53	56	57	58	61	62	63	64	65	66	67	68	69	70	71	72	73	74	75	76	77	78	79	80	81	82	84	86	89	91	92
Frequency	1	2	1	1	1	3	1	1	3	1	2	2	2	6	1	4	3	4	2	3	1	1	2	3	1	1	2	2	1	1	1

a. Organize the pulse rates by frequency in the provided table.

Pulse rate	53–56	57–60	61–64	65–68	69–72	73–76	77–80	81–84	85–88	89–92
Frequency										

b. Use the data in your frequency table to complete the histogram.

c. Do the pulse rates appear to you to be fairly close to a normal distribution?

*d. *Standard deviation* (σ) is a measure of the variation and spread of a distribution. One property of a normal distribution is that 68 percent of the measurements are within 1 standard deviation on either side of the mean, 95 percent are within 2 standard deviations on either side of the mean, and 99.7 percent of the measurements are within 3 standard deviations on either side of the mean, as illustrated below. The set of pulse rates has a mean of 72 and a standard deviation of 8.7. Determine the percentage of pulse rates within ±1 standard deviation, ±2 standard deviations and ±3 standard deviations of the mean, and record your results below. Does the distribution of pulse rates approximately satisfy the 68–95–99.7 property?

Normal Curve   Pulse Rates

±1 standard deviation _____%

±2 standard deviations _____%

±3 standard deviations _____%

e. Even smaller collections of measurements may tend to be normally distributed. Draw a bar graph of your classmates' pulse rates taken over a 10-second interval. One property of approximately normal curves is that the mean, median, and mode are approximately equal. Determine the mean, median, and mode for the pulse rates of your class. Are they approximately equal?

Mean _____   Median _____   Mode _____

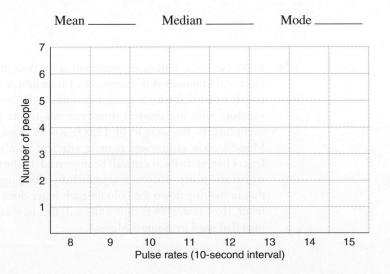

3. Some people are not aware of the uneven distribution of letters which occurs in words. One such person may have been Christofer Sholes, the inventor of the typewriter. He gave the left hand 56 percent of all the strokes, and he gave the two most agile fingers on the right hand two of the least often used letters of the alphabet, *j* and *k*. This table shows the frequencies, in terms of percentages of occurrence, of letters in large random samples.

E	12.3%	S	6.6%	U	3.1%	B	1.6%	J	0.1%
T	9.6%	R	6.0%	P	2.3%	G	1.6%	Z	0.1%
A	8.1%	H	5.1%	F	2.3%	V	0.9%		
O	7.9%	L	4.0%	M	2.2%	K	0.5%		
N	7.2%	D	3.7%	W	2.0%	Q	0.2%		
I	7.2%	C	3.2%	Y	1.9%	X	0.2%		

*a. There are 350 letters in the preceding paragraph. Count the number of times that *e, s, c, w,* and *k* occur and compute their percentages. Compare your answer with the percentages that have been computed for large random samples.

	Tally	Frequency	Percent
e			
s			
c			
w			
k			

b. The most frequently occurring letter in the English language is *e*. In 1939, a 267 page novel entitled *Gadsby* was released by the Wetzel Publishing Company. The novel was known not for its literary merit, but rather for one distinctive feature: Not one of its 50,000 words contained the letter *e*. Compose a sentence of at least ten words that does not use the letter *e*. (It is interesting for classmates to share their sentences.)

*c. In Morse code, letters are represented by dots and dashes so that they can be sent by electrical impulses. A dot consumes 1 time unit, a dash consumes 3 time units, and 1 time unit is needed for each space between symbols. In 1938, Samuel Morse assigned the symbols with the shortest time intervals to the letters that occurred most frequently, according to his sample of 12,000 words from a Philadelphia newspaper. Although Morse's code assignment is more efficient than it would have been if he had assigned letters haphazardly, it can still be improved. In the table at the top of the next page, devise a new and more efficient assignment by changing and reassigning the code symbols so that in moving down the column each letter does not use more time units than the next letter. How many fewer time units will this new assignment require for these nine letters than that used by Samuel Morse?

Code Symbol	Number of Time Units	Letters	Reassigned Code Symbol
•	1	e	_____
—	3	t	_____
•—	5	a	_____
— — —	11	o	_____
—•	5	n	_____
••	3	i	_____
•••	5	s	_____
•—•	7	r	_____
••••	7	h	_____

4. It is surprising to learn that the leading digits of any numerous set of large numbers *do not occur with the same frequency*—that is, are not evenly distributed.[†] Find a partner to help you tally the first digit in the list of metropolitan populations below and play the following game. For each number in the table beginning with a 1, 2, 3, or 4, you win; for each number beginning with a 5, 6, 7, 8, or 9, your partner wins. Record your tallies in the table at the end of the next page and determine the total for each digit to see who wins. Then answer the questions on page 233.

Populations of 166 Selected Metropolitan Areas

Philadelphia to Atlantic City

Cecil	99,926
Chester	491,489
New Castle	529,641
Bucks	621,643
Gloucester	287,860
Burlington	445,475
Montgomery	950,680
Atlantic	270,681
Cape May	95,838
Cumberland	312,696
Camden	517,234
Salem	66,141
Delaware	553,619
Philadelphia	1,447,395

Phoenix-Mesa

Maricopa	3,954,598
Pinal	327,301

Pittsburgh

Butler	182,902
Westmoreland	361,589
Washington	206,407
Fayette	143,925
Beaver	172,476
Allegheny	1,215,103

Portland-Salem

Clark	432,002
Washington	529,216
Yamhill	98,168
Polk	77,074
Clackamas	380,576
Columbia	49,408
Marion	314,606
Multnomah	714,567

Providence-Warwick-Pawtucket

Washington	126,264
Bristol	49,838
Kent	168,058
Providence	626,150

Raleigh-Durham-Chapel Hill

Wake	866,410
Johnston	163,428
Franklin	58,927
Orange	126,532
Chatham	63,077
Durham	262,715

Richmond-Petersburg

Powhatan	28,006
Hanover	99,716
Goochland	20,956
New Kent	17,825
Chesterfield	303,469
Henrico	292,599
Charles City	7,212
Dinwiddie	26,082
Prince George	36,089
Colonial Heights	17,768
Hopewell	23,142
Richmond	202,002
Petersburg	32,916

Rochester

Wayne	91,564
Orleans	42,135
Livingston	63,154
Ontario	104,475
Genesee	57,821
Monroe	732,762

(continues)

[†]An explanation of this phenomenon can be found in W. Weaver, *Lady Luck*, pp. 270–277.

(continued)

Sacramento-Yolo

Placer	341,945
El Dorado	176,075
Sacramento	1,394,154
Yolo	197,658

St. Louis

St. Charles	349,407
Lincoln	52,775
Warren	31,214
Monroe	32,804
Jefferson	217,679
Franklin	100,898
Clinton	36,711
Jersey	22,622
Madison	268,078
St. Louis County	991,830
St. Clair	262,291
St. Louis	354,361

Salt Lake City-Ogden

Davis	295,332
Salt Lake County	1,022,651
Weber	227,487

San Antonio

Comal	109,635
Wilson	40,398
Guadalupe	117,172
Bexar	1,622,899

San Diego

San Diego	3,001,072

San Francisco Bay Area

Contra Costa	1,029,703
Sonoma	466,741
Solano	407,234
Santa Clara	1,764,499
San Mateo	712,690
Napa	133,433
Alameda	1,474,368
Santa Cruz	253,137
San Francisco	808,976
Marin	248,794

Sarasota-Bradenton

Manatee	315,766
Sarasota	372,057

Scranton-Wilkes-Barre-Hazleton

Wyoming	27,759
Columbia	65,004
Luzerne	311,983
Lackawanna	209,408

Seattle Area

Snohomish	683,655
Thurston	245,181
Kitsap	239,769
Island	81,424
Pierce	785,639
King	1,875,519

Springfield, Massachusetts

Hampshire	154,983
Hampden	460,840
Worcester	783,806
Berkshire	129,395

Syracuse

Madison	69,441
Oswego	121,395
Cayuga	79,823
Onondaga	452,633

Tampa-St. Petersburg-Clearwater

Hernando	171,689
Pasco	471,028
Hillsborough	1,180,784
Pinellas	910,260

Toledo

Fulton	42,485
Wood	125,340
Lucas	440,456

Tucson

Pima	1,012,018

Tulsa

Rogers	84,300
Wagoner	68,960
Creek	69,822
Tulsa	591,982
Osage	45,489

Washington-Baltimore

Loudoun	289,995
Spotsylvania	120,031
Stafford	121,736
Calvert	88,698
Manassas Park City	11,319
King George	23,170
Manassas City	35,205
Howard	274,995
Frederick	225,721
Carroll	169,353
Prince William	364,734
Berkeley	102,044
Culpeper	46,203
Harford	240,351
Queen Anne's	47,958
Charles	140,764
Warren	36,663
Jefferson	51,615
Fredericksburg	22,818
Fairfax County	1,015,302
Anne Arundel	512,790
Fauquier	66,839
Montgomery	950,680
Prince George's	834,560
Alexandria	143,885
Clarke	14,458
Falls Church	11,169
Washington County	53,038
Baltimore County	785,618
Fairfax	24,665
Arlington	209,969
Baltimore	636,919
Washington	53,038

West Palm Beach-Boca Raton

Palm Beach	1,265,293

Wichita

Butler	63,562
Sedgwick	482,863
Harvey	33,675

Youngstown-Warren

Columbiana	107,873
Trumbull	211,317
Mahoning	237,978

Leading Digit of Number	1	2	3	4	5	6	7	8	9
Tallies									
Totals									

a. Would you have won the game if you had used the digits 1, 2, and 3 only? Justify your answer by showing the percentage of numbers with these leading digits.

b. Use the results from the table to make one or more conjectures regarding the occurrence of the leading digits of large numbers from sets of data.

c. The populations in the list of metropolitan areas are four-, five-, six-, and seven-digit numbers. The least number is 7,212 and the greatest number is 3,954,598. In the table below, all numbers from 7,212 to 3,954,598 have been separated into six intervals. There are 2,788 numbers (9,999 − 7,212 + 1) in the first interval and all have leading digits of 7, 8, or 9. The second interval has numbers with leading digits 1, 2, 3, 4. Determine the number of numbers in each of the remaining intervals and whether you win or lose the game with leading digits 1, 2, 3, and 4.

Interval	Number of Numbers	Win or Lose
7,212 to 9,999	2,788	LOSE
10,000 to 49,999	_____	_____
50,000 to 99,999	_____	_____
100,000 to 499,999	_____	_____
500,000 to 999,999	_____	_____
1,000,000 to 3,954,598	_____	_____

*d. Considering *all* numbers from 7,212 to 3,954,598, how do the number of numbers with leading digits 1, 2, 3, and 4 compare to those with leading digits of 5, 6, 7, 8, and 9? Describe how this result can explain why it is likely that the person choosing digits 1, 2, 3, and 4 will win using the list of populations of metropolitan areas or any numerous set of large numbers.

JUST FOR FUN

CRYPTANALYSIS

Cryptanalysis is the analysis and deciphering of crypto-grams, codes, and other secret writings. Successful crypt-analysis has been important in gaining many military victories and in preventing crime and espionage. One of the earliest cryptographic systems known was used by Julius Caesar and is called the Caesar cipher. Enciphering a message using this system involves replacing each letter of the alpha-bet by the letter that is 3 letters beyond it: A is replaced by D, B by E, C by F, etc. Use the Caesar cipher to decipher the statement on this scroll.

It is not known why Caesar selected 3 as the number of places to shift the alphabet. Any whole number greater than 1 can be used.

One way of improv-ing cryptograms is to eliminate word lengths. The message below is written in groups of 5 letters. It was enciphered by shifting each letter of the alphabet the same number of letters to the right.

L FDPH L VDZ
L FRQTXHUHG

OITQT	MWAPW	EMLUM	VWNAK	QMVKM	BPIBE	MQOPQ	VOIVL	UMIAC
ZQVOI	ZMEWZ	BPEPQ	TMVME	BWVKW	VDQVK	MLITI	ZOMXZ	WXWZB
QWVWN	BPMUB	PIBEM	QOPQV	OIVLU	MIACZ	QVOIZ	MBPMW	VTGQV
DMABQ	OIBQW	VABPI	BIZME	WZBPE	PQTMK	PIZTM	AAQVO	MZ

One method of determining the amount of shift is to make a frequency distribution of the letters in the message and compare it to a frequency distribution of letters in com-mon use. The following bar graph shows the percentage of occurrence of each letter (rounded to the nearest whole num-ber) in a large sample of unencrypted words. There are some important patterns. Among the high-frequency letters, we see that three (A, E, and I) are 4 letters apart; two (N and O) are next to each other; and three (R, S, and T) are side by side. Among the low-frequency letters, two (J and K) occur as a pair, and six (U, V, W, X, Y, and Z) are side by side.

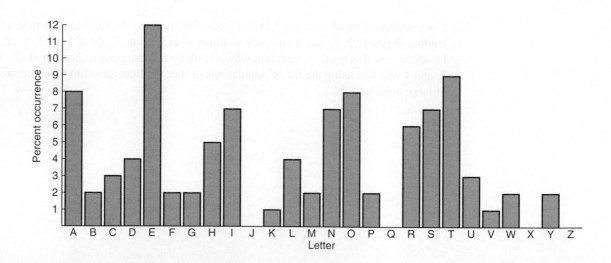

Make a frequency distribution of letters in the coded message. Predict the amount of shift by comparing this dis-tribution with the one above, and by looking for patterns of high- and low-frequency letters. Try your prediction by deci-phering a few words. When you have found the correct amount of shift, decipher the message.[†]

[†]For further techniques in cryptography, see A. Sinkov, *Elementary Cryptanalysis*.

DISTRIBUTIONS APPLET

If the blue chip shown at the bottom of this grid moves randomly up the grid to the right (the square labeled R) or left (the square labeled L), in which lettered square will it most likely end? This applet will help you find patterns in different size grids in order to help you predict the final square on which a tile will most likely land. It is interesting that such random movements, when applied many times, produce dependable patterns.

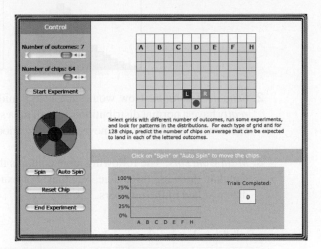

Distributions Applet, Chapter 7
www.mhhe.com/bbn

Exercises and Activities **7.3**

1. *School Classroom:* A middle school student is confused by the term "skewed to the right" when the data are "piled up" on the left and "skewed to the left" when the data are "piled up" on the right. Explain how you would help the student make sense out of these terms.

Skewed left   Skewed right

2. *School Classroom:* How would you help a middle school student who states you can never *really* have a normal distribution since all data sets will be finite and the frequency histogram will always be bumpy and never perfectly smooth like a normal distribution?

3. *Math Concepts:* The following table contains the results of using a table of random digits to simulate throwing three dice, 30 times. For example, in roll #1, the simulated throw of three dice resulted in the numbers 3, 3, and 2.

Roll #	1	2	3	4	5	6	7	8	9	10
Dice	332	356	642	332	234	225	353	311	365	411

Roll #	11	12	13	14	15	16	17	18	19	20
Dice	211	243	423	343	422	416	234	332	414	234

Roll #	21	22	23	24	25	26	27	28	29	30
Dice	324	221	352	212	426	551	214	153	415	141

   a. Use the table to determine the sum of each roll of the dice. Tabulate the sum data and sketch a bar graph showing the sum data. Clearly label the graph. Does the sum data appear to be approximately normally distributed? Explain the reasons for your conclusion.

   b. The set of dice sums has a mean of 8.8 and a standard deviation of 2.5. Determine the percentage of sums ±1 standard deviation from the mean, ±2 standard deviations from the mean, and ±3 standard deviations from the mean.

   c. Based on your calculations in part b, is the data set approximately normally distributed? Explain your reasons for your conclusion.

4. *Math Concepts:* Read the **Just for Fun Activity** in this section and:

   a. Use the Caesar cipher to decipher the message on the pictured scroll.

   b. Follow the instructions and use a frequency distribution to help decipher the secret message given on the top of page 234.

L FDPH L VDZ
L FRQTXHUHG

5. *Math Concepts:*

  a. Using an organized table, list all of the possible results for tossing five coins (there are 32 possibilities). What percentage of your outcomes are 0 heads, 1 head, 2 heads, 3 heads, 4 heads, and 5 heads?

  b. Using the number of heads as the outcome of each possible toss, plot the frequency of each outcome on a grid similar to the grid used for activity 1b in this activity set.

  c. Given a mean of 2.5 heads and a standard deviation of 1.1 heads, does the distribution of number of heads seem approximately normally distributed? Explain your reasoning.

6. *NCTM Standards:* Read the first *Expectation* in the **Grade 3–5 Data Analysis and Probability Standard** under "Formulate Questions." Then propose a statistical investigation that you think would be of interest for elementary students to pursue in which they formulate questions and then collect, analyze, and interpret data to answer the questions. With regard to the *Expectation,* how could, "data-collection methods affect the nature of the data set" for the investigation you suggest?

7. *NCTM Standards:* Go to http://illuminations.nctm.org/ and under "Lessons" select grade levels 3–5 and the **Data Analysis and Probability Standard.** Choose a lesson that involves graphing data.

  a. State the title of the lesson and briefly summarize the lesson.

  b. Referring to the **Standards Summary** in the back pages of this book as necessary, list the **Data Analysis and Probability Standard Expectations** that the lesson addresses and explain how the lesson addresses these *Expectations.*

---

www.mhhe.com/bbn

bennett-burton-nelson website

Virtual Manipulatives	Grid and Dot Paper	Links and Readings
Interactive Chapter Applets	Color Transparencies	Geometer Sketchpad Modules
Puzzlers	Extended Bibliography	

ACTIVITIES FOR THE ELEMENTARY SCHOOL CLASSROOM

Finding Averages with Color Tiles

Purpose: To provide elementary school students with a visual introduction and meaning to finding the average of whole numbers.

Connections: Ask the class what the word "average" means. They may suggest several meanings, such as an average person or an average score. Discuss a few meanings of this word and tell them that today we are going to discover the meaning of the word "average" in mathematics.

Materials: Sets of color tiles may be created by copying 2-centimeter grid paper on four different colors of cardstock or by copying the color tile images from the companion website. Color tile transparencies can also be made with the color tile images. Sets of 20 of each of four colors can be placed in plastic sealable bags for storage. Each group of two to four students will need one set of color tiles. Students will also need centimeter grid paper for recording averages with fractional parts.

7   3

1. Place two towers of tile on the overhead, one of height 7 and the other of height 3 and have the students form the same towers at their tables. Ask the students to level off the towers by shifting tiles so that towers both have the same height. Tell them that this leveling off process can be used to find the average of numbers. Ask them, "What is the average of 7 and 3?"

2. Ask the students to find the average of 1 and 5 by building two towers and leveling them off. Then, without building towers, ask them to imagine towers of heights 20 and 26 and mentally find the average of 20 and 26. Have student volunteers share the different ways they determined the average was 23.

3. Ask the students to find the average of 5 and 8 by building towers or doing it mentally. Discuss that it is permissible to use half tiles (or fractions of tiles). Allow students to use grid paper to record this new idea. See the two towers at the left.

8   5   6.5   6.5

4. Place the five towers shown at the left on the overhead and ask the students to find the average of the five numbers by leveling off the towers. Discuss the average and then pose questions like the following (keep the original towers of heights 4, 5, 2, 1, and 3 on your overhead so students can refer back to the original towers):

   a. Tell the students that each tower represents the feet of snow that fell in Nisswa, Minnesota, for each of the past 5 years. Ask each group to discuss and report what they believe is the average snowfall for Nisswa during this 5-year period.

   b. If it snowed 6 feet the next year, have them use their tile and grid paper to determine the 6-year average.

   c. If it did not snow at all during the sixth year ask them to discuss and determine what the 6-year average would be.

4   5   2   1   3

Students find the average of 7, 2, and 6 by leveling off towers of 7 cubes, 2 cubes, and 6 cubes to a height of 5 cubes.

8 Probability

In prekindergarten through grade 2, the treatment of probability ideas should be informal. Teachers should build on children's developing vocabulary. . . . We'll probably have recess this afternoon, or It's unlikely to rain today. . . . In grades 3–5 students can consider ideas of chance through experiments—using coins, dice, or spinners—with known theoretical outcomes or through designating familiar events as impossible, unlikely, likely, or uncertain. . . . Middle grade students should learn and use appropriate terminology and should be able to compute probabilities for simple compound events. . . .[†]

Activity Set 8.1 ## PROBABILITY EXPERIMENTS

PURPOSE

To determine probabilities experimentally and then analyze the experiments to determine the theoretical probabilities, when possible.

MATERIALS

A penny, 10 identical tacks, Two-Penny and Three-Penny Game Grids on Material Cards 22 and 23 respectively, and the Table of Random Digits on Material Card 21.

INTRODUCTION

The word *stochastic,* strange sounding but currently very popular in scientific circles, means random, chancy, chaotic. It is pronounced "stoh-kastic." The stochastization of the world (forgive this tongue-twister) means the adoption of a point of view wherein randomness, chance or probability is perceived as real, objective and a fundamental aspect of the world. . . .

Of the digits that crowd our daily papers many have a stochastic basis. We read about the percentage of families in New York City that are childless, the average number of cars owned by four-person families in Orlando, Florida, the probability that a certain transplant operation will succeed. . . . It is implied that a certain attitude is to be engendered by these disclosures, that a course of action should be set in motion. If it is reported that the English scores of Nebraskan tenth-graders are such and such, while that of Iowan tenth-graders are this and that, then presumably someone believes that something ought to be done about it.

The stochastization of the world so permeates our thinking and our behavior that it can be said to be one of the characteristic features of modern life. . . .[‡]

[†]*Principles and Standards for School Mathematics,* p. 51.
[‡]P. J. Davis and R. Hersh, *Descartes Dream,* pp. 18–19.

15-1   Probability

GET READY to Learn

One cube is drawn from each bag without looking. Write *certain*, *impossible*, or *equally likely* to make each a true sentence.

Bag 1	Bag 2	Bag 3

It is ___?___ that a black cube will be drawn.

It is ___?___ that a yellow cube will be drawn.

It is ___?___ that a yellow cube will be drawn.

MAIN IDEA

I will determine the likelihood of an event.

New Vocabulary

probability
certain
impossible
equally likely
outcome
probability experiment

Math Online

macmillanmh.com

• Extra Examples
• Personal Tutor
• Self-Check Quiz

Probability is the chance that an event will happen.

Probability		
Description	**Meaning**	**Example**
Certain	The event will definitely happen.	Drawing a yellow cube from Bag 2.
Impossible	There is no chance the event will happen.	Drawing a yellow cube from Bag 3.
Equally likely	There is an equal chance the event will happen.	Drawing a black cube from Bag 1.

An **outcome** is a possible result in a **probability experiment**. So, when drawing a cube from Bag 1 above, the possible outcomes are a black cube and a green cube.

EXAMPLE   List Outcomes

① **Cole spins the spinner at the right. List the possible outcomes.**

The spinner could land on the red space, the blue space, or the orange space.

outcomes: red, blue, orange

The importance of an understanding of probability and the related area of statistics to becoming an informed citizen is widely recognized. The *Principles and Standards for School Mathematics* recommends probability activities at all grade levels, K–12, and that a spirit of investigation, exploration, experimentation, and discussion permeate this study. Probability is rich in interesting problems and provides opportunities for using fractions, decimals, ratios, and percents.

In this activity set, we will consider both *experimental probabilities,* which are determined by observing the outcomes of experiments, and *theoretical probabilities,* which are determined by mathematical calculations. The theoretical probability of rolling a 4 on a die is $\frac{1}{6}$ because there are 6 faces on a die, each of which is equally likely to turn up, and only one of these faces has a 4. The experimental probability of obtaining a 4 is found by rolling a die many times and recording the results. Dividing the number of times a 4 comes up by the total number of rolls gives us the experimental probability.

1. Suppose someone wanted to bet that a tack would land with its point up when dropped on a hard surface. Would you accept the bet? Before you wager any money, try the following experiment. Take 10 identical tacks and drop them on a hard surface. Count the number of tacks that land point up. Do this experiment 10 times and record your results in the following table.

Trial Number	1	2	3	4	5	6	7	8	9	10
Number with points up	—	—	—	—	—	—	—	—	—	—

a. Out of the 100 tacks you dropped, how many landed point up? On the basis of this experiment, explain why you would or would not accept the bet.

b. Based on your results, what is the experimental probability that this type of tack will land point up?

$$\frac{\text{Number with point up}}{\text{Total number dropped}} =$$

c. Based on your results, about how many tacks would you expect to land point up if you dropped 300 tacks?

d. Based on your results, what is the experimental probability that this type of tack will land point down? How is this probability related to the probability in part b?

2. Games of chance like the following are common at carnivals and fairs. A penny is spun on a square grid, and if it lands inside a square you win a prize. Compare the diameter of a penny to the width of the Two-Penny Grid (Material Card 22). Do you think there is a better chance that the penny will land inside a square or on a line? Make and record a conjecture before you begin the experiment in part a below.

Conjecture:

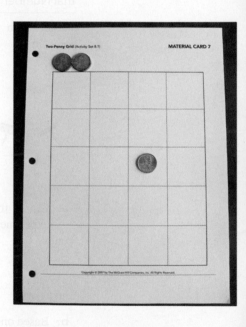

a. Spin a penny 24 times on the Two-Penny Grid and tally the results below.

	Tally	Total
Penny inside square	_____	_____
Penny on line	_____	_____

b. Based on your experiment, compute and record the experimental probability that a penny will land inside a square.

$$\frac{\text{Number inside squares}}{\text{Total number of spins}} =$$

c. The length of a side of each square in the Two-Penny Grid is twice the diameter of a penny. Which of the points to the left labeled *A*, *B*, and *C* will be winning points if they represent the center of a penny?

d. Shade the region of the square in which the center of every *winning* penny must fall. What fractional part of the square is the shaded region? This is the theoretical probability that a penny will land inside the square.

*e. Is this a fair game, in the sense that there is a 50 percent chance of winning?

3. The sides of the squares on the Three-Penny Grid (Material Card 23) are three times the diameter of a penny. When a penny is spun on this grid, do you think the chances of its landing inside the lines are better than the chances of its landing on a line? Make and record a conjecture before you begin the experiment.

Conjecture:

a. Spin a penny 24 times, tally your results, and compute the experimental probability of not landing on a line.

	Tally	Total
Penny inside square		
Penny on line		

$$\frac{\text{Number inside squares}}{\text{Total number of spins}} =$$

b. Shade the region of the square in which the centers of winning pennies must fall. What is the theoretical probability that a penny will land inside the square?

c. Explain why this is or is not a fair game.

JUST FOR FUN

RACETRACK GAME (2 or 3 players)

Each player chooses three tracks on the race track game board and places a marker on its starting square. In turn, the players roll two dice. If the sum of the numbers on the dice matches the number of a track on which the player's marker is located, the player may move one square toward the finish line on this track. The first player to have a marker reach the last square on the track is the winner. Play the game a few times. What are the three tracks that are most likely to produce a winner, and which of the three gives the best chance of winning?

Variation: Use the sum of the numbers on three dice rather than on two dice and the following game board. Which tracks give you the best chance of winning?

Exercises and Activities 8.1

1. *School Classroom:* After a class of students played the penny spin games described in activities 2 and 3 of this activity set, some wanted to know the grid square width for which the game becomes a fair game. Determine this size and write a description of how you would help students discover and understand this result.

2. *School Classroom:* Suppose that you wanted your students to play the *Racetrack Game* described in the **Just for Fun Activity** in this section but had no dice in the classroom. Devise two ways that you could have the students simulate the random roll of a pair of dice to successfully play the game. Describe your methods in detail.

3. *Math Concepts:* For the card game described in activity 4 of this activity set, does the probability that the letter facing up will be different than the letter facing down increase or decrease as you increase the number of cards and letters? Explore this idea and find the theoretical probability that the letter facing up will be different than the letter facing down on a randomly selected card from the following set of cards. Explain your thinking.

Six Card Set

Card 1: A on both sides	Card 4: One side A, one side B
Card 2: B on both sides	Card 5: One side A, one side C
Card 3: C on both sides	Card 6: One side B, one side C

4. *Math Concepts:* Design a game similar to the *Racetrack Game* in the **Just for Fun Activity** in this section. Instead of sums, use the product of the numbers when two dice are rolled.

   a. List the set of numbers that must be placed in the start boxes for the game (order the list from least to greatest).

   b. What is the theoretical probability of obtaining each of the different products? Explain your reasoning.

5. *Math Concepts:*

   a. Suppose the Penny Spin game in activity 3 in this activity set uses a Four-Penny diameters wide by Three-Penny diameters high Grid instead of a Three-Penny Grid. Is the game fair now? Explain your reasoning and support your answer with theoretical probability calculations.

   b. Suppose the Penny Spin game in activity 3 in this activity set uses a Four-Penny Grid instead of a Three-Penny Grid. Is the game fair now? Explain your reasoning and support your answer with theoretical probability calculations.

6. *NCTM Standards:* Go to http://illuminations.nctm.org/ and under "Lessons" select grade levels 6–8 and the **Data Analysis and Probability Standard.** Choose a lesson that involves probability.

   a. State the title of the lesson and briefly summarize the lesson.

   b. Referring to the **Standards Summary** in the back pages of this book as necessary, list the **Number and Operation Standard** *Expectations* that the lesson addresses and explain how the lesson addresses these *Expectations*.

d. *Theoretical Probability of Winning if Sticking:* The contestant always starts off by choosing a door at random. If you are sticking with your first choice, you will win if you pick the door with a prize. What is the theoretical probability of winning the prize if you always stick with your first choice? How does this compare to your experimental probability of winning while sticking?

Theoretical Probability of Winning if Sticking: _____

e. *Theoretical Probability of Winning if Switching:* Even if the contestant uses the switch strategy, they still choose a door at random to begin the game. With the switch strategy, they win if the pointer stops on "junk," but they lose if the pointer stops on "prize." Explain why this happens. What is the theoretical probability of winning the prize with a switch strategy?

Theoretical Probability of Winning if Switching: _____

f. *Theoretical Probability of Winning if Randomly Sticking or Switching:* This two-stage tree diagram below represents picking a door at random and then deciding to stick or switch at random. The uppermost branch shows that if you randomly choose a junk door and then randomly spin "switch," you win the prize. Finish labeling the outcomes of the second stage and determine the theoretical probability of winning a prize with the random selection of stick or switch.

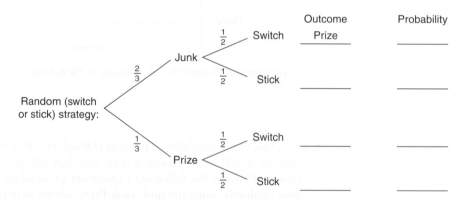

Theoretical Probability of Winning if Randomly Sticking or Switching: _____

g. *Best Strategy:* If you were the contestant, would you stick, switch, or choose the options at random? Explain your reasoning.

JUST FOR FUN

TRICK DICE

The four dice shown below have the following remarkable property: No matter which die your opponent selects, you can always select one of the remaining three dice so that the probability of winning when you each roll your die is in your favor. (Winning means having a greater number of dots facing up.) Make a set of these dice, either by altering regular dice or by using the dice on Material Card 25.

Die 1   Die 2   Die 3   Die 4

Try the following experiment with die 2 and die 4. Roll both dice 21 times and record the resulting numbers in the appropriate boxes of the following table. Then circle the numbers for which die 4 wins over die 2. Before beginning the experiment, try to predict which die has the better chance of winning.

Die 2																					
Die 4																					

1. For the winning die in the experiment above, what is the experimental probability of winning.

*2. Complete table below to show all 36 pairs of numbers that can result from the two dice. Circle the pairs in which die 4 has the greater number. What is the theoretical probability that die 4 will win over die 2? Compare this result to the experimental probability in question 1.

Die 2

	5	5	5	1	1	1
2	2, 5	2, 5	2, 5	(2,1)	(2,1)	(2,1)
2						
2						
2						
6						
6						

(Die 4 labels the rows on the left side)

*3. If a 2 is rolled on die 4 and a 1 is rolled on die 2, then die 4 wins. What is the probability of these events happening? (*Hint*: Multiply the 2 probabilities.)

*4. If a 6 is rolled on die 4, it wins over every number on die 2. What is the chance of rolling a 6 on die 4?

*5. The theoretical probability that die 4 will win over die 2 is the sum of the probabilities in questions 3 and 4. What is this probability? Compare this result to your answer in problem 2.

Similar approaches can be used to show that die 2 wins over die 1, die 1 wins over die 3, and die 3 wins over die 4. Surprisingly, the first die of each of these pairs has a $\frac{2}{3}$ probability of winning over the second die. Try this experiment with some of your friends. Let them choose a die first, and you will always be able to select one with a greater chance of winning.

DOOR PRIZES APPLET: STICK OR SWITCH?

You may have heard of the TV game show where the contestant picks one of three doors in hopes there is a prize behind it. The host then opens one of the remaining doors with junk behind it and asks if the contestant wishes to stick with the original choice or switch. Would you *Stick* or *Switch*? This applet will help you discover the winning strategy. The results may be surprising.

Door Prizes Applet, Chapter 8
www.mhhe.com/bbn

Exercises and Activities 8.2

1. *School Classroom:* When asked to determine the probability of drawing two green tiles from a box containing three red tiles and three green tiles, one pair of students disagreed about an approach to the problem. One student said you must reach into the container and randomly pull out two tiles in one draw. The other said that you reach in and randomly draw one tile, then reach in again and randomly draw the second tile. Explain how you would help the students settle this difference without simply telling them what to do.

2. *School Classroom:* Several of your students insist that the probability of rolling two dice and obtaining a 2 on one die and a 3 on the other, is $\frac{1}{6} + \frac{1}{6}$. Explain how you can help them understand the error in their reasoning and how you can help them discover the correct probability.

3. *School Classroom:* Read the discussion of the *Fundamental Counting Principle* on the **Elementary School Text** page at the beginning of this section. Suppose a student asked what he or she should do if the shoes also came in four sizes (small, medium, large, and extra-large). Describe what you would say or do as the teacher to help the student connect the ideas of a tree diagram and the *Fundamental Counting Principle* to answer the question without simply drawing a large tree diagram.

4. *Math Concepts:* Suppose you are dealing cards from a 16-card set with 4 each of the cards numbered 1, 2, 3, and 4.

    a. What is the probability of being dealt a pair (two cards with the same number) if you are dealt two cards at a time? Set up a probability tree to explore this idea. Show your procedure and explain your thinking.

    b. What is the probability of being dealt two cards that sum to at most 5? Set up a probability tree to explore this idea. Show your procedure and explain your thinking.

5. *Math Concepts:*

    a. Does rolling two four-sided tetrahedral dice with sides numbered 1, 2, 3, and 4 instead of two standard cubical dice with sides numbered 1, 2, 3, 4, 5, and 6 increase or decrease your chances of rolling doubles? Set up a probability tree to explore this idea. Show your procedure and explain your thinking.

    b. Does rolling two eight-sided octahedral dice with sides numbered 1, 2, 3, 4, 5, 6, 7, and 8 instead of two standard cubical dice with sides numbered 1, 2, 3, 4, 5, and 6 increase or decrease your chances of rolling doubles? Set up a probability tree to explore this idea. Show your procedure and explain your thinking.

6. *NCTM Standards:* Design a simple probability experiment that you believe is appropriate for an elementary school class. Describe your experiment and write a few questions for the students. For the probability experiment you designed, state the *Standards* and *Expectations* from the **Data Analysis and Probability Standards** in the back pages of this book that your experiment addresses. Explain how your experiment addresses these *Expectations*.

---

www.mhhe.com/bbn

bennett-burton-nelson website

Virtual Manipulatives	Grid and Dot Paper	Links and Readings
Interactive Chapter Applets	Color Transparencies	Geometer Sketchpad Modules
Puzzlers	Extended Bibliography	

ACTIVITIES FOR THE ELEMENTARY SCHOOL CLASSROOM

Probability Experiments with Dice

Purpose: To provide elementary school students with an example of an experimental approach to understanding simple probability.

Connections: Ask the class the meaning of the following phrase "There is a 50–50 chance it will rain." They may suggest several meanings such as, there is a good chance it will rain; or they don't know for sure; etc. Then discuss what it means to say, "There is a less than a 50–50 chance it will rain." Tell them that the chance something will happen is sometimes difficult to determine and that today they will perform an experiment to look at the chance of getting certain numbers when rolling two dice.

Materials: One pair of dice per pair of students, overheads or poster paper for creating class probability charts, and one or two probability charts per pair of students like the probability chart below.

1. Post a probability chart like the one below in front of the class and then follow the steps below the chart.

This third grade student conjectured that the 6-column would fill up first.

Sum of Two Dice Probability Chart

2	3	4	5	6	7	8	9	10	11	12

   (i) Have each pair of students roll their dice and write down the sum.
   (ii) Ask each pair of students what sum they rolled and record an X in the table above that number.
   (iii) Repeat these steps until one column on the chart is filled.

2. Pass out the blank probability charts and pairs of dice to each pair of students and have them repeat the experiment until one of their columns is filled.

3. Now repeat the experiment described in #1 with the whole class and with a new chart, but first ask each student to pick the number of the column they think will fill up first. Record the student names (or initials) under the column they choose. When the experiment is completed, start a discussion by asking the students why they chose the columns they did.

4. Repeat the experiment, if desired, always asking the students to choose the column they think will fill up first and asking the students why they are choosing this number. Discuss the results of each experiment. The experiments should lead the students to the conclusion that some sums have a greater chance of occurring than others. Ask them to list the numbers of the columns that appear to fill up fastest and the numbers that have the least chance of filling a column.

9

Geometric Figures

The study of geometry in grades 3–5 requires thinking and doing. As students sort, build, draw, model, trace, measure, and construct, their capacity to visualize geometric relationships will develop. At the same time they are learning to reason and to make, test, and justify conjectures about these relationships.[†]

FIGURES ON RECTANGULAR AND CIRCULAR GEOBOARDS

PURPOSE

To use rectangular geoboards to illustrate geometric figures and circular geoboards to study inscribed and central angles.

Virtual Manipulatives

www.mhhe.com/bbn

MATERIALS

Rectangular and circular geoboards and rubber bands (optional). Templates for making rectangular and circular geoboards are on Material Cards 8 and 27, respectively, and are also available in the Virtual Manipulatives. Recording paper for activity 1 is on Material Card 26 and the three-circle Venn diagram is on Material Card 6. A protractor is on Material Card 20. Scissors are needed for activity 1.

INTRODUCTION

The geoboard is a popular physical model for illustrating geometric concepts and solving geometric investigations. The most familiar type of geoboard has a square shape, with 25 pins arranged in a 5-pin × 5-pin array. Rubber bands can be placed around the pins to form models for segments, angles, and polygons. For example, here is an 8-sided polygon.

The circular geoboard is very helpful for developing angle concepts. The one shown at the top of page 265 has a pin at the center and an outer circle of 24 pins. Many of the angles and polygons that can be formed on this circular geoboard cannot be made on the rectangular geoboard. The circular geoboard will be used to form central and inscribed angles and to establish an important relationship between them.

[†]*Principles and Standards for School Mathematics,* p. 165.

Extend 7-1

Geometry Lab
Investigating Arcs and Angles

In Lesson 6-1, you learned about angle relationships. Angles can also be placed in circles. A **central angle** is an angle that intersects a circle in two points and has its vertex at the center of the circle. It separates the circle into two parts, each of which is an **arc**.

The measure of a central angle is equivalent to the measure of its corresponding arc. There are three types of arcs.

MAIN IDEA

Find measures of arcs and inscribed angles.

New Vocabulary

central angle
arc
minor arc
major arc
semicircle
inscribed angle

A **minor arc** measures less than 180°.	A **major arc** measures more than 180°.	A **semicircle** measures 180°.

An **inscribed angle** is an angle that has its vertex on the circle, and its sides contain chords of the circle.

ACTIVITY   Measure of Inscribed Angles

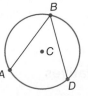

1. **STEP 1** Use a compass to draw a circle and label the center C.

STEP 2 Use a straightedge to draw chords BA and BD that do not go through the center of the circle.

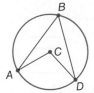

STEP 3 Use a straightedge to draw $\overline{AC}$ and $\overline{CD}$.

STEP 4 Measure ∠ABD and ∠ACD.

ANALYZE THE RESULTS

1. What seems to be the relationship between m∠ABD and m∠ACD?

2. Repeat Steps 1–4 with several different inscribed angles.

3. **MAKE A PREDICTION** Draw a circle with a radius of 3 inches. Then draw a central angle that measures 60° and an inscribed angle that intercepts the same arc. Without measuring, predict the measure of the inscribed angle. Then check your prediction by measuring.

Reading Math

Arcs and Segments
The symbol $\overset{\frown}{AC}$ is read *arc AC*. The symbol $\overline{AC}$ is read *segment AC*.

Since most geoboard activities can be carried out on dot paper by drawing figures, the use of geoboards is optional in the following activities. However, geoboards provide insights because of the ease with which figures can be shaped and reshaped during an investigation. They also encourage experimentation and creativity. If geoboards are not available, you may wish to make them from boards and thumb tacks or finishing nails using the templates on Material Cards 8 and 27.

Rectangular Geoboards

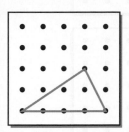

1. This figure shows a geoboard triangle with its base along the bottom row of pins. Determine all possible geoboard triangles that have the same base and the third vertex on a pin. Record your results by drawing each triangle on geoboard recording paper (Material Card 26).

   a. If each small square is 1 square unit of area, determine the area of each of the triangles you drew using methods developed in Activity Set 6.4. Record the area inside the triangle.

   *b. Cut out each geoboard that has a triangle drawn on it. (Cut around the entire geoboard, not just the triangles.) Group the triangles that have the same area. Describe the characteristics that triangles of equal area have in common.

   *c. The two triangles shown below are **congruent** because they have the same size and shape and one can be cut out and placed on the other so that they coincide. Sort all of the triangles into sets of congruent triangles. Select one triangle from each set of congruent triangles to form a new collection of noncongruent triangles. How many noncongruent triangles are there?

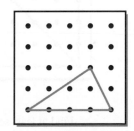

   d. Label the three-circle Venn diagram, Material Card 6, as shown at the right. Sort the collection of noncongruent triangles from part c by placing each of them in the appropriate regions of the Venn diagram. Record the number of triangles in each region on the diagram at the right. (Note: A **scalene triangle** has all sides of different length; an **isosceles triangle** has at least two sides of equal length; and a **right triangle** has one right angle.)

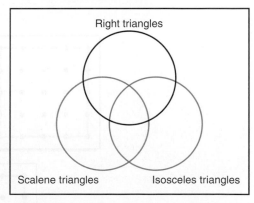

   e. For the regions of the Venn diagram in part d which have no entries, can triangles that cannot be constructed on a 5-pin × 5-pin geoboard be drawn that belong to those regions? Explain how you arrived at your answer.

2. The first geoboard below shows three segments of different lengths. A geoboard segment has its endpoints on geoboard pins. Use your geoboard to determine how many geoboard segments of *different* lengths can be constructed. Record your solutions on these geoboards.

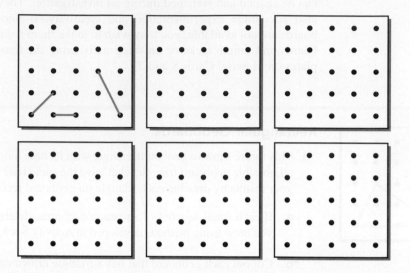

3. The following geoboards have a rubber band around the outer pins to form as large a square as possible. Additional rubber bands have been used to divide the squares into two *congruent* halves.

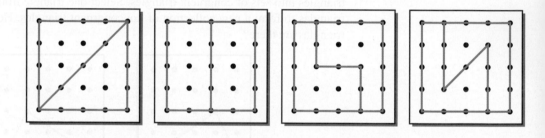

Find at least seven other ways to divide the square into congruent halves, and draw them below.

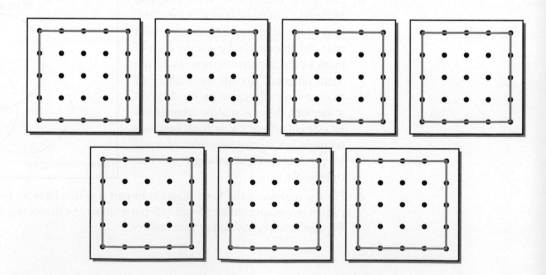

*4. There are 16 noncongruent quadrilaterals that can be formed on a 3-pin × 3-pin geoboard. Each of the quadrilaterals has its vertices at geoboard pins. Sketch them here.

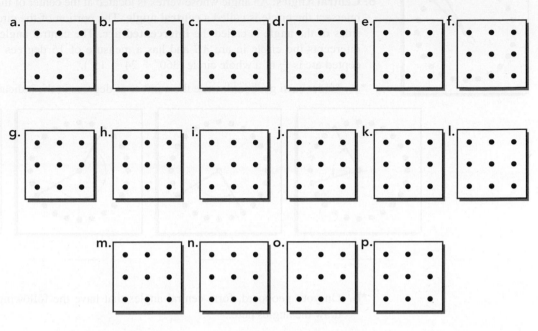

Classify each of the preceding quadrilaterals by recording the letter of its geoboard after each description that applies to it. (A **parallelogram** has two pairs of opposite parallel sides, a **trapezoid** has exactly one pair of parallel sides, a **convex polygon** is not "caved in," i.e., the line segment connecting any pair of points on the polygon lies within the polygon and a **concave polygon** is a nonconvex polygon.)

Square   _____

Rectangle, but not square   _____

Parallelogram, but not rectangle   _____

Trapezoid   _____

Convex   _____

Concave   _____

5. On each geoboard, sketch a polygon whose vertices are points of the geoboard and which satisfies the given conditions. (An **octagon** is an 8-sided polygon, a **nonagon** is 9-sided, a **decagon** is 10-sided, and a **dodecagon** is 12-sided.)

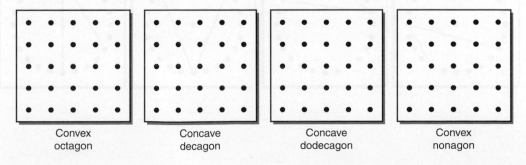

Convex   Concave   Concave   Convex
octagon   decagon   dodecagon   nonagon

Circular Geoboards

6. **Central Angles:** An angle whose vertex is located at the center of the circle and whose sides intersect the circle is called a **central angle.** The portion of the circle that is cut off by the sides of the angle is called the **intercepted arc.** The central angle *AOB* on this geoboard intercepts the circle in arc *AB* and has a measure of 15 degrees (15°) because its intercepted arc is $\frac{1}{24}$ of a whole circle (360° ÷ 24 = 15°).

*a. Under each geoboard, write the number of degrees in the indicated central angle.

_____　　　_____　　　_____　　　_____

*b. On your geoboard, form central angles that have the following angle measures. Then draw the angles here.

　45°　　　　　　165°　　　　　　195°　　　　　　105°

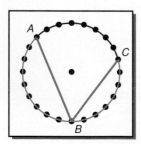

7. **Inscribed Angles:** An angle is **inscribed** in an arc of a circle when the vertex of the angle is on the arc and its sides contain endpoints of the arc. In the figure at the left, angle *ABC* is *inscribed* in the dark blue arc *ABC* and angle *ABC intercepts* the red arc *AC*.

*a. Construct the following inscribed angles on your circular geoboard and measure them with your protractor. (There is a protractor on Material Card 20. If you do not have a circular geoboard, draw the angles lightly, in pencil, on the geoboard template on Material Card 27.)

_____　_____　_____　_____　_____

*b. Look at the inscribed angles in part a that have the same angle measure. Make and record a conjecture about the *equality* of inscribed angles and the size of their corresponding intercepted arcs. Test your conjecture by drawing and measuring more inscribed angles. Record your conclusions.

Conjecture:

*c. Angle *PQR* is inscribed in a semicircle (half a circle). Using your circular geoboard and protractor, form and measure angle *PQR* as well as several other inscribed angles whose sides intersect the ends of a diameter. Record the angles and their measures below. Make and record a conjecture about the measure of these angles.

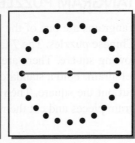

_____   _____   _____   _____   _____

Conjecture:

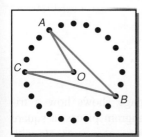

8. Form central angle *AOC* and inscribed angle *ABC* (left) on your circular geoboard (or draw them on your circular geoboard template). Determine the measure of central angle *AOC*. Measure angle *ABC* with your protractor. Record both measures here.

Inscribed angle *ABC* _____   Central angle *AOC* _____

*a. Form each of the following inscribed angles on your geoboard, measure the angle with your protractor, and record the inscribed angle measure below the figure. Then, on each geoboard, form and determine the measure of the central angle that intercepts the same arc as the inscribed angle and record it.

Inscribed angle _____   Inscribed angle _____   Inscribed angle _____   Inscribed angle _____

Central angle _____   Central angle _____   Central angle _____   Central angle _____

*b. There is a relationship between the measure of an inscribed angle and that of its corresponding central angle. Write a conjecture about that relationship.

Conjecture:

JUST FOR FUN

TANGRAM PUZZLES

Tangrams are one of the oldest and most popular of ancient Chinese puzzles. The 7 tangram pieces are shown in the following square. There are 5 triangles, 1 square, and 1 parallelogram. Fold a standard piece of paper to get a square and cut out the square. Then fold the paper to obtain the 7 tangram pieces and cut them out for the following activities.

*1. The 7 pieces are used in Chinese puzzles called *tangram puzzles*. The object of tangram puzzles is to use all of the tangram pieces to form figures. The tangram pieces should be placed so that they do not overlap. Try to form the following figures. There are many tangram figures.† You may wish to create and record a few of your own.

2. The 7 tangram pieces also can be used to create geometric shapes. For example:

a. Use the 2 small triangles to make a square, a larger triangle, and a parallelogram. Sketch the results here.

b. Use the 2 small triangles and the medium-size triangle to make a rectangle, a parallelogram that is not a rectangle, and a larger triangle. Sketch the results here.

3. The chart on the following page shows how a triangle can be created with 3 tangram pieces, a square with 5 tangram pieces, and a nonsquare rectangle with 4 pieces. Record your results from question 2 above and then complete the chart. (There are no solutions for the spaces that are crossed out.)

†R. Reed's *Tangrams* contains 330 tangram figures and their solutions.

Number of pieces used	Triangle	Square	Rectangle	Parallelogram
1			✕	
2			✕	
3	◢			
4			◪	
5		◪		
6	✕	✕		
7				

CROSS SECTIONS OF A CUBE APPLET

How would you cut this cube into two parts with one straight slice so that the cross section is a triangle? A trapezoid? This applet lets you select points on the edges of the cube for your slices and rotate the cube for a better perspective of the resulting cross section.

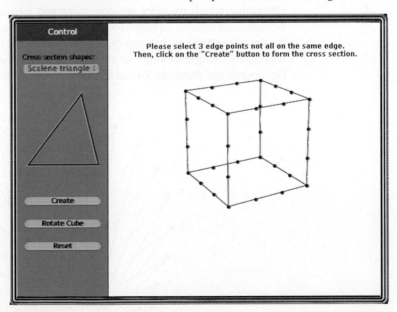

Cross Sections of a Cube Applet, Chapter 9
www.mhhe.com/bbn

Exercises and Activities **9.1**

1. *School Classroom:* While working on an activity to divide geoboard squares into two congruent halves, several students could see that halves as in figures *A* and *B* were congruent but could not see that the parts of figures *C* and *D* were also congruent halves. Explain how you can help students determine when two plane figures are congruent so they can apply this knowledge to geoboard figures as well as other plane figures.

2. *School Classroom:* Several of your students insist that the following is a nonsquare rhombus because the sides are at a diagonal. How can you help your students resolve this issue?

3. *School Classroom:* Read the activity, *Measure of Inscribed Angles,* on the **Elementary School Text** page at the beginning of this section. Describe several advantages for introducing this activity using a circular geoboard before using the compass and protractor to construct the circles and angles. Explain your thinking.

4. *Math Concepts:* Each triangle in the following family of triangles formed on a circular geoboard has base T_1T_{23}.

Determine which triangles are congruent and which triangles are acute, obtuse, scalene, isosceles, equilateral, or right; identify each triangle by its vertex angle (T_2 through T_{22}) and list the triangles in each category. Sketch or print the triangles you have formed and explain why each triangle belongs in the category you have put it in. Downloadable Circular Geoboards and printable Virtual Geoboards are available at the companion website.

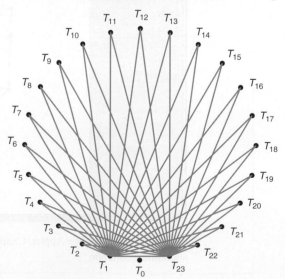

5. *Math Concepts:* Which regular polygons (all sides congruent and all angles congruent) can you form on a 24-pin circular geoboard? Illustrate each regular polygon on a circular geoboard and explain how you know it is a regular polygon. Circular Geoboards are available for download at the companion website.

6. *Math Concepts:* Downloadable Rectangular Geoboards and printable Virtual Geoboards are available at the companion website.
   a. Form polygons with 13, 14, 15, and 16 sides whose vertices are pins of a 5-pin × 5-pin geoboard. Sketch or print your work.
   b. Classify the polygons in part a as convex or concave.
   c. What is the polygon with the greatest number of sides you can form with vertices on the pins of a 5-pin × 5-pin geoboard? Is the polygon convex or concave? Sketch or print your work.

7. *NCTM Standards:* Go to http://illuminations.nctm.org/ and under "Lessons" select grade levels 3–5 and the **Geometry Standard.** Choose a lesson that involves polygons.
   a. State the title of the lesson and briefly summarize the lesson.
   b. Referring to the **Standards Summary** in the back pages of this book as necessary, list the *Geometry Standard Expectations* that the lesson addresses and explain how the lesson addresses these *Expectations.*

---

www.mhhe.com/bbn

bennett-burton-nelson website

Virtual Manipulatives   Grid and Dot Paper   Links and Readings
Interactive Chapter Applets   Color Transparencies   Geometer Sketchpad Modules
Puzzlers   Extended Bibliography

Activity Set **9.2** # REGULAR AND SEMIREGULAR TESSELLATIONS

Virtual Manipulatives

www.mhhe.com/bbn

PURPOSE

To study regular and semiregular tessellations of the plane.

MATERIALS

Pattern Blocks and Polygons for Tessellations from the Manipulative Kit or from the Virtual Manipulatives. You may wish to use scissors for activity 4.

Giant's Causeway, County Antrim, Ireland

INTRODUCTION

The hexagonal-shaped basalt columns in the photographs above occur off the coast of Northern Ireland. The partitioning of surfaces by hexagons or nearly hexagonal figures is common in nature.[†] A figure, such as a regular hexagon, that can be used repeatedly to cover a surface without gaps or overlaps is said to *tile* or *tessellate* the surface. The resulting pattern is called a *tessellation*. An infinite variety of shapes can be used as the basic figure for a tessellation. The famous Dutch artist Maurits C. Escher (1898–1972) is noted for his tessellations with drawings of birds, fish, and other living creatures. Techniques for creating Escher-type tessellations are developed in Activity Set 11.2.

Pattern Block Tessellations

1. Figure 1 below shows the beginnings of a tessellation with the yellow hexagon pattern block and figures 2 and 3, on the next page, show the beginnings of two different tessellations with the red trapezoid.

(1)

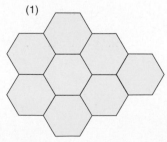

[†]For examples of hexagonal patterns and a discussion of why they occur in nature, see H. Weyl, *Symmetry*, pp. 83–89.

(2) (3)

a. Find at least one other way to tessellate with the red trapezoid. Record your pattern.

b. All of the pattern block pieces other than the hexagon have more than one tessellation pattern like the trapezoid. For the square and for the blue parallelogram, sketch enough of at least two patterns so that a reader will be able to extend your patterns.

*2. When 3 acute angles (an angle measuring between 0° and 90°) of tan rhombuses are put together at a point, the sum of their measures is the same as one of the angles of an orange square. Since each angle of the square measures 90°, the acute angle of the tan rhombus measures 30°.

By comparing the angles of the various pieces (and using no angle-measuring instruments), determine the measures of the other seven different angles of the pieces in the pattern block collection. Draw pattern block sketches below each figure to show briefly how you reached your conclusions. Then record the angle measures in the provided blanks. (An **obtuse** angle measures between 90° and 180°.)

(1) _____ (obtuse)

___30°___ (acute)

(2) _____

(3) _____ (obtuse)

(4) _____ (acute)

(5) _____

(6) _____ (obtuse)

(7) _____ (acute)

3. Both of the figures at the right have been formed by taping two pattern blocks together to form new shapes. The first figure, which uses a trapezoid and a blue parallelogram, is a hexagon (6 sides and 6 interior angles) and the second, which uses a triangle and a tan parallelogram, is a pentagon (5 sides and 5 interior angles).

a. On the diagrams, record the measure of each interior angle in the new shapes.

b. Use tape and pattern blocks to form the hexagon and pentagon shown on the previous page and test each of them to see if they will tessellate. If so, sketch enough of the beginnings of a pattern so the reader has sufficient information to extend it. If not, explain why it will not work.

c. Tape two other pattern block pieces together to create a new shape that will not tessellate. Sketch your figure and explain why it will not tessellate.

Tessellations with Regular Polygons

4. Six regular polygons are shown in the following figures. For each polygon, trace additional copies of that polygon around the enlarged vertex point, as if to begin a tessellation, and then answer the questions on the next page. The triangle, square, hexagon, and octagon are included with the Polygons for Tessellation in your Manipulative Kit. You will need to trace and cut out a regular pentagon and a regular heptagon from below to use while tracing in this activity.

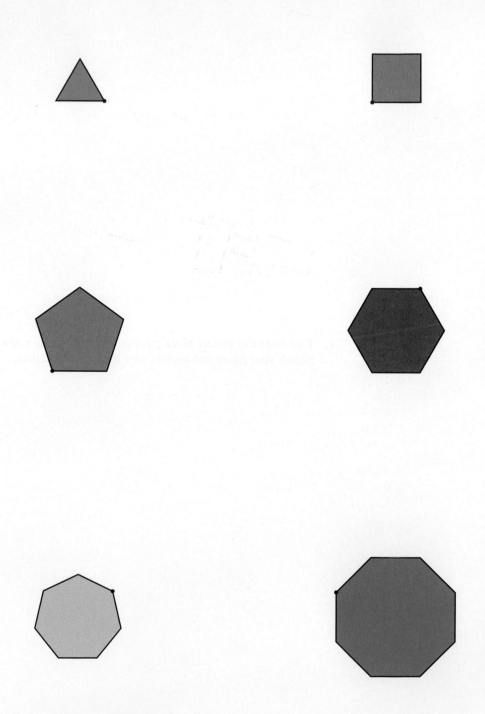

a. Which of the regular polygons on the previous page will tessellate?

b. A tessellation created from one regular polygon is called a **regular tessellation.** What condition must the angles of a regular polygon satisfy in order for the polygon to tessellate?

*c. Explain why regular polygons with more than 6 sides will not tessellate.

5. More interesting tessellations can be formed by using two or three different regular polygons. A square and two octagons are around each vertex point (for example, see vertex point *A*) of the tessellation shown here. Notice that the vertex angle of a square is 90° and of an octagon is 135°, and 90° + 135° + 135° = 360°.

   A tessellation that has two or more types of regular polygons arranged in the same order around every vertex point is called a **semiregular tessellation.** There are only five regular polygons that can be used in semiregular tessellations and they are shown below. The number of degrees in a vertex angle of each polygon is recorded above the polygon. There are multiple copies of these polygons in the Manipulative Kit. Use them for the tessellations in parts a and b on the next page.

a. There are six semiregular tessellations that can be formed using combinations of two different regular polygons about each vertex. Find and sketch at least one of these tessellations. (*Hint:* Look for combinations of angles whose measures add up to 360°.)

b. There are two semiregular tessellations that use combinations of three different regular polygons about each vertex. Find and sketch one of these tessellations. (*Hint:* Look for combinations of angles whose measures add up to 360°.)

*c.   Pattern Block Tessellations: It is possible to tile a plane with combinations of polygons that do not form a semiregular tessellation. These tilings may have a regular pattern, but not every vertex point is surrounded by the same arrangement of polygons and not every polygon need be regular. Use your pattern blocks to create such a tiling and sketch it here.

JUST FOR FUN

THE GAME OF HEX (2 players)

Hex, a game of deductive reasoning, is played on a game board of hexagons similar to the 11 by 11 grid shown below (see Material Card 28). Player 1 and player 2 take turns placing their markers or symbols on any unoccupied hexagon. Player 1 attempts to form an unbroken chain or string of symbols from the left side of the grid to the right, and player 2 tries to form a chain of symbols from the top of the grid to the bottom. The first player to complete a chain is the winner. In this sample game, player 2 (using Os) won against player 1 (using Xs).

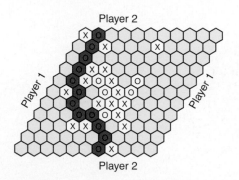

Winning Strategy: There will always be a winner in the game of Hex, since the only way a player can prevent the other from winning is to form an unbroken chain of markers from one side of the grid to the other. On a 3 by 3 game board, the person who plays first can easily win in 3 moves. What should be the first move? Find a first move on the 4 by 4 and 5 by 5 game boards that will ensure a win regardless of the opponent's moves.

It is tempting to conclude that a winning strategy on an 11 by 11 game board begins with a first move on the center hexagon. However, there are so many possibilities for plays on a grid of this size that no winning strategy has yet been found. There is a type of proof in mathematics, called an *existence proof*, which shows that something exists even though no one is able to find it. It has been proved that a winning strategy does exist for the first player in a game of Hex on an 11 by 11 grid, but just what that strategy is, no one knows.[†]

[†]For an elementary version of this proof, see M. Gardner, "Mathematical Games," *Scientific American* 197 (1), p. 145.

Exercises and Activities 9.2

1. *School Classroom:* Bees form tessellations when they create their honeycombs. How might you use this idea to design an activity for your classroom? Explain your activity ideas and your thinking.

(a)   (b)

2. *School Classroom:* One of your students claims that she has formed regular polygons of 3, 4, and 6 sides on her rectangular geoboard and shows you the following figures. Explain how you would help her determine which of these figures are regular and which are not.

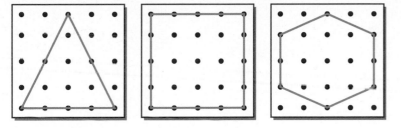

3. *School Classroom:* Do an Internet search and find a website that features a game or math applet focused on tessellations for kids. Print a one-page view of the game or applet, describe the game or applet, and discuss how you would use such an activity in your own class. Give the URL of the game or math applet you found.

4. *Math Concepts:* On Dot Paper or Grid Paper draw a seven-sided polygon that tessellates and show the tessellation. Dot Paper and Grid Paper are available for download at the companion website.

5. *Math Concepts:* Copy this concave quadrilateral in the center of a page of dot paper. Dot Paper is available for download at the companion website.

a. Form a tessellation with the figure above. Draw enough of the tessellation so it is obvious that the tessellation can be continued in all directions.

b. What observations can you make about the angles around the points where the vertices of the quadrilaterals meet?

6. *Math Concepts:* Use Polygons for Tessellations and create a semiregular tessellation different from the tessellation you produced for activity 5a in this activity set. Sketch or print your work. Printable Virtual Polygons for Tessellations are available at the companion website.

7. *NCTM Standards:* Read over the **Standards Summary** in the back pages of this book. Tessellations are not mentioned. What *Content Standards* and *Expectations* does the study of these topics address? List the *Standards* and *Expectations* and explain your thinking.

---

www.mhhe.com/bbn

bennett-burton-nelson website

Virtual Manipulatives	Grid and Dot Paper	Links and Readings
Interactive Chapter Applets	Color Transparencies	Geometer Sketchpad Modules
Puzzlers	Extended Bibliography	

MODELS FOR REGULAR AND SEMIREGULAR POLYHEDRA

PURPOSE

To construct and use models in order to observe and examine the properties of regular and semi-regular polyhedra.

MATERIALS

Scissors and patterns for constructing regular polyhedra on Material Cards 29 and 30. Two-Centimeter Grid Paper from Material Card 31.

INTRODUCTION

The term polyhedron comes from Greek and means "many faces." A *regular polyhedron* is a convex polyhedron whose faces are regular polygons and whose vertices are each surrounded by the same number of these polygons. The regular polyhedra are also called *Platonic solids* because the Greek philosopher Plato (427–347 B.C.E.) immortalized them in his writings. Euclid (340 B.C.E.) proved that there were exactly five regular polyhedra. Can you identify the Platonic solids in M.C. Escher's wood engraving *Stars?*

11-2

1 Introduce

Activity Choice 1 • Hands-On

Display the following items in a row: board eraser, soccer ball, tissue box, tennis ball, crayon box.

- **What shapes are in this pattern?** rectangular prisms and spheres

- **What object could I put next to continue the pattern?** Sample answer: globe

- **How are the tissue box and the crayon box alike?** Sample answer: Both have corners.

- **How is the soccer ball different from the crayon box?** Answers will vary; the ball is round with no corners. The box has corners.

Activity Choice 2 • Literature

Introduce the lesson with Stuart J. Murphy's *Captain Invincible and the Space Shapes.* For a related math activity, see p. TR59.

2 Teach

Display a cube and use it to teach the following definitions:

- **face** a flat surface, some faces are called bases

- **edge** where 2 faces meet

- **vertex** where 3 or more faces meet

- Give each student a cube and ask students to count the number of faces (6), edges (12), and vertices (8) on the cube. Record their results on the board.

Get Ready Use the section at the top of p. 347 to teach the lesson concept. Guide students in identifying faces, edges, and vertices.

Check Observe students as you work through Exercises 1–6 as a class.

💬 **Exercise 7** Assess student comprehension before assigning practice exercises.

⚠️ **COMMON ERROR!**
Students may be confused as to why spheres have no faces. Remind them that a face is flat. Lead them to understand that spheres are round and can roll.

Name _____

Faces, Edges, and Vertices

 Hands-On Activity

Get Ready

Main Idea
I will describe three-dimensional figures using faces, edges, and vertices.

Vocabulary
face
edge
vertex (vertices)

You can describe three-dimensional figures by the number of faces, edges, and vertices.

A **face** is a flat surface.

An **edge** is where 2 faces meet.

A **vertex** is where 3 or more faces meet.

Check

7. Sample answer: Both have the same number of faces, edges, and vertices.

Use three-dimensional figures to count the faces, edges, and vertices.

Shape	Faces	Edges	Vertices
1. cube	6	12	8
2. rectangular prism	6	12	8
3. pyramid	5	8	5
4. cylinder	2	0	0
5. cone	1	0	1
6. sphere	0	0	0

7. **Talk About It** How are a rectangular prism and a cube alike?

Chapter 11   Lesson 2

three hundred forty-seven   347

Reteach (p. 13) BL

11-2 **Reteach**
Faces, Edges, and Vertices

12 edges — 6 faces (sides)
— 8 vertices (corners)

Write how many faces, vertices, and edges.

Solid Figure	Faces	Vertices	Edges
1.	5	5	8
2.	6	8	12

3. Find the figure that has one face and a point. Color it blue.
4. Find the figures with the same number of faces. Color them red.
5. Circle the figures that can roll.

Grade 2   13   Chapter 11

Skills Practice (p. 14) OL

11-2 **Skills Practice**
Faces, Edges, and Vertices

Circle the three-dimensional figure that is named. Write how many faces, vertices, and edges it has.

Name	Figure	Faces	Vertices	Edges
1. rectangular prism		6	8	12
2. cone		1	1	0
3. cube		6	8	12
4. pyramid		5	5	8
5. sphere		0	0	0

Grade 2   14   Chapter 11

Platonic Solids

1. There are several common methods for constructing the five Platonic solids. The polyhedra pictured here are see-through models similar to those in Escher's wood engraving. They can be made from drinking straws that are threaded or stuck together.

Another method is to cut out regular polygons and glue or tape them together. Material Cards 29 and 30 contain regular polygonal patterns for making the Platonic solids. Cut out the patterns, use a ballpoint pen or sharp point to score the dashed lines, and assemble them by folding on the dashed lines and taping the edges. For each Platonic solid, record the number of faces (polygonal regions) and the name of the polygon used as the face.

	Number of Faces	Type of Face
Tetrahedron	————	————
Cube	————	————
Octahedron	————	————
Dodecahedron	————	————
Icosahedron	————	————

2. The faces of the icosahedron in the photo were made from colorful greeting cards. (The triangular pattern for the faces are also shown. The vertices of these patterns were cut with a paper punch and scissors, and the edges bent up along the dashed lines. Adjoining faces of the polyhedra are held together by one rubber band.)

Icosahedron created by a student at the University of New Hampshire

a. If you were to make your Platonic solids from greeting cards as described on the previous page, how many rubber bands would you need to make each one? (One band is used for each edge.)

Tetrahedron   _____

Cube   _____

Octahedron   _____

Dodecahedron   _____

Icosahedron   _____

b. You may enjoy planning colors for your Platonic solids so that no two faces with a common edge have the same color. For this condition to be satisfied, what is the least number of colors needed for the octahedron? Explain.

3. Euler's Formula

*a. In the following table, record the numbers of vertices, faces, and edges for each of the Platonic solids you constructed in activity 1.

	Vertices (V)	Faces (F)	Edges (E)
Tetrahedron	_____	_____	_____
Cube	_____	_____	_____
Octahedron	_____	_____	_____
Dodecahedron	_____	_____	_____
Icosahedron	_____	_____	_____

b. There is a relationship among the numbers of vertices, faces, and edges. Make and record a conjecture about this relationship and express it in terms of the letters *V*, *F*, and *E*.

Conjecture:

*c. The following polyhedra are not Platonic solids. Count their vertices, faces, and edges and record your results. Test your conjecture from part b on these polyhedra.

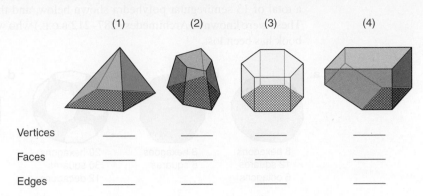

	(1)	(2)	(3)	(4)
Vertices	_____	_____	_____	_____
Faces	_____	_____	_____	_____
Edges	_____	_____	_____	_____

4. **Net Patterns for Cubes:** A two-dimensional pattern that can be folded into a three-dimensional shape without overlap is called a **net** for the three-dimensional shape. The shaded areas in parts a–f below were formed by joining 6 squares along their edges. Three of the following patterns are nets for a cube and three are not. (i) Identify the patterns in parts a–f that are nets for a cube. (ii) Use Two-Centimeter Grid Paper (Material Card 31) to create at least five more nets for a cube (there are 11 different nets in total that have 6 squares adjoined along their edges that can be folded into a cube). You may wish to cut your patterns out to test them. Sketch the additional nets for a cube in the provided grids.

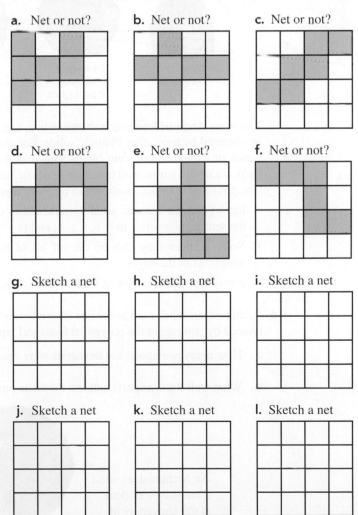

a. Net or not?

b. Net or not?

c. Net or not?

d. Net or not?

e. Net or not?

f. Net or not?

g. Sketch a net

h. Sketch a net

i. Sketch a net

j. Sketch a net

k. Sketch a net

l. Sketch a net

5. Archimedean Solids: A *semiregular polyhedron* is a polyhedron that has as faces two or more regular polygons and the same arrangement of polygons about each vertex. There are a total of 13 semiregular polyhedra shown below, and they are called *Archimedean solids*. These were known to Archimedes (287–212 B.C.E.) who wrote a book on these solids, but the book has been lost.

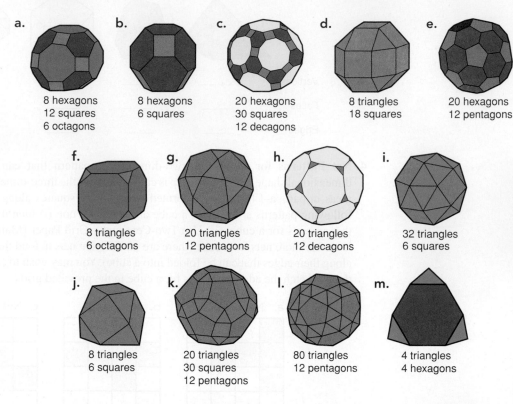

a.
8 hexagons
12 squares
6 octagons

b.
8 hexagons
6 squares

c.
20 hexagons
30 squares
12 decagons

d.
8 triangles
18 squares

e.
20 hexagons
12 pentagons

f.
8 triangles
6 octagons

g.
20 triangles
12 pentagons

h.
20 triangles
12 decagons

i.
32 triangles
6 squares

j.
8 triangles
6 squares

k.
20 triangles
30 squares
12 pentagons

l.
80 triangles
12 pentagons

m.
4 triangles
4 hexagons

The seven Archimedean solids shown in b, e, f, g, h, j, and l can be obtained by truncating Platonic solids. For example, if each vertex of a tetrahedron is cut off, as shown in the figure at the right, we obtain a truncated tetrahedron whose faces are regular hexagons and triangles, as shown in figure m above.

- Identify which Platonic solid is truncated to obtain each of the semiregular solids in b, e, f, g, h, and j.
- Note: Vertices may also be cut off all of the way to the midpoints of the edges.
- It may be helpful to look at the Platonic solids you constructed in activity 1.

Truncated Tetrahedron

6. Archimedean solids such as the one shown below (made by a student using this book) can be created by cutting out the polygonal faces and taping them together.

a. How many pentagons and hexagons were needed to make this model?

b. What well-known sports ball has the same number of pentagon and hexagon faces?

An Archimedean solid
created by a student
at the University of
New Hampshire

JUST FOR FUN

INSTANT INSANITY

Instant Insanity is a popular puzzle that consists of four cubes with their faces colored either red, yellow, blue, or green. The object of the puzzle is to stack the cubes so that each side of the stack (or column) has one of each of the four colors.

Material Card 32 contains patterns for a set of four cubes. Cut out and assemble the cubes and try to solve the puzzle. Note; the arrangement of the cubes in the photo to the right is not a solution to this puzzle.

Cube A   Cube B   Cube C   Cube D

Robert E. Levin described the following method for solving this puzzle.[†] He numbered the faces of the cubes, using 1 for red, 2 for yellow, 3 for blue, and 4 for green, as shown below. To solve the puzzle you must get the numbers 1, 2, 3, and 4 along each side of the stack. The sum of these numbers is 10, and the sum of the numbers on opposite sides of the stack must be 20.

Levin made the table at the bottom of this page showing opposite pairs of numbers on each cube and their sums. For example, 4 and 2 are on opposite faces of cube A and their

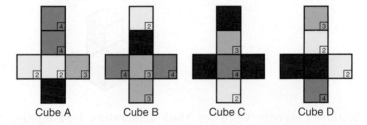

Cube A   Cube B   Cube C   Cube D

sum is 6. The bottom row of the table contains the sums of opposite faces for each cube. For one combination of numbers whose sum is 20, the sums have been circled. Notice that above these circled numbers, the numbers 1, 2, 3, and 4 each occur only twice. This tells you how to stack the cubes so that two opposite sides of the stack will have a total sum of 20. (Both of these sides will have all four colors.) The two remaining sides of the stack must also have a sum of 20. Find four more numbers from the bottom row (one for each cube) such that their sum is 20 and each of the numbers 1, 2, 3, and 4 occurs exactly twice among the faces. The remaining two faces of each cube will be its top and bottom faces when it is placed in the stack.

	Cube A	Cube B	Cube C	Cube D
Pairs of opposite faces	4 4 3	4 1 2	1 1 3	1 1 4
	2 1 2	4 3 3	1 4 2	3 2 2
Sums of pairs	⑥5 5	8 4⑤	2⑤5	④3 6

[†]R. Levin, "Solving Instant Insanity," *Journal of Recreational Mathematics*, pp. 189–192.

Exercises and Activities 9.3

1. *School Classroom:* Suppose that your students are using sticks and gumdrops to create models of the five Platonic solids. How will you help them decide how many sticks and how many gumdrops they need and how to assemble their solids?

2. *School Classroom:* When asked to make a net for a cube, a drawing like net A is the usual response. Design an activity for middle school students that will lead them to draw nets like net B that are formed without using all squares. Describe your activity in such a way that another person could follow your directions. Submit a few designs for a net by sketching them on 2-Centimeter Grid Paper. 2-Centimeter Grid Paper is available for download at the companion website.

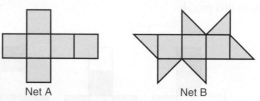

Net A   Net B

3. *School Classroom:* Read the definitions of face, edge, and vertex in the *Get Ready* box at the top of the **Elementary School Text** page at the beginning of this section. Review the answers in the *Check* table for the number of faces, edges, and vertices for each shape and compare them to the definitions. Make a list of at least three questions you anticipate that your students will ask about these ideas. Describe how you will answer those questions.

4. *Math Concepts:* Design a two-dimensional net for the following figure that is composed of four cubes. Describe your procedure for constructing this net and submit a copy of the net with your response.

5. *Math Concepts:* Open the **Math Laboratory Investigation 9.3: Read Me—Pyramid Patterns Instructions** from the companion website and investigate the pyramid patterns described in question 1 of the *Starting Points for Investigations 9.3*. Show your procedures and explain your thinking.

6. *Math Concepts:* Check your conjecture for Euler's formula (activity 3a in this activity set) on the two-polygon Archimedean solids in activity 5 of this activity set (parts b, d, e, f, g, h, i, j, and m) by listing and comparing the number of edges, vertices, and faces. You may wish to do an Internet search on a site such as Math World (mathworld.wolfram.com) to find movable three-dimensional views of the solids pictured in activity 5.

7. *NCTM Standards:* Read over the **Geometry Standards** in the back pages of this book. Pick one *Expectation*, from each grade level that the activities in this activity set address. State the *Expectations* and the *Standards* they are under. Explain which activities address these *Expectations* and how they do so.

---

bennett-burton-nelson website

Virtual Manipulatives	Grid and Dot Paper	Links and Readings
Interactive Chapter Applets	Color Transparencies	Geometer Sketchpad Modules
Puzzlers	Extended Bibliography	

Activity Set **9.4**

CREATING SYMMETRIC FIGURES: PATTERN BLOCKS AND PAPER FOLDING

Virtual Manipulatives

ww.mhhe.com/bbn

PURPOSE

To introduce investigations of symmetry.

MATERIALS

Pattern Blocks from the Manipulative Kit or the Virtual Manipulatives, Material Card 33, scissors and pieces of blank or scratch paper.

INTRODUCTION

The *wind rose,* shown below on the left, is a mariner's device for charting the direction of the wind. The earliest known wind rose appeared on the ancient sailing charts of the Mediterranean pilots, who charted eight principal winds. These are marked Nord, NE, EST, SE, Sud, SO, Ovest, and NO on the wind rose. Later, half-winds led to a wind rose with 16 points, and quarter-winds brought the total number of points to 32.[†]

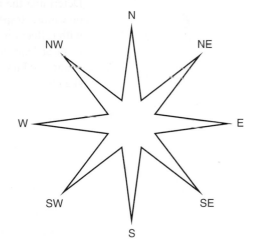

The eight-pointed wind rose shown above at the right is highly symmetric. It has eight lines of symmetry and eight rotational symmetries. For example, a line through any two opposite vertices of the wind rose is a **line of symmetry** because when the wind rose is folded on this line, the two sides will coincide. When a figure has a line of symmetry, the figure is also said to have *reflection symmetry.* The wind rose has **rotational symmetries** of 45°, 90°, 135°, 180°, 225°, 270°, 315°, and 360° because, when rotated about its center through any one of these angles, the figure will coincide with the original position of the wind rose.

In activities 1 and 2 you will be using pattern blocks to construct symmetric figures, and activities 3 to 6 have several basic patterns for cutting out symmetric figures. The variety of figures that can be obtained from slight changes in the angles of the cuts is surprising. The eight-pointed wind rose can be cut from one of these patterns. As you cut out these figures try to predict which one will produce the eight-pointed wind rose.

[†]M. C. Krause, "Wind Rose, the Beautiful Circle," *Arithmetic Teacher,* p. 375.

Pattern Block Symmetries

1. Use the square and the tan rhombus from your pattern block pieces to form figure 1. Notice that when another rhombus is attached as in figures 2 and 3, the new figures each have one line of symmetry. When the rhombus is attached as in figure 4, there are no lines of symmetry but there is rotational symmetry of 180°. Finally, when the rhombus is attached as in figure 5, there are no lines of symmetry or rotational symmetries (other than 360°).

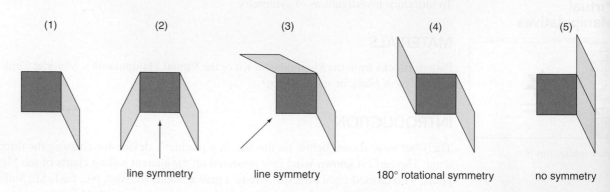

| (1) | (2) | (3) | (4) | (5) |

line symmetry   line symmetry   180° rotational symmetry   no symmetry

*a. Form this figure with your pattern block pieces. Determine the different ways you can attach exactly one more trapezoid to this figure to create figures with reflection symmetry. Use your pattern blocks to form at least four of these figures and sketch your results. Mark the lines of symmetry on your sketches.

b. Do the same as in part a but find two ways to create figures with rotational symmetry (other than 360°) by attaching exactly one more trapezoid to the figure above. List the rotational symmetries for each figure.

*c. By attaching 6 trapezoids to one hexagon, create the following four figures that have the given properties. Sketch your results.

Figure 1: One line of symmetry and no rotational symmetries (other than 360°)

Figure 2: Six rotational symmetries but no lines of symmetry

Figure 3: Three rotational symmetries and three lines of symmetry

Figure 4: No rotational symmetries (other than 360°) and no lines of symmetry

2. a. Use your pattern blocks and Material Card 33 to build this design. Complete the design by adding additional pattern blocks so that the design has reflection symmetry about both perpendicular lines. Sketch the completed design on the given axes. Does the completed design have any rotational symmetries? If so, what are they?

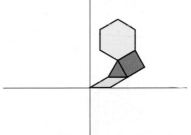

b. Build the design shown here and use additional pattern blocks to complete a design which has rotational symmetries of 90°, 180°, and 270° about the intersection of the perpendicular lines. Sketch the completed design on the given axes. Does the completed design have reflection symmetries? If so, how many? Mark any lines of symmetry on your sketch.

c. Arrange pattern blocks as shown in this figure. Add additional pattern blocks so that the completed design has rotational symmetry of 90°, 180°, and 270°. Sketch the completed design on the given axes.

Paper-Folding Symmetries

3. Fold a rectangular piece of paper in half twice, making the second fold perpendicular to the first. Let C be the corner of all folded edges. Hold the folded paper at corner C and make one cut across as shown by segment AB on the diagram. Before opening the folded corner, predict what the shape (shaded part in unfolded paper) will be and how many lines of symmetry it will have.

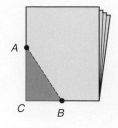

	Predicted Figure	Actual Result
Type of polygon	_____	_____
Number of lines of symmetry	_____	_____

a. Is it possible to draw a segment AB and make one cut across the folds so that the piece will unfold to a square? If so, describe how you made your cut. If not, explain why it cannot be done.

b. Using a new piece of paper each time, experiment with other single cuts that start at point A but which exit from any of the other three sides of the twice-folded paper. Continue to predict before you unfold. Make a list of the different types of figures you obtain.

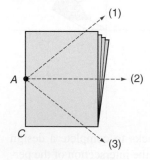

Cut	Predicted Figure	Actual Result
(1)	_____	_____
(2)	_____	_____
(3)	_____	_____

4. Fold a rectangular piece of paper in half twice, making the second fold perpendicular to the first as in activity 3. Let C be the corner of all the folded edges. Make two cuts from the edges to an inside point, as shown here. Before cutting the paper, predict what kind of polygon you will get, how many lines of symmetry the figure will have, and whether the figure will be convex or nonconvex. Cut and check your predictions.

	Predicted Figure	Actual Result
Type of polygon	_____	_____
Number of lines of symmetry	_____	_____
Convex or not	_____	_____

*a. Find a way to make two cuts into an inside point so that you get a regular octagon; a regular hexagon. Sketch the location of your cuts on these folded-paper diagrams.

C   Octagon   C   Hexagon

b. Make a sketch of the figure you think will result when you cut a piece of double-folded paper as shown at the left. Then cut the paper and sketch the result.

C

Predicted Figure	Actual Result

c. Vary the angle of the cuts in part b so that the two cuts are not parallel to each other. Experiment with cuts that will result in a rhombus inside a square; a square inside a rhombus. Sketch these lines on the folded-paper diagrams below.

Cuts for rhombus   Sketch of rhombus   Cuts for square   Sketch of square
inside square   inside square   inside rhombus   inside rhombus

5. The following pattern leads to a variety of symmetrical shapes. Begin with a standard sheet of paper as in figure a, and fold the upper right corner down to produce figure b. Then fold the upper vertex R down to point S to obtain figure c. To get figure d, fold the two halves inward so that points S and T are on line ℓ.

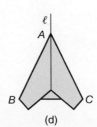

(a)   (b)   (c)   (d)

Make a horizontal cut, as indicated on this diagram, and draw a sketch of the resulting figure.

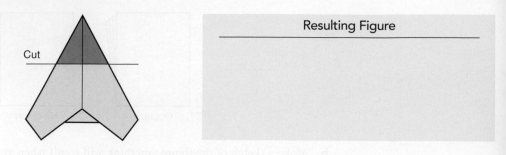

Cut

Resulting Figure

For each part a–d, draw a sketch of the figure you predict will result from the indicated cut. Then fold the paper, make the cut, and draw the actual result. Determine the number of lines of symmetry for each.

a. Slanted cut

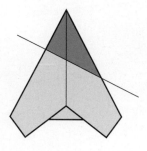

Predicted Figure	Actual Result

Number of lines of symmetry _____

b. Slanted cut (reversed)

Predicted Figure	Actual Result

Number of lines of symmetry _____

c. Combination of two slanted cuts

Predicted Figure	Actual Result

Number of lines of symmetry _____

*d. Two cuts to an inside point on the center line

Predicted Figure	Actual Result

Number of lines of symmetry _____

*e. Find two cuts from the slanted sides of the following figure into a point on the center line that will produce a regular 16-sided polygon. Sketch the cuts on this diagram.

6. The five-pointed star has been used for badges and national symbols for centuries. It appears on the flags of over 40 countries and was once used on the back of a United States $4 piece.

The steps pictured in figures a through d illustrate a paper-folding approach to making a five-pointed star. To obtain figure a, fold a standard sheet of *paper* perpendicular to its longer side. Next, fold point *C* over to midpoint *M* of side $\overline{AD}$, as shown in figure b. To get figure c, fold up the corner containing point *D* and crease along $\overline{MZ}$. The final fold line is shown in figure d. Fold the right side of figure d over to the left side so that edge *NZ* lies along edge *MZ* resulting in figure e.

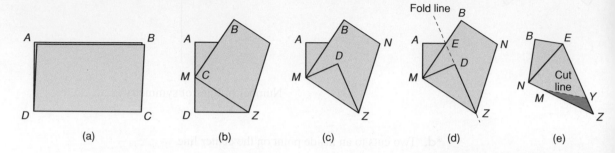

(a)   (b)   (c)   (d)   (e)

a. Using your folded paper, as in figure e, make a cut from *Y* to *M* (not *N*) and sketch the resulting figure here. Changing the position of *Y* will alter the thickness of the points on your star. Hold the paper tightly when cutting so it doesn't slip.

b. Begin with a new piece of paper and use the preceding steps to obtain the pattern in figure e. Find a way to make a single cut so that the resulting figure is a regular pentagon; a regular decagon. Sketch the cut lines on the figures below.

JUST FOR FUN

SNOWFLAKES

Snow is the only substance that crystallizes in many different figures. Yet, in spite of the variations in the figures, all snow crystals have a common characteristic—their hexagonal shape.

A New England farmer, W. A. Bentley, began looking at snowflakes when he was given a microscope at the age of 15. A few years later he was given a camera, which he adapted to his microscope to take photographs of snowflakes. Shortly before his death in 1931, Bentley published a book containing 2500 pictures of snow crystals. His work has been used by artists, photographers, illustrators, jewelers, meteorologists, and crystallographers.[†]

To create your own snowflake, fold a standard-size sheet of paper according to the following directions.

1. Fold the paper in half twice, making the second fold perpendicular to the first as in activity 3. In figure a the corner C is also the center of the original piece of paper.

2. Fold to find the center line parallel to the longer edges, as indicated in figure b.

3. Bring corner X up to the center line and crease the paper along CY, as shown in figure c.

4. Fold corner B back until side $\overline{CB}$ lies along side $\overline{CY}$, and crease along $\overline{CX}$, as in figure d.

5. Cut off the portion of paper above $\overline{XY}$, as shown in figure e.

Now cut out designs along sides $\overline{CY}$, $\overline{CX}$, and $\overline{XY}$. Unfold the finished product carefully to examine your snowflake design. What is its shape? What lines of symmetry and what rotational symmetries does it have? Experiment with other designs to obtain a variety of snowflakes.

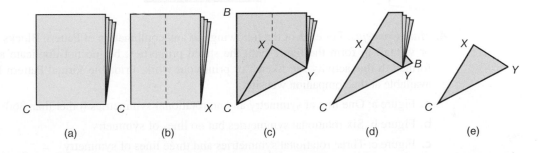

(a)	(b)	(c)	(d)	(e)

[†]F. Hapgood, "When Ice Crystals Fall from the Sky, Art Meets Science," *Smithsonian*, pp. 67–72.

Exercises and Activities 9.4

1. *School Classroom:* One of your students claims that any line drawn through the center of a square is a line of symmetry for the square. Describe what you believe this student was thinking and how you would help her determine the lines of symmetry of a square without actually showing her these lines.

2. *School Classroom:* Rydell has found a wonderful pattern. Squares have four lines of symmetry and four rotational symmetries, nonsquare rectangles have two lines of symmetry and two rotational symmetries. He is sure this pattern (the number of lines of symmetry equals the number of rotational symmetries) holds for all quadrilaterals. Is he correct and if not, how can you help him resolve this issue?

3. *School Classroom:* Determine and describe the rotational and line symmetries for each of the following three figures.

   a.   b.   c.

4. *Math Concepts:* For each of the following use any combination of Pattern Blocks (cardstock or virtual) to form the figure with the stated properties; but do not duplicate any figures formed in this activity set. Sketch or print your work. Printable Virtual Pattern Blocks are available at the companion website.

   a. Figure a: One line of symmetry and no rotational symmetries (other than 360°)
   b. Figure b: Six rotational symmetries but no lines of symmetry
   c. Figure c: Three rotational symmetries and three lines of symmetry
   d. Figure d: No rotational symmetries (other than 360°) and no lines of symmetry

5. *Math Concepts:* How many symmetrical shapes can be made by joining one more square to the ten square shape below? Use color tiles from the Manipulative Kit to find the shapes and record your answers on centimeter grid paper. Describe the type of symmetry. Centimeter Grid Paper is available for download at the companion website.

6. *Math Concepts:* Open the **Math Laboratory Investigation 9.4: Read Me—Mirror Cards Instructions** from the companion website and investigate the mirror patterns described in 1, 2, and 3 of the *Starting Points for Investigations 9.4*. Show your procedures and explain your thinking. A small handheld mirror will be helpful.

7. *NCTM Standards:* Go to http://illuminations.nctm.org/ and under "Lessons" select grade levels 3–5 and the **Geometry Standard.** Choose a lesson involving symmetry.

   a. State the title of the lesson and briefly summarize the lesson.

   b. Referring to the **Standards Summary** in the back pages of this book as necessary, list the *Geometry Standard Expectations* that the lesson addresses and explain how the lesson addresses these *Expectations*.

ACTIVITIES FOR THE ELEMENTARY SCHOOL CLASSROOM

Tiling with Pattern Blocks

Purpose: To introduce elementary school students to creating tessellations with pattern block pieces.

Connections: Ask the students to describe some tiles that they have in the floors, kitchens, or bathrooms of their homes. Ask them what shapes the tiles in their homes have and why they think that these shapes are used for tiling. Ask if any of their homes have tile shapes other than squares. Tell them that today they will do some tiling with pattern blocks.

Materials: A set of pattern blocks for each student. Masters for pattern blocks can be downloaded from the companion website. Pattern block transparencies can also be made with the pattern block images. Sets of pattern blocks can be placed in plastic sealable bags.

1. Distribute a set of pattern blocks to each student. If the students are not familiar with pattern blocks, allow time for them to sort, group by color, and manipulate the blocks. Discuss the names of the various pattern block shapes.

2. Ask the students to use their orange squares to show how they can be used for tiling. Select a student volunteer to show a tiling pattern. Ask for volunteers to show different ways of tiling with squares. Stress that when tiling there can be no gaps or overlaps.

3. Have students test the yellow hexagons to see if they can be used for tiling. Is there more than one tiling pattern with the hexagons? Discuss.

4. Ask the students to create ways of tiling with the red trapezoids. Share and discuss different tiling patterns.

Forming tessellations with pattern blocks is a natural activity for children as early as the first grade.

5. Have the students select two different shapes and tile the surface using both shapes. Give the students the opportunity to see the tiling patterns created by their classmates.

6. (Optional) The students can trace their pattern blocks and color the shapes to create a record of their tile patterns. The results can be posted in the room. Some students may wish to create tiling patterns using more than two pattern blocks. For some grade levels, it may be appropriate to call these tiling patterns "tessellations" and the process of creating a pattern is called "tessellating."

10 Measurement

Since the customary English system of measurement is still prevalent in the United States, students should learn both customary and metric systems and should know some rough equivalences between the metric and customary systems. . . .

Students should begin to develop formulas for perimeter and area in the elementary grades. Middle-grade students should formalize these techniques, as well as develop formulas for the volume and surface area of objects like prisms and cylinders.[†]

Activity Set **10.1** ## MEASURING WITH METRIC UNITS

PURPOSE

To use estimation and measurement activities to introduce the basic metric units.

MATERIALS

The Metric Ruler from Material Card 20, the Metric Measuring Tape from Material Card 34, and pieces of paper.

© 1974 United Feature Syndicate, Inc.

INTRODUCTION

The metric system of measurement is used by most nations of the world. The basic metric units for length, mass, and volume are the *meter* (a little longer than a yard), the *gram* (about the weight of a paper clip), and the *liter* (a little more than a quart). If larger and smaller measures

[†]*Principles and Standards for School Mathematics,* pp. 45–46.

12-1

① Introduce

Activity Choice 1 • Hands-On

Show students a 24-inch length of yarn. Explain that you will use **nonstandard units**—a paper clip and a craft stick—to measure it. Have students guess if you will use more craft sticks or paper clips.

- **How many craft sticks long do you think this yarn is?** about 5 craft sticks
- **How many paper clips long do you think this yarn is?** about 20 paper clips

Ask volunteers to **measure** the yarn, using both craft sticks and paper clips.

Activity Choice 2 • Literature

Introduce the lesson with *Super Sand Castle Saturday* by Stuart J. Murphy. For a related math activity, see p. TR60.

② Teach

Draw a three-column table on the board. Label the second and third columns "Unit of Measure" and "Measurement."

- **What are some things in our classroom that we can measure with paper clips?** Sample answers: stapler, books, desk, shoes, notebooks

Write the items students mention in the first column.

- **What objects can we use to measure length?** Sample answers: paper clips, blocks, hands

Record different units of measure in the "Units of Measure" column of the table. Then have volunteers use those units to measure the items and record the results in the "Measure" column.

Get Ready Use the section at the top of p. 379 to teach the lesson concept. Guide students as they measure length using nonstandard units.

Check Observe students as you work through Exercises 1–2 as a class.

 Exercise 3 Assess student comprehension before assigning practice exercises.

⚠️ **COMMON ERROR!**
Students may fail to lay out nonstandard units in a straight line. Have them use a straightedge to help keep the units lined up. They can also start at the exact end of an object, lining up the units next to the object.

Name _____

Nonstandard Units

*I will use **nonstandard units**, like cubes and paper clips, to measure the pencil.*

Get Ready

Main Idea
I will select and use nonstandard units to describe length.

Vocabulary
nonstandard unit
measure
length

You can use different units to **measure length**.

Remember
Line up the end of the pencil with the end of your unit of measure.

The pencil measures

about **6** cubes long or

about **8** paper clips long.

Check   1, 2. See students' answers.

Find the object. Select and draw your unit of measure. Use your unit to measure the object.

1.   Unit of measure: _____

          Measurement: about _____

2.   Glue Stick   Unit of measure: _____

          Measurement: about _____

3. **Talk About It** How would your measurement in Exercise 2 be different if you used a smaller unit of measure?
The measure would be a greater number.

Chapter 12   Lesson 1   three hundred seventy-nine   379

Reteach (p. 6)   **BL**

12-1 Reteach
Nonstandard Units

Different units make different measurements.
A ▢ will give a different measurement than a ⬭ for the same object.

Estimate. Then use ▢ and ⬭ to measure.   Answers will vary depending on size of classroom objects.

Skills Practice (p. 7)   **OL**

12-1 Skills Practice
Nonstandard Units

Find the object. Estimate. Then use ⬭ to measure.

Estimate: about _____   Measure: about _____

2.   glue   Answers will vary depending on size of classroom objects.

Estimate: about _____   Measure: about _____

Solve.
3. Jim wants to measure his marker with cubes and paper clips. About how many of each unit?

about _____   about _____

Are your answers the same or different? Explain why.
Answers will vary depending on size of classroom objects.

are needed in the metric system, they are obtained by using the following prefixes. The four prefixes marked with an asterisk are most commonly used. There are additional prefixes that extend this system to even larger and smaller measures for scientific purposes.

kilo*	1000 times
hecto	100 times
deka	10 times
deci*	$\frac{1}{10}$
centi*	$\frac{1}{100}$
milli*	$\frac{1}{1000}$

The prefixes differ by powers of 10. For example,

$$10 \text{ millimeters (mm)} = 1 \text{ centimeter (cm)}$$

$$10 \text{ centimeters} = 1 \text{ decimeter (dm)}$$

$$10 \text{ decimeters} = 1 \text{ meter (m)}$$

$$1000 \text{ meters} = 1 \text{ kilometer (km)}$$

1 cm
1 cm
1 cm

One cubic centimeter (1 cm^3) equals 1 milliliter (mL) and, if water, has a mass of about 1 gram (g).

Here is one simple relationship among the metric units for length, mass, and volume: One cubic centimeter of water equals one milliliter of water and has a mass of about one gram.

The following activities involve the metric units for length and volume. If you are not familiar with the metric system and are unaccustomed to thinking of length in terms of centimeters and meters, the estimation and measuring game in activity 1 will give you expertise quickly. Another measuring game is in *Just for Fun,* at the end of this activity set.

---

1. **Centimeter and Meter Guessing Games** (2 players): One player marks two points on a sheet of paper. The opponent guesses the distance in centimeters between these two points. The distance is then measured with a centimeter ruler. If the guess is within 1 centimeter of being correct, the guessing player scores 1 point. If not, there is no score. The players alternate picking points and guessing distances until someone has scored 11 points. Use the score chart on the next page and play the game with a partner.

   Challenging: If a player thinks an opponent's guess is not within 1 centimeter, that player may challenge the guess by giving his or her own estimate of the distance. If the challenger's estimate is within 1 centimeter and the opponent's is not, then the challenger receives 1 point and the opponent receives no score. However, if the opponent is within 1 centimeter, he or she receives 2 points for the insult, regardless of the challenger's estimate, and the challenger receives no score.

   Variation 1: Players estimate the lengths of objects around them. Since they will be estimating in centimeters, these objects should be reasonably small, such as pencils, books, width and length of desks, etc.

   Variation 2: This game is called the Meter Guessing Game. On a player's turn, he or she selects an object in the room, and the opponent guesses its length in meters. If the guess is within $\frac{1}{2}$ meter, the guessing player scores 1 point. If not, there is no score. The players alternate picking objects and guessing lengths. As before, a player's guess may be challenged.

Guess in cm	Actual Distance in cm	Score Player 1	Player 2
_____	_____	_____	_____
_____	_____	_____	_____
_____	_____	_____	_____
_____	_____	_____	_____
_____	_____	_____	_____
_____	_____	_____	_____
_____	_____	_____	_____
_____	_____	_____	_____
_____	_____	_____	_____
_____	_____	_____	_____
_____	_____	_____	_____
_____	_____	_____	_____

2. Your handspan is a convenient ruler for measuring lengths. Stretch out your fingers and use your metric ruler (Material Card 20) to measure the maximum distance from your little finger to your thumb in centimeters.

a. Use your handspan to approximate the width and length of this page in centimeters. Record your results below and then check your approximations by measuring.

	Width	Length
Approximation	_____	_____
Measurement	_____	_____

b. Select some objects around you and estimate their lengths in centimeters. Check your estimates by measuring. Repeat this activity 10 times, and see how many lengths you can predict to within 1 centimeter. Record the objects, your estimates of lengths, and your measurements. In the last column record the difference between your estimation and measurement as a positive number, and then compute the average difference.

Object	Estimation	Measurement (nearest cm)	Difference
_____	_____	_____	_____
_____	_____	_____	_____
_____	_____	_____	_____
_____	_____	_____	_____
_____	_____	_____	_____
_____	_____	_____	_____
_____	_____	_____	_____
_____	_____	_____	_____
_____	_____	_____	_____
_____	_____	_____	_____

Average of differences _____

3. A millimeter is the smallest unit on your metric ruler. Obtain the measurements of the objects in parts a through c to the nearest millimeter.

  ***a.** The length of a dollar bill.

  ***b.** The diameter of a penny.

  c. The width of one of your fingernails. Do you have one with a width of 1 centimeter?

  d. What fraction of a millimeter is the thickness of one page of this book? (*Hint:* Measure several pages at once.)

4. This table contains some body measurements that are useful for buying and making clothes. Estimate or use your handspan to approximate these measurements. Then use your metric measuring tape and your metric ruler to obtain these measurements to the nearest centimeter.

	Estimate	Measurement
Waist		
Height		
Arm length		
Foot length		
Width of palm		
Circumference of head		

5. Use your metric measuring tape (Material Card 34) for the following.

  a. Measure the distance from the middle of your chest to your fingertips with your arm outstretched. Is this distance greater than or less than 1 meter? This body distance was once used by merchants to measure cloth. It is the origin of the English measure called the yard.

  b. Measure the distance from the floor up to your waist. How does this distance compare with a meter?

c. Select some objects around you whose lengths are greater than 1 meter, and try to estimate their length to within $\frac{1}{2}$ meter (50 cm). For example, estimate the height, width, and length of a room and then measure these distances with your metric measuring tape. Repeat this activity for 10 different objects. Record the objects, your estimates of lengths, and the measurements in the following table. In the last column of the table, record the difference between your estimation and measurement, as a positive number, and then compute the average of the differences.

Object	Estimation	Measurement (nearest $\frac{1}{2}$ m)	Difference

Average of differences _____

6. Your *pace* is the distance you cover in one normal step. The single pace shown here is approximately 51 centimeters. To gather information about your pace, measure off a distance of 10 meters. Record the time in seconds and the number of paces it takes you to walk this distance.

Number of paces needed to walk 10 meters: _____

Time, in seconds, needed to walk 10 meters: _____

Using this information, explain how to determine each of the following.

a. The length of a single pace, in centimeters.

b. The number of paces it will take you to walk 1 kilometer.

c. The time in minutes that it will take you to walk 1 kilometer.

7. A liter is very close to the English measure the quart. A liter is equal to 1000 cubic centimeters (1000 milliliters), the volume of a 10 cm by 10 cm by 10 cm cube.

One-quart container

19.3 cm

7 cm   7 cm

   *a. Use the dimensions on this drawing of a quart container to approximate the number of cubic centimeters in a quart. Which is greater, a liter or a quart?

   *b. Suppose you wanted to cut off the top of a two-quart milk container to use for measuring 1 liter. What height (from the bottom of the container) should be marked as a cut line to measure 1 liter?

Two-quart container

Milk
Half Gallon (1.89 L)

Milk

Half Gallon (1.89 L)

20.5 cm

9.6 cm

9.6 cm

JUST FOR FUN

CENTIMETER RACING GAME (2 or more players)

This game is played on a racing mat (Material Card 35). The object of the game is to go from the center of the circle to a point inside the triangle, square, pentagon, and hexagon, in that order. Each player in turn rolls two dice. The two numbers may be added, subtracted, multiplied, or divided. The resulting computation is the number of centimeters the player moves. A metric ruler (Material Card 20) should be used to draw the line segment whose length is the player's number.

   On each subsequent turn, players draw another line segment, beginning at the end of their last line segment. Before players can pass through a polygon or proceed from one polygon to the next, they must land inside the polygon with the end of a line segment. The first player to draw a line segment that ends inside the hexagon is the winner.

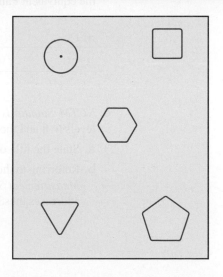

Exercises and Activities 10.1

1. *School Classroom:* In a half page or more, make a case for one of the following approaches to teaching the metric system.

   a. The metric system should be taught from the point of view that it is secondary to the standard English system and learning how to convert between the two systems is the primary goal.

   b. The metric system should be taught so students can operate in the metric system with the facility we expect them to have with the standard English system.

2. *School Classroom:* While doing a measurement activity, one of your students asks you what it means to record a measurement to the nearest centimeter. Explain how you would help him understand what it means to measure "to the nearest centimeter."

3. *School Classroom:* The **Elementary School Text** page at the beginning of this section directs students to choose their own units of measure to measure the lengths of various objects. Explain what you believe is the purpose of this activity. Why not just give the students rulers (centimeter and inch) and teach them how to measure lengths using standard units?

4. *Math Concepts:* In the metric system of measures, "meters" are used instead of "yards" from the English system. What used to be the 100-yard dash in track has now become the 100-meter dash (even though the distances are different).

   a. What lengths in the metric system do you think are used instead of these common units of length in the English system: quarter of an inch, inch, foot, and mile?

   b. Give examples to explain the advantage of the metric system over the English system with respect to the numerical relationship between the common units of length within each system.

5. *Math Concepts:* The Celsius scale is used for temperature in the metric system. Freezing is 0°C and boiling is 100°C on the Celsius scale. The corresponding temperatures on the Fahrenheit scale are 32°F and 212°F, respectively. Viewing the two temperature scales side-by-side as below, and using arithmetic but no formulas, explain how you can determine the equivalent Fahrenheit temperature for 20°C.

0°C	20°C	100°C
32°F		212°F

6. *NCTM Standards:* Go to http://illuminations.nctm.org/ and under "Lessons" select grade levels 6–8 and the **Measurement Standard.** Choose a lesson involving measurement.

   a. State the title of the lesson and briefly summarize the lesson.

   b. Referring to the **Standards Summary** in the back pages of this book as necessary, list the *Measurement Standard Expectations* that the lesson addresses and explain how the lesson addresses these *Expectations*.

7. *NCTM Standards:* Using the **Standards Summary** at the back of this book, describe what metric measuring experiences are being suggested at each level: Pre-K–2, grades 3–5, and grades 6–8.

bennett-burton-nelson website

Virtual Manipulatives   Grid and Dot Paper   Links and Readings
Interactive Chapter Applets Color Transparencies   Geometer Sketchpad Modules
Puzzlers   Extended Bibliography

Activity Set **10.2**   AREAS ON GEOBOARDS

PURPOSE

To use rectangular geoboards to develop area concepts.

MATERIALS

A Rectangular Geoboard and rubber bands (optional). There is a template for making a rectangular geoboard on Material Card 8 or you may wish to use the Rectangular Geoboard in the Virtual Manipulatives.

Virtual Manipulatives

www.mhhe.com/bbn

INTRODUCTION

The virtual geoboard shown to the left has a rectangular array of 25 pins around which rubber bands have been placed. Notice the red polygon on the geoboard is divided into 6 squares and 7 half squares by blue bands. If one small square serves as a unit of area, then the total area of the polygon is $9\frac{1}{2}$ unit squares or $9\frac{1}{2}$ square units.

In the following activities you will examine different methods for determining areas of polygons and discover how the formulas for the areas of rectangles, parallelograms, and triangles are related. The unit square for the areas in these activities is the smallest square with pins at its corners (1 unit by 1 unit) and the area of a polygon is the number of unit squares needed to cover the polygon.

---

1. In the figure for part a, the upper shaded triangle has an area of 1 square unit because it is half of a 2-unit by 1-unit rectangle. Similarly, the lower shaded triangle has an area of $1\frac{1}{2}$ square units because it is half of a 3-unit by 1-unit rectangle. Determine the areas of these figures by subdividing them into squares, halves of squares, and triangles that are halves of rectangles.

    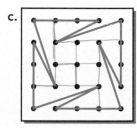

Area of figure: _____   _____   _____

2. Sometimes it is easier to find the area outside a figure than the area inside. The hexagon in part a has been enclosed inside a square. What is the area of the shaded region? Subtract this area from the area of the 3-unit by 3-unit square to find the area of the hexagon. Use this technique to find the areas of the other figures.

    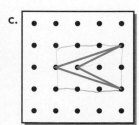

Area of figure: _____   _____   _____

3. The **height,** or **altitude,** of a triangle is the perpendicular distance from a vertex to the line containing the opposite side. The **height** of a parallelogram is the perpendicular distance from a line containing one side to the line containing the opposite side. Using the length between two consecutive vertical or horizontal pins as the unit length, determine the heights, base length, and area of each triangle and each parallelogram.

   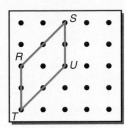

Height from vertex *A:* _____   Height from vertex *E:* _____   Height from side $\overline{ZW}$: _____   Height from side $\overline{RS}$: _____

Base $\overline{BC}$ length: _____   Base $\overline{FG}$ length: _____   Base $\overline{ZW}$ length: _____   Base $\overline{RS}$ length: _____

Area: _____   Area: _____   Area: _____   Area: _____

4. Use your geoboard techniques to determine the area and the perimeter of each of these parallelograms.

       a.   **b.**   **c.**   **d.**

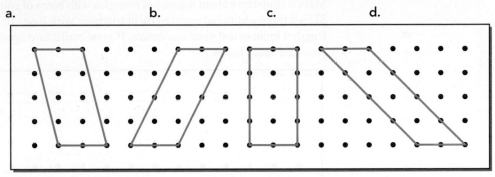

Area: _____   _____   _____   _____

Perimeter: _____   _____   _____   _____

e. The parallelograms in parts a–d all have the same height, and each has two sides of length 2 units. Make a conjecture about how to determine the area of a parallelogram if you know the length of a side and the height from that side. Sketch three additional parallelograms here with different areas to test your conjecture. If your conjecture appears to be valid, record it in the provided space.

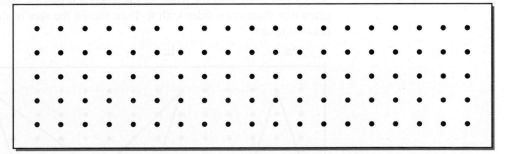

Conjecture:

f. It is a common thought that the area of some polygons is directly connected to the perimeter of the polygon. That is, when the perimeter of a polygon increases or decreases, so does the area. Is this true for parallelograms? Explain your thinking.

5. Use geoboard techniques to determine the areas of these triangles.

a.　　　　　　**b.**　　　　　　　　**c.**　　　　　　　　**d.**

Triangle Area: _____　　　　_____　　　　_____　　　　_____

Make a conjecture about the area of triangles with bases of equal length and common heights. Sketch three additional noncongruent triangles with bases of length 5 units and altitudes of length 4 units to test your conjecture. If your conjecture appears to be valid, record it in the provided space below.

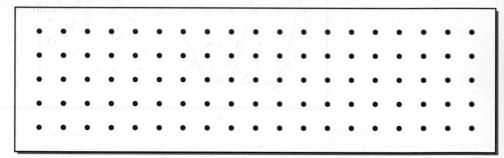

Conjecture:

6. One approach to discovering the formula for the area of a triangle is to use the formula for the area of a parallelogram. The triangle in part a below is enclosed in a parallelogram that shares two sides with the triangle. Enclose each triangle (parts b, c, and d) in a parallelogram that shares two sides with it. Then record the area of the triangle and the area of the parallelogram.

*a.　　　　　　**b.**　　　　　　***c.**　　　　　　**d.**

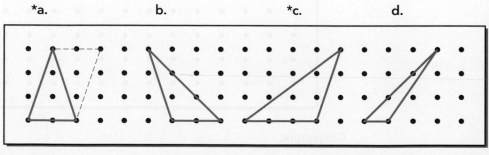

Triangle area: _____　　_____　　_____　　_____

Parallelogram area: _____　　_____　　_____　　_____

*7. The formula for the area of a triangle is one-half of the base length times the height to that base $[A = (\frac{1}{2})bh]$. Based on the observations you have made in activities 3, 4, 5, and 6, write a statement that explains why this formula works.

JUST FOR FUN

PENTOMINOES

Pentominoes are shapes that can be formed by joining five squares along their edges. Surprisingly, there are 12 such shapes. Pentominoes are used in puzzles, games, tessellations, and other problem-solving activities.

A complete set of pentomino pieces is on Material Card 36. Material Card 37 has a grid that can be used for questions 2, 3, and 4. (*Note:* Pieces can be turned over for the activities.)

1. Selecting the appropriate pieces from your pentomino set, form the 4 by 5 rectangular puzzle shown here. Outline this rectangle with pencil, and see how many other combinations of pieces you can find that will exactly fill the outline. There are at least five others.

2. The best-known challenge is to use all 12 pieces to form a 6 by 10 rectangle. Supposedly there are over 2000 different solutions. Find one solution and record it on this grid.

3. The 12 combined pentomino pieces have a total of 60 squares; therefore, it is possible to create puzzle grids from an 8 by 8 grid with 4 squares removed. One of these puzzles has a square removed from each corner as shown here. Use all 12 pieces to cover a grid with this shape. Record your solution here.

*4. Pentomino Game (2 players): This game is played on an 8 by 8 grid. The players take turns placing a pentomino on uncovered squares of the grid. Play continues until someone is unable to play or all the pieces have been used. The player who makes the last move wins the game. The first seven plays of a game are shown on this board. Player A has made four moves, and player B has made three moves. Find a way player B can make the eighth move (with one of the remaining pentominoes) so that no more moves can be made. Play a few games and look for strategies.

*5. It is possible to place 5 different pentomino pieces on an 8 by 8 grid so that no other piece from the same set can be placed on the grid. Find 5 such pieces.

Exercises and Activities **10.2**

Downloadable Dot Paper, Rectangular Geoboards, and printable Virtual Rectangular Geoboards are available at the companion website.

1. *School Classroom:* One of your students says that she can find the area of any geoboard figure that has no pins inside of it by counting the number of pins on the boundary of the figure, subtracting 2, and then dividing that number by 2. Form and record several figures that satisfy her conditions and determine their areas to test her conjecture. What would you say to this student?

2. *School Classroom:* Design a geoboard activity connecting the exploration of perimeter and area in parallelograms that you believe is appropriate for an elementary school student and write a few questions that you can ask about your activity. Try this activity on an elementary school age child of your choice. Describe your activity and record your questions and the student's responses.

3. *Math Concepts:* Determine the areas of the following figures using any technique or combination of techniques from the activities in this activity set. Notice that the hexagon in part a has a vertical line of symmetry, so you can determine the area of half the hexagonal region and then double the result to obtain the area of the entire hexagonal region.

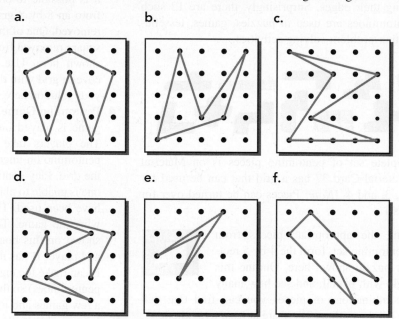

a.   b.   c.

d.   e.   f.

4. *Math Concepts:*

   a. Use geoboard techniques to determine the areas of these six trapezoids without using any known formulas (see Activity Set 9.1 for the definition of trapezoid).

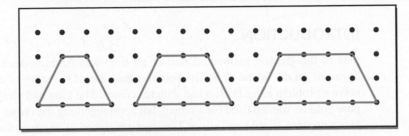

   b. Make a conjecture about the area of trapezoids with upper bases of equal length and lower bases of equal length but with different heights.

   c. Sketch three additional noncongruent trapezoids and determine their areas to test your conjecture.

5. *Math Concepts:* On a 5-pin × 5-pin geoboard:

   a. Determine a triangle of *least* area that can be formed with vertices on pins. Repeat for the triangle of greatest area. Record your triangles and justify your answers.

   b. Is it possible to form a triangle with area 1 square unit and a triangle with area 8 square units on a geoboard? Is it possible to form triangles with area 2, 3, 4, 5, 6, or 7 square units on a geoboard? Record your triangles and justify your answers.

6. *NCTM Standards:* Using the **Standards Summary** at the back of this book, list the *Expectations* that suggest using activities with nonstandard units of measurements (such as the width of your handspan) for Pre-K–2. Determine if these ideas extend to grades 3–5 and grades 6–8 and describe your results.

---

www.mhhe.com/bbn

bennett-burton-nelson website

Virtual Manipulatives   Grid and Dot Paper   Links and Readings
Interactive Chapter Applets   Color Transparencies   Geometer Sketchpad Modules
Puzzlers   Extended Bibliography

MODELS FOR VOLUME AND SURFACE AREA

PURPOSE

To construct three-dimensional figures and measure their volume.

MATERIALS

Patterns for a Prism, Pyramid, and Cylinder from Material Card 38; a Centimeter Ruler, a Compass, and a Protractor from Material Card 20; sand or rice for activity 6; and pieces of standard paper. For activity 7 an unopened cylindrical can, a baseball, and a container that can be used to submerge the baseball and the can in water.

INTRODUCTION

One of the greatest mathematicians of all time was Archimedes (287–212 B.C.E.), a native of Syracuse on the Island of Sicily. You may have heard the story of how Archimedes was able to solve a problem King Hieron had with his crown. The king had weighed out the exact amount of pure gold he wanted used for a crown, but upon receiving the crown he became suspicious that it was a mixture of gold and silver. The crown weighed as much as the original amount of gold, so there seemed to be no way of exposing the fraud. Archimedes was informed of the problem, and a solution occurred to him while he was taking a bath. He noticed that the amount of water that overflowed the tub depended on the extent to which his body was immersed. In his excitement to try his solution with gold and silver, Archimedes leaped from the tub and ran naked to his home, shouting, "Eureka! Eureka!"

As Archimedes discovered, the volume of a submerged object is equal to the volume of the displaced water. Finding the volumes of objects by submerging them in water is especially convenient with metric units, because the number of milliliters of water that is displaced is equal to the volume of the object in cubic centimeters. This relationship will be used in the following activities. You will also need the formulas for volumes of prisms and cylinders (area of base $\times$ height), pyramids and cones ($\frac{1}{3} \times$ area of base $\times$ height), and spheres [$(\frac{4}{3})\pi r^3$].

*1. To understand Archimedes' solution, consider two cubes both weighing the same amount, one of pure gold and one of pure silver. Since gold is about twice as heavy as silver, the cube of gold will be smaller than the cube of silver. Therefore, when each is submerged in water, there will be more water displaced for the cube of silver. To apply his theory, Archimedes used the crown and an amount of pure gold weighing the same as the crown. He submerged them separately in water and measured the amount of overflow. There was more water displaced for the crown than for the pure gold. What does this show about the volume of the crown as compared to the volume of the gold? Was King Hieron cheated?

Gold   Silver

*2. Patterns for prisms, pyramids, and cylinders are easy to make. Three such patterns are contained on Material Card 38. Cut them out and tape their edges. Complete the first two lines of the table below and then determine the volumes and surface areas of these figures. You may wish to fill them with sand or rice to check your volume answers. (The area of the base of a cylinder is πr^2.)

	Hexagonal Prism	Hexagonal Pyramid	Cylinder
Area of base	_____	_____	_____
Height (altitude)	_____	_____	_____
Volume	_____	_____	_____
Surface area	_____	_____	_____

*3. A standard 21.5 cm × 28 cm sheet of paper can be made into a cylinder in the two ways shown in the following figures. Make a cylinder (without bases) so that its circumference is 21.5 centimeters and its height is 28 centimeters. Then use another sheet of paper to form a cylinder with a circumference of 28 centimeters and a height of 21.5 centimeters. Predict which cylinder has the greater volume. As you compute the volume of each cylinder, record your methods and answers below the figures.

Cylinder A   Cylinder B

Volume _____   Volume _____

4. Cut a standard sheet of paper in half lengthwise and tape the two halves end to end, as shown below. Make a cylinder without bases and compute its volume. Compare the volume of this cylinder with that of cylinder B in activity 3. What happens to the volume of a cylinder as the height is halved and the circumference (thus, radius and diameter) is doubled?

Cut

Top half

Bottom half

Two halves taped end to end

12-5 Surface Area of Cylinders

MAIN IDEA

Find the surface area of a cylinder.

Math Online

glencoe.com
- Extra Examples
- Personal Tutor
- Self-Check Quiz

▷ MINI Lab

STEP 1 Trace the top and bottom of the can on grid paper. Then cut out the shapes.

STEP 2 Cut a long rectangle from the grid paper. The width of the rectangle should be the same as the height of the can. Wrap the rectangle around the side of the can. Cut off the excess paper so that the edges just meet.

1. Make a net of the cylinder.
2. Name the shapes in the net.
3. How is the length of the rectangle related to the circles?

You can put two circles and a rectangle together to make a cylinder.

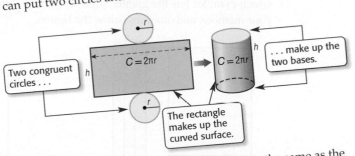

In the diagram above, the length of the rectangle is the same as the circumference of the circle. Also, the width of the rectangle is the same as the height of the cylinder.

$$S = 2(\pi r^2) + 2(\pi r)h$$

surface area = two bases + curved surface

Key Concept

Surface Area of a Cylinder

Words The surface area S of a cylinder with height h and radius r is the sum of the areas of the circular bases and the area of the curved surface.

Model

Symbols $S = 2\pi r^2 + 2\pi rh$

5. Make a set of six different cones by cutting out three disks, each of radius 10 centimeters. (There is a compass and protractor on Material Card 20.) Each disk can be used for making two cones, as shown here. Cut sectors from these disks with central angles of 45°, 90°, 135°, 225°, 270°, and 315°, and *number the sectors from 1 to 6 according to the size of the central angle*. After cutting each disk into two parts, bend and tape the edges to form the cones.

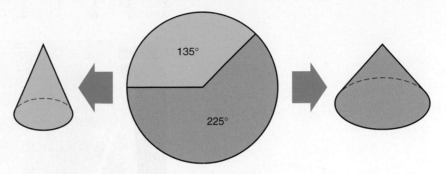

a. Without computing, line the cones up from left to right in what you estimate to be increasing volumes. Record your estimated order by recording the numbers of the cones.

_____   _____   _____   _____   _____   _____

Least volume   Greatest volume

*b. Compute the base areas and volumes (to the nearest two decimal places) of the cones, and enter them in the following table. Compare the results with the estimated order of the cones in part a. (The area of the base of a cone is πr^2.)

Computations:

	1	2	3	4	5	6
Central angle of disk	45°	90°	135°	225°	270°	315°
Radius (cm) of base	1.25	2.50	3.75	6.25	7.50	8.75
Base area (cm²)	_____	_____	_____	_____	_____	_____
Height (cm) of cone	9.92	9.68	9.27	7.81	6.61	4.84
Volume (cm³) of cone	_____	_____	_____	_____	_____	_____

*c. What will happen to the volume of the cone as sectors with central angles of less than 45° are used? As sectors with central angles of greater than 315° are used?

Central angles less than 45°:   Central angles greater than 315°:

6. Choose one of your cones from activity 5, and place a mark on the surface halfway from the vertex to the base (moving along the height from the vertex to the center of the cone).

    a. If the cone were filled to this mark, estimate what fractional part of the total volume of the cone would be filled. Circle the fraction that best represents your estimate.

$$\frac{1}{8} \qquad \frac{1}{7} \qquad \frac{1}{6} \qquad \frac{1}{5} \qquad \frac{1}{4} \qquad \frac{1}{3} \qquad \frac{1}{2}$$

    b. To experimentally test your estimate, fill the cone up to the mark with water (or sand or rice) and then pour its contents into an identical cone, repeating the process until the second cone is full. How many "fillings" are required?

    *c. Determine the radius and height of your "half-cone" and compute its volume. Compare this volume to the volume of the whole cone. Assume the cone has radius r and height h and that the half-cone has radius $\frac{r}{2}$ and height $\frac{h}{2}$. What fraction in part a represents the relationship between the volume of the half-cone compared to the volume of the whole cone? Show all of your work here.

7. The basketball and hand together displace 7715 milliliters of water and the hand alone displaces 480 milliliters. The marked line shows the original height of the water.

Original height of water

*a. What is the volume of the basketball in cubic centimeters?

b. What is the diameter of this ball to the nearest centimeter? [Sphere volume $= \left(\frac{4}{3}\right)\pi r^{3}$, where r is the radius.] Explain how you arrived at your conclusions.

c. Submerge a baseball in water and measure the displaced water in milliliters. According to this experiment, what is the volume of a baseball in cubic centimeters? A baseball has a diameter of approximately 7.3 centimeters. Compute its volume in cubic centimeters, and compare this answer with the results of your experiment. Record your results.

d. Submerge an unopened cylindrical can in water and measure the overflow. Then measure the diameter and height of the can and compute its volume. Compare the computed volume with the results of your experiment. Record your results.

8. Spherical objects such as Christmas tree ornaments and basketballs are packed in cube-shaped compartments and boxes.

a. If a sphere just fits into a box, estimate what fraction of the box is "wasted space." Circle the fraction that best represents your estimate.

$$\frac{1}{6} \qquad \frac{1}{5} \qquad \frac{1}{4} \qquad \frac{1}{3} \qquad \frac{1}{2}$$

Compute the amount of wasted space when a sphere of diameter 25 centimeters is placed in a 25 cm × 25 cm × 25 cm box. What fraction of the total volume of this box is wasted space?

b. Spheres are also packed in cylinders. A cylinder provides a better fit than a box, but there is still extra space. If 3 balls are packed in a cylindrical can whose diameter equals that of a ball and whose height is 3 times the diameter of a ball, estimate what fraction of the space is unused.

$$\frac{1}{6} \qquad \frac{1}{5} \qquad \frac{1}{4} \qquad \frac{1}{3} \qquad \frac{1}{2}$$

Compute the amount of unused space. Assume that each ball and the cylinder have radius r and then express the height of the can in terms of r.

*c. Tennis ball cans hold 3 balls. Determine the amount of wasted space in these cans if the balls have a diameter of 6.3 centimeters and the can has a diameter of 7 centimeters and a height of 20 centimeters. What fraction from part b is closest to representing the amount of wasted space? Check the reasonableness of your answer by experimenting with a can of balls and water.

JUST FOR FUN

SOMA CUBES

Soma cubes are a seven-piece puzzle invented by the Danish author Piet Hein. Piece 1 has 3 cubes, and the other pieces each have 4 cubes. Soma cubes can be purchased, or they can be constructed by gluing together cubes, such as sugar cubes, wooden cubes, or dice.

Surprisingly, these 7 pieces can be assembled to form a 3 by 3 by 3 cube. You may wish to try this challenging puzzle.

A common activity with soma cubes is constructing certain well-known figures. Each of the shapes in Figure 1 requires all 7 pieces. Try to build them.

There are several elementary techniques for determining when a figure cannot be constructed with soma cubes. The simplest of these is counting the number of cubes. For example, a figure with 18 cubes cannot be formed because there is no combination of 4s and one 3 that adds up to 18.[†]

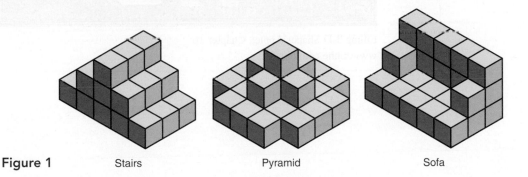

Figure 1   Stairs   Pyramid   Sofa

[†]Additional techniques can be found in G. Carson, "Soma Cubes," *The Mathematics Teacher* 66, pp. 583–592.

FILLING 3-D SHAPES APPLET

How does the volume of a cube compare with the volume of a square pyramid that just fits into the cube? (Their bases have the same area and their altitudes are equal.) This applet enables you to experiment by pumping water from one figure to another to discover relationships. In a similar manner, you can compare the volumes of other solids.

Filling 3-D Shapes Applet, Chapter 10
www.mhhe.com/bbn

Exercises and Activities **10.3**

1. *School Classroom:* Katrina is convinced that the two cylinders made by rolling a standard piece of paper left-to-right or top-to-bottom must have the same volume. Describe how you can help Katrina explore this concept without using any formulas.

2. *School Classroom:* Make paper models to illustrate the following relationships and explain how you would illustrate the relationships in classroom experiences with maximum student involvement.

   a. The volume of a square pyramid is one-third the volume of a box with the same base and the same height as the pyramid.

   b. The volume of a right circular cone is one-third the volume of a cylinder with the same base and the same height as the cone.

   c. The volume of an inverted right circular cone has eight times the volume as an identical inverted cone that is filled to one-half its height.

Full cone h $\frac{h}{2}$ Cone filled to $\frac{1}{2}$ its height

3. *School Classroom:* The surface area *Mini-Lab* described on the **Elementary School Text** page at the beginning of this section asks students to make a net for a cylinder.

   a. Using a soup can or similar cylinder for your model, make a net for the cylinder on centimeter graph paper; include both the top and bottom of the cylinder in your net. Compute the approximate area of your cylinder by counting squares and partial squares on the graph paper. Downloadable centimeter graph paper is available at the companion website.

   b. Carefully measure your original cylinder (in centimeters) and use formulas to compute the exact surface area of the cylinder.

   c. Find the difference between your approximate (part a) and exact (part b) surface areas and determine the percent of error (difference ÷ exact).

4. *Math Concepts:* If you have a cubical box that measures 3 inches on each edge and want to make a box with three times the volume, how long must each edge of the larger box be (to the nearest tenth of an inch)? Explain your thinking.

5. *Math Concepts:* Imagine that you have a cube of modeling clay that measures 4 inches on each edge.

   a. What is the surface area of that cube of clay?

   b. If you formed the same piece of clay (same volume) into a sphere, predict which clay object would have more surface area, the cube or the sphere. Then compute the surface area of the sphere to test your prediction (surface area of a sphere is $4\pi r^2$). Explain in detail how you determined the surface area of the clay sphere.

6. *Math Concepts:* Go to the companion website and open the Chapter 10 Applet: Filling 3-D Shapes. Compare the volumes of the various shapes and record your observations.

7. The **Standards Summary** at the back of this book mentions *Volume* at every grade level. Give three simple examples of grade level appropriate activities exploring volume, one each for Pre-K–2, grades 3–5, and grades 6–8. Explain how these activities address *Expectations* in the **Geometry Standards.** State the *Expectations* with your explanation.

---

www.mhhe.com/bbn

bennett-burton-nelson website

Virtual Manipulatives   Grid and Dot Paper   Links and Readings
Interactive Chapter Applets Color Transparencies   Geometer Sketchpad Modules
Puzzlers   Extended Bibliography

ACTIVITIES FOR THE ELEMENTARY SCHOOL CLASSROOM

Finding Areas on Geoboards

Purpose: To introduce elementary school students to finding areas of figures by dividing regions into square units.

Connections: Ask the class if they know the meaning of the word "area" or if they can use the word in a sentence. Maybe they have heard the expression "work area" or "play area" or maybe they have seen signs such as: "This area is for construction workers" or "This area is closed." Tell them that today they will use the word "area" in a different way.

Materials: Per student or pair of students: One geoboard, one large rubber band, and 10 to 12 small rubber bands.

1. Show the students a geoboard with the two figures at the left marked with rubber bands and ask them to form both figures on their geoboards using their rubber bands. Tell the students to use more bands to divide the large figure into small squares the size of the small square on their geoboard. When this has been done, select a student to show his or her geoboard to the class. Ask the students to count the number of small squares contained in the large figure. Tell them that this shows that the area of the large figure is 10 square units.

2. Show the students the following figures, ask them to form the figures on their geoboards and determine the area of each figure. Ask volunteers to state the areas they found and to explain their methods. Some students may find it helpful to subdivide the figures into small squares, while others may have different methods.

3. The areas of the following figures can be found by dividing the figures into squares and half-squares. Show the students the figures and ask them to form the figures and determine their areas. Discuss each by asking volunteers to explain their methods.

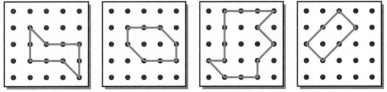

4. (Optional) The areas of each of the triangles on these geoboards can be found by enclosing the triangle in a rectangle and taking half the area of the rectangle. Have the students form the first geoboard figure and ask for suggestions as to how its area can be found. Some students may say that the lower part of the triangle is almost one square unit and the top half of the triangle can be used to make a whole square. If no one suggests the method of using rectangles, have the students enclose the triangle in the smallest possible rectangle and find the area of the rectangle. Ask how this can be used to find the area of the triangle. (Area is 1 square unit.)

Student is determining area of geoboard figure by placing squares and half-squares in the figure.

11

Motions in Geometry

> Students need to learn to physically and mentally change the position, orientation, and size of objects in systematic ways as they develop their understandings about congruence, similarity, and transformations.[†]

LOCATING SETS OF POINTS IN THE PLANE

PURPOSE

To locate and sketch sets of points in a plane that satisfy given conditions.

MATERIALS

A ruler, compass, and protractor from Material Card 20, pieces of paper, two index cards, and scissors.

INTRODUCTION

Look at the two identical coins here. If the left coin is carefully rolled halfway around the other, what will be the position of the point *A*? Make a conjecture and test it by experimenting with two identical coins.

In this activity set, we will be locating the positions of points in the plane. Many geometric figures are described or defined as sets of points with certain conditions placed on them. Suppose, for example, that we are asked to locate and sketch *the set of points in the plane that are 2 cm from a given point P*. We can begin to identify points by using a ruler to locate points 2 cm from

[†]*Principles and Standards for School Mathematics*, p. 43.

Circumference and Area of Circles

MAIN IDEA

Find the circumference and area of circles.

New Vocabulary

circle
center
radius
chord
diameter
circumference
pi

Math Online

glencoe.com

- Extra Examples
- Personal Tutor
- Self-Check Quiz

▷ **MINI Lab**

STEP 1 Measure and record the distance d across the circular part of an object, such as a battery or a can, through its center.

STEP 2 Place the object on a piece of paper. Mark the point where the object touches the paper on both the object and on the paper.

STEP 3 Carefully roll the object so that it makes one complete rotation. Then mark the paper again.

STEP 4 Finally, measure the distance C between the marks.

1. What distance does C represent?
2. Find the ratio $\frac{C}{d}$ for this object.
3. Repeat the steps above for at least two other circular objects and compare the ratios of C to d. What do you observe?
4. Graph the data you collected as ordered pairs, (d, C). Then describe the graph.

A **circle** is a set of points in a plane that are the same distance from a given point in the plane, called the **center**. The segment from the center to any point on the circle is called the **radius**. A **chord** is any segment with both endpoints on the circle. A **diameter** is a chord that passes through the center. It is the longest chord.

The diameter of a circle is twice its radius or $d = 2r$.

The distance around the circle is called the **circumference**. The ratio of the circumference of a circle to its diameter is always 3.1415926…. It is represented by the Greek letter **π (pi)**. The numbers 3.14 and $\frac{22}{7}$ are often used as approximations for π. So, $\frac{C}{d} = \pi$. This can also be written as $C = \pi d$ or $C \approx 3.14d$.

point P, as shown in figure a. As more and more points are added to the collection of points, we can see that a smooth curve drawn through the points, as in figure b, visually describes the set of all points 2 cm from P as a circle with center P and radius 2 cm.

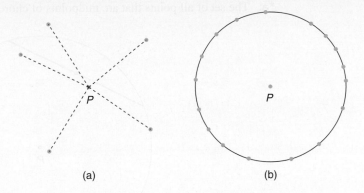

(a)   (b)

1. For parts a and b, place 10 to 20 points on each figure that satisfy the stated condition. Then draw a smooth curve through all points satisfying the condition and describe the outcome in your own words.

   a. The set of all points in the plane that are the same distance from point K as from point L.

   K •

   L •

   *b. The set of all points in the plane that are the same distance from line m as from line n. (The distance from a point to a line is along the perpendicular from the point to the line.)

2. A *chord* is a line segment joining two points on a circle. Parts a through c involve chords of circles. Locate as many points as you need to feel confident about sketching the curve that satisfies the conditions. Describe each result in words, as specifically as possible.

   *a. The set of all points that are midpoints of chords of length 4 cm on this circle.

   b. The midpoints of all chords of this circle that have point *R* as one endpoint.

   *c. The midpoints of all chords of this circle that pass through point *S*.

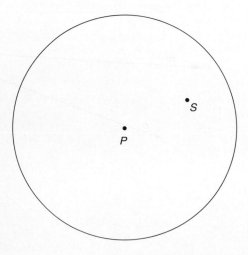

3. Draw and cut out a circle with radius 1.5 cm.

    a. Suppose the circle rolls around the inside of the square shown below, always tangent to at least 1 edge. Sketch the path traced by the center of the circle and then describe it in words.

    b. Sketch and describe the path of the circle's center if the circle rolls around the outside of the square.

*4. Point *B* is the center of a circle with radius 1 cm, and point *A* is the center of a circle with radius 2 cm. Both *X* and *Y*, which are the intersections of these two circles, are twice as far from point *A* as from point *B*. Find more points that are twice as far from *A* as from *B*. Sketch and describe the set of all points in the plane that satisfy the conditions. (*Hint:* You may find it helpful to locate these points by drawing circles about *A* and *B*, with the radius about *A* twice the radius about *B*.)

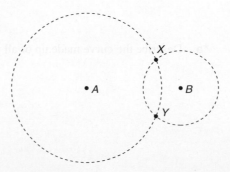

5. Cut out a narrow strip of cardstock or paper having a length of 5 cm and punch a small hole at its midpoint. Place this strip on the two perpendicular lines so that each end touches one of the lines as illustrated in Figure 1 below. Place a pencil at the midpoint, *M*, and with the help of a classmate, move the strip so that its endpoints always touch the two perpendicular lines in Figure 2. What curve is traced by point *M*?

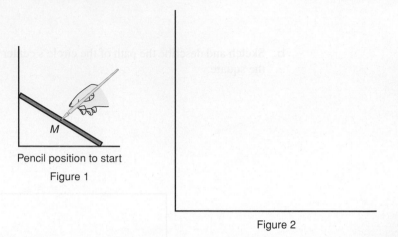

Pencil position to start

Figure 1

Figure 2

6. On a piece of paper draw a line segment $\overline{PQ}$ of length 7 cm. Place an index card (any piece of paper with a 90° corner will work) on top of segment $\overline{PQ}$ so that its adjacent sides pass through points *P* and *Q*. It is possible to shift the index card to new positions so that *P* and *Q* are still on adjacent edges of the index card but the corner of the card is at different points, such as point *X* and point *Y* in the following figure. Locate and mark several other different corner points by repositioning the index card in this manner.

*a. Describe the curve made up of all possible corner points.

b. Bisect one corner of the index card, and cut along the angle bisector to obtain a 45° angle. The point W is the vertex point of the 45° angle. This card is placed on top of segment $\overline{RS}$ so that its sides pass through points R and S. Shift the card to locate other vertex points with R and S on the adjacent sides of the 45° angle. Describe the set of all such vertex points.

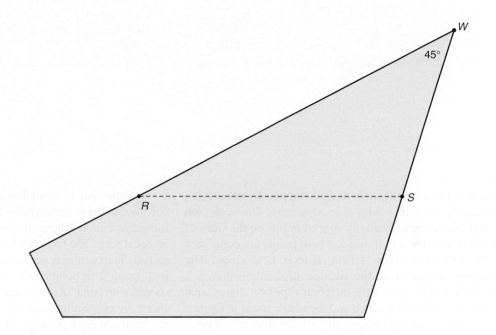

c. Suppose the vertex angle W of the card in part b were greater than 90°, for example, 110°. Draw a sketch of what you think the set of vertex points would look like. Test your conjecture by cutting an angle greater than 90° and locating points on segment $\overline{AB}$.

JUST FOR FUN

LINE DESIGNS

Line designs are geometric designs formed by connecting sequences of points with line segments. One common method is to connect equally spaced points on the sides of an angle, as shown in figure a. These points are connected in the following order: A to a, B to b, C to c, etc. The resulting design gives the illusion of a curve that is a parabola. Experiment with different types of angles such as the acute angle in figure b and the obtuse angle in figure c to see if the resulting designs give similar illusions of parabolas. Combining several angles, as in the figure above, and varying the colors can lead to interesting and beautiful designs.

Another way to create line designs is to draw chords in a circle according to certain rules. The design in figure d is being formed in a circle whose circumference has been divided into 36 equal parts. The first chord connects point 1 to point 2; the second chord connects point 2 to point 4; the third chord connects point 3 to point 6; etc. This figure shows the first 18 chords, with point 18 connected to point 36. Continue drawing chords by connecting point 19 to point 2, point 20 to point 4, etc., until you reach point 36. The resulting figure has the shape of a heart. A curve with this shape is called a *cardioid*. The front ends of the chords for this cardioid traveled twice as fast around the circle as the back ends of the chords.

(a)   (b)   (c)   (d)

In the next figure let the front ends of the chords travel 3 times as fast. That is, connect point 1 to point 3, 2 to 6, 3 to 9, etc. Continue drawing these chords until the back ends of the chords have made one revolution and the front ends have made three revolutions. The cardioid on the preceding page has 1 *cusp* (inward point). How many cusps will this curve have?

Experiment with some more patterns. For example, let the front ends of the chords move 4 times faster ($1 \rightarrow 4, 2 \rightarrow 8, 3 \rightarrow 12, \dots$) or 5 times faster ($1 \rightarrow 5, 2 \rightarrow 10, \dots$). Can you predict the number of cusps in each case? (The 36 spaces around a circle will work for 2, 3, 4, or 6 cusps. For 5 cusps, use 40 spaces or some other multiple of 5 that conveniently divides into 360.) Many of these designs can be stitched with colored thread or yarn on cloth or poster-board, or formed with nails and string or rubber bands. Below is an example of a variety of line art designs stitched on poster board with multicolored thread. The student who made this piece used a compass and protractor to sketch geometric shapes and mark points on the back of the poster before stitching the final art piece.

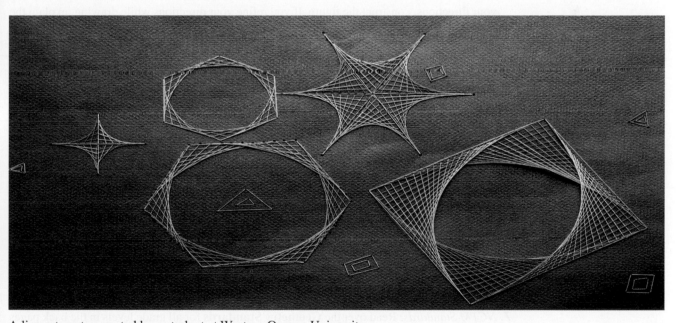

A line art poster created by a student at Western Oregon University

Exercises and Activities 11.1

1. *School Classroom:* Cresedeo is having trouble sorting out the following four geometric terms: circle, diameter, chord, and arc. Describe several hands-on ways you might use to help Cresedeo and other students make sense of these terms.

2. *School Classroom:* One way to introduce students to definitions involving sets of points in the plane is to ask them to place or locate small objects (beans, rice, counters, etc.) that satisfy certain conditions. For example, placing a bean on a table and having your students place many pieces of rice, all an equal distance from the bean leads to the definition of a circle. Create two activities concerning the location of sets of points that are appropriate for the elementary school classroom. Describe your activities in detail and accompany them with diagrams.

3. *School Classroom:* Obtain several small cylinders and follow the four steps for measuring circles in the *Mini-Lab* on the **Elementary School Text** page at the beginning of this section. Answer questions 1 through 4 and show your results. Explain the value of this activity for understanding the meaning of π and understanding how to use π to find the measure of the circumference of a circle.

4. *Math Concepts:* Analyze the line design at the beginning of the **Just for Fun Activity** in this section. Write a set of directions that will enable your reader to construct this figure. Using your directions, construct the figure. If you refine your directions while drawing, explain the refinement.

5. *Math Concepts:* Suppose a point P is placed above a line and many line segments are drawn from P to the line. Describe the shape the set of midpoints of all of the line segments would form. Draw a sketch to accompany your conclusion.

6. *Math Concepts:* Open the **Math Laboratory Investigation 11.1: Read Me—Paper Folding Instructions** from the companion website and investigate the triangle constructions as described in 1, 2, 3, and 4 of the *Starting Points for Investigations 11.1.* Describe your investigation and explain your thinking.

7. *NCTM Standards:* Read over the **Geometry Standards** for all grade levels in the back pages of this book; list any *Expectations* that you believe are satisfied by activities that ask students to describe sets of points whose location is determined by given conditions. State the *Expectations,* the *Standards,* and the grade levels they are under.

---

bennett-burton-nelson website

Virtual Manipulatives	Grid and Dot Paper	Links and Readings
Interactive Chapter Applets	Color Transparencies	Geometer Sketchpad Modules
Puzzlers	Extended Bibliography	

Activity Set **11.2** DRAWING ESCHER-TYPE TESSELLATIONS

PURPOSE

To create nonstandard tessellations and Escher-type drawings that illustrate motions in geometry.

MATERIALS

Tracing paper and a ruler and compass from Material Card 20.

Tessellations created by students at Portland State University

INTRODUCTION

The Dutch artist M.C. Escher was fascinated by the tile patterns he observed on the walls, floors, and ceilings of the Alhambra—a thirteenth-century Moorish palace in Granada, Spain. He considered pure geometric tessellations his "richest source of inspiration." Many of his own works are filled with images of living things as is the following Escher-type student drawing.

A tessellation involving life forms created by a student at Portland State University

Escher-type drawings can be constructed by altering polygons that tessellate (triangles, quadrilaterals, and regular hexagons) by using congruence mappings (translations, rotations, reflections, and glide reflections). In this activity set, you will devise drawings and have the opportunity to create your own artistic work.

Extend 10-8

Geometry Lab
Tessellations

In this lab, you will create tessellations.

MAIN IDEA
Create tessellations.

ACTIVITY

STEP 1 Draw a square on the back of an index card. Then draw a triangle on the inside of the square and a trapezoid on the bottom of the square as shown.

STEP 2 Cut out the square. Then cut out the triangle and slide it from the right side of the square to the left side of the square. Cut out the trapezoid and slide it from the bottom to the top of the square.

STEP 3 Tape the figures together to form a pattern.

STEP 4 Trace this pattern onto a sheet of paper as shown to create a tessellation.

 CHECK Your Progress

Create a tessellation using each pattern.

a.
b.

c.

ANALYZE THE RESULTS

1. Design and describe your own tessellation pattern.
2. **MAKE A CONJECTURE** *Congruent figures* have corresponding sides of equal length and corresponding angles of equal measure. Explain how congruent figures are used in your tessellation.

1. Translation Tessellations: The rectangle in figure a tessellates. In figure b, one side of the rectangle is modified by a jagged line design. The design is then *translated* to the opposite side of the rectangle as a modification in figure c.

(a)   (b)   (c)

*a. Explain why the new shape in figure c will also tessellate the plane.

In figure d, one of the remaining parallel sides of the rectangle is altered by a different design. This design is then translated to the opposite side in figure e, producing the final shape in figure f.

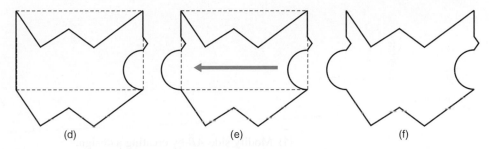

(d)   (e)   (f)

The tessellation formed by the modified rectangle is shown in Figure 1. This tessellation becomes an Escher-type drawing when details and/or color are added to the basic design. In Figure 2, the tessellation has been rotated 90° and a few details have been added to make a simple Escher-type drawing.

Figure 1

Figure 2

b. Create your own translation tessellation pattern by modifying and translating the sides of this parallelogram according to steps 1 through 3 given below.

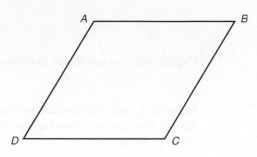

(1) Modify side $\overline{AB}$ by creating a design.

(2) Translate the design to $\overline{DC}$ by carrying out the following steps: Place a piece of tracing paper over the parallelogram. Mark points A and B and trace your modification for side $\overline{AB}$. Slide the tracing paper so that point A coincides with D and point B coincides with C. Use a pointed object (ballpoint pen or compass point) to make enough imprints through the tracing paper so that when you remove the paper you can draw the translated design on $\overline{DC}$.

(3) Repeat steps 1 and 2 to translate a modification of side $\overline{AD}$ to side $\overline{BC}$.

c. Use the pattern you have just created to form a tessellation. An easy way to do this is to place a clean piece of tracing paper over the pattern you created and carefully trace the pattern. Then move the tracing paper up, down, right, or left, and trace additional patterns adjacent to your first copy on the tracing paper. Make an Escher-type drawing by sketching in details.

2. Rotation Tessellations: The following figures illustrate the modification and rotation of the sides of an equilateral triangle. First, side $\overline{AB}$ is modified as in figure a. Then the design is rotated about vertex A to adjacent side $\overline{AC}$, as shown in figure b, so that vertex B is mapped onto vertex C.

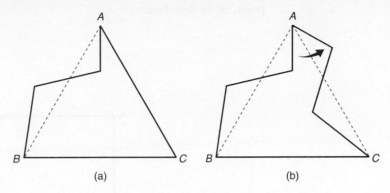

(a)   (b)

Side $\overline{BC}$ can be modified by rotating a design about its midpoint. In figure c, a design is created between the midpoint M and vertex C. The pattern is completed by rotating this design $180°$ about midpoint M so that vertex C is mapped onto vertex B, as shown in figure d.

(c)   (d)

This pattern was used to create the following tessellation. Notice that this tessellation can be mapped onto itself by rotations about certain vertex points.

List all the rotations about point P that will map this tessellation onto itself.

a. Create a rotation tessellation pattern from square *ABCD* by first modifying side $\overline{AB}$ and rotating the design about vertex *B* to adjacent side $\overline{BC}$ and then modifying side $\overline{AD}$ and rotating the design about vertex *D* to adjacent side $\overline{DC}$. Use your pattern to form a tessellation and list all the rotations of the tessellation onto itself about one of the vertex points of the tessellation.

b. Use the following scalene triangle to design a rotation tessellation pattern. Because no two sides have equal length, you cannot rotate one side to another about a vertex, as in figure b at the beginning of activity 2. However, half a side can be rotated about the mid-point of that side, as was done in figures c and d of activity 2. The midpoint of each side has been marked. For each side, create a design between a vertex and the midpoint, and then rotate the design 180° about the midpoint. Show that this pattern tessellates by forming a tessellation. For a vertex point of the tessellation, what is the number of rotations of the tessellation into itself?

c. Convert one or both of your tessellation patterns from part a and part b to an Escher-type drawing.

3. Glide-Reflection Tessellations: A *glide reflection* can be used to create a tessellating figure from parallelogram *ABCD*. Side $\overline{AD}$ is modified in figure a, and the design is translated to side $\overline{BC}$ in figure b. Next, side $\overline{DC}$ is modified as shown in figure c.

(a)   (b)   (c)

The design on $\overline{DC}$ is then translated to side $\overline{AB}$, as shown in figure d. Finally, the design along side $\overline{AB}$ is reflected about a line ℓ perpendicular to the midpoint of AB, as illustrated in figure e. The two motions (translation followed by reflection) shown in figures d and e produce a *glide reflection*.

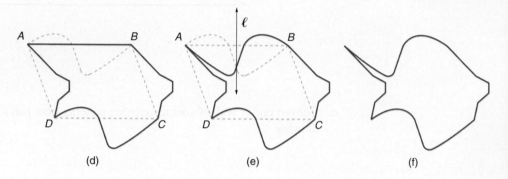

(d)   (e)   (f)

a. The pattern created above in figures a–f was used to form the following tessellation. What single mapping will map each row of this tessellation onto the row below it?

Mapping:

b. Modify the square *ABCD* below, using two glide reflections to produce a figure that tessellates. To do this create a design along side $\overline{AD}$, translate the design to side $\overline{BC}$, and then reflect it about a line perpendicular to the midpoint of $\overline{BC}$. Similarly, modify side $\overline{AB}$ and translate that design to side $\overline{DC}$ through a glide reflection. (*Suggestion:* Use tracing paper to perform the glide reflection.)

JUST FOR FUN

PAPER PUZZLE 1: PAPER-STRIP CUBE

Draw a strip of eight squares that each measure 3 cm on a side. Cut out the strip of squares, and fold it to make a cube that measures 3 cm on each edge.

PAPER PUZZLE 2: FOLDING NUMBERS IN ORDER

The following rectangle with the eight numbered squares can be folded so that the numbers are in order from 1 through 8 by carrying out the three folds shown in figures a, b, and c. (*Note:* The numbers will be in order, but not all will be facing up.)

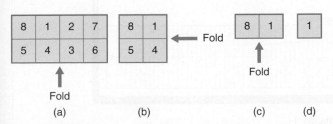

Each of these four numbered rectangles below can be folded so that the numbers from 1 to 8 are in order. Make copies of the rectangles, and fold them to get the numbers in order. Devise a way, perhaps similar to that shown in the previous column, to record your solutions so that another person can understand your procedures.

2	1	3	4
7	8	6	5

6	7	5	8
3	2	4	1

8	7	2	5
1	6	3	4

1	8	7	4
2	3	6	5

Design a similar puzzle. One method is to *work backwards* by creatively folding a rectangle with blank squares, numbering the squares in order, and then unfolding it to write the numbers right side up on the rectangle.

PAPER PUZZLE 3: STEPPING THROUGH A PIECE OF PAPER

It is possible to cut a piece of $8\frac{1}{2}$ inch by 11 inch paper in such a way that you create a hole large enough to step through. A paper and scissors are all you need. No taping, gluing, or refastening the paper is needed or permitted. Try it.

Hint: Fold a sheet of paper and mark three points, *A, B,* and *C,* on the fold line. Make three cuts, as indicated by the dotted lines. Note that the cuts pass through points *A* and *C*

on the fold and the cut in line with *B* passes through the edge of the paper but not through the fold. Then cut along the fold from *A* to *C*. Carefully unfold the piece of paper to see the size of the hole you have created. To create a larger hole with a new sheet of paper, extend this procedure by making more cuts, alternating cutting from the fold and cutting from the edge.

 TESSELLATIONS APPLET

If you have ever formed a tessellation by tracing figures on paper or at a window, you will be amazed at the power of this applet. By creating one of several different polygons, you will be able to quickly modify its sides and then to click and see the resulting tessellation. You will be pleasantly surprised.

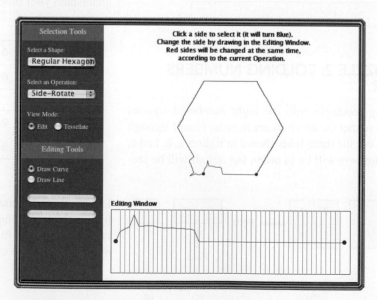

Tessellations Applet, Chapter 11
www.mhhe.com/bbn

Exercises and Activities 11.2

1. *School Classroom:* Make a list of the geometric knowledge and skills that you believe elementary school students will learn by successfully creating a translation tessellation. What can you add to your list if students also successfully create rotation tessellations and glide reflection tessellations? Explain in detail.

2. *School Classroom:* Find and copy at least two Escher-type drawings that you believe would be appropriate to discuss with elementary students. Accompany the drawings with a list of questions you could pose to an elementary class to begin a discussion of the mathematical aspects of the drawings. Explain what you would like the students to notice.

3. *Math Concepts:* Every quadrilateral tessellates the plane. However, can an arbitrary quadrilateral such as the one shown below have all its sides altered and still tessellate the plane? Decide which methods described in this activity set you can use to alter the sides of this quadrilateral and tessellate the plane. In the pictured quadrilateral, no sides are of equal length and no sides are parallel. For each method you use, make a template for your figure and determine whether or not it will tessellate the plane. Describe your results and include any clarifying diagrams.

4. *Math Concepts:* Go to the companion website and launch the Tessellation Applet in Chapter 11. Choose one of the tessellations discussed in this activity set and create it online. Print your results.

5. *Math Concepts:* One way to create a shape for tessellation is to use tracing paper to trace and reproduce the transformed edges as demonstrated in activity 1 in this activity set. Another way is to use an index card or cardstock paper, and tape and follow the four steps in the activity described on the **Elementary School Text** page at the beginning of this section.

   a. Which tessellation-shaping techniques described in this activity set can be accomplished with this cut and tape process? Explain your thinking.

   b. Alter an isosceles trapezoid like the trapezoid shown below and use the cut-and-tape method described on the **Elementary School Text** page at the beginning of this section to form a template. Use the template to form an Escher-type tessellation; sketch enough of the beginnings of a pattern so the reader has sufficient information to extend your pattern.

6. *NCTM Standards*: In the **Standards Summary** in the back pages of this book there are five **Process Standards.** The **Process Standards** discuss ways of acquiring and using content knowledge. Describe in detail how an activity in this activity set addresses an *Expectation* in one of the **Process Standards.** State the *Expectation* and the *Standard.*

---

www.mhhe.com/bbn

bennett-burton-nelson website

Virtual Manipulatives	Grid and Dot Paper	Links and Readings
Interactive Chapter Applets	Color Transparencies	Geometer Sketchpad Modules
Puzzlers	Extended Bibliography	

DEVICES FOR INDIRECT MEASUREMENT

PURPOSE

To devise methods and simple instruments for measuring distances based on knowledge of similar triangles.

MATERIALS

Tape, drinking straws, string, paper-towel tube, small weights, yardstick, push-pins, hypsometer-clinometer from Material Card 39, and ruler and protractor from Material Card 20 (depending on which instruments you make). Cardstock or heavy weight paper for activity 4.

INTRODUCTION

It was in the second century B.C.E. that the Greek astronomer Hipparchus applied a simple theorem from geometry to measure distances indirectly. He computed the distance to the moon and many other astronomical distances. The theorem that Hipparchus applied states that if two triangles are *similar* (have the same shape), their sides are proportional. This important theorem is used in surveying, map-making, and navigation.

All that is needed to establish that two triangles are similar is that two angles of one are congruent to two angles of the other. The two triangles shown below are similar because ∡A is congruent to ∡D and ∡C is congruent to ∡F. (When two angles of one triangle are congruent to two angles of another, the remaining angles also must be congruent. Why?)

Hipparchus knew that for two similar triangles their side lengths are proportional. For example, side $\overline{DF}$ corresponds to side $\overline{AC}$ and is 2.5 times as long. You can check by measuring that this same relationship holds for all three pairs of corresponding sides. That is,

$$DF = 2.5 \times AC = 10 \text{ cm} \qquad FE = 2.5 \times CB = 5 \text{ cm} \qquad ED = 2.5 \times BA = 7.5 \text{ cm}$$

Notice also that the ratios of the lengths of sides in one triangle are equal to the corresponding ratios in a similar triangle. Use the measurements from the corresponding sides of the two triangles above to verify the following proportions:

$$\frac{AB}{AC} = \frac{DE}{DF}, \quad \frac{AB}{BC} = \frac{DE}{EF}, \quad \text{and} \quad \frac{BC}{AC} = \frac{EF}{DF}$$

All of the estimating methods and instruments in this activity set use the fact that the lengths of corresponding sides of similar triangles are proportional.

4-9 Indirect Measurement

MAIN IDEA

Solve problems involving similar triangles.

New Vocabulary

indirect measurement

Math Online

glencoe.com

- Extra Examples
- Personal Tutor
- Self-Check Quiz

▷ GET READY for the Lesson

HISTORY Thales is known as the first Greek scientist, engineer, and mathematician. Legend says that he was the first to determine the height of the pyramids in Egypt by examining the shadows made by the Sun. He considered three points: the top of the objects, the lengths of the shadows, and the bases.

1. What appears to be true about the corresponding angles in the two triangles?

2. If the corresponding sides are proportional, what could you conclude about the triangles?

Indirect measurement allows you to use properties of similar polygons to find distances or lengths that are difficult to measure directly. The type of indirect measurement Thales used is called *shadow reckoning*. He measured his height and the length of his shadow then compared it with the length of the shadow cast by the pyramid.

$$\frac{\text{Thales' shadow}}{\text{pyramid's shadow}} = \frac{\text{Thales' height}}{\text{pyramid height}}$$

EXAMPLE   Use Shadow Reckoning

1 **CITY PROPERTY** A fire hydrant 2.5 feet high casts a 5-foot shadow. How tall is a street light that casts a 26-foot shadow at the same time? Let h represent the height of the street light.

| Shadow | Height |

hydrant →
street light →
$\dfrac{5}{26} = \dfrac{2.5}{h}$ ← hydrant ← street light

$5h = 2.5 \cdot 26$ Find the cross products.

$5h = 65$ Multiply.

$\dfrac{5h}{5} = \dfrac{65}{5}$ Divide each side by 5.

$h = 13$

The street light is 13 feet tall.

1. **Sighting Method:** Distances can be estimated when the size of an object at that distance is roughly known. For example, stretch your arm out in front of you, holding a ruler in a vertical position. Select some distant object such as a person and estimate his or her height. Hold the ruler so that the top is in line with your eye and the top of the person's head. Position your thumb on the ruler so that it is in line with the person's feet.

*a. The lines of sight from your eye (point *E*) to the top of your ruler and your thumb form triangle *EAB*. The lines of sight from *E* to the head and feet of the observed person form triangle *EA'B'*. *Why are these triangles similar?*

b. Obtain the length of $\overline{EA}$ by measuring the distance from your eye to the ruler, as shown in the figure. Obtain the length of $\overline{AB}$ from the ruler. Record these two lengths and your estimate of the height of the person ($\overline{A'B'}$) you are measuring the distance to.

c. Use the fact that triangle *EAB* is similar to triangle *EA'B'* to estimate the distance to the person, $\overline{EA'}$.

2. Scout Sighting Method: Here is an old scout trick for getting a rough estimate of the distance to an object. This variation of the sighting method does not require a ruler. The scout stretches out his or her arm and, with the left eye closed, sights with the right eye along the tip of one finger to a distant object, *T*, to determine the unknown distance. Next, the scout closes the right eye and sights with the left eye along the unmoved finger to a second object, *R*. The scout then estimates the distance between the two objects and multiplies by 10 to estimate the distance to these objects.[†]

a. In the following diagram, E_1 and E_2 represent the eyes, *A* the finger, *T* the tree, and *R* the rock. Why is triangle E_1E_2A similar to triangle *TRA*?

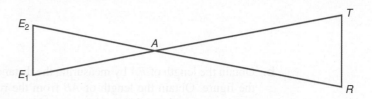

b. Assume the distance between the scout's eyes is 7.5 cm, and the distance from the scout's eye to fingertip (E_1A) is 75 cm. If the scout estimates the distance between the tree and the rock to be about 90 meters (the length of a football field), how far is it from the scout's finger to the tree? That is, what is length *AT*? Explain your thinking.

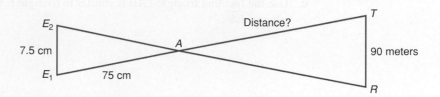

[†]For several more sighting methods, see C. N. Shuster and F. L. Bedford, *Field Work in Mathematics*, pp. 56–57.

c. The scout sighting method is based on the assumption that E_1A (the distance from the scout's eye to fingertip) is 10 times E_1E_2 (the distance between the scout's eyes). Stretch your arm out in front of you and measure the distance from your eye to your raised index finger. Then measure the distance between your eyes. Record your distances on the following diagram. Should you be using the number 10 for the scout sighting method? If not, what number should you be using?

$$\frac{E_1A}{E_1E_2} = \underline{\qquad}$$

*d. When you measure your distance from an object you are fairly close to, such as something in a room, you should add the distance from eye to finger to the result obtained from the scout sighting method. In approximating greater distances, you can ignore the distance from eye to finger, E_1A. Explain why.

3. Stadiascope: The stadiascope works on the same principle as the sighting method with the ruler (see activity 1). This instrument has a peep sight at one end and cross threads at the other. The stadiascope shown here was made from a paper-towel tube having a length of 27 cm. At one end of the tube, six threads have been taped in horizontal rows. These threads are 1 cm apart. A piece of paper has been taped over the other end, and a peep sight has been punched on the same level as the lowest thread.

Peep sight

27 cm

Threads, 1 cm apart

Stadiascope

The following diagram shows a stadiascope being used to measure the distance to a truck. The truck fills 4 spaces at the end of the stadiascope. Let's assume that the truck has a height (*CD*) of 3 m.

a. Point *E* is the peep sight, and points *A* and *B* mark the upper thread and lower thread of the 4 spaces of the stadiascope between which the truck is seen. Triangle *EBA* and triangle *EDC* are right triangles. Explain why they are similar.

*b. Since triangle *EBA* is similar to triangle *EDC*, the ratios of their corresponding sides are equal. Use the proportion given here to compute the length of *ED* in meters. (*Note: EB* and *AB* can be left in centimeters and *CD* in meters.)

$$\frac{ED}{EB} = \frac{CD}{AB}$$

*c. Suppose you sight a person who fills 2 spaces of the stadiascope and you estimate this person's height to be 180 cm. How many meters is this person from you?

d. Make a stadiascope and use it to measure some heights or distances indirectly. Check your results with direct measurements.

4. Clinometer: The clinometer, used to measure heights of objects, is an easy device to construct (see Material Card 39). It is a simplified version of the quadrant, an important instrument in the Middle Ages, and the sextant, an instrument used for locating the positions of ships. Each of these devices has arcs that are graduated in degrees for measuring angles of elevation. The arc of the clinometer is marked from 0 to 90°. When an object is sighted through the straw, the number of degrees in angle *BVW* can be read from the arc. Angle *BAC* is the angle of elevation of the clinometer.

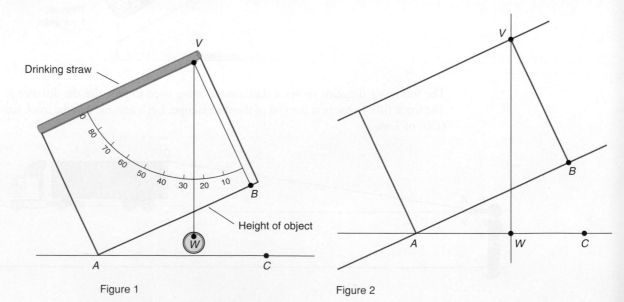

Figure 1   Figure 2

a. Use Figure 2 on the previous page to determine the relationship of angle *BVW* on the clinometer to the angle of elevation, angle *BAC*.

b. In the following diagram, a clinometer was used to determine that the angle of elevation, angle *TER*, from the observer's eye to the top of the tree, is 18°. This knowledge enables us to correctly draw the scale model right triangle *ETR*. Explain why scale model triangle *ETR* is similar to the actual triangle *ETR* formed by the observer's eye and the two parts of the tree.

60 meters

*c. Assume the distance from the observer's feet to the base of the tree is 60 m. Use a ruler to set up a scale on $\overline{ET}$. For example, $\overline{ET}$ can be marked off in millimeters. If *ET* represents a distance of 60 m, what distance does each millimeter unit of your scale represent? Use your scale to find the length of $\overline{TR}$.

d. The observer's eye is 150 cm above the ground. What is the height of the tree?

e. Make a clinometer by pasting Material Card 39 onto a solid backing and attaching a straw, string, and small weight as shown in Figure 1 on the previous page. Use this device to measure the angle of elevation to a tall object. Measure the horizontal distance from your feet to the object. Draw a right triangle that has the same angle of elevation, use a ruler to measure the legs of the triangle to set up a scale, and use similar triangles to determine the height of the object from your eye level. Add the distance from the ground to your eye level to determine the total height of the object.

5. Hypsometer: The hypsometer is used for the same purpose as the clinometer, but it eliminates the need to measure angles (see Material Card 39). The grid is used to set up a scale on the sides of the hypsometer. For example, suppose that you sight to the top of a building and that the string of the hypsometer falls in the position shown below. If you are standing 55 m from the base of the building, this distance can be scaled on the right side of the hypsometer by letting each space be 10 m. This same scale should be used on the lower edge of the hypsometer. Now by beginning at distance 55 on the right side of the hypsometer and following the arrow in to the plumb line (weighted string) and then down to the lower edge of the grid, you can see that the height of the building is 25 m plus the distance from the ground to the viewer's eye.

a. Explain why triangle ABC is similar to triangle $A'B'C'$ and explain why $\overline{B'C'} \cong \overline{B''D}$.

b. Use a similar triangle argument to explain why the hypsometer works.

*c. Given the position of the string shown on this hypsometer, determine the height of an object that is at a distance of 70 m, if the distance from the ground to the eye is 1.5 m.

d. If you know the height of an object, you can use the hypsometer to find the distance to its base. Given the position of the string on the above hypsometer, determine the distance to the base of a tree that is 30 m tall, if the distance from the ground to the eye is 1.5 m.

e. Make a hypsometer from Material Card 39 and use it to measure the heights of some objects. Describe how you obtained the height of one of these objects, including the scale and the position the string falls on the hypsometer.

6. Transit: The transit (or theodolite) is one of the most important instruments for measuring horizontal and vertical angles in civil engineering. In its earliest form, this instrument was capable of measuring only horizontal angles, much like the simplified version shown below. To make a transit, tape a protractor (Material Card 20) to one end of a meterstick (or long thin board) and pin a drinking straw at the center point of the protractor.

The following diagram shows how the transit can be used to find the distance between two points. Line segment $\overline{AB}$ has been marked by posts on the left bank of the river. By standing at point B and holding the stick of the transit parallel to $\overline{AB}$, you can measure angle FBA. Similarly, by standing at point A and holding the stick parallel to $\overline{AB}$, you can measure angle FAB. The distance between the posts can be found by using a tape measure or by pacing off. This distance is 500 m. On paper, a similar triangle can be drawn to represent the real triangle formed by the Fort and the posts. This small triangle will be similar to the real triangle if angle A and angle B have been drawn to be congruent to the angles measured with the transit.

a. Use a ruler to set up a scale on $\overline{AB}$ in the diagram below to represent 500 m. The actual distance from A to the fort, point F, can be found by using your scale. What is this distance to the nearest meter?

Fort

A   F

500 meters

B

*b. Explain how you would use the transit to make a map of the objects in this field. What is the least number of angles and distances you would have to measure?

Pine tree   Bush   Rock   Old wagon

Well   Fir tree

Land marker

JUST FOR FUN

ENLARGING DRAWINGS

Figure a shows a drawing of a rabbit. Suppose you wish to copy and double the size of the drawing. Here is one method that works when you do not have immediate access to a copy machine that automatically enlarges. Draw or place a transparent grid over the bunny as shown in figure b.

A grid whose edges are 2 times the length of those in figure b is drawn on the next page. The sketch of the rabbit is then copied square by square from the small grid to the

(a)

(b)

larger grid. On the grid below, five squares have been copied from figure b on the previous page. Complete the enlargement by copying the remaining squares.

Choose a picture, cartoon, or drawing and enlarge it using the grid method. You can make it as large as you wish by choosing an appropriate grid.

Exercises and Activities **11.3**

1. *School Classroom:* One of your students asks you if all squares are similar. Explain how you would explore this idea with your student.

2. *School Classroom:* A student says that a way to test whether or not two rectangles are similar is to put the smaller rectangle on the corner of the larger rectangle (as shown in the figure below). Then, if the corner X on the smaller rectangle is on the diagonal AC of the larger rectangle, the two rectangles are similar. Explain whether or not this student is correct and why.

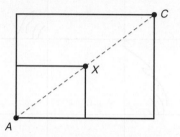

3. *School Classroom:* Explain, as you would to an elementary school student, how the proportion using Thales' height, the pyramid height, and the length of both of their shadows on the **Elementary School Text** page at the beginning of this section can be used to estimate the height of the Great Pyramid. Use 1.8 meters for Thales' height, 2.7 meters for the length of his shadow, and 203 meters for the length of the shadow of the Great Pyramid. Include labeled triangle sketches with your explanation.

4. *Math Concepts:* A typical stop sign is about 9.5 feet tall.

   a. Use a ruler and the sighting method described in activity 1 in this activity set to estimate the length of a typical city block. With a partner, stand on one end of the block, sight the top and base of a stop sign using a ruler and your thumb, and measure the distance from your eye to the ruler. Estimate the length of the block using similar triangles. Include clearly labeled triangles with your solution. Explain your thinking.

b. Use the scout sighting method described in activity 2 in this activity set to estimate the same city block length you estimated in part a. Use your personal scout ratio as determined in activity 2c as your scaling factor. Include clearly labeled diagrams of your work and explain which second object you used to set up the similar triangles. Explain your thinking.

5. *Math Concepts:* Use your pattern blocks to form figure 1 below. Then use pattern blocks to form a new figure similar to figure 1 whose sides are in a ratio of 2 to 1 to figure 1. Sketch your resulting figure.

(1)

6. *Math Concepts:* On Centimeter Grid paper draw a new figure, similar to figure 2 below, so that the ratio from the sides of figure 2 to the sides of the new figure is 2 to 3. Compare the area of the new figure to the area of figure 2; how many times larger is the area of the new figure than figure 2? Centimeter Grid paper is available for download at the companion website.

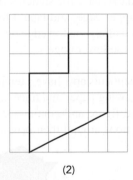

(2)

7. *NCTM Standards:* Give an example of an activity for exploring similarity for grades 3–5. What *Expectations* and *Standards* does your activity address? State the *Expectations* and *Standards* and explain why your activity addresses these recommendations.

ACTIVITIES FOR THE ELEMENTARY SCHOOL CLASSROOM

Creating Escher-Type Tessellations

Purpose: To introduce elementary school students to methods for creating an Escher-type tessellation.

Connections: Books, posters or calendars of Escher's tessellation artwork are available in libraries and bookstores. Bring examples of his artwork to class for students to examine. Many students may have seen some of his work already. Ask students to look at the shapes of the interlocking pieces. Tell them that today they will be creating their own Escher-type drawings.

Materials: Scotch tape, scissors, and rulers for each group of students. A cardstock rectangle and large sheet of drawing paper for each student. (Cut a cardstock rectangle (2" by 4") ahead of time for each student—old file folders work well.)

This Escher-type tessellation was created by a fourth grader, who is putting in some finishing touches.

1. Distribute the rectangles and other materials to the students. Have the students put two points (like P and Q) on their rectangle and draw line segments from the points to the vertices and edge of the rectangle as shown. You may wish to illustrate the process for your students using an overhead.

2. Ask the students to cut out the triangle from the end of their rectangle and carefully tape the triangle on the other end of the rectangle without turning it.

3. Similarly, have the students cut out their bottom triangle, slide it to the upper edge, and tape it to the top of the rectangle. (It must be placed along the top edge directly above the place where it was cut from the lower edge.)

4. The students now have a template. Ask them to place the template in the center of their piece of drawing paper and trace around it with a pencil. Then fit the template to the edges of the traced figure and continue tracing to create a tessellation by expanding the drawing in all directions around their original figure.

Proudly displaying her tessellation.

5. After completing the tessellation, the students can use their imagination to color and/or create repeating figures (such as faces, wings, ears, fins, or simply designs) within their tessellation.

6. (Optional) Some students may wish to start over or create other tessellations. The beginning shape can be a square, parallelogram, or rectangle. The shapes cut from the end and bottom edges can be shapes other than triangular, but they must be taped directly across, as described above.

References

Chapter 1

National Council of Teachers of Mathematics. *Principles and Standards for School Mathematics,* p. 159. Reston, VA: National Council of Teachers of Mathematics, 2000.

Steen, L. A. *On the Shoulders of Giants: New Approaches to Numeracy,* pp.1–8. Washington, DC: National Academy Press, 1990.

Chapter 2

Johnson, D., and R. Johnson. "Cooperative Learning in Mathematics Education." In *New Directions for Elementary School Mathematics,* p. 235. 1989 Yearbook. Reston, VA: National Council of Teachers of Mathematics, 1989.

National Council of Teachers of Mathematics. *Curriculum and Evaluation Standards for School Mathematics,* p. 29. Reston, VA: National Council of Teachers of Mathematics, 1989.

National Council of Teachers of Mathematics. *Principles and Standards for School Mathematics,* p. 56. Reston, VA: National Council of Teachers of Mathematics, 2000.

Chapter 3

National Council of Teachers of Mathematics. *Principles and Standards for School Mathematics,* p. 80. Reston, VA: National Council of Teachers of Mathematics, 2000.

Chapter 4

Bennett, A. B., Jr. "Star Patterns." *Arithmetic Teacher* 25 (January 1978): 12–14.

Bradford, C. L. "Keith's Secret Discovery of the Sieve of Eratosthenes." *Arithmetic Teacher* 21 (March 1974): 239–241.

National Council of Teachers of Mathematics. *Principles and Standards for School Mathematics,* pp. 91–93. Reston, VA: National Council of Teachers of Mathematics, 2000.

Chapter 5

Carpenter, T. P., H. Kepner, M. K. Corbitt, M. M. Lindquist, and R. E. Reys. "Results and Implications of the Second NAEP Mathematics Assessment: Elementary School." *Arithmetic Teacher* 27 (April 1980): 10–12, 44–47.

Driscoll, M. J. "The Role of Manipulatives in Elementary School Mathematics." In *Research within Reach: Elementary School Mathematics,* p. 1. St. Louis, MO: Cemrel Inc., 1983.

Drizigacker, R. "FRIO, or Fractions In Order." *Arithmetic Teacher* 13 (December 1966): 684–685.

National Council of Teachers of Mathematics. *Principles and Standards for School Mathematics,* pp. 150, 218. Reston, VA: National Council of Teachers of Mathematics, 2000.

Chapter 6

Carpenter, T. P., H. Kepner, M. K. Corbitt, M. M. Lindquist, and R. E. Reys. "Decimals: Results and Implications from National Assessment." *Arithmetic Teacher* 28 (April 1981): 34–37.

Grossman, A. "Decimal Notation: An Important Research Finding." *Arithmetic Teacher* 30 (May 1983): 32–33.

National Assessment of Educational Progress (NAEP). "Math Achievement Is Plus and Minus." *NAEP Newsletter* 12(5) (October 1979): 2.

National Council of Teachers of Mathematics. *Curriculum and Evaluation Standards for School Mathematics,* p. 59. Reston, VA: National Council of Teachers of Mathematics, 2000.

National Research Council. *Everybody Counts: A Report to the Nation on the Future of Mathematics Education,* pp. 47–48. Washington, DC: The National Academy Press, 1989.

Wiebe, J. H. "Manipulating Percentages." *The Mathematics Teacher* (January 1986): 23–26.

Chapter 7

Foreman, L. C., and A. B. Bennett Jr. *Math Alive,* pp. 399–417. Salem, OR: The Math Learning Center, 1998.

Gnanadesikan, M., R. Scheaffer, and J. Swift. *The Art and Techniques of Simulation.* Palo Alto, CA: Dale Seymour Publications, 1987.

Mosteller, F. et al. *Statistics: A Guide to the Unknown,* pp. 164–175. New York: Holden-Day, 1972.

National Council of Teachers of Mathematics. *Curriculum and Evaluation Standards for School Mathematics,* p. 105. Reston, VA: National Council of Teachers of Mathematics, 2000.

Sinkov, A. *Elementary Cryptanalysis.* Washington, DC: Mathematical Association of America, 1966.

Weaver, W. *Lady Luck,* pp. 270–277. New York: Doubleday, 1963.

Chapter 8

Davis, P. J., and R. Hersh. *Descartes Dream,* pp. 18–19. New York: Harcourt Brace Jovanovich, 1986.

National Council of Teachers of Mathematics. *Principles and Standards for School Mathematics,* p. 51. Reston, VA: National Council of Teachers of Mathematics, 2000.

Chapter 9

Gardner, M. "Mathematical Games." *Scientific American* 197(1) (1957):145.

Hapgood, F. "When Ice Crystals Fall from the Sky Art Meets Science." *Smithsonian* (January 1976): 67–72.

Krause, M. C. "Wind Rose, the Beautiful Circle." *Arithmetic Teacher* 20 (May 1973): 375.

Levin, R. "Solving Instant Insanity." *Journal of Recreational Mathematics* 2 (July 1969): 189–192.

National Council of Teachers of Mathematics. *Principles and Standards for School Mathematics,* p. 165. Reston, VA: National Council of Teachers of Mathematics, 2000.

Reed, R. *Tangrams.* New York: Dover, 1965.

Weyl, H. *Symmetry,* pp. 83–89. Princeton: Princeton University Press, 1952.

Chapter 10

Carson, G. "Soma Cubes." *The Mathematics Teacher* 66 (November 1973): 583–592.

National Council of Teachers of Mathematics. *Principles and Standards for School Mathematics,* pp. 45–46. Reston, VA: National Council of Teachers of Mathematics, 2000.

Chapter 11

National Council of Teachers of Mathematics. *Principles and Standards for School Mathematics,* p. 43. Reston, VA: National Council of Teachers of Mathematics, 2000.

Shuster, C. N., and F. L. Bedford. *Field Work in Mathematics,* pp. 56–57. East Palestine, OH: Yoder Instruments, 1935.

Activity Set 3.4

1. b.

132   132 ÷ 12 = 11

2. b.

114 ÷ 12 = 9 with a remainder of 6

4. c.

529 ÷ 23 = 23

6. c.

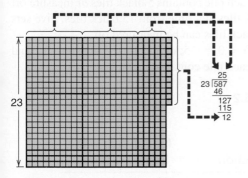

$$\begin{array}{r} 25 \\ 23\overline{\smash)587} \\ 46 \\ \hline 127 \\ 115 \\ \hline 12 \end{array}$$

Activity Set 4.1

2. b. The 125th even number has two rows of 125 tiles. The 125th even number is 250.

3. b. The 15th odd number has a horizontal row of 15 tiles on the bottom and a row of 14 tiles on the top. The 15th odd number is 29.

  d. 79 is the 40th position; 117 is in the 59th position.

4. b. Even   **e.** Even

5. b. The L-shapes representing the first 10 consecutive odd numbers form a 10 by 10 square, so the sum of the first 10 consecutive odd numbers is 100.

8. b. 1 is the only nonzero whole number with exactly 1 factor.

  e. Numbers with an odd number of factors have a square among their rectangles. That is, they are square numbers.

Activity Set 4.2

1. b. 1, 2, 3, 4, 6, 12

2. b. GCF(18, 25) = 1

4. a. 8

5. GCF(40, 24) = 8   GCF(42, 28) = 14
  GCF(21, 12) = 3

6. b. GCF(280, 168) = GCF(112, 168) = GCF(112, 56) = GCF(56, 56) = 56

  d. GCF(306, 187) = GCF(119, 187) = GCF(119, 68) = GCF(51, 68) = GCF(51, 17) = GCF(34, 17) = GCF(17, 17) = 17

7. b. LCM(14, 21) = 42

  d. LCM(8, 10) = 40

14
21

8
10

8. a.

	A	B	GCF(A, B)	LCM(A, B)	A × B
(3)	14	21	7	42	294
(5)	8	10	2	40	80

9. a. GCF(9, 15) = 3 and 9 × 15 = 135, 135 ÷ 3 = 45. So LCM(9, 15) = 45.

  c. GCF(140, 350) = 70 and (140 × 350) ÷ 70 = 70. So LCM(140, 350) = 700.

Just for Fun 4.2

1. Yes

Star (8, 3)

Star (9, 4)

Star (7, 2)

Star (7, 4)

2. Star (n, s) is congruent to (has the same size and shape as) star (n, r).

Star (12, 5)   Star (12, 7)   Star (10, 3)   Star (10, 7)

3. Star $(5, 1)$ has 1 path; star $(10, 4)$ has 2 paths; star $(12, 4)$ has 4 paths; and star $(6, 3)$ has 3 paths.

Star (5, 1)   Star (10, 4)   Star (12, 4)   Star (6, 3)

4. n and s must be relatively prime; that is, GCF$(n, s) = 1$. These stars have 1 continuous path: (1) star $(15, 2) =$ star $(15, 13)$; (2) star $(15, 4) =$ star $(15, 11)$; and (3) star $(15, 7) =$ star $(15, 8)$.

Star (15, 2)   Star (15, 4)   Star (15, 7)

5. Star $(9, 2)$ has 1 path and requires 2 orbits. Star $(8, 6)$ has 2 paths and each path requires 3 orbits. Star $(14, 4)$ has 2 paths and each path requires 2 orbits.

Star (9, 2)   Star (8, 6)   Star (14, 4)

6. b. The number of orbits for star (n, s) is LCM(n, s) divided by n.

7. b. 11

Activity Set 5.1

2. a. 37   8   29 $^+21$
   c. 20   6   14 $^+8$
   f. 24   13   11 $^-2$

3. c. 13; $^-59$; $^-62$

4. b. If there are more red tiles than black tiles, subtract the number of black tiles from the number of red tiles and make the answer negative. If the number of black tiles is greater than or equal to the number of red tiles, subtract the number of red tiles from the number of black tiles.

5. b.

       $^+5$ $^+5$ $^+5 - {}^-2 = 7$

6. Notice that in each of the preceding examples, taking out a given number of tiles of one color is equivalent to putting in the same number of tiles of the opposite color. For example, in 5b, 2 red tiles and 2 black tiles were put in the set and then 2 red tiles were withdrawn from the set. The same result could be accomplished by simply adding 2 black tiles to the set.

7. b.

0                     $^+8$

$^-2 \times {}^-4 = {}^+8$

9. c. In the sharing approach, $^-3$ represents the number of groups, which is not possible. In the measurement approach, groups of 3 red tiles cannot be formed from 12 black tiles.

10. c. i. $15 \div 3 = 5$; divide 15 black tiles into 3 equal piles, each pile contains 5 black tiles *or* measure off 3 black tiles at a time from 15 black tiles. Five sets of 3 black tiles can be measured off.
      iii. $^-15 \div 3 = {}^-5$; divide 15 red tiles into 3 equal piles, each pile contains 5 red tiles.

Activity Set 5.2

1. a.

Fraction	No. of Bars with Equal Fractions
$\frac{0}{4}$	5
$\frac{1}{2}$	4
$\frac{2}{3}$	3
$\frac{6}{6}$	5
$\frac{1}{4}$	2

2. a. $\frac{1}{12} < \frac{1}{6} < \frac{1}{4} < \frac{1}{3} < \frac{5}{12} < \frac{1}{2} < \frac{7}{12} < \frac{2}{3} < \frac{3}{4} < \frac{5}{6} < \frac{11}{12}$

3. b. The $\frac{7}{12}$ bar; this is the "cheapest" way to win the $\frac{1}{2}$ bar.

4. a. Nearest whole number is 5

  c. Nearest whole number is 1

5. b.

$\dfrac{6}{7} = \dfrac{18}{21}$ $\dfrac{5}{8} = \dfrac{15}{24}$ $\dfrac{1}{6} = \dfrac{3}{18}$

6. b. $\dfrac{2}{3} = \dfrac{2 \times 17}{3 \times 17} = \dfrac{34}{51}$

  d.

$\dfrac{5}{6} = \dfrac{10}{12}$ $\dfrac{5}{6} = \dfrac{15}{18}$ $\dfrac{5}{6} = \dfrac{20}{24}$

7. a.

$\dfrac{1}{2} = \dfrac{7}{14}$

$\dfrac{5}{7} = \dfrac{10}{14}$

8. d. $\dfrac{7}{9} = \dfrac{70}{90}$ and $\dfrac{8}{10} = \dfrac{72}{90}$ so $\dfrac{8}{10} > \dfrac{7}{9}$

  f. $\dfrac{11}{15} = \dfrac{121}{165}$ and $\dfrac{8}{11} = \dfrac{120}{165}$ so $\dfrac{11}{15} > \dfrac{8}{11}$

9. b. $2 \div 3 = \dfrac{2}{3}$

Activity Set 5.3

1. a.

$\dfrac{1}{3} + \dfrac{2}{4} = \dfrac{10}{12} = \dfrac{5}{6}$

  c.

$\dfrac{1}{3} + \dfrac{8}{9} = 1\dfrac{2}{9}$

  e.

$\dfrac{3}{8} + \dfrac{1}{4} = \dfrac{5}{8}$

2. c. Here are four pairs of fractions that sum to 1; there are others: $\dfrac{1}{2} + \dfrac{2}{4} = 1$, $\dfrac{2}{12} + \dfrac{5}{6}$, $\dfrac{2}{3} + \dfrac{2}{6}$, $\dfrac{3}{4} + \dfrac{3}{12}$.

3. a.

  d. $\dfrac{13}{12} = 1\dfrac{1}{12}$ **g.** $\dfrac{7}{12}$

$\dfrac{5}{6} - \dfrac{1}{4} = \dfrac{7}{12}$

4. b.

$\dfrac{1}{3} \times \dfrac{1}{4} = \dfrac{1}{12}$ $\dfrac{2}{3} \times \dfrac{1}{6} = \dfrac{2}{18}$ $\dfrac{2}{3} \times \dfrac{4}{5} = \dfrac{8}{15}$

5. b. 5

|← 5 →|

  d. $1\dfrac{1}{2}$

|← 1 →| $\frac{1}{2}$

6. b.

$$\frac{5}{8} - \frac{1}{6} \approx \frac{4}{8} = \frac{1}{2}$$

d.

$$\frac{2}{3} \times \frac{5}{6} \approx \frac{3}{6}$$

7. a. $\frac{1}{6} + \frac{1}{4} = \frac{5}{12}$　　$3 \times \frac{3}{12} = \frac{3}{4}$　　$\frac{2}{4} - \frac{1}{2} = \frac{0}{3}$　　$\frac{2}{3} \div \frac{2}{6} = 2$

or

$\frac{2}{4} + \frac{0}{3} = \frac{1}{2}$　　$3 \times \frac{1}{4} = \frac{3}{4}$　　$\frac{5}{12} - \frac{3}{12} = \frac{1}{6}$　　$\frac{2}{3} \div \frac{2}{6} = 2$

Activity Set 6.1

1. b.

.75 = Seventy-five hundredths

2. b. .33　　**f.** .954, nine-hundred fifty four thousandths

4. c. 3 parts out of 10 is equal to 30 parts out of 100; .3 = .30

　　e. 470 parts out of 1000 is equal to 47 parts out of 100; .470 = .47

　　g. 1 part out of 100 is equal to 10 parts out of 1000; .01 = .010

5. b.

.055

Tenths	Hundredths	Thousandths
0	5	5

　　d. Every collection of 10 like parts (thousandths, hundredths, or tenths) can be regrouped to form 1 larger part and is recorded in the adjacent column, to the left.

6. b. Each part would be $\frac{1}{100,000}$ of the unit square. The decimal is written as .00001 and named 1 hundred-thousandth.

7. b. .042 > .04

9. c.

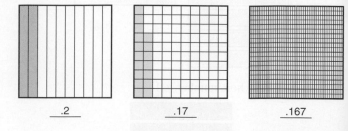

.2　　　　　　.17　　　　　　.167

Activity Set 6.2

5. b. $4 \times .725 = 2.9$ because 4 thousandth squares, each with 725 parts shaded, yield a total of 2900 shaded parts. Since there are 1000 parts in 1 whole square, the total shaded amount would be equal to 2 whole squares and 900 parts shaded out of 1000.

　　c. Multiplying by 10 makes each shaded tenth column of a decimal square equal to a unit square. Similarly, multiplying by 10 makes each hundredth square equal to a tenth column and each thousandth piece equal to a hundredth square.

7. b.

1 unit square, 7 tenths, and 12 hundredths
$1.4 \times 1.3 = 1.82$

9. d. The decimal 2.87 can be represented by 2 whole squares and a square with 87 hundredths shaded (8 tenth columns and 7 hundredth squares). Dividing a unit square by 10 results in a region equivalent to 1 tenth column. Dividing a tenth column by 10 results in a region equal to 1 hundredth square, and dividing a hundredth square by 10 results in a region equal to 1 thousandth piece. When the squares representing 2.87 are divided by 10, the result is 2 tenth columns, 8 hundredth squares, and 7 thousandth pieces.

10. b. .70 ÷ .05 = 14

　　d. Five tenths can be measured off or subtracted from each unit twice. Since there are 250 units, .5 can be subtracted 500 times.

Activity Set 6.3

1. a. 30%　　　**c.** 103%　　　**d.** 130%

2. a.　　　**c.**　　　　　　　　　　　　**f.**

3. a. The value is 3. 300 ÷ 100 = 3.

　　c. The value is 288. Each small square has value 3 and 300 − 12 = 288.

4. a. Value 45: Each strip (10%) has value 15 so three strips (30%) have value 45.

　　c. Value 10.5: Every pair of small squares has value 3, and 3 + 3 + 3 + 1.5 = 10.5.

5. a. 45 is 10% of 450: Each strip has value 45 and is 10% of 450.

　　c. 441 is 98% of 450: Each small square has value 4.5, so 98 (98%) small squares have value 441.

6. a. Value of grid is 400: Since 6% has value 24, 1% has value 4, and the value of the 10 by 10 grid is 400.

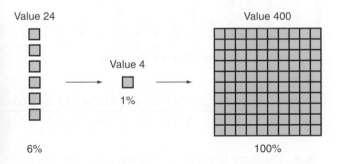

c. Value of the grid is 240: Since 55% has value 132, 1% has value 2.4 (132 ÷ 55), and 100% has value 240.

7. a. Some possible observations: There are 208 women employees; 35% of the employees are men; there are 112 men employees.

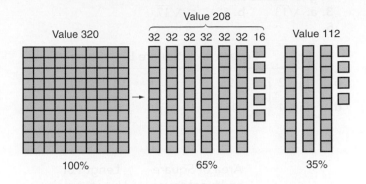

b. Some observations: 35% of the students were absent; 65% of the students were present.

8. b. $\frac{2}{4} = \frac{40}{100} = 40\% = .4$

d. $\frac{13}{20} = \frac{65}{100} = .65\% = .65$

9. b. $\frac{5}{6} \approx 85\% = .85$

Activity Set 6.4

1. b. 4 square units   **e.** 2 square units
   g. 10 square units
3. a. $\sqrt{13}$ **b.** 5   **c.** $\sqrt{17}$
5.

		Square A	Square B	Square C
b.	Fig. 2	9	4	13
d.	Fig. 4	45	20	65

6. c.

		Area of Square on Hypotenuse	Length of Hypotenuse
*(2)	Fig. 2	13	$\sqrt{13}$
*(4)	Fig. 4	65	$\sqrt{65}$

7. b.

e.

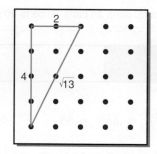

Activity Set 7.1

1. a. A typical bar graph display of eye color might look like

b. A typical distribution and pie graph might look like

Eye Color	Number	Percentage	Central Angle (degrees)
Brown	10	30.3	109.1
Blue	5	15.2	54.5
Green	7	21.2	76.4
Hazel	8	24.2	87.3
Gray	3	9.1	32.7
Total	33	100.0	360

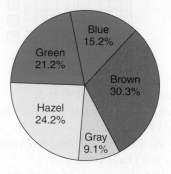

2. a. A typical line plot might look like

3. c.

Interval	15–24	25–34	35–44	45–54	55–64	65–7~
Frequency	1	5	14	6	17	7

6. a. The trend line for this data has a negative slope. It indicates that the taller the father, the shorter the mother.

b. The horizontal trend line for this data has zero slope. Short fathers are paired with short and tall mothers and the same is true for taller fathers. There seems to be no apparent trend.

Heights of fathers

Just for Fun 7.1

1. There is a negative relationship. As the number of blue increases the number of brown decreases. (A correlation of about −.5.)
2. Based on the scatter plot trend line, if you had 14 blue you could expect between 3 to 5 brown. If you had 10 brown you could expect 3 to 5 blue.
3. There is also a negative relationship between yellow and green. (A correlation of about −.4.)

Activity Set 7.2

1. a. Some possible observations:
   - Short and long time intervals alternate.
   - The shortest time interval is 51 minutes and the longest is 98 minutes.
   - There is a difference of 47 minutes between the shortest and longest time intervals.
   - The table does not show how long an eruption lasts, just the time between eruptions.
   - Among the 15 time intervals there are four pairs of equal time intervals.

2. a.

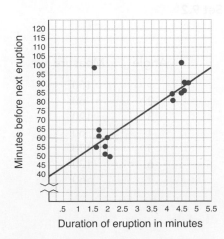

Duration of eruption in minutes

b.

Starting Time	Duration	Predicted Interval Before Next Eruption	Predicted Time of Next Eruption
11:22 a.m.	1 min 50 sec	Between 55 and 65 min	12:17 p.m. to 12:27 p.m.
8:30 a.m.	4 min 26 sec	Between 80 and 90 min	9:50 a.m. to 10:00 a.m.
12:40 a.m.	3 min 46 sec	Between 75 and 85 min	1:55 p.m. to 2:05 p.m.

4. b. $287,000 is the average for the 6 greatest housing prices; $120,667 is the average for the 6 smallest housing prices.
   d. $264,167 is the greatest average and $139,667 is the least average. Both are closer to the mean of $195,611 than the greatest average and least average from part b.

Activity Set 7.3

1. c. *At least* 3 means 3, 4, 5, or 6 girls. Count the number of outcomes in the chart that have 3, 4, 5, or 6 heads and divide that number by 64.
2. d. The pulse rate distribution comes close to satisfying this property because 68.3% of the pulse rates are within ±1 standard deviation of the mean, and 95% are within ±2 standard deviations of the mean.
3. a.

Letter	e	s	c	w	k
Percent	16.3%	7.2%	2.6%	1.7%	.6%

   c. This assignment of code symbols requires 43 time units, as compared to 47 time units for Morse code.

e	t	a	o	n	i	s
•	—	• •	• —	— •	• • •	— —

s	r	h	h
• • —	• — •	• • • •	— • •

4. d. There are 3,947,387 numbers from 7,212 to 3,954,598. Approximately 70% $\left(\frac{117}{166}\right)$ begin with the digits 1, 2, 3, or 4. If the populations are randomly distributed you would expect a greater number of those populations to start with digits 1, 2, 3, or 4.

Activity Set 8.1

2. e. No. There is only a 25% chance of winning.
4. a. 2   **c.** $A_1 A_2 A$ **e.** No
$A_2 A_1 B$

Just for Fun 8.1

Variation: Tracks 9, 10, 11, and 12 most likely to win with probabilities 11.5%, 12.5%, 12.5%, and 11.5%, respectively.

Activity Set 8.2

1. c. Theoretical probability of 2 of different colors: $\frac{3}{5}$

Theoretical probability of 2 of the same color: $\frac{2}{5}$

e. From the probability tree, we see that the probability of drawing first a red and then a green is $\frac{1}{2} \times \frac{3}{5} = \frac{3}{10}$, and the probability of drawing first a green and then a red is $\frac{1}{2} \times \frac{3}{5} = \frac{3}{10}$. So, the theoretical probability of drawing 2 squares of different colors is $\frac{3}{10} + \frac{3}{10} = \frac{3}{5}$.

2. c. $\frac{6}{16}$ or $\frac{3}{8}$

4. b. $\frac{49}{100}$

5. a. $\frac{1}{36}$ **c.** $\frac{35}{36} \times \frac{35}{36}$ or $\left(\frac{35}{36}\right)^2$

e. Approximately $1 - .51 = .49$

Just for Fun 8.2

2. $\frac{2}{3}$ **3.** $\frac{1}{3}$ **4.** $\frac{1}{3}$ **5.** $\frac{2}{3}$

Activity Set 9.1

1. b. All triangles that have their third vertex on the same row parallel to the base have the same area.

c. There are 12 noncongruent triangles that can be formed on the given base.

4.

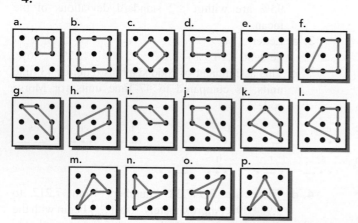

Figures a, b, and c are squares; figure d is a rectangle but not a square; figures h and i are parallelograms but not rectangles; figures e, f, and g are trapezoids; figures a, b, c, d, e, f, g, h, i, j, k, and l are convex; figures m, n, o, and p are concave.

6. a. 75°; 90°; 210°; 120°

b.

45°

165°

195°

105°

7. a. 45°; 30°; 45°; 30°; 45°

b. Inscribed angles that intercept arcs of equal length in the same or congruent circles have the same measure.

c. Inscribed angles whose sides intersect the ends of a diameter are right angles.

8. a.

Inscribed angle 105.0°   Inscribed angle 60.0°   Inscribed angle 75.0°   Inscribed angle

Central angle 210.0°   Central angle 120.0°   Central angle 150.0°   Central angle

b. The measure of an inscribed angle is half the measure of the central angle that intercepts the same arc.

Just for Fun 9.1

1. The 7 tangram pieces have been numbered (see the square below) in the solutions to the puzzles.

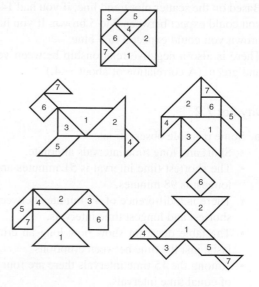

Activity Set 9.2

2.

Angle	Measure
1	150°
2	60°
3	120°
4	60°
5	120°
6	120°
7	60°

4. c. Each interior angle of a regular polygon with more than 6 sides is greater than 120° and less than 180°. The measures of such angles are not factors of 360.

5. c. Here are two examples of pattern block tessellations that are neither regular nor semi-regular.

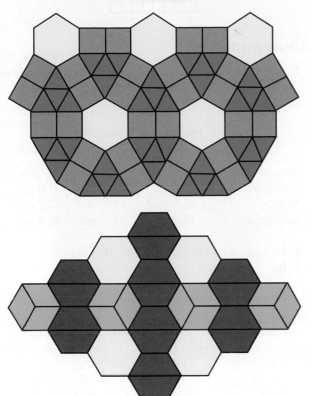

Just for Fun 9.2

The winning strategy on a 3 by 3 or 5 by 5 grid is to occupy the center hexagon on the first move. On a 4 by 4 grid, the winning first move is any of those marked here.

4 by 4

Activity Set 9.3

3. a.

	Vertices (V)	Faces (F)	Edges (E)
Tetrahedron	4	4	6
Cube	8	6	12
Octahedron	6	8	12
Dodecahedron	20	12	30
Icosahedron	12	20	30

c.

	(1)	(2)	(3)	(4)
Vertices	5	10	12	10
Faces	5	7	8	7
Edges	8	15	18	15

5. b. Octahedron **e.** Icosahedron **f.** Cube
g. Icosahedron or dodecahedron
h. Dodecahedron **j.** Cube or octahedron

Activity Set 9.4

1. a.

c. There are other ways besides the ones shown.

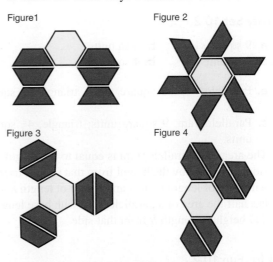

4. a. Angle *ABC* has a measure of 135°; *AD* = *DC* and *AB* = *BC*.

Angle *EFG* has a measure of 120°; *FG* = *HG* = *HF* and *EF* = $\frac{1}{2}$ of *FG*.

Hexagon

5. d. The eight-pointed wind rose.

e. A regular 16-sided polygon can be obtained by cutting a 157.5° angle as shown here, with *AB* = *AC* = *AD*. *Note:* Some of the lines of symmetry are not crease lines.

Activity Set 10.1

3. a. 156 mm   **b.** 19 mm

7. a. A quart contains approximately 946 cm³. A liter contains slightly more than a quart.

b. Approximately 10.9 cm

Activity Set 10.2

1. a. 9 sq units   **b.** 6 sq units
2. a. 3 sq units   **b.** 4 sq units

6. a. Parallelogram, 6 square units; triangle, 3 square units.

c. Parallelogram, 9 square units; triangle, $4\frac{1}{4}$ square units.

7. The area of a parallelogram is equal to the length of a side multiplied by the height from that side. A triangle with base of length *b* units and height of length *h* units has half the area of a parallelogram with base length *b* and height of length *h* from that side.

Just for Fun 10.2

4. The squares with an *X* in the following figure show one possible final move in the pentomino game.

5. Here are 5 pieces that work.

Activity Set 10.3

1. The volume of the crown was greater than the volume of the gold. King Hieron was cheated.

2.

	Hexagonal Prism	Hexagonal Pyramid	Cylinder
Area of base	9.1 cm²	9.1 cm²	12.6 cm²
Height (altitude)	5.0 cm	5.0 cm	3.0 cm
Volume	45.5 cm³	15.2 cm³	37.7 cm³
Surface area	75.2 cm²	38.7 cm²	62.8 cm²

3. Cylinder A: 1030 cm³; cylinder B: 1341 cm³

5. b.

	1	2	3	4	5	6
Central angle of disk	45°	90°	135°	225°	270°	315°
Radius of base (cm)	1.25	2.50	3.75	6.25	7.50	8.75
Base area (cm²)	4.91	19.63	44.18	122.72	176.71	240.53
Height of cone (cm)	9.92	9.68	9.27	7.81	6.61	4.84
Volume of cone (cm³)	16.24	63.34	136.52	319.48	389.35	388.06

c. For central angles of less than 45°, the smaller the angle is, the smaller the volume is. For central angles of more than 315°, the larger the angle is, the smaller the volume is. The maximum volume of approximately 403 cm³ occurs with a central angle of 294°.

6. c. A cone with a base of radius *r* and a height of *h* has a volume of $\frac{1}{3} \times \pi r^2 h$. The "half cone" has a base of radius $\frac{r}{2}$ and a height of $\frac{h}{2}$. Its volume is $\frac{1}{3} \times \pi(\frac{r}{2})^2(\frac{h}{2})$, which is equal to $\frac{1}{3} \times \pi r^2 h \times \frac{1}{8}$.

Therefore, the volume of the "half cone" is $\frac{1}{8}$ of the volume of the original cone.

7. a. 7235 cm³

8. c. The volume of the 3 balls is $3 \times \frac{4}{3} \times \pi(3.15)^3 \approx$ 393 cm³. The volume of the can is $20 \times \pi(3.5)^2 \approx$ 770 cm³. Therefore, approximately $\frac{1}{2}$ of the space is wasted.

Activity Set 11.1

1. b. The points form 2 perpendicular lines that pass through the intersection of lines m and n and bisect the angles formed by the intersection of m and n.

2. a. The points form a circle with P as center and radius equal to the distance from P to the midpoint of the chords.

c. The points form a circle whose center is the midpoint of segment $\overline{PS}$ and whose diameter is $\overline{PS}$.

4. A circle

6. a. A semicircle on diameter $\overline{PQ}$ (a circle if you reverse the card and repeat the process on the other side of segment $\overline{PQ}$).

Activity Set 11.2

1. a. The new figure will tessellate because the exact shape that has been adjoined to one edge of the rectangle was deleted from the opposite side of the rectangle.

Activity Set 11.3

1. a. Both triangles contain the angle at E, and the angles at A and A' are right angles. When two angles of one triangle are congruent to two angles of another, the triangles are similar.

2. d. When you are estimating large distances, the distance from eye to finger is relatively small and ignoring it will not significantly affect the estimate. However, when you are estimating small distances, which may be only a few times greater than the distance from eye to finger, ignoring the distance from the eye to the finger will give a larger error. In the latter case, the distance should be added to the estimated distance.

3. b. 20.25 m   **c.** 24.3 m

4. c. $\overline{ET}$ in the figure measures 80 mm. So, 80 mm represents 60 m, or 1 mm represents .75 m. The height of the tree from T to R in the diagram is 24 mm, so the height of the actual tree between those two points is $24 \times .75 = 18$ m.

5. c. Approximately 33 m plus 1.5 m, the height of the hypsometer above the ground, for a total of 34.5 m.

6. b. Use a line from the land marker to the pine tree as a base line and measure the distance between these two points. From the pine tree, measure the 5 angles between the base line and the remaining 5 objects. From the landmark, measure the 5 angles between the base line and the remaining 5 objects. With the 10 angles, a map can be made of the locations of each object. Using the distance from the pine tree to the landmark, a scale can be set up to determine all distances between any pairs of objects in the field.

Photo Credits

Chapter 1
Page 11: © The Granger Collection; p. 15 (top): © Vol. 6 PhotoDisc/Getty RF; p. 15 (middle): © Dr. Parvind Sethi; p. 15 (bottom left): © PhotoAlto/PunchStock RF; p. 15 (bottom right): *Patterns in Nature* by Peter S. Stevens, Atlantic Monthly/Little Brown, 1974. Reprinted by permission of Peter S. Stevens; p. 26: Photo by Albert B. Bennett, Jr.

Chapter 2
Page 34 and p. 57: Photo by Albert B. Bennett, Jr.

Chapter 3
Page 59 (all), p. 79, p. 95, and p. 97: Photo by Albert B. Bennett, Jr.

Chapter 4
Page 115 and p. 118: Photo by Albert B. Bennett, Jr.; p. 120: Courtesy Hamid Buhmard, Western Oregon University; p. 122: Photo by Albert B. Bennett, Jr.

Chapter 5
Page 130 and p. 151: Photo by Albert B. Bennett, Jr.

Chapter 6
Page 163: Photo by Albert B. Bennett, Jr.; p. 196: © Getty RF; p. 199: Photo by Albert B. Bennett, Jr.

Chapter 7
Page 224 (left & right): Library of Congress; p. 226 (all): © Image Club RF; p. 238 (all): Photo by L. Ted Nelson.

Chapter 8
Page 241 and p. 242: Photo by Albert B. Bennett, Jr.; p. 243 (all): © Image Club RF; p. 245 and p. 246: Photo by Albert B. Bennett, Jr.; p. 249 (top): © Comstock/Alamy RF; p. 249 (middle): © Vol. 25 PhotoDisc/Getty RF; p. 249 (bottom): Photo by Albert B. Bennett, Jr.; p. 253 (all): © Image Club RF; p. 255, p. 256, p. 259 (left & right), and p. 262: Photo by Albert B. Bennett, Jr.

Chapter 9
Page 263, p. 265, and p. 270 (all): Photo by Albert B. Bennett, Jr.; p. 274 (left & right): © Stockbyte/Getty RF; p. 283a: © Comstock/PunchStock RF; p. 283b: © Digital Vision, Ltd. RF; p. 285: M.C. Escher's "Stars" © 2008 The M.C. Escher Company—Baarn—Holland. All rights reserved. www.mcescher.com; p. 287 (top & bottom), p. 290, and p. 291: Photo by Albert B. Bennett, Jr.; p. 293: © Getty RF; p. 304: Photo by Albert B. Bennett, Jr.

Chapter 10
Page 308 and p. 310: Photo by Albert B. Bennett, Jr.; p. 311 (top): © The McGraw-Hill Companies, Inc./Dot Box, Inc.; p. 311 (bottom): © The McGraw-Hill Companies, Inc./Jacques Cornell, photographer; p. 317: Photo by Albert B. Bennett, Jr.; p. 320: © Comstock/Alamy RF; p. 324, p. 325, and p. 326 (top): Photo by Albert B. Bennett, Jr.; p. 326 (bottom): © The McGraw-Hill Companies, Inc./Ken Karp, photographer; p. 327 and p. 331: Photo by Albert B. Bennett, Jr.

Chapter 11
Page 333: © Image Club RF; p. 341: Photo courtesy Hamid Behmard, Western Oregon University; p. 343 (all): Photo by L. Ted Nelson; p. 363 and p. 368 (top & bottom): Photo by Albert B. Bennett, Jr.

Material Cards
MC10 (all): © Vol. 116 PhotoDisc/Getty RF and © Children's Portraits Punchstock/Stockbyte RF; MC11 (all): © Vol. 116 PhotoDisc/Getty RF; © Children's Portraits Punchstock/Stockbyte RF; and © IS490/Image Source Black RF; MC22 and MC23 (all): © Image Club RF; MC36: Photo by Albert Bennett, Jr.

Illustrations and Text

Chapter 5
Page 133: Fraction Bar model from the Fraction Bars® materials by Albert B. Bennett, Jr., and Patricia Davidson © 2003. Permission of American Education Products, LLC. Fort Collins, Colorado.

Chapter 6
Page 153: Decimal Squares model from the Decimal Squares® materials by Albert B. Bennett, Jr., © 2003. Permission of American Education Products, LLC. Fort Collins, Colorado.

Chapter 7
Page 225: Graphs from *A Guide to the Unknown,* by Frederick Mosteller et al., copyright 1972. Reprinted by courtesy of Holden-Day, Inc.

Chapter 11
Page 342: Line designs from *Line Designs* by Dale Seymour, Linda Libey, and Joyce Snider. Reprinted by permission of Creative Publications, Palo Alto.

Index

Note: Page numbers preceded by A refer to the Appendix; those preceded by M refer to the Material Cards section.

Material Cards

1. Algebra Pieces (1.3)
2. Algebraic Expression Cards (1.3)
3. Attribute Label Cards (2.1)
4. Attribute-Game Grid (2.1)
5. Two-Circle Venn Diagram (2.1)
6. Three-Circle Venn Diagram (2.1, 9.1)
7. Exercises and Activities No. 3 (2.1)
8. Rectangular Geoboard Template (2.2, 6.4, 9.1, 10.2)
9. Coordinate Guessing and Hide-a-Region Grids (2.2)
10. Logic Problem Clue Cards and People Pieces (Problem 1) (2.3)
11. Logic Problem Clue Cards and People Pieces (Problem 2) (2.3)
12. Logic Problem Clue Cards, Prize and People Pieces (Problem 3) (2.3)
13. Logic Problem Clue Cards, Career, Singer, People, and Location Pieces (Problem 4) (2.3)
14. Logic Problem Clue Cards (Problem 5) (2.3)
15. Logic Problem Object Pieces (Problem 5) (2.3)
16. Pica-Centro Recording Sheet (2.3)
17. Mind-Reading Cards (3.1)
18. Interest Gameboard (6.3)
19. Pythagorean Puzzle Visual Proof and Square Me Puzzle (6.4)
20. Metric Ruler, Protractor, and Compass (7.1, 9.1, 10.1, 10.3, 11.1, 11.2, 11.3)
21. Table of Random Digits (7.2, 7.3, 8.1)
22. Two-Penny Grid (8.1)
23. Three-Penny Grid (8.1)
24. Simulation Spinners (8.2)
25. Trick Dice (8.2)
26. Geoboard Recording Paper (9.1)
27. Circular Geoboard Template (9.1)
28. Grids for Game of Hex (9.2)
29. Regular Polyhedra (9.3)
30. Regular Polyhedra (9.3)
31. Two-Centimeter Grid Paper (9.3)
32. Cube Patterns for Instant Insanity (9.3)
33. Perpendicular Lines for Symmetry (9.4)
34. Metric Measuring Tape (10.1)
35. Centimeter Racing Mat (10.1)
36. Pentominoes (10.2)
37. Pentomino Game Grid (10.2)
38. Prism, Pyramid, and Cylinder (10.3)
39. Hypsometer-Clinometer (11.3)

VARIABLE PIECE
VARIABLE PIECE
VARIABLE PIECE
VARIABLE PIECE
VARIABLE PIECE
VARIABLE PIECE
VARIABLE PIECE
VARIABLE PIECE
VARIABLE PIECE
VARIABLE PIECE
VARIABLE PIECE
VARIABLE PIECE
VARIABLE PIECE
VARIABLE PIECE
VARIABLE PIECE
VARIABLE PIECE

UNIT	UNIT	UNIT
UNIT	UNIT	UNIT
UNIT	UNIT	UNIT
UNIT	UNIT	UNIT
UNIT	UNIT	UNIT
UNIT	UNIT	UNIT
UNIT	UNIT	UNIT
UNIT	UNIT	UNIT
UNIT	UNIT	UNIT
UNIT	UNIT	UNIT
UNIT	UNIT	UNIT
UNIT	UNIT	UNIT

Algebraic Expression Cards (Activity Set 1.3 JUST FOR FUN)

Team A

I have $n + 1$ **Who has** two less than a number	**I have** $4n + 5$ **Who has** two more than the square root of a number
I have $n - 2$ **Who has** one more than two times a number	**I have** $\sqrt{n} + 2$ **Who has** five less than eight times a number
I have $2n + 1$ **Who has** five less than seven times a number	**I have** $8n - 5$ **Who has** one more than four times the square of a number
I have $7n - 5$ **Who has** seven more than the square of a number	**I have** $4n^2 + 1$ **Who has** four more than one-third of a number
I have $n^2 + 7$ **Who has** three more than half of a number	**I have** $\frac{n}{3} + 4$ **Who has** seven less than the cube of a number
I have $\frac{n}{2} + 3$ **Who has** five more than four times a number	**I have** $n^3 - 7$ **Who has** one more than a number

Team B

I have $n + 2$ **Who has** five less than a number	**I have** $5n + 3$ **Who has** one more than three times the square of a number
I have $n - 5$ **Who has** two more than three times a number	**I have** $3n^2 + 1$ **Who has** two more than one-third of a number
I have $3n + 2$ **Who has** five less than six times a number	**I have** $\frac{n}{3} + 2$ **Who has** six less than the cube of a number
I have $6n - 5$ **Who has** eight more than the square of a number	**I have** $n^3 - 6$ **Who has** nine more than four times a number
I have $n^2 + 8$ **Who has** five less than half of a number	**I have** $4n + 9$ **Who has** seven less than half of a number
I have $\frac{n}{2} - 5$ **Who has** three more than five times a number	**I have** $\frac{n}{2} - 7$ **Who has** two more than a number

Attribute Label Cards (Activity Set 2.1)

MATERIAL CARD 3

TRIANGULAR

HEXAGONAL

CIRCULAR

SQUARE

AND   RED

AND   BLUE

NOT   YELLOW

LARGE   SMALL   NOT   OR   LARGE

SMALL   NOT   OR   LARGE

Rows, 1 difference (1 point)   Columns, 2 differences (2 points)   Diagonals, 3 differences (3 points)

		Place attribute piece here to start game		

a.

SMALL   TRIANGULAR

RED

Description

d.

SMALL   TRIANGULAR

RED

Description

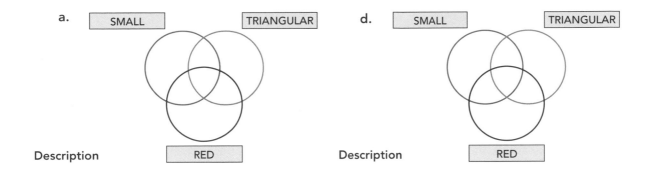

b.

SMALL   TRIANGULAR

RED

Description

e.

SMALL   TRIANGULAR

RED

Description

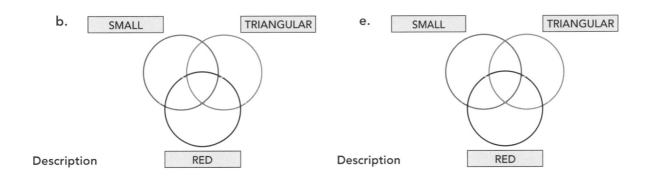

c.

SMALL   TRIANGULAR

RED

Description

f.

SMALL   TRIANGULAR

RED

Description

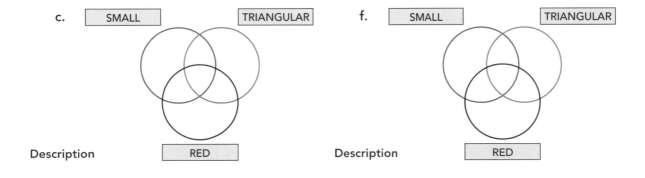

Rectangular Geoboard Template

(Activity Sets 2.2, 6.4, 9.1, and 10.2)

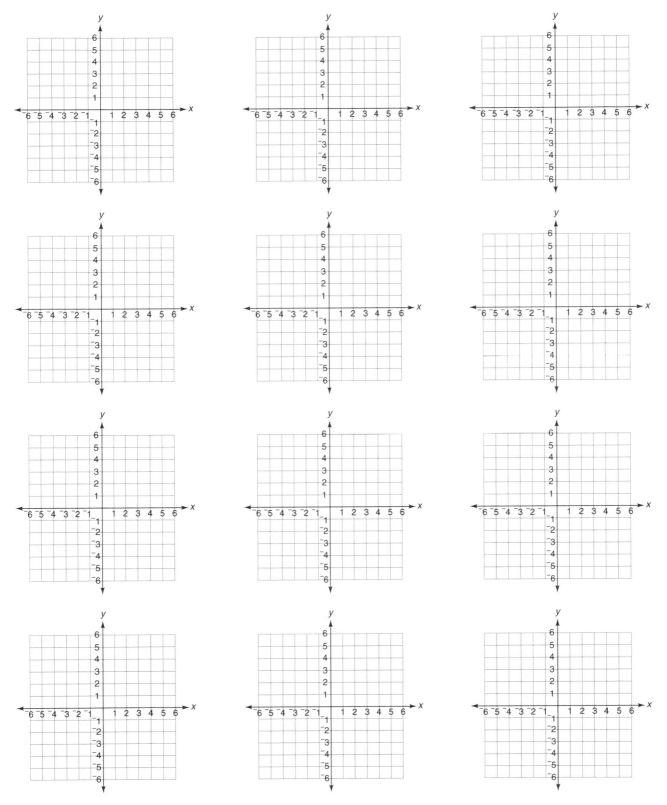

Logic Problem Clue Cards and People Pieces

PROBLEM 1 (Activity Set 2.3)

Paul, Nicky, Sally, Uri, Jane, Veneta, Monty, Marc, and Edith are standing in a row according to height, but not necessarily in the order given.

Edith is closer to Sally than she is to Nicky.

LOGIC PROBLEM 1   CARD A

Veneta, Edith, Marc, Sally, Monty, and Jane are shorter than Paul, Nicky, and Uri.

There is just one person between Uri and Paul.

Name the 9 people in order from shortest to tallest.

LOGIC PROBLEM 1   CARD B

Edith, Marc, Monty, Jane, and Veneta are shorter than the other four.

Uri is between Sally and Nicky.

Monty and Paul have 7 people between them.

LOGIC PROBLEM 1   CARD C

Uri, Nicky, Jane, Paul, and Sally are taller than the others.

Veneta and Monty are the only two people shorter than Edith.

LOGIC PROBLEM 1   CARD D

 Nicky

 Paul

 Sally

 Marc

 Uri

 Edith

 Jane

 Monty

 Veneta

Logic Problem Clue Cards and People Pieces

PROBLEM 2 (Activity Set 2.3)

Mr. Racquet is coach of the tennis team.

McKenna said, "I won't play if Tyrone is on the team."

LOGIC PROBLEM 2   CARD A

Juan, McKenna, Tyrone, Derek, Ida and Anna play mixed doubles.

Tyrone said, "I won't play if either Derek or Ida is chosen."

LOGIC PROBLEM 2   CARD B

How can Mr. Racquet select four compatible players (two men and two women) for a road trip?

Derek said, "I'll only play if Anna plays."

LOGIC PROBLEM 2   CARD C

Juan said, "I'll only play if McKenna plays."

Anna had no likes or dislikes.

LOGIC PROBLEM 2   CARD D

Juan

Anna

Tyrone

Derek

McKenna

Ida

Logic Problem Clue Cards, Prize and People Pieces

PROBLEM 3 (Activity Set 2.3)

Smith, Brown, Jones, and Robinson are told that they have each won one of four academic prizes, but none of them knows which, so they are speculating.

Smith thinks that Robinson has won the logic prize.

LOGIC PROBLEM 3   CARD A

The four academic prizes are for outstanding work in mathematics, English, French, and logic.

Jones feels confident that Smith has not won the mathematics prize.

Who won each prize?

LOGIC PROBLEM 3   CARD B

Robinson is of the opinion that Brown has won the French prize.

The winners of the mathematics and logic prizes were correct in their speculations.

LOGIC PROBLEM 3   CARD C

The English and French prize winners were not correct in their predictions of the prize winners.

Brown thinks that Jones has won the English prize.

The math prize was awarded to Robinson.

LOGIC PROBLEM 3   CARD D

Math

Jones

English

Smith

French

Robinson

Logic

Brown

Logic Problem Clue Cards, Career, Singer, People, and
Location Pieces PROBLEM 4 (Activity Set 2.3)

On a plane, Smith, Jones, and
Robinson are pilot, copilot, and
engineer, but not necessarily in that
order.

The copilot has the same name as
the singer living in the same town.

LOGIC PROBLEM 4   CARD A

On the plane there is a singing group,
The 3-Ms, whose names are M. Smith,
M. Robinson, and M. Jones.

The copilot lives in the city between
that of M. Jones and that of the
engineer.

LOGIC PROBLEM 4   CARD B

M. Robinson lives in New York City.

Jones consistently beats the engineer
in racquetball.

LOGIC PROBLEM 4   CARD C

The singers each reside in a different
city, New York, San Francisco, and
Chicago, as do the members of the
plane crew.

What is the pilot's name?

LOGIC PROBLEM 4   CARD D

Pilot	Chicago
Copilot	New York
Engineer	San Francisco
M. Jones	Jones
M. Smith	Smith
M. Robinson	Robinson

The Chevrolet owner lives in the house next door to the house where the horses are kept.

The person in the red house is English.

The Japanese drives a Ford.

Each house is occupied by a person of different nationality.

The person in the ivory house does not drink milk.

LOGIC PROBLEM 5   CARD A

The Plymouth driver lives next door to the person with the fox.

The Honda owner drinks orange juice.

The Norwegian lives next to the blue house.

Coffee is drunk in the green house.

Who owns the skunk?

LOGIC PROBLEM 5   CARD B

The Chevrolet owner lives in the yellow house.

Milk is drunk in the middle house.

The Norwegian lives in the first house.

The Spaniard owns a dog.

If each person has one home, one pet, one car, a different nationality and a different drink, who drinks the water?

LOGIC PROBLEM 5   CARD C

The Ukrainian drinks tea.

The green house is immediately to the right of the ivory house.

The Mercedes driver owns snails.

The fox lives with the owner of the house farthest from the green house.

The five houses are in a row.

LOGIC PROBLEM 5   CARD D

Logic Problem Object Pieces

PROBLEM 5 (Activity Set 2.3)

English

Dog

Green House

Mercedes

Norwegian

Horse

Red House

Honda

Japanese

Skunk

Ivory House

Plymouth

Ukrainian

Snails

Blue House

Chevrolet

Spaniard

Fox

Yellow House

Ford

Water

Coffee

Orange Juice

Tea

Milk

Pica-Centro Recording Sheet
(Activity Set 2.3 JUST FOR FUN)

THREE-DIGIT RECORDING SHEETS

GUESSES			RESPONSES			GUESSES			RESPONSES			GUESSES			RESPONSES	
Digits			Pica	Centro		Digits			Pica	Centro		Digits			Pica	Centro

FOUR-DIGIT RECORDING SHEETS

GUESSES				RESPONSES			GUESSES				RESPONSES			GUESSES				RESPONSES	
Digits				Pica	Centro		Digits				Pica	Centro		Digits				Pica	Centro

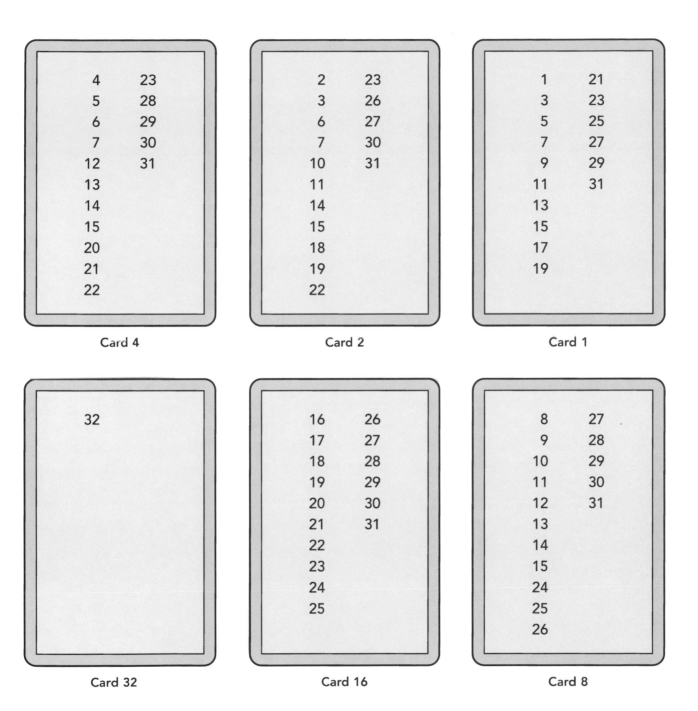

4	23
5	28
6	29
7	30
12	31
13	
14	
15	
20	
21	
22	

Card 4

2	23
3	26
6	27
7	30
10	31
11	
14	
15	
18	
19	
22	

Card 2

1	21
3	23
5	25
7	27
9	29
11	31
13	
15	
17	
19	

Card 1

32

Card 32

16	26
17	27
18	28
19	29
20	30
21	31
22	
23	
24	
25	

Card 16

8	27
9	28
10	29
11	30
12	31
13	
14	
15	
24	
25	
26	

Card 8

INTEREST GAMEBOARD

	$50	$100	$200	$300	$400	$500	$600
	.5	1	2	2.5	3.5	4	5
	1	2	4	5	7	8	10
	2	4	8	10	14	16	20
	3	6	12	15	21	24	30
	4	8	16	20	28	32	40
	5	10	20	25	35	40	50
	6	12	24	30	42	48	60

Pythagorean Puzzle Visual Proof and Square
Me Puzzle (Activity Set 6.4)

PYTHAGOREAN PUZZLE VISUAL PROOF

SQUARE ME PUZZLE

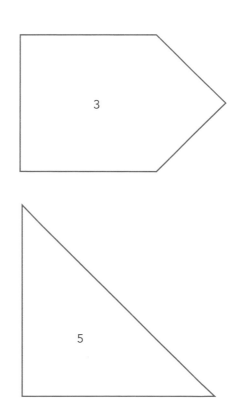

Metric Ruler, Protractor, and Compass

(Activity Sets 7.1, 9.1, 10.1, 10.3, 11.1, 11.2, and 11.3)

Compass

| C | 1 | 2 | 3 | 4 | 5 | 6 | 7 | 8 | 9 | 10 |

Punch out holes C, 1, 2, 3, ..., 10. Hold point C fixed for the center of a circle and place a pencil at hole 8 to draw a circle of radius 8 centimeters.

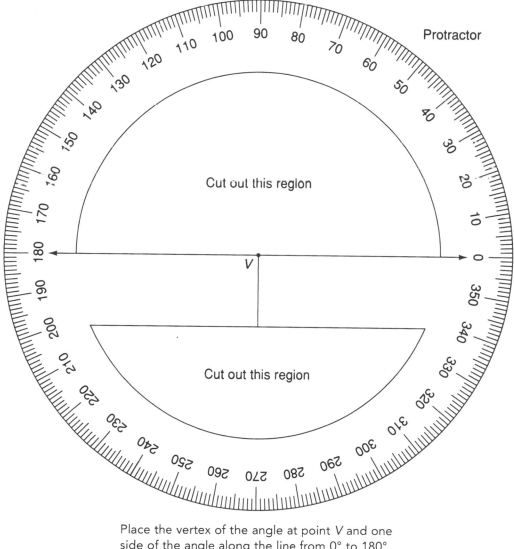

Protractor

Cut out this region

V

Cut out this region

Place the vertex of the angle at point V and one side of the angle along the line from 0° to 180°.

69588	18885	24831	28185	84019	91168	62187	69079	86492	24195
19797	27708	70288	72541	10576	79693	28704	97678	95777	46759
50212	65574	17333	21694	47617	71881	88513	62695	76222	42544
16380	57486	86835	82724	23964	77540	93652	75555	77283	29473
29826	51673	28082	85640	43062	21997	77247	14653	13471	03865
51427	10863	96787	43214	68955	13735	72107	63399	15951	53968
36037	55838	30244	28819	19794	72893	43642	89344	72686	17378
52421	74281	44363	37701	25103	06701	33100	00483	38208	57711
64936	77559	27432	27412	89263	50899	68524	54274	35905	40343
05013	22060	17792	96536	74156	88924	19652	84311	92236	18008
69970	37423	22837	28337	06347	84836	68812	06121	23216	64020
96601	64066	87785	41608	32193	67850	46509	70020	18435	75427
30984	17658	07126	96234	66401	05691	55657	29217	61037	83086
93775	97887	39692	84605	98008	43174	07226	17637	63106	11806
10975	47371	37928	71999	19339	87802	88208	23697	57359	64825
34487	51270	55303	80666	63115	97793	01883	46650	10668	04238
77876	02108	02420	23983	49776	29281	01665	04908	78948	09727
38781	58184	25008	00962	80002	22962	92127	49898	24259	61862
83788	62480	44711	21815	84629	06939	67646	06948	04529	45214
89704	30361	15988	83311	78147	00323	49940	68820	24291	44077
24113	92774	25852	01814	44175	64734	25392	58525	88314	97199
23041	81334	43410	28285	59247	22853	24395	17770	61573	30097
43123	25825	91840	79914	41137	99165	33796	95374	25960	35135
20585	11696	84826	43878	74239	98734	35854	82082	97416	20039
45699	87633	29489	57614	52384	88793	24228	60107	83502	28129
42060	77709	09509	58712	21415	38415	10841	93372	53568	70864
23038	92956	27304	20825	70350	33151	93654	81710	34692	58456
72936	52909	92458	61567	72380	00931	49994	38711	12237	49788
24631	18803	35690	70000	10040	38204	67146	85913	48332	86757
62397	54028	77523	24891	27989	02289	74513	26279	85382	82180
75724	78027	60675	01294	37607	84053	41144	94743	85633	50356
44997	49702	68073	99166	05851	22239	76340	79458	25968	75875
20733	42897	05445	46195	97046	16120	41546	04463	34074	05515
90448	49154	27693	90607	98476	50924	25067	01233	64588	31287
50151	76497	10878	87213	84640	35943	46320	03267	15324	95455
33944	22308	60879	07308	10759	75179	05130	66184	69554	65891
42837	55847	75893	54245	38752	68095	33158	81860	56469	84190
39357	40544	25447	96260	87283	22483	78031	91393	38040	82382
45673	87347	44240	61458	87338	62039	71825	52571	27146	86404
97714	52538	91976	52406	19711	99248	23073	43926	81889	47540

Two-Penny Grid (Activity Set 8.1)

Three-Penny Grid (Activity Set 8.1)

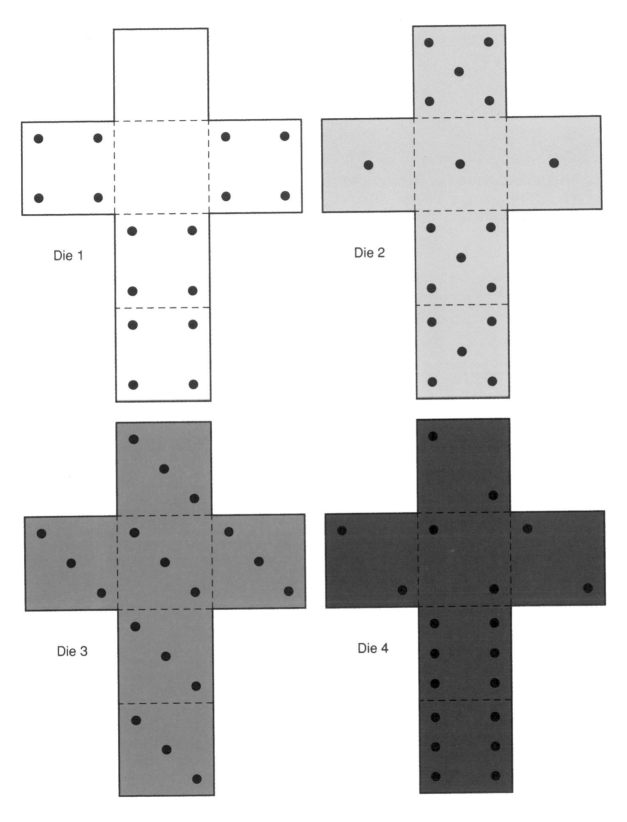

Die 1

Die 2

Die 3

Die 4

Geoboard Recording Paper (Activity Set 9.1)

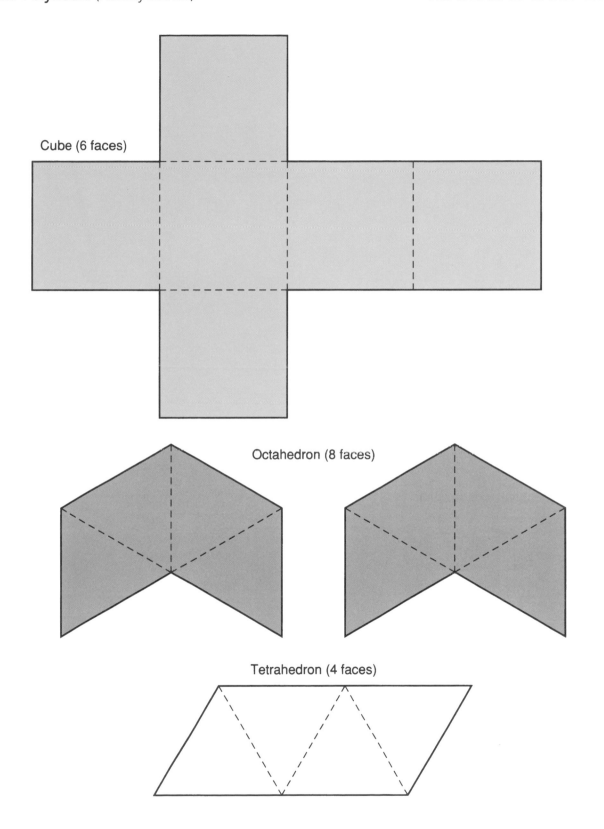

Cube (6 faces)

Octahedron (8 faces)

Tetrahedron (4 faces)

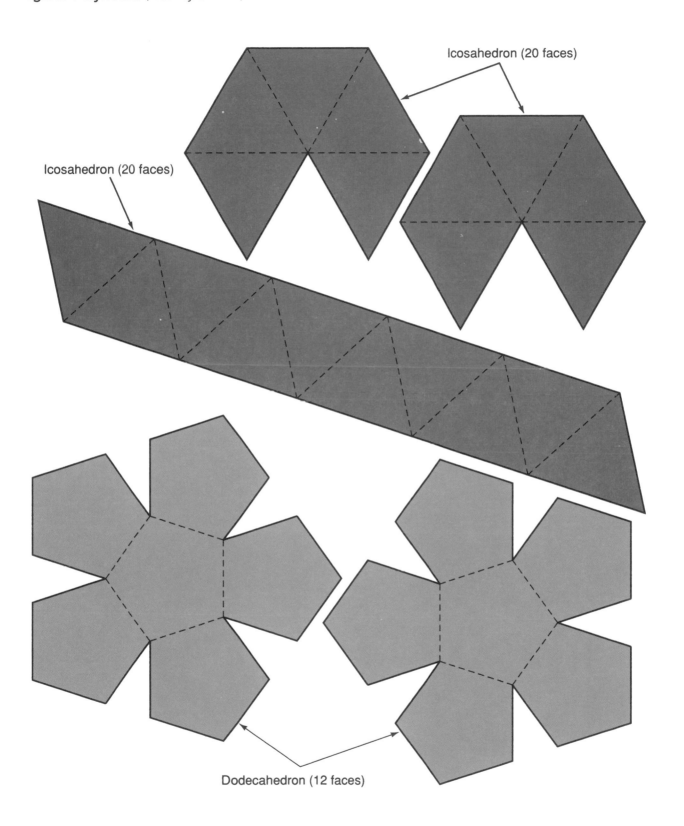

Icosahedron (20 faces)

Icosahedron (20 faces)

Dodecahedron (12 faces)

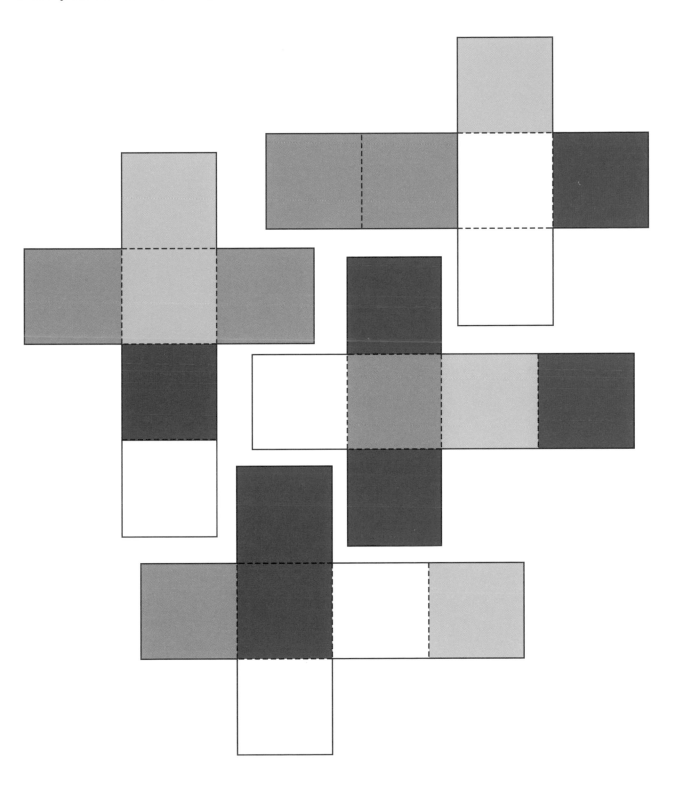

Metric Measuring Tape (Activity Set 10.1)

MATERIAL CARD 34

Cut out the five vertical strips and then tape or glue tab 2 under the edge labeled 2, tab 4 under the edge labeled 4, tab 6 under the edge labeled 6, and tab 8 under the edge labeled 8, to form a metric tape that is 100 centimeters long.

2	4	6	8	100 cm
15 cm	35 cm	55 cm	75 cm	95 cm
10 cm	30 cm	50 cm	70 cm	90 cm
5 cm	25 cm	45 cm	65 cm	85 cm
20	40	60	80

Tabs ⟶

CENTIMETER RACING MAT

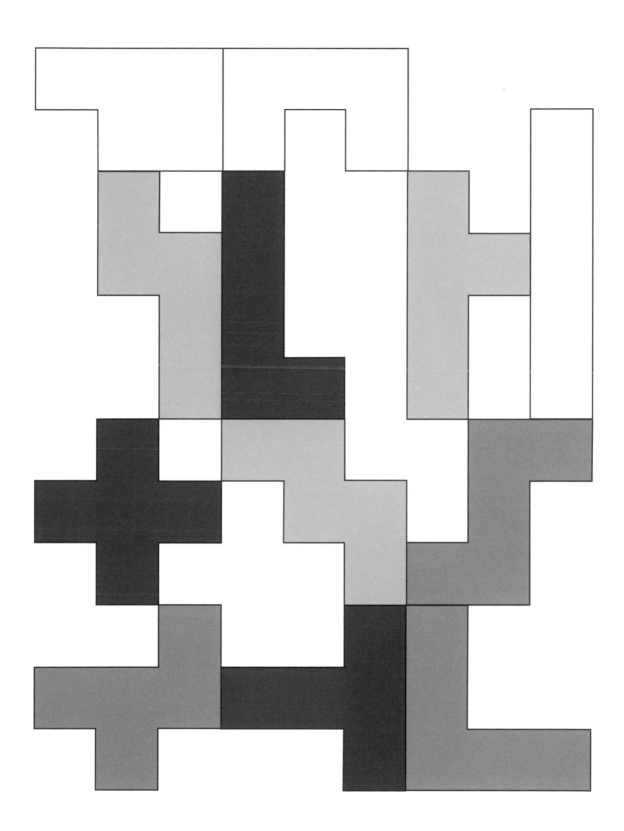

Pentomino Game Grid (Activity Set 10.2 JUST FOR FUN)   **MATERIAL CARD 37**

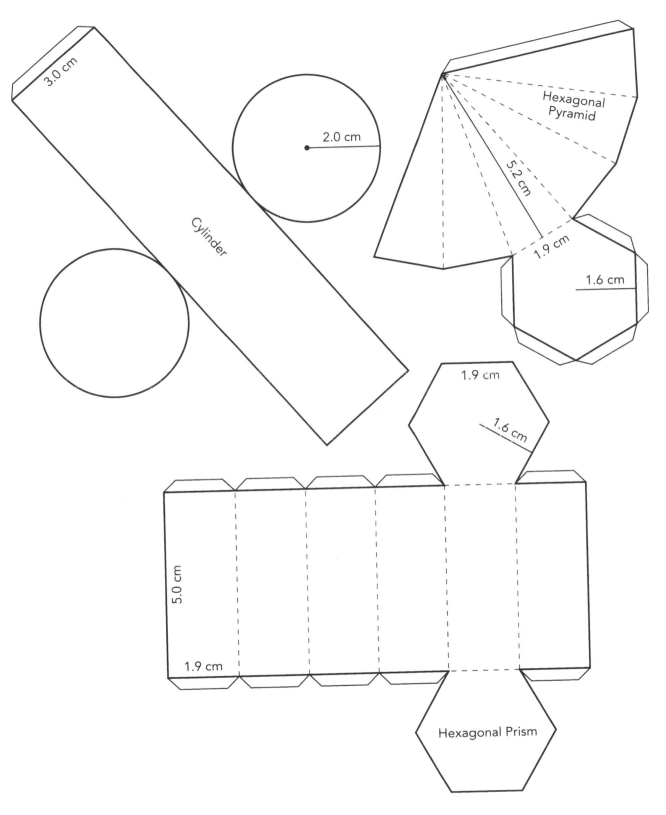

3.0 cm

Cylinder

2.0 cm

Hexagonal
Pyramid

5.2 cm

1.9 cm

1.6 cm

1.9 cm

1.6 cm

5.0 cm

1.9 cm

Hexagonal Prism

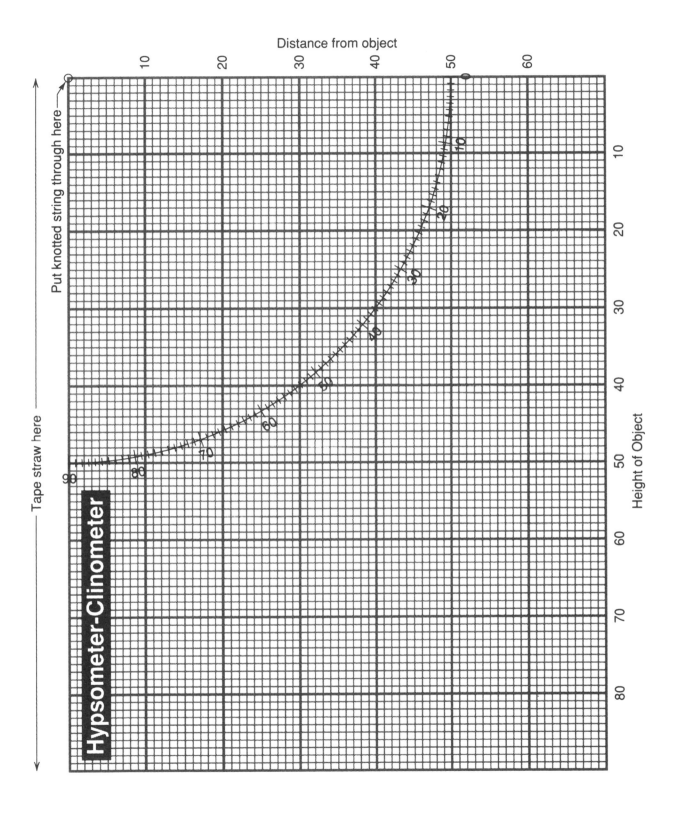

Hypsometer-Clinometer

Appendix

Table of NCTM Standards and Expectations

Content Standards

Number and Operations

STANDARD	Pre-K–2	Grades 3–5
Instructional programs from prekindergarten through grade 12 should enable all students to—	**Expectations** In prekindergarten through grade 2 all students should—	**Expectations** In grades 3–5 all students should—
Understand numbers, ways of representing numbers, relationships among numbers, and number systems	• count with understanding and recognize "how many" in sets of objects; • use multiple models to develop initial understandings of place value and the base-ten number system; • develop understanding of the relative position and magnitude of whole numbers and of ordinal and cardinal numbers and their connections; • develop a sense of whole numbers and represent and use them in flexible ways, including relating, composing, and decomposing numbers; • connect number words and numerals to the quantities they represent, using various physical models and representations; • understand and represent commonly used fractions, such as 1/4, 1/3, and 1/2.	• understand the place-value structure of the base-ten number system and be able to represent and compare whole numbers and decimals; • recognize equivalent representations for the same number and generate them by decomposing and composing numbers; • develop understanding of fractions as parts of unit wholes, as parts of a collection, as locations on number lines, and as divisions of whole numbers; • use models, benchmarks, and equivalent forms to judge the size of fractions; • recognize and generate equivalent forms of commonly used fractions, decimals, and percents; • explore numbers less than 0 by extending the number line and through familiar applications; • describe classes of numbers according to characteristics such as the nature of their factors.
Understand meanings of operations and how they relate to one another	• understand various meanings of addition and subtraction of whole numbers and the relationship between the two operations; • understand the effects of adding and subtracting whole numbers; • understand situations that entail multiplication and division, such as equal groupings of objects and sharing equally.	• understand various meanings of multiplication and division; • understand the effects of multiplying and dividing whole numbers; • identify and use relationships between operations, such as division as the inverse of multiplication, to solve problems; • understand and use properties of operations, such as the distributivity of multiplication over addition.
Compute fluently and make reasonable estimates	• develop and use strategies for whole-number computations, with a focus on addition and subtraction; • develop fluency with basic number combinations for addition and subtraction; • use a variety of methods and tools to compute, including objects, mental computation, estimation, paper and pencil, and calculators.	• develop fluency with basic number combinations for multiplication and division and use these combinations to mentally compute related problems, such as 30×50; • develop fluency in adding, subtracting, multiplying, and dividing whole numbers; • develop and use strategies to estimate the results of whole number computations and to judge the reasonableness of such results; • develop and use strategies to estimate computations involving fractions and decimals in situations relevant to students' experience; • use visual models, benchmarks, and equivalent forms to add and subtract commonly used fractions and decimals; • select appropriate methods and tools for computing with whole numbers from among mental computation, estimation, calculators, and paper and pencil according to the context and nature of the computation and use the selected method or tool.

Number and Operations

Instructional programs from prekindergarten through grade 12 should enable all students to—	Grades 6–8 **Expectations** In grades 6–8 all students should—	Grades 9–12 **Expectations** In grades 9–12 all students should—
Understand numbers, ways of representing numbers, relationships among numbers, and number systems	• work flexibly with fractions, decimals, and percents to solve problems; • compare and order fractions, decimals, and percents efficiently and find their approximate locations on a number line; • develop meaning for percents greater than 100 and less than 1; • understand and use ratios and proportions to represent quantitative relationships; • develop an understanding of large numbers and recognize and appropriately use exponential, scientific, and calculator notation; • use factors, multiples, prime factorization, and relatively prime numbers to solve problems; • develop meaning for integers and represent and compare quantities with them.	• develop a deeper understanding of very large and very small numbers and of various representations of them; • compare and contrast the properties of numbers and number systems, including the rational and real numbers, and understand complex numbers as solutions to quadratic equations that do not have real solutions; • understand vectors and matrices as systems that have some of the properties of the real-number system; • use number-theory arguments to justify relationships involving whole numbers.
Understand meanings of operations and how they relate to one another	• understand the meaning and effects of arithmetic operations with fractions, decimals, and integers; • use the associative and commutative properties of addition and multiplication and the distributive property of multiplication over addition to simplify computations with integers, fractions, and decimals; • understand and use the inverse relationships of addition and subtraction, multiplication and division, and squaring and finding square roots to simplify computations and solve problems.	• judge the effects of such operations as multiplication, division, and computing powers and roots on the magnitudes of quantities; • develop an understanding of properties of, and representations for, the addition and multiplication of vectors and matrices; • develop an understanding of permutations and combinations as counting techniques.
Compute fluently and make reasonable estimates	• select appropriate methods and tools for computing with fractions and decimals from among mental computation, estimation, calculators or computers, and paper and pencil, depending on the situation, and apply the selected methods; • develop and analyze algorithms for computing with fractions, decimals, and integers and develop fluency in their use; • develop and use strategies to estimate the results of rational-number computations and judge the reasonableness of the results; • develop, analyze, and explain methods for solving problems involving proportions, such as scaling and finding equivalent ratios.	• develop fluency in operations with real numbers, vectors, and matrices, using mental computation or paper-and-pencil calculations for simple cases and technology for more-complicated cases. • judge the reasonableness of numerical computations and their results.

Algebra

Instructional programs from prekindergarten through grade 12 should enable all students to—	Pre-K–2	Grades 3–5
	Expectations	**Expectations**
	In prekindergarten through grade 2 all students should—	In grades 3–5 all students should—
Understand patterns, relations, and functions	• sort, classify, and order objects by size, number, and other properties; • recognize, describe, and extend patterns such as sequences of sounds and shapes or simple numeric patterns and translate from one representation to another; • analyze how both repeating and growing patterns are generated.	• describe, extend, and make generalizations about geometric and numeric patterns; • represent and analyze patterns and functions, using words, tables, and graphs.
Represent and analyze mathematical situations and structures using algebraic symbols	• illustrate general principles and properties of operations, such as commutativity, using specific numbers; • use concrete, pictorial, and verbal representations to develop an understanding of invented and conventional symbolic notations.	• identify such properties as commutativity, associativity, and distributivity and use them to compute with whole numbers; • represent the idea of a variable as an unknown quantity using a letter or a symbol; • express mathematical relationships using equations.
Use mathematical models to represent and understand quantitative relationships	• model situations that involve the addition and subtraction of whole numbers, using objects, pictures, and symbols.	• model problem situations with objects and use representations such as graphs, tables, and equations to draw conclusions.
Analyze change in various contexts	• describe qualitative change, such as a student's growing taller; • describe quantitative change, such as a student's growing two inches in one year.	• investigate how a change in one variable relates to a change in a second variable; • identify and describe situations with constant or varying rates of change and compare them.

Algebra

STANDARD

Instructional programs from prekindergarten through grade 12 should enable all students to—	Grades 6–8	Grades 9–12
	Expectations In grades 6–8 all students should—	**Expectations** In grades 9–12 all students should—
Understand patterns, relations, and functions	• represent, analyze, and generalize a variety of patterns with tables, graphs, words, and. when possible, symbolic rules; • relate and compare different forms of representation for a relationship; • identify functions as linear or nonlinear and contrast their properties from tables, graphs, or equations.	• generalize patterns using explicitly defined and recursively defined functions; • understand relations and functions and select, convert flexibly among, and use various representations for them; • analyze functions of one variable by investigating rates of change, intercepts, zeros, asymptotes, and local and global behavior; • understand and perform transformations such as arithmetically combining, composing, and inverting commonly used functions, using technology to perform such operations on more-complicated symbolic expressions; • understand and compare the properties of classes of functions, including exponential, polynomial, rational, logarithmic, and periodic functions; • interpret representations of functions of two variables.
Represent and analyze mathematical situations and structures using algebraic symbols	• develop an initial conceptual understanding of different uses of variables; • explore relationships between symbolic expressions and graphs of lines, paying particular attention to the meaning of intercept and slope; • use symbolic algebra to represent situations and to solve problems, especially those that involve linear relationships; • recognize and generate equivalent forms for simple algebraic expressions and solve linear equations.	• understand the meaning of equivalent forms of expressions, equations, inequalities, and relations; • write equivalent forms of equations, inequalities, and systems of equations and solve them with fluency—mentally or with paper and pencil in simple cases and using technology in all cases; • use symbolic algebra to represent and explain mathematical relationships; • use a variety of symbolic representations, including recursive and parametric equations, for functions and relations; • judge the meaning, utility, and reasonableness of the results of symbol manipulations, including those carried out by technology.
Use mathematical models to represent and understand quantitative relationships	• model and solve contextualized problems using various representations, such as graphs, tables, and equations.	• identify essential quantitative relationships in a situation and determine the class or classes of functions that might model the relationships; • use symbolic expressions, including iterative and recursive forms, to represent relationships arising from various contexts; • draw reasonable conclusions about a situation being modeled.
Analyze change in various contexts	• use graphs to analyze the nature of changes in quantities in linear relationships.	• approximate and interpret rates of change from graphical and numerical data.

Geometry

STANDARD

Instructional programs from prekindergarten through grade 12 should enable all students to—	Pre-K–2	Grades 3–5
	Expectations In prekindergarten through grade 2 all students should—	**Expectations** In grades 3–5 all students should—
Analyze characteristics and properties of two- and three-dimensional geometric shapes and develop mathematical arguments about geometric relationships	• recognize, name, build, draw, compare, and sort two- and three-dimensional shapes; • describe attributes and parts of two- and three-dimensional shapes; • investigate and predict the results of putting together and taking apart two- and three-dimensional shapes.	• identify, compare, and analyze attributes of two- and three-dimensional shapes and develop vocabulary to describe the attributes; • classify two- and three-dimensional shapes according to their properties and develop definitions of classes of shapes such as triangles and pyramids; • investigate, describe, and reason about the results of subdividing, combining, and transforming shapes; • explore congruence and similarity; • make and test conjectures about geometric properties and relationships and develop logical arguments to justify conclusions.
Specify locations and describe spatial relationships using coordinate geometry and other representational systems	• describe, name, and interpret relative positions in space and apply ideas about relative position; • describe, name, and interpret direction and distance in navigating space and apply ideas about direction and distance; • find and name locations with simple relationships such as "near to" and in coordinate systems such as maps.	• describe location and movement using common language and geometric vocabulary; • make and use coordinate systems to specify locations and to describe paths; • find the distance between points along horizontal and vertical lines of a coordinate system.
Apply transformations and use symmetry to analyze mathematical situations	• recognize and apply slides, flips, and turns; • recognize and create shapes that have symmetry.	• predict and describe the results of sliding, flipping, and turning two-dimensional shapes; • describe a motion or a series of motions that will show that two shapes are congruent; • identify and describe line and rotational symmetry in two- and three-dimensional shapes and designs.
Use visualization, spatial reasoning, and geometric modeling to solve problems	• create mental images of geometric shapes using spatial memory and spatial visualization; • recognize and represent shapes from different perspectives; • relate ideas in geometry to ideas in number and measurement; • recognize geometric shapes and structures in the environment and specify their location.	• build and draw geometric objects; • create and describe mental images of objects, patterns, and paths; • identify and build a three-dimensional object from two-dimensional representations of that object; • identify and draw a two-dimensional representation of a three-dimensional object; • use geometric models to solve problems in other areas of mathematics, such as number and measurement; • recognize geometric ideas and relationships and apply them to other disciplines and to problems that arise in the classroom or in everyday life.

Geometry

STANDARD

Instructional programs from prekindergarten through grade 12 should enable all students to—

	Grades 6–8	Grades 9–12
	Expectations	**Expectations**
	In grades 6–8 all students should—	In grades 9–12 all students should—
Analyze characteristics and properties of two- and three-dimensional geometric shapes and develop mathematical arguments about geometric relationships	• precisely describe, classify, and understand relationships among types of two- and three-dimensional objects using their defining properties; • understand relationships among the angles, side lengths, perimeters, areas, and volumes of similar objects; • create and critique inductive and deductive arguments concerning geometric ideas and relationships, such as congruence, similarity, and the Pythagorean relationship.	• analyze properties and determine attributes of two- and three-dimensional objects; • explore relationships (including congruence and similarity) among classes of two- and three-dimensional geometric objects, make and test conjectures about them, and solve problems involving them; • establish the validity of geometric conjectures using deduction, prove theorems, and critique arguments made by others; • use trigonometric relationships to determine lengths and angle measures.
Specify locations and describe spatial relationships using coordinate geometry and other representational systems	• use coordinate geometry to represent and examine the properties of geometric shapes; • use coordinate geometry to examine special geometric shapes, such as regular polygons or those with pairs of parallel or perpendicular sides.	• use Cartesian coordinates and other coordinate systems, such as navigational, polar, or spherical systems, to analyze geometric situations; • investigate conjectures and solve problems involving two- and three-dimensional objects represented with Cartesian coordinates.
Apply transformations and use symmetry to analyze mathematical situations	• describe sizes, positions, and orientations of shapes under informal transformations such as flips, turns, slides, and scaling; • examine the congruence, similarity, and line or rotational symmetry of objects using transformations.	• understand and represent translations, reflections, rotations, and dilations of objects in the plane by using sketches, coordinates, vectors, function notation, and matrices; • use various representations to help understand the effects of simple transformations and their compositions.
Use visualization, spatial reasoning, and geometric modeling to solve problems	• draw geometric objects with specified properties, such as side lengths or angle measures; • use two-dimensional representations of three-dimensional objects to visualize and solve problems such as those involving surface area and volume; • use visual tools such as networks to represent and solve problems; • use geometric models to represent and explain numerical and algebraic relationships; • recognize and apply geometric ideas and relationships in areas outside the mathematics classroom, such as art, science, and everyday life.	• draw and construct representations of two- and three-dimensional geometric objects using a variety of tools; • visualize three-dimensional objects from different perspectives and analyze their cross sections; • use vertex-edge graphs to model and solve problems; • use geometric models to gain insights into, and answer questions in, other areas of mathematics; • use geometric ideas to solve problems in, and gain insights into, other disciplines and other areas of interest such as art and architecture.

Measurement

STANDARD

Instructional programs from prekindergarten through grade 12 should enable all students to—	Pre-K–2	Grades 3–5
	Expectations In prekindergarten through grade 2 all students should—	**Expectations** In grades 3–5 all students should—
Understand measurable attributes of objects and the units, systems, and processes of measurement	• recognize the attributes of length, volume, weight, area, and time; • compare and order objects according to these attributes; • understand how to measure using nonstandard and standard units; • select an appropriate unit and tool for the attribute being measured.	• understand such attributes as length, area, weight, volume, and size of angle and select the appropriate type of unit for measuring each attribute; • understand the need for measuring with standard units and become familiar with standard units in the customary and metric systems; • carry out simple unit conversions, such as from centimeters to meters, within a system of measurement; • understand that measurements are approximations and understand how differences in units affect precision; • explore what happens to measurements of a two-dimensional shape such as its perimeter and area when the shape is changed in some way.
Apply appropriate techniques, tools, and formulas to determine measurements	• measure with multiple copies of units of the same size, such as paper clips laid end to end; • use repetition of a single unit to measure something larger than the unit, for instance, measuring the length of a room with a single meterstick; • use tools to measure; • develop common referents for measures to make comparisons and estimates.	• develop strategies for estimating the perimeters, areas, and volumes of irregular shapes; • select and apply appropriate standard units and tools to measure length, area, volume, weight, time, temperature, and the size of angles; • select and use benchmarks to estimate measurements; • develop, understand, and use formulas to find the area of rectangles and related triangles and parallelograms; • develop strategies to determine the surface areas and volumes of rectangular solids.

Measurement

Instructional programs from prekindergarten through grade 12 should enable all students to—	Grades 6–8	Grades 9–12
	Expectations	**Expectations**
	In grades 6–8 all students should—	In grades 9–12 all students should—
Understand measurable attributes of objects and the units, systems, and processes of measurement	• understand both metric and customary systems of measurement; • understand relationships among units and convert from one unit to another within the same system; • understand, select, and use units of appropriate size and type to measure angles, perimeter, area, surface area, and volume.	• make decisions about units and scales that are appropriate for problem situations involving measurement.
Apply appropriate techniques, tools, and formulas to determine measurements	• use common benchmarks to select appropriate methods for estimating measurements; • select and apply techniques and tools to accurately find length, area, volume, and angle measures to appropriate levels of precision; • develop and use formulas to determine the circumference of circles and the area of triangles, parallelograms, trapezoids, and circles and develop strategies to find the area of more-complex shapes; • develop strategies to determine the surface area and volume of selected prisms, pyramids, and cylinders; • solve problems involving scale factors, using ratio and proportion; • solve simple problems involving rates and derived measurements for such attributes as velocity and density.	• analyze precision, accuracy, and approximate error in measurement situations; • understand and use formulas for the area, surface area, and volume of geometric figures, including cones, spheres, and cylinders; • apply informal concepts of successive approximation, upper and lower bounds, and limit in measurement situations; • use unit analysis to check measurement computations.

Data Analysis and Probability

Instructional programs from prekindergarten through grade 12 should enable all students to—	Pre-K–2	Grades 3–5
	Expectations In prekindergarten through grade 2 all students should—	**Expectations** In grades 3–5 all students should—
Formulate questions that can be addressed with data and collect, organize, and display relevant data to answer them	• pose questions and gather data about themselves and their surroundings; • sort and classify objects according to their attributes and organize data about the objects; • represent data using concrete objects, pictures, and graphs.	• design investigations to address a question and consider how data-collection methods affect the nature of the data set; • collect data using observations, surveys, and experiments; • represent data using tables and graphs such as line plots, bar graphs, and line graphs; • recognize the differences in representing categorical and numerical data.
Select and use appropriate statistical methods to analyze data	• describe parts of the data and the set of data as a whole to determine what the data show.	• describe the shape and important features of a set of data and compare related data sets, with an emphasis on how the data are distributed; • use measures of center, focusing on the median, and understand what each does and does not indicate about the data set; • compare different representations of the same data and evaluate how well each representation shows important aspects of the data.
Develop and evaluate inferences and predictions that are based on data	• discuss events related to students' experiences as likely or unlikely.	• propose and justify conclusions and predictions that are based on data and design studies to further investigate the conclusions or predictions.
Understand and apply basic concepts of probability		• describe events as likely or unlikely and discuss the degree of likelihood using such words as *certain, equally likely,* and *impossible;* • predict the probability of outcomes of simple experiments and test the predictions; • understand that the measure of the likelihood of an event can be represented by a number from 0 to 1.

Data Analysis and Probability

STANDARD

Instructional programs from prekindergarten through grade 12 should enable all students to—	Grades 6–8 **Expectations** In grades 6–8 all students should—	Grades 9–12 **Expectations** In grades 9–12 all students should—
Formulate questions that can be addressed with data and collect, organize, and display relevant data to answer them	• formulate questions, design studies, and collect data about a characteristic shared by two populations or different characteristics within one population; • select, create, and use appropriate graphical representations of data, including histograms, box plots, and scatterplots.	• understand the differences among various kinds of studies and which types of inferences can legitimately be drawn from each; • know the characteristics of well-designed studies, including the role of randomization in surveys and experiments; • understand the meaning of measurement data and categorical data, of univariate and bivariate data, and of the term variable; • understand histograms, parallel box plots, and scatterplots and use them to display data; • compute basic statistics and understand the distinction between a statistic and a parameter.
Select and use appropriate statistical methods to analyze data	• find, use, and interpret measures of center and spread, including mean and interquartile range; • discuss and understand the correspondence between data sets and their graphical representations, especially histograms, stem-and-leaf plots, box plots, and scatterplots.	• for univariate measurement data, be able to display the distribution, describe its shape, and select and calculate summary statistics; • for bivariate measurement data, be able to display a scatterplot, describe its shape, and determine regression coefficients, regression equations, and correlation coefficients using technological tools; • display and discuss bivariate data where at least one variable is categorical; • recognize how linear transformations of univariate data affect shape, center, and spread; • identify trends in bivariate data and find functions that model the data or transform the data so that they can be modeled.
Develop and evaluate inferences and predictions that are based on data	• use observations about differences between two or more samples to make conjectures about the populations from which the samples were taken; • make conjectures about possible relationships between two characteristics of a sample on the basis of scatterplots of the data and approximate lines of fit; • use conjectures to formulate new questions and plan new studies to answer them.	• use simulations to explore the variability of sample statistics from a known population and to construct sampling distributions; • understand how sample statistics reflect the values of population parameters and use sampling distributions as the basis for informal inference; • evaluate published reports that are based on data by examining the design of the study, the appropriateness of the data analysis, and the validity of conclusions; • understand how basic statistical techniques are used to monitor process characteristics in the workplace.
Understand and apply basic concepts of probability	• understand and use appropriate terminology to describe complementary and mutually exclusive events; • use proportionality and a basic understanding of probability to make and test conjectures about the results of experiments and simulations; • compute probabilities for simple compound events, using such methods as organized lists, tree diagrams, and area models.	• understand the concepts of sample space and probability distribution and construct sample spaces and distributions in simple cases; • use simulations to construct empirical probability distributions; • compute and interpret the expected value of random variables in simple cases; • understand the concepts of conditional probability and independent events; • understand how to compute the probability of a compound event.

Process Standards

Problem Solving

STANDARD

Instructional programs from prekindergarten through grade 12 should enable all students to—

- Build new mathematical knowledge through problem solving
- Solve problems that arise in mathematics and in other contexts
- Apply and adapt a variety of appropriate strategies to solve problems
- Monitor and reflect on the process of mathematical problem solving

Reasoning and Proof

STANDARD

Instructional programs from prekindergarten through grade 12 should enable all students to—

- Recognize reasoning and proof as fundamental aspects of mathematics
- Make and investigate mathematical conjectures
- Develop and evaluate mathematical arguments and proofs
- Select and use various types of reasoning and methods of proof

Communication

STANDARD

Instructional programs from prekindergarten through grade 12 should enable all students to—

- Organize and consolidate their mathematical thinking through communication
- Communicate their mathematical thinking coherently and clearly to peers, teachers, and others
- Analyze and evaluate the mathematical thinking and strategies of others
- Use the language of mathematics to express mathematical ideas precisely

Connections

STANDARD

Instructional programs from prekindergarten through grade 12 should enable all students to—

- Recognize and use connections among mathematical ideas
- Understand how mathematical ideas interconnect and build on one another to produce a coherent whole
- Recognize and apply mathematics in contexts outside of mathematics

Representation

STANDARD

Instructional programs from prekindergarten through grade 12 should enable all students to—

- Create and use representations to organize, record, and communicate mathematical ideas
- Select, apply, and translate among mathematical representations to solve problems
- Use representations to model and interpret physical, social, and mathematical phenomena